Taste of Home
quick COOKING
ANNUAL RECIPES

Taste of Home

RDA ENTHUSIAST BRANDS, LLC • MILWAUKEE, WI

Taste of Home quick COOKING
ANNUAL RECIPES

■ EDITORIAL
Editor-in-Chief **Catherine Cassidy**
Vice President, Content Operations **Kerri Balliet**
Creative Director **Howard Greenberg**

Managing Editor, Print & Digital Books **Mark Hagen**
Associate Creative Director **Edwin Robles Jr.**

Editor **Christine Rukavena**
Art Director **Maggie Conners**
Graphic Designer **Courtney Lovetere**
Editorial Services Manager **Dena Ahlers**
Editorial Production Coordinator **Jill Banks**
Copy Chief **Deb Warlaumont Mulvey**
Copy Editors **Dulcie Shoener (senior),
Ronald Kovach, Chris McLaughlin, Ellie Piper**

Content Director **Julie Blume Benedict**
Food Editors **Gina Nistico; James Schend;
Peggy Woodward, RDN**
Recipe Editors **Sue Ryon (lead), Irene Yeh**
Editorial Services Administrator **Marie Brannon**

Culinary Director **Sarah Thompson**
Test Cooks **Nicholas Iverson (lead),
Matthew Hass**
Food Stylists **Kathryn Conrad (lead),
Lauren Knoelke, Shannon Roum**
Prep Cooks **Bethany Van Jacobson (lead),
Melissa Hansen, Aria C. Thornton**
Culinary Team Assistant **Maria Petrella**

Photography Director **Stephanie Marchese**
Photographers **Dan Roberts, Jim Wieland**
Photographer/Set Stylist **Grace Natoli Sheldon**
Set Stylists **Melissa Franco (lead), Stacey Genaw,
Dee Dee Schaefer**
Set Stylist Assistant **Stephanie Chojnacki**

Business Architect, Publishing Technologies
Amanda Harmatys
Business Analyst, Publishing Technologies
Kate Unger
Junior Business Analyst, Publishing Technologies
Shannon Stroud

Editorial Business Manager **Kristy Martin**
Rights & Permissions Associate
Samantha Lea Stoeger
Editorial Business Associate **Andrea Meiers**

Editor, *Simple & Delicious* **Emily Betz Tyra**
Art Director, *Simple & Delicious* **Kristen Johnson**

■ BUSINESS
Vice President, Group Publisher **Kirsten Marchioli**
Publisher, *Simple & Delicious* **Donna Lindskog**
Business Development Director, Taste of Home Live
Laurel Osman
Strategic Partnerships Manager, Taste of Home Live
Jamie Piette Andrzejewski

■ TRUSTED MEDIA BRANDS, INC.
President & Chief Executive Officer
Bonnie Kintzer
Chief Financial Officer **Dean Durbin**
Chief Marketing Officer **C. Alec Casey**
Chief Revenue Officer **Richard Sutton**
Chief Digital Officer **Vince Errico**
Senior Vice President, Global HR
& Communications **Phyllis E. Gebhardt,
SPHR; SHRM-SCP**
General Counsel **Mark Sirota**
Vice President, Magazine Marketing
Christopher Gaydos
Vice President, Product Marketing **Brian Kennedy**
Vice President, Operations **Michael Garzone**
Vice President, Consumer Marketing Planning
Jim Woods
Vice President, Digital Product & Technology
Nick Contardo
Vice President, Financial Planning & Analysis
William Houston

Cover Photography
Taste of Home Photo Studio

© 2017 RDA Enthusiast Brands, LLC
1610 N. 2nd St., Suite 102, Milwaukee WI 53212-3906

International Standard Book Number:
978-1-61765-640-8
International Standard Serial Number: 1552-6603

Component Number: 117800062H

All rights reserved.

Taste of Home is a registered trademark of
Trusted Media Brands, Inc.

Printed in USA
1 3 5 7 9 10 8 6 4 2

Easy
MEALS *for* BUSY
· FAMILIES ·

PICTURED ON FRONT COVER Balsamic Beef Hoagies (p. 47); Berry & Ganache Cheesecake Bars (p. 244); Wintertime Braised Beef Stew (p. 260); Spicy Turkey Lettuce Wraps (p. 117) and Puff Pastry Chicken Potpie (p. 142).
PICTURED ON PAGE 1 Bacon and Spinach Pizza (p. 111).
PICTURED AT LEFT Brownie Affogato Sundae (p. 250); Bacon, Egg & Avocado Sandwiches (p. 186) and Cheesy Summer Squash Flatbreads (p. 83).
PICTURED ON BACK COVER Strawberry-Blue Cheese Steak Salad (p. 22); Asparagus & Cheese Frittata (p. 187); Traditional Meat Loaf (p. 155); Key Lime Cupcakes (p. 257) and Chicken with Mango-Cucumber Salsa (p. 300).

contents

Express your love with home cooking that's *quick* & *easy!*

BEEFY CHILI DOGS (p. 276)

TWO-BERRY PAVLOVA (p. 248)

QUINOA & BLACK BEAN-STUFFED PEPPERS (p. 145)

BRUNCH BUDDIES ENCHILADAS (p. 187)

Memorable dishes are just moments away when you crack open this gorgeous, all-new edition of *Quick Cooking Annual Recipes*.

SMART COOKS KNOW that good home cooking comes from the heart, and that a treasured recipe doesn't have to take a lot of work in order to leave an enduring impression. That's why they turn to the fast and fabulous dishes found in *Quick Cooking Annual Recipes* for mealtime solutions they know their families will adore.

Inside, we've included a full year of recipes from *Simple & Delicious* magazine, plus over 100 bonus dishes specially selected for time-crunched cooks who appreciate wholesome, homemade fare. Shared by home cooks from across the country, each dish is simple to prepare and uses common, everyday ingredients.

ICONS IN THIS BOOK

FAST FIX
Recipes that are table-ready in 30 minutes or less.

(5)INGREDIENTS
Recipes that use five or fewer ingredients (they may also call for water, salt, pepper, and canola or olive oil).

EAT SMART
Dietitian-approved recipes that are lower in calories, fat and sodium.

FREEZE IT
Freezer-friendly recipes that include directions for freezing and reheating.

SLOW COOKER
Recipes that use a slow cooker.

EASY CONFETTI PIE (p. 285)

FAJITA IN A BOWL (p. 304)

Serve up cherished family favorites with
650+ RECIPES & TIPS.

FRESH IN THIS EDITION
Weeknight Solutions
Hundreds of quick dinners are in store for your busiest nights. Find over 40 complete menus in the 30-Minute Menus chapter and dozens more entrees that are table-ready in a half-hour or less, plus speedy casseroles, oven dishes and 5-ingredient dinners.

Expert Techniques
Step-by-step photos and helpful hints throughout this volume allow readers to master beautiful, simple classics such as Two-Berry Pavlova (pictured on facing page) and Puff Pastry Chicken Potpie (on the cover; see recipe on page 142). You'll love adding these easy dishes to your home-cooking repertoire.

Effortless Entertaining
For shortcut Italian wedding soup, a slow-cooked sandwich inspired by Vietnamese banh mi, over-the-top nachos and more, look no further than this smartly curated chapter.

Lightened-Up Classics
If you're looking to eat smarter and reduce the calories, fat and added sugar in your diet, turn here for healthy takes on beloved comfort-food classics. Turns out you really can have it all.

Breakfast & Brunch
This expanded chapter is brimming with creative options, such as savory biscuit waffles, oatmeal breakfast cookies and an asparagus-ham strata that's ideal for overnight guests.

Cooking for Kids
With its whimsical rainbow sprinkles and sugar cone crust, Easy Confetti Pie (pictured above) is guaranteed to create excitement! Find this 25-minute icebox treat and dozens more amazing dishes that children will celebrate.

Nutrition Insights
Our registered dietitian nutritionist shares her best secrets to help you make healthy eating choices. Look for the **HEALTH TIP** icon.

PLUS...
Discover wow-factor holiday menus, handcrafted breads, comforting soups, slow cooker specialties, cookout favorites, showstopping desserts and more!

**Belinda Gibson's
Buffalo Chicken Dip**
PAGE 19

Appetizers & Beverages

Look here for the easiest, tastiest, most crowd-pleasing snacks, dips and drinks. Whether you need a winning potluck appetizer or a fun game-time munchie, these dishes are sure to make any gathering special. Give one a try this weekend!

**Denise Hazen's
Antipasto Kabobs**
PAGE 9

**Wendi Wavrin Law's
Championship Bean Dip**
PAGE 11

**Mike Dietiker's
Manmosa**
PAGE 12

(5) INGREDIENTS
MEXICAN CHOCOLATE DIP

Chocolate, cinnamon and a touch of heat are a classic Mexican trio. Any fruit goes in this fudgy dip. And don't forget the churros!

—TASTE OF HOME TEST KITCHEN

START TO FINISH: 10 MIN.
MAKES: ABOUT ½ CUP

- ¾ **cup semisweet chocolate chips**
- ⅓ **cup heavy whipping cream**
- ⅛ **teaspoon ground cinnamon**
- ⅛ **teaspoon cayenne pepper**
  Assorted fresh fruit

In a small heavy saucepan, combine chocolate chips and cream. Using a whisk, heat and stir over medium-low heat 4-5 minutes or until smooth. Remove from heat; stir in cinnamon and cayenne. Cool slightly. Serve with fruit.

NOTE *Dip will become firmer as it cools. If desired, warm gently in the microwave to soften.*

PER SERVING *2 tablespoons dip (calculated without fruit): 221 cal., 17g fat (10g sat. fat), 27mg chol., 11mg sodium, 21g carb. (18g sugars, 2g fiber), 2g pro.*

ICED HONEYDEW MINT TEA

MEXICAN CHOCOLATE DIP

ICED HONEYDEW MINT TEA

I grow mint in the garden on my balcony. For this drink, I blend two of my favorite beverages—Moroccan mint tea and honeydew agua fresca.

—SARAH BATT THRONE EL CERRITO, CA

START TO FINISH: 20 MIN.
MAKES: 10 SERVINGS

- 4 **cups water**
- 24 **fresh mint leaves**
- 8 **individual green tea bags**
- ⅔ **cup sugar**
- 5 **cups diced honeydew, divided**
- 3 **cups ice cubes, divided**
  Additional ice cubes

1. In a large saucepan, bring water to a boil; remove from heat. Add mint leaves and tea bags; steep, covered, 3-5 minutes according to taste, stirring occasionally. Discard mint and tea bags. Stir in sugar.

2. Place 2½ cups honeydew, 2 cups tea and 1½ cups ice in a blender; cover and process until blended. Serve over additional ice. Repeat with remaining ingredients.

PER SERVING *1 cup: 83 cal., 0 fat (0 sat. fat), 0 chol., 15mg sodium, 21g carb. (20g sugars, 1g fiber), 0 pro.* **Diabetic Exchanges:** *1 starch, ½ fruit.*

TOP TIP

HANDY TOOL

A curved grapefruit knife is the best tool for taking the rind off of cantaloupe or honeydew wedges or watermelon slices.

—RUTH M. MILFORD, NH

MOROCCAN EMPANADAS

My family goes for Moroccan flavors, so I make empanadas using beef, apricot preserves and pastry. This is a flaky hand pie with a spicy dipping sauce.

—**ARLENE ERLBACH** MORTON GROVE, IL

PREP: 30 MIN. • **BAKE:** 15 MIN.
MAKES: 20 SERVINGS

- ¾ **pound ground beef**
- 1 **medium onion, chopped**
- 3 **ounces cream cheese, softened**
- ⅓ **cup apricot preserves**
- ¼ **cup finely chopped carrot**
- ¾ **teaspoon Moroccan seasoning (ras el hanout) or ½ teaspoon ground cumin plus ¼ teaspoon ground coriander and dash cayenne pepper**
- ¼ **teaspoon salt**
- 3 **sheets refrigerated pie pastry**
- 1 **large egg yolk, beaten**
- 1 **tablespoon sesame seeds**

SAUCE
- ½ **cup apricot preserves**
- ½ **cup chili sauce**

1. Preheat oven to 425°. In a large skillet, cook beef and onion over medium heat 5-7 minutes or until beef is no longer pink, breaking up beef into crumbles; drain. Stir in cream cheese, preserves, carrot and seasonings. Cool slightly.

2. On a lightly floured work surface, unroll pastry. Cut 40 circles with a floured 3-in. cookie cutter, rerolling dough as necessary. Place half of the circles 2 in. apart on parchment paper-lined baking sheets. Top each with 1 rounded tablespoon beef mixture. Top with remaining pastry circles; press edges with a fork to seal.

3. Brush tops with egg yolk; sprinkle with sesame seeds. Cut slits in tops. Bake empanadas for 12-15 minutes or until golden brown. Remove from pan to a wire rack.

4. Meanwhile, in a microwave, warm sauce ingredients, stirring to combine. Serve with empanadas.

FREEZE OPTION *Cover and freeze unbaked empanadas on waxed paper-lined baking sheets until firm. Transfer to resealable plastic freezer bags; return to freezer. To use, bake empanadas as directed, increasing time as necessary. Prepare sauce as directed.*

NOTE *This recipe was tested with McCormick Gourmet Moroccan Seasoning (ras el hanout).*

PER SERVING *1 empanada with about 2 teaspoons sauce: 215 cal., 11g fat (5g sat. fat), 30mg chol., 256mg sodium, 25g carb. (8g sugars, 0 fiber), 5g pro.*

ANTIPASTO KABOBS

My husband and I met at a cooking class, and we've loved creating menus and entertaining together ever since. These make-ahead appetizers are always a hit.

—**DENISE HAZEN** CINCINNATI, OH

PREP: 35 MIN. + MARINATING
MAKES: 40 APPETIZERS

- 1 **package (9 ounces) refrigerated cheese tortellini**
- 40 **pimiento-stuffed olives**
- 40 **large pitted ripe olives**
- ¾ **cup Italian salad dressing**
- 40 **thin slices pepperoni**
- 20 **thin slices hard salami, halved**
  Fresh parsley sprigs, optional

1. Cook the tortellini according to package directions; drain and rinse in cold water. In a large resealable plastic bag, combine the tortellini, olives and salad dressing. Seal the bag and turn to coat; refrigerate 4 hours or overnight.

2. Drain and discard marinade. For each appetizer, thread a stuffed olive, folded pepperoni slice, tortellini, folded salami piece, ripe olive and, if desired, a parsley sprig on a toothpick or short skewer.

PER SERVING *2 kabobs: 138 cal., 10g fat (3g sat. fat), 18mg chol., 671mg sodium, 8g carb. (1g sugars, 1g fiber), 5g pro.*

MOROCCAN EMPANADAS

CHEESY SNACK MIX

ROASTED BUTTERNUT SQUASH DIPPERS

When it comes to fries, I've made everything from apple and carrot to pumpkin and zucchini. The sour cream sauce is just heavenly.

—**PAULA MARCHESI** LENHARTSVILLE, PA

PREP: 10 MIN. • **BAKE:** 25 MIN.
MAKES: 4 SERVINGS (⅔ CUP DIP)

- 1 **small butternut squash (about 2 pounds)**
- 2 **teaspoons olive oil**
- 1 **teaspoon Cajun seasoning**
- ¼ **teaspoon salt**
- ¼ **teaspoon pepper**

DIP
- ½ **cup sour cream**
- 2 **tablespoons maple syrup**

1. Preheat oven to 425°. Peel, halve and seed squash; cut into 3x½-in. strips. Spread in a greased foil-lined 15x10x1-in. pan; toss with oil. Roast until tender and lightly browned, 25-30 minutes, stirring once.
2. Sprinkle with seasonings. Mix dip ingredients; serve with squash.
PER SERVING *208 cal., 7g fat (4g sat. fat), 20mg chol., 303mg sodium, 34g carb. (13g sugars, 8g fiber), 3g pro.*

ROASTED BUTTERNUT SQUASH DIPPERS

CHEESY SNACK MIX

Our love for Mexican food inspired me to add taco seasoning to my party mix. The flavor is mild enough to make this a kid-friendly snack.

—**ELIZABETH WYNNE** AZTEC, NM

PREP: 10 MIN. • **COOK:** 5 MIN. + COOLING
MAKES: 2½ QUARTS

- 3 **cups Corn Chex**
- 3 **cups Rice Chex**
- 3 **cups cheddar miniature pretzels**
- ¼ **cup butter, melted**
- 1 **envelope cheesy taco seasoning**
- 2 **cups white cheddar popcorn**

1. In a large microwave-safe bowl, combine cereal and pretzels. In a small bowl, mix melted butter and taco seasoning; drizzle over cereal mixture and toss to coat.
2. Microwave, uncovered, on high for 3-3½ minutes or until heated through, stirring once every minute. Stir in popcorn. Transfer to a baking sheet to cool completely. Store in an airtight container.
NOTE *This recipe was tested in a 1,100-watt microwave.*
PER SERVING *¾ cup: 151 cal., 5g fat (3g sat. fat), 11mg chol., 362mg sodium, 23g carb. (2g sugars, 1g fiber), 3g pro.* **Diabetic Exchanges:** *1½ starch, 1 fat.*

WATERMELON-LIME
COOLER

CHAMPIONSHIP BEAN DIP

My friends and neighbors expect me to bring this irresistible dip to every gathering. When I arrive, they ask, "You brought your bean dip, didn't you?" If there are any leftovers, I use them to make bean and cheese burritos the next day. I've given out this recipe probably a hundred times.

—**WENDI WAVRIN LAW** OMAHA, NE

PREP: 10 MIN. • **COOK:** 2 HOURS
MAKES: 4½ CUPS

- 1 can (16 ounces) refried beans
- 1 cup picante sauce
- 1 cup shredded Monterey Jack cheese
- 1 cup shredded cheddar cheese
- ¾ cup sour cream
- 3 ounces cream cheese, softened
- 1 tablespoon chili powder
- ¼ teaspoon ground cumin
  Tortilla chips and salsa

1. In a large bowl, combine the first eight ingredients; transfer to a 1½-qt. slow cooker.

2. Cover and cook on high 2 hours or until heated through, stirring once or twice. Serve bean dip with tortilla chips and salsa.

PER SERVING *2 tablespoons: 57 cal., 4g fat (2g sat. fat), 12mg chol., 151mg sodium, 3g carb. (1g sugars, 1g fiber), 2g pro.*

⑤ INGREDIENTS   FAST FIX

WATERMELON-LIME COOLER

When the weather heats up, chill some glasses and cool down with a slushy blend of watermelon, lime and ginger ale. Slurp and repeat.

—*TASTE OF HOME* **TEST KITCHEN**

START TO FINISH: 10 MIN.
MAKES: 12 SERVINGS

- 12 cups cubed seedless watermelon, frozen, divided
- ¾ teaspoon grated lime peel, divided
- 6 cups chilled ginger ale, divided

Place 4 cups frozen watermelon, ¼ teaspoon lime peel and 2 cups ginger ale in a blender; cover and process until slushy. Serve immediately. Repeat twice.

PER SERVING *1 cup: 82 cal., 0 fat (0 sat. fat), 0 chol., 14mg sodium, 24g carb. (23g sugars, 1g fiber), 1g pro.*

HARVEST PUMPKIN DIP

Beat 8 ounces softened cream cheese, 2 cups confectioners' sugar, 3 teaspoons pumpkin pie spice, 1 teaspoon vanilla and ½ teaspoon ground ginger until blended. Gradually beat in 1 can (15 ounces) pumpkin until smooth. Serve with apple and pear slices. Refrigerate leftovers. Makes 12 servings.

—**CHRISTY JOHNSON** COLUMBUS, OH

THREE CHEESE PEPPERONCINI SPREAD

BLUE CHEESE POTATO CHIPS

Game day calls for something bold. I top potato chips with tomatoes, bacon and tangy blue cheese. I make two big pans, and they always disappear.

—**BONNIE HAWKINS** ELKHORN, WI

START TO FINISH: 15 MIN.
MAKES: 10 SERVINGS

- 1 package (8½ ounces) kettle-cooked potato chips
- 2 medium tomatoes, seeded and chopped
- 8 bacon strips, cooked and crumbled
- 6 green onions, chopped
- 1 cup crumbled blue cheese

1. Preheat broiler. In a 15x10x1-in. baking pan, arrange the potato chips in an even layer. Top with the remaining ingredients.
2. Broil 4-5 in. from heat 2-3 minutes or until cheese begins to melt. Serve immediately.
PER SERVING *215 cal., 14g fat (5g sat. fat), 17mg chol., 359mg sodium, 16g carb. (2g sugars, 1g fiber), 6g pro.*

MANMOSA

Here's a fun adaptation of the beloved brunch beverage, the sweet and fruity mimosa. This delightful combination of orange juice and beer is a tasty kickoff to Dad's special day.

—**MIKE DIETIKER** ELBURN, IL

START TO FINISH: 5 MIN.
MAKES: 2 SERVINGS

- 1 bottle (12 ounces) beer, chilled
- 1 cup orange juice
- 2 ounces Triple Sec

Divide beer between two tall glasses. Add ½ cup orange juice and 1 ounce Triple Sec to each glass.
PER SERVING *1⅓ cups: 229 cal., 0 fat (0 sat. fat), 0 chol., 7mg sodium, 31g carb. (28g sugars, 0 fiber), 1g pro.*

THREE CHEESE PEPPERONCINI SPREAD

Our big family loves to celebrate with food. Here's my take on a cheesy Greek spread called *Kopanisti*. We serve it with pita crisps or crackers.

—**MICHAEL HALL** GOODLAND, IN

PREP: 10 MINUTES + CHILLING
MAKES: 16 SERVINGS

- 1 package (8 ounces) cream cheese, cubed and softened
- 1 cup crumbled feta cheese
- ½ cup crumbled blue cheese
- ½ cup coarsely chopped pepperoncini
- 1 tablespoon juice from pepperoncini
- 3 tablespoons olive oil
- ½ teaspoon minced garlic clove
- ½ teaspoon pepper
- ½ teaspoon crushed red pepper flakes, optional
  Assorted crackers

1. Place first eight ingredients in a food processor; if desired, add pepper flakes. Pulse just until combined (do not process until smooth).
2. Remove to a bowl; refrigerate, covered, at least 1 hour. Serve with crackers.
PER SERVING *2 tablespoons: 105 cal., 10g fat (5g sat. fat), 23mg chol., 172mg sodium, 1g carb. (0 sugars, 0 fiber), 3g pro.*

BLUE CHEESE
POTATO CHIPS

EAT SMART FAST FIX ▶
GOAT CHEESE MUSHROOMS

Stuffed mushrooms are superstars in the hot appetizer category. I use baby portobellos and load them up with goat cheese and sweet red peppers.

—**MIKE BASS** ALVIN, TX

START TO FINISH: 30 MIN.
MAKES: 2 DOZEN

- 24 **baby portobello mushrooms (about 1 pound), stems removed**
- ½ **cup crumbled goat cheese**
- ½ **cup chopped drained roasted sweet red peppers**
  Pepper to taste
- 4 **teaspoons olive oil**
  Chopped fresh parsley

1. Preheat oven to 375°. Place the mushroom caps in a greased 15x10x1-in. baking pan. Fill each with 1 teaspoon cheese and top with 1 teaspoon chopped red pepper. Sprinkle with pepper; drizzle with oil.
2. Bake for 15-18 minutes or until tender. Sprinkle with parsley.

PER SERVING *1 stuffed mushroom: 19 cal., 1g fat (0 sat. fat), 3mg chol., 31mg sodium, 1g carb. (1g sugars, 0 fiber), 1g pro.*

GOAT CHEESE MUSHROOMS

ASIAGO BEEF TART

I love simple recipes that still feel fancy enough for guests. To achieve the velvety texture in this tart, I use creme fraiche, but sour cream works, too.

—**VERONICA CALLAGHAN** GLASTONBURY, CT

PREP: 25 MIN. • **BAKE:** 15 MIN.
MAKES: 16 SERVINGS

- 1 **sheet refrigerated pie pastry**
- ¾ **pound lean ground beef (90% lean)**
- 1 **shallot, finely chopped**
- 2 **large eggs**
- ¾ **cup sour cream or creme fraiche**
- ½ **teaspoon salt**
- ¼ **teaspoon pepper**
- ¾ **cup shredded part-skim mozzarella cheese**
- ⅔ **cup shredded Asiago cheese**
- ⅓ **cup oil-packed sun-dried tomatoes, coarsely chopped**
- ¼ **cup coarsely chopped fresh basil**
- 1 **teaspoon minced fresh rosemary or ¼ teaspoon dried rosemary, crushed**

TOPPINGS
- 2 **tablespoons pine nuts, toasted**
  Thinly sliced fresh basil, optional

1. Preheat oven to 400°. On a work surface, unroll pastry sheet; roll to a 12-in. circle. Press pastry onto bottom and up sides of an ungreased 11-in. tart pan with removable bottom. Refrigerate while preparing filling.
2. In a large skillet, cook the beef and shallot over medium heat 5-7 minutes or until the meat is no longer pink, breaking up beef into crumbles. Remove from heat.
3. In a small bowl, whisk eggs, sour cream, salt and pepper until blended. Stir in cheeses, sun-dried tomatoes, chopped basil and rosemary. Stir into beef mixture; pour into tart shell.
4. Bake tart on a lower oven rack for 15-20 minutes or until crust is golden brown and filling is set. Just before serving, add toppings as desired.

NOTE *To toast nuts, cook in a skillet over low heat until lightly browned, stirring occasionally.*

PER SERVING *1 slice: 172 cal., 11g fat (5g sat. fat), 54mg chol., 202mg sodium, 9g carb. (1g sugars, 0 fiber), 9g pro.*

JALAPENO-PECAN CHEESE SPREAD

I like to shape this cheesy spread like a Christmas tree around the holidays, but it's a recipe I make year-round.

—CHAROLETTE WESTFALL HOUSTON, TX

PREP: 15 MIN. + CHILLING ● **COOK:** 5 MIN.
MAKES: 2 CUPS

- 1 package (8 ounces) cream cheese, softened
- 1 cup shredded sharp white cheddar cheese
- 1 cup finely chopped pecans
- 4 green onions, finely chopped
- ¼ cup jalapeno pepper jelly
  Assorted crackers

1. In a bowl, beat cream cheese, cheddar cheese, pecans and green onions until blended. On a serving plate, form mixture into desired shape. Refrigerate, covered, at least 2 hours.

2. In a microwave, warm jelly until melted; spread over cheese spread. Serve with crackers.

PER SERVING *2 tablespoons (calculated without crackers): 139 cal., 12g fat (5g sat. fat), 23mg chol., 99mg sodium, 6g carb. (4g sugars, 1g fiber), 3g pro.*

FAST FIX ▶
FROTHY MEXI-MOCHA COFFEE

Who needs a gourmet coffeehouse when you can whip up your own delicious treat at home? This will wow your friends.

—MARIA REGAKIS SAUGUS, MA

START TO FINISH: 15 MIN.
MAKES: 4 SERVINGS

- 1 cup packed brown sugar
- 4 ounces semisweet chocolate, chopped
- 2 orange peel strips (1 to 3 inches)
- ½ teaspoon ground cinnamon
- ¼ teaspoon ground allspice
- 3 cups hot strong brewed coffee
- ½ cup half-and-half cream, warmed
  Optional garnishes: cinnamon sticks, orange peel and whipped cream

1. Place the first five ingredients in a blender; cover and process until chocolate is finely chopped. Add the coffee; cover and process 1-2 minutes or until chocolate is melted. Transfer to a small saucepan; heat through.

2. Return mixture to blender; add the cream. Cover and process until frothy. Strain mixture, discarding solids; serve coffee in mugs. Garnish as desired.

PER SERVING *1 cup (calculated without garnishes): 392 cal., 12g fat (7g sat. fat), 15mg chol., 37mg sodium, 71g carb. (68g sugars, 2g fiber), 3g pro.*

JALAPENO-PECAN CHEESE SPREAD

LEMON-HERB OLIVES
WITH GOAT CHEESE

LEMON-HERB OLIVES WITH GOAT CHEESE

Greek olives have a fruity flavor that comes into play when you mix them with lemon and fresh herbs. Spoon over goat cheese and serve with crackers.

—JEANNE AMBROSE MILWAUKEE, WI

START TO FINISH: 15 MIN.
MAKES: 6 SERVINGS

- 3 tablespoons olive oil
- 2 teaspoons grated lemon peel
- 1 garlic clove, minced
- ½ teaspoon minced fresh oregano or rosemary
- ¼ teaspoon crushed red pepper flakes
- ½ cup assorted pitted Greek olives
- 1 package (5.3 ounces) fresh goat cheese
- 1 tablespoon minced fresh basil
  Assorted crackers

1. In a small skillet, combine the first five ingredients; heat over medium heat 2-3 minutes or just until fragrant, stirring occasionally. Stir in olives; heat through, allowing flavors to blend. Cool completely.
2. To serve, place cheese on a serving plate. Stir basil into olive mixture; spoon over cheese and serve with crackers.
PER SERVING (*calculated without crackers*): *135 cal., 13g fat (3g sat. fat), 17mg chol., 285mg sodium, 2g carb. (0 sugars, 0 fiber), 3g pro.*

BLT BITES

These quick hors d'oeuvres may be mini, but their bacon and tomato flavor is full-size. I serve them at parties, brunches and picnics, and they're always a hit. My kids love them, too!

—KELLIE REMMEN DETROIT LAKES, MN

PREP: 25 MIN. + CHILLING
MAKES: 16-20 APPETIZERS

- 16 to 20 cherry tomatoes
- 1 pound sliced bacon, cooked and crumbled
- ½ cup mayonnaise
- ⅓ cup chopped green onions
- 3 tablespoons grated Parmesan cheese
- 2 tablespoons snipped fresh parsley

1. Cut a thin slice off of each tomato top. Scoop out and discard pulp. Invert the tomatoes on a paper towel to drain.
2. In a small bowl, combine the remaining ingredients. Spoon or pipe into tomatoes. Refrigerate for several hours.
PER SERVING *1 piece: 113 cal., 10g fat (3g sat. fat), 11mg chol., 206mg sodium, 1g carb. (1g sugars, 0 fiber), 3g pro.*

MILD TOMATO SALSA

I got this salsa recipe from my sister, and my children and I have been making it ever since. We pair pint jars with bags of tortilla chips for zesty Christmas gifts. When the kids give this present to their teachers, they can truly say they helped make it.

—PAMELA LUNDSTRUM BIRD ISLAND, MN

PREP: 40 MIN. + SIMMERING
PROCESS: 20 MIN. •**MAKES:** 10 PINTS

- 10½ pounds tomatoes (about 35 medium), peeled and quartered
- 4 medium green peppers, chopped
- 3 large onions, chopped
- 2 cans (12 ounces each) tomato paste
- 1¾ cups white vinegar
- ½ cup sugar
- 1 medium sweet red pepper, chopped
- 1 celery rib, chopped
- 15 garlic cloves, minced
- 4 to 5 jalapeno peppers, seeded and chopped
- ¼ cup canning salt
- ¼ to ½ teaspoon hot pepper sauce

1. In a stockpot, cook tomatoes, uncovered, over medium heat for 20 minutes. Drain, reserving 2 cups liquid. Return tomatoes to the pot.
2. Stir in the green peppers, onions, tomato paste, vinegar, sugar, red pepper, celery, garlic, jalapenos, canning salt, hot pepper sauce and reserved tomato liquid. Bring to a boil. Reduce heat; simmer, uncovered, for 1 hour, stirring frequently.
3. Ladle hot mixture into 10 hot 1-pint jars, leaving ½-in. headspace. Remove air bubbles and adjust headspace, if necessary, by adding hot mixture. Wipe rims. Center lids on jars; screw on bands until fingertip tight.
4. Place the jars into canner with simmering water, ensuring that they are completely covered with water. Bring to a boil; process for 20 minutes. Remove jars and cool.
NOTES *Wear disposable gloves when cutting hot peppers; the oils can burn skin. Avoid touching your face. The processing time listed is for altitudes of 1,000 feet or fewer. For altitudes up to 3,000 feet, add 5 minutes; 6,000 feet, add 10 minutes; 8,000 feet, add 15 minutes; 10,000 feet, add 20 minutes.*
PER SERVING *2 tablespoons: 14 cal., 0 fat (0 sat. fat), 0 chol., 182mg sodium, 3g carb. (2g sugars, 1g fiber), 0 pro.*

MILD TOMATO SALSA

BUTTERNUT-GOUDA
POT STICKERS

bottoms are crisp and the water is evaporated, 1-2 minutes. Repeat twice.

FREEZE OPTION *Cover and freeze uncooked pot stickers on lightly floured baking sheets until firm. Transfer to resealable plastic freezer bags; return to freezer. To use, cook pot stickers as directed, increasing time as necessary to heat through.*

NOTE *This recipe was tested in a 1,100-watt microwave.*

PER SERVING *1 pot sticker: 55 cal., 3g fat (1g sat. fat), 7mg chol., 84mg sodium, 7g carb. (1g sugars, 1g fiber), 2g pro.*

APPETIZER TORTILLA PINWHEELS

A friend gave me the recipe for this attractive and tasty appetizer. You can prepare the pinwheels in advance and slice just before serving to save time for other party preparations.

—**PAT WAYMIRE** YELLOW SPRINGS, OH

PREP: 20 MIN. + CHILLING
MAKES: ABOUT 4 DOZEN

- 1 cup (8 ounces) sour cream
- 1 package (8 ounces) cream cheese, softened
- 1 can (4¼ ounces) chopped ripe olives
- 1 can (4 ounces) chopped green chilies, well drained
- 1 cup shredded cheddar cheese
- ½ cup chopped green onions
  Garlic powder to taste
  Seasoned salt to taste
- 5 flour tortillas (10 inches), room temperature
  Fresh parsley for garnish
  Salsa

1. In a large bowl, beat the first eight ingredients until blended. Spread over the tortillas; roll up tightly. Wrap each with plastic, twisting ends; refrigerate for several hours.
2. Unwrap; cut into ½-in. to ¾-in. slices. Discard ends. Garnish with parsley. Serve with salsa if desired.

PER SERVING *3 pinwheels: 180 cal., 11g fat (7g sat. fat), 33mg chol., 305mg sodium, 12g carb. (1g sugars, 2g fiber), 5g pro.*

FREEZE IT

BUTTERNUT-GOUDA POT STICKERS

My family can't get enough butternut squash. I had some left over, so I used pot sticker wraps and veggies to create these fun little appetizers.

—**CARLA MENDRES** WINNIPEG, MB

PREP: 45 MIN. • **COOK:** 15 MIN.
MAKES: ABOUT 4 DOZEN

- 1 small butternut squash (about 2½ pounds)
- 1 tablespoon butter
- 1 small sweet red pepper, finely chopped
- 1 small onion, finely chopped
- 2 cups shredded Gouda cheese
- ½ teaspoon salt
- ½ teaspoon minced fresh thyme or ⅛ teaspoon dried thyme
- ½ teaspoon pepper
- 1 package (10 ounces) pot sticker or gyoza wrappers
- 3 tablespoons canola oil, divided
- ¾ cup water, divided

1. Halve squash lengthwise; discard seeds. Place squash in a microwave-safe dish, cut side down; add ½ in. water. Microwave, covered, on high until soft, 15-20 minutes; cool slightly. Scoop out pulp and mash.
2. In a skillet, heat butter over medium heat; saute pepper and onion until tender, 4-6 minutes. Add to the squash; stir in the cheese, salt, thyme and pepper.
3. Place 1 tablespoon filling on each wrapper (keep remaining wrappers covered with a damp towel). Moisten edge of wrapper with water; fold over to enclose filling while pleating the front side to form a pouch. Stand on a work surface to flatten the bottom, curving ends slightly.
4. In a large nonstick skillet, heat 1 tablespoon oil over medium heat. Place a third of the pot stickers in the pan; cook until the bottoms are lightly browned, 1-2 minutes. Add ¼ cup of water (water may spatter); cook, covered, until filling is heated through, 3-4 minutes. Uncover; cook until the

VIDALIA ONION
SWISS DIP

1. Preheat oven to 350°. Spread cream cheese into an ungreased shallow 1-qt. baking dish. Layer with chicken, wing sauce and salad dressing. Sprinkle with cheese.

2. Bake, uncovered, 20-25 minutes or until cheese is melted. Serve with baguette slices.

PER SERVING *2 tablespoons dip (calculated without dippers): 156 cal., 13g fat (7g sat. fat), 38mg chol., 484mg sodium, 2g carb. (1g sugars, 0 fiber), 7g pro.*

⑤INGREDIENTS

CRANBERRY FIZZ

With just five ingredients, this wonderfully tangy punch couldn't be much simpler to stir together.
—**SUZETTE JURY** KEENE, CA

PREP: 5 MIN. + CHILLING
MAKES: 2 QUARTS

- 1 bottle (32 ounces) cranberry juice
- 1 cup orange juice
- 1 cup ruby red grapefruit juice
- ½ cup sugar
- 2 cups ginger ale, chilled

In a pitcher, combine the cranberry, orange and grapefruit juices with the sugar. Refrigerate until chilled. Just before serving, stir in ginger ale.

PER SERVING *1 cup: 154 cal., 0 fat (0 sat. fat), 0 chol., 7mg sodium, 40g carb. (36g sugars, 0 fiber), 1g pro.*

VIDALIA ONION SWISS DIP

I make one of those sweet, creamy, cheesy dips you can't resist. Bake it in the oven, or use the slow cooker to make it ooey-gooey marvelous.
—**JUDY BATSON** TAMPA, FL

PREP: 5 MIN. ● **COOK:** 25 MIN.
MAKES: 20 SERVINGS (¼ CUP EACH)

- 3 cups chopped Vidalia or other sweet onion (about 1 large)
- 2 cups shredded Swiss cheese
- 2 cups mayonnaise
- ¼ cup prepared horseradish
- 1 teaspoon hot pepper sauce
  Fresh coarsely ground pepper, optional
  Assorted crackers or fresh vegetables

1. Preheat oven to 375°. In a large bowl, mix the first five ingredients. Transfer to a deep-dish pie plate.

2. Bake, uncovered, 25-30 minutes or until edges are golden brown and onion is tender. If desired, sprinkle with pepper. Serve warm with crackers or fresh vegetables.

PER SERVING *¼ cup (calculated without crackers and vegetables): 212 cal., 21g fat (4g sat. fat), 18mg chol., 143mg sodium, 3g carb. (1g sugars, 1g fiber), 3g pro.*

FAST FIX

BUFFALO CHICKEN DIP

Buffalo wing sauce, cream cheese and ranch make a great party dip. Everywhere I take it, people want the recipe.
—**BELINDA GIBSON** DRY RIDGE, KY

START TO FINISH: 30 MIN.
MAKES: ABOUT 2 CUPS

- 1 package (8 ounces) cream cheese, softened
- 1 can (10 ounces) chunk white chicken, drained
- ½ cup Buffalo wing sauce
- ½ cup ranch or blue cheese salad dressing
- 2 cups shredded Colby-Monterey Jack cheese
  French bread baguette slices, celery ribs or tortilla chips

READER RAVE

"Easy and tasty. I don't drink alcohol, but some of our guests added white rum for an adult beverage. Everyone liked it and I appreciate that this drink works for kids and adults. Many punches I run into at parties either have ice cream, which makes them kid-friendly but too sweet for my tastes, or they are spiked with alcohol. This is a versatile drink for all ages."

—**CORWIN44** TASTEOFHOME.COM

**Sue Gronholz's
Basil & Heirloom Tomato Toss**
PAGE 30

Side Dishes & Salads

Here are dozens of simple, healthy, satisfying recipes that are ideal for rounding out weeknight menus, holiday feasts and more. You'll discover light but hearty main-dish salads, the perfect picnic sides and the best potato salad on the block.

Cindy Heinbaugh's Gingered Spaghetti Salad
PAGE 26

Jenny Dawson's Salmon & Spinach Salad with Avocado *PAGE 29*

Ellie Martin Cliffe's Lemony Zucchini Ribbons
PAGE 25

BACON & BLUE STUFFED
SWEET POTATOES

STRAWBERRY-BLUE CHEESE STEAK SALAD

START TO FINISH: 30 MIN.
MAKES: 4 SERVINGS

- 1 **beef top sirloin steak (¾ inch thick and 1 pound)**
- ½ **teaspoon salt**
- ¼ **teaspoon pepper**
- 2 **teaspoons olive oil**
- 2 **tablespoons lime juice**

SALAD

- 1 **bunch romaine, torn (about 10 cups)**
- 2 **cups fresh strawberries, halved**
- ¼ **cup thinly sliced red onion**
- ¼ **cup crumbled blue cheese**
- ¼ **cup chopped walnuts, toasted**
  Reduced-fat balsamic vinaigrette

1. Season steak with salt and pepper. In a large skillet, heat oil over medium heat. Add steak; cook 5-7 minutes on each side until desired doneness (for medium-rare, a thermometer should read 145°; medium, 160°; well-done, 170°). Remove from pan; let stand 5 minutes. Cut steak into bite-size strips; toss with lime juice.

2. On a platter, combine romaine, strawberries and onion; top with steak. Sprinkle with cheese and nuts. Serve with vinaigrette.

PER SERVING (*calculated without vinaigrette*): *289 cal., 15g fat (4g sat. fat), 52mg chol., 452mg sodium, 12g carb. (5g sugars, 4g fiber), 29g pro.* ***Diabetic Exchanges:*** *4 lean meat, 2 vegetable, 2 fat, ½ fruit.*

HEALTH TIP *If you're looking to trim calories, leave off the walnuts and blue cheese; they're adding almost 40 calories per serving.*

BACON & BLUE STUFFED SWEET POTATOES

Give sweet potatoes the good stuff like pear, bacon, honey and fresh tarragon. If Gorgonzola isn't your thing, swap in some shredded plain or smoked Gouda.
—**JEANNE HOLT** MENDOTA HEIGHTS, MN

PREP: 20 MIN. • **BAKE:** 65 MIN.
MAKES: 4 SERVINGS

- 4 **medium sweet potatoes (about 10 ounces each)**
- 3 **tablespoons butter, softened**
- 2 **teaspoons honey**
- ½ **teaspoon salt**
- ⅛ **teaspoon cayenne pepper**
- ⅛ **teaspoon pepper**
- 1 **small ripe pear, peeled and chopped**
- 4 **bacon strips, cooked and chopped, divided**
- ¼ **cup plus 3 tablespoons crumbled Gorgonzola cheese, divided**
- 2 **green onions, thinly sliced**
- 2 **teaspoons minced fresh tarragon or ¼ teaspoon dried tarragon**

1. Preheat oven to 375°. Scrub the potatoes; pierce several times with a fork. Bake on a foil-lined baking sheet until tender, 45-60 minutes. Cool potatoes slightly.

2. Cut a thin slice from top of each potato. Scoop out pulp, leaving ¼-in.-thick shells. Mash pulp with butter, honey and seasonings. Stir in pear, ⅓ cup chopped bacon, ¼ cup cheese, green onions and tarragon. Spoon into shells; return to pan. Top with remaining cheese.

3. Bake until heated through, 20-25 minutes. Sprinkle with remaining bacon.

PER SERVING *1 stuffed potato: 388 cal., 16g fat (9g sat. fat), 42mg chol., 696mg sodium, 55g carb. (25g sugars, 7g fiber), 9g pro.*

CILANTRO GINGER CARROTS

Slice 1 pound carrots on the diagonal. Saute in 1 tablespoon butter until crisp-tender. Add 1½ teaspoons minced fresh ginger; cook 1 minute longer. Stir in 2 tablespoons chopped fresh cilantro, ½ teaspoon salt and ¼ teaspoon pepper.
—***TASTE OF HOME*** TEST KITCHEN

At lunch with a friend one day, she told me about a steak salad she'd had at a party. It sounded so fantastic, I had to try it for myself. My family would eat it nonstop if we could. We can't seem to get enough of that dressing! —**ALMA WINBERRY** GREAT FALLS, MT

STRAWBERRY-BLUE CHEESE STEAK SALAD

DILL-MARINATED
BROCCOLI

CUCUMBER AND
RED ONION SALAD

EAT SMART ⑤**INGREDIENTS**

DILL-MARINATED BROCCOLI

A co-worker tipped me off to this splashy marinade for broccoli. The longer you wait, the better it gets. Add some fresh cauliflower if you have it.
—**TIFFONY BUSH** HUNTINGDON, PA

PREP: 15 MIN. + MARINATING
MAKES: 8 SERVINGS

- 6 **cups fresh broccoli florets (about ¾ pound)**
- 1 **cup canola oil**
- 1 **cup cider vinegar**
- 2 **tablespoons snipped fresh dill**
- 2 **teaspoons sugar**
- 1 **teaspoon garlic salt**
- 1 **teaspoon salt**

1. Place broccoli in a large resealable plastic bag. Whisk together remaining ingredients; add to broccoli. Seal bag and turn to coat; refrigerate 4 hours or overnight.
2. To serve, drain broccoli, discarding the marinade.

PER SERVING *79 cal., 7g fat (1g sat. fat), 0 chol., 119mg sodium, 3g carb. (0 sugars, 2g fiber), 2g pro.* **Diabetic Exchanges:** *1½ fat, 1 vegetable.*

EAT SMART ⑤**INGREDIENTS**

CUCUMBER AND RED ONION SALAD

My go-to salad for parties and picnics uses the bumper crop of cucumbers from my garden. I pile it on top of sandwiches and burgers, too.
—**BRYNN STECKMAN** NEW ALBANY, OH

PREP: 15 MIN. + CHILLING
MAKES: 4 SERVINGS

- 2 **small English cucumbers, thinly sliced**
- 1 **cup thinly sliced red onion**
- 2 **tablespoons white wine vinegar or rice vinegar**
- 1 **tablespoon white vinegar**
- ¼ **teaspoon salt**
- ¼ **teaspoon pepper**
- ¼ **teaspoon sesame oil**

Place all ingredients in a bowl; toss to combine. Refrigerate, covered, about 1 hour. Serve with a slotted spoon.
PER SERVING *¾ cup: 31 cal., trace fat (trace sat. fat), 0 chol., 151mg sodium, 7g carb. (2g sugars, 1g fiber), 1g pro.* **Diabetic Exchanges:** *1 vegetable.*

TOP TIP

CUKE KNOW-HOW

Most cucumbers are coated with a protective wax to prolong freshness, so you should peel them before eating. There's no need to peel English cucumbers that come wrapped in plastic, though. Ditto for cukes from the farmers market or your own garden. Whether or not to peel these is a matter of preference.

FETA GARBANZO BEAN SALAD

This quick chickpea salad is a hit with my crowd. If there are any leftovers (rarely happens), put them into a pita pocket for lunch.

—**JUDY DOEPEL** CHARLTON, NY

START TO FINISH: 15 MIN.
MAKES: 4 SERVINGS

- 1 **can (15 ounces) garbanzo beans, rinsed and drained**
- 1½ **cups coarsely chopped English cucumber (about ½ medium)**
- 1 **can (2¼ ounces) sliced ripe olives, drained**
- 1 **medium tomato, seeded and chopped**
- ¼ **cup thinly sliced red onion**
- ¼ **cup chopped fresh parsley**
- 3 **tablespoons olive oil**
- 1 **tablespoon lemon juice**
- ¼ **teaspoon salt**
- ⅛ **teaspoon pepper**
- 5 **cups torn mixed salad greens**
- ½ **cup crumbled feta cheese**

Place the first 11 ingredients in a large bowl; toss to combine. Sprinkle with feta cheese.
PER SERVING *2 cups: 268 cal., 16g fat (3g sat. fat), 8mg chol., 586mg sodium, 24g carb. (4g sugars, 7g fiber), 9g pro.* **Diabetic Exchanges:** *3 fat, 1 starch, 1 lean meat, 1 vegetable.*

FETA GARBANZO
BEAN SALAD

LEMONY ZUCCHINI RIBBONS

Fresh zucchini gets a drizzle of lemony goodness in this fab salad. Sprinkle on the goat cheese or feta and dive in.

—**ELLIE MARTIN CLIFFE** MILWAUKEE, WI

START TO FINISH: 15 MIN.
MAKES: 4 SERVINGS

- 1 **tablespoon olive oil**
- ½ **teaspoon grated lemon peel**
- 1 **tablespoon lemon juice**
- ½ **teaspoon salt**
- ¼ **teaspoon pepper**
- 3 **medium zucchini**
- ⅓ **cup crumbled goat or feta cheese**

1. For dressing, in a small bowl, mix the first five ingredients. Using a vegetable peeler, shave zucchini lengthwise into very thin slices; arrange on a serving plate.
2. To serve, drizzle with dressing and toss lightly to coat. Top with cheese.
PER SERVING *¾ cup: 83 cal., 6g fat (2g sat. fat), 12mg chol., 352mg sodium, 5g carb. (3g sugars, 2g fiber), 3g pro.* **Diabetic Exchanges:** *1 fat, 1 vegetable.*
HEALTH TIP *Making this colorful salad with zucchini instead of cooked pasta saves 130 calories per serving.*

FAST & FABULOUS
THAI CHICKEN SALAD

FAST & FABULOUS THAI CHICKEN SALAD

This delicious, healthful recipe looks time-consuming, but it's as simple as can be. Aside from the mixing, the only prep work is chopping a red pepper and some green onions. It's always a crowd-pleaser.

—**ELINOR IVES** FISKDALE, MA

START TO FINISH: 20 MIN.
MAKES: 6 SERVINGS

- 1 **package (14 ounces) coleslaw mix**
- ⅓ **cup sesame ginger salad dressing**
- 2 **cups cubed cooked chicken**
- ½ **cup Thai peanut sauce**
- 1 **medium sweet red pepper, julienned**
- ½ **cup chow mein noodles**
- 2 **green onions, chopped**

In a large bowl, combine coleslaw mix and salad dressing. Transfer to a serving platter. Combine chicken and peanut sauce; place over coleslaw mixture. Top with red pepper, noodles and onions.
PER SERVING *230 cal., 12g fat (3g sat. fat), 42mg chol., 588mg sodium, 13g carb. (7g sugars, 3g fiber), 17g pro.* **Diabetic Exchanges:** *2 lean meat, 1 vegetable, 1 fat, ½ starch.*

CHICKEN PASTA
CAESAR SALAD

1 small sweet yellow pepper, chopped
1 small red onion, finely chopped
3 green onions, sliced

1. Cook spaghetti according to package directions, adding edamame during the last 5 minutes of cooking. Rinse in cold water and drain well. Meanwhile, stir ginger into salad dressing.

2. In a large bowl, combine spaghetti, chicken, cucumber, peppers and red onion. Add dressing; toss to coat. Sprinkle with green onions.

PER SERVING *1¾ cups: 353 cal., 5g fat (1g sat. fat), 40mg chol., 432mg sodium, 53g carb. (6g sugars, 8g fiber), 26g pro.*

HEALTH TIP *Make this meatless by omitting the chicken and tossing in more edamame, a legume that is higher in protein than most.*

⑤ INGREDIENTS

CREAMY TWICE-BAKED SWEET POTATOES

I like prepping these sweet potatoes ahead of time so I can focus on the main dish. The cream cheese makes them extra luscious.
—**LINDA CALL** FALUN, KS

PREP: 15 MIN. ● **BAKE:** 1 HOUR
MAKES: 2 SERVINGS

2 medium sweet potatoes (about 10 ounces each)
2 ounces cream cheese, softened
1 tablespoon brown sugar
¼ teaspoon ground cinnamon
2 tablespoons chopped pecans

1. Preheat oven to 375°. Scrub potatoes; pierce several times with a fork. Bake on a foil-lined baking sheet until tender, 45-60 minutes. Cool slightly.

2. Cut off a thin slice from top of each potato. Scoop out pulp, leaving ¼-in.-thick shells. Mash pulp with cream cheese, brown sugar and cinnamon. Spoon into shells; return to pan. Top with pecans. Bake until heated through, 15-20 minutes.

PER SERVING *1 stuffed potato: 297 cal., 16g fat (7g sat. fat), 32mg chol., 100mg sodium, 36g carb. (18g sugars, 4g fiber), 5g pro.*

EAT SMART **FAST FIX** ▶

CHICKEN PASTA CAESAR SALAD

My colleagues and I made a pact to eat healthier, and we took turns sharing dishes. I'm happy to report that, thanks to recipes like this crisp and tangy salad, we all trimmed down.
—**TERESA JORDAN** SPRINGVILLE, UT

START TO FINISH: 30 MIN.
MAKES: 6 SERVINGS

3 cups uncooked whole wheat spiral pasta (about 8 ounces)
6 cups torn romaine
3 cups coarsely shredded rotisserie chicken
2 medium tomatoes, chopped
½ cup shredded Parmesan cheese
½ cup creamy Caesar salad dressing
⅓ cup slivered almonds, toasted

Cook pasta according to the package directions. Drain; rinse with cold water and drain again. Toss with the remaining ingredients. Serve immediately.

NOTE *To toast nuts, bake in a shallow pan in a 350° oven for 5-10 minutes or cook in a skillet over low heat until lightly browned, stirring occasionally.*
PER SERVING *2 cups: 422 cal., 22g fat (5g sat. fat), 75mg chol., 416mg sodium, 26g carb. (3g sugars, 5g fiber), 30g pro.*

EAT SMART **FAST FIX** ▶

GINGERED SPAGHETTI SALAD

On sunny spring days, this chilled chicken salad brimming with veggies is perfect for a backyard picnic.
—**CINDY HEINBAUGH** AURORA, CO

START TO FINISH: 30 MIN.
MAKES: 8 SERVINGS

1 package (16 ounces) whole wheat spaghetti
1 cup frozen shelled edamame
1 teaspoon minced fresh gingerroot
1 cup reduced-fat sesame ginger salad dressing
3 cups cubed cooked chicken breast
1 English cucumber, chopped
1 medium sweet red pepper, chopped

ROASTED
VEGETABLES
WITH SAGE

EAT SMART

ROASTED VEGETABLES WITH SAGE

When I can't decide what vegetable to serve, I just roast a variety. That's how we boost the veggie love at our house.
—**BETTY FULKS** ONIA, AR

PREP: 20 MIN. • **BAKE:** 35 MIN.
MAKES: 8 SERVINGS

- 5 cups cubed peeled butternut squash
- ½ pound fingerling potatoes (about 2 cups)
- 1 cup fresh Brussels sprouts, halved
- 1 cup fresh baby carrots
- 3 tablespoons butter
- 1 tablespoon minced fresh sage or 1 teaspoon dried sage leaves
- 1 garlic clove, minced
- ½ teaspoon salt

1. Preheat the oven to 425°. Place the vegetables in a large bowl. In a microwave, melt the butter; stir in the remaining ingredients. Add to vegetables and toss to coat.
2. Transfer to a greased 15x10x1-in. baking pan. Roast 35-45 minutes or until tender, stirring occasionally.
PER SERVING ¾ cup: 122 cal., 5g fat (3g sat. fat), 11mg chol., 206mg sodium, 20g carb. (4g sugars, 3g fiber), 2g pro. **Diabetic Exchanges:** 1 starch, 1 fat.

SWEET POTATO WEDGES WITH CHILI MAYO

Cajun spices bring the zing to roasted sweet potatoes. They're delicious dunked in chili-spiced mayo.
—**RAYMONDE BOURGEOIS** SWASTIKA, ON

PREP: 15 MIN. • **BAKE:** 30 MIN.
MAKES: 8 SERVINGS (1 CUP DIP)

- 6 small sweet potatoes
- 2 tablespoons olive oil
- 2 to 3 tablespoons Cajun seasoning

DIP
- 1 cup mayonnaise
- 4 teaspoons lemon juice
- 2 teaspoons chili powder or chili garlic sauce
- 2 teaspoons Dijon mustard

1. Preheat oven to 400°. Peel and cut each potato lengthwise into eight wedges. Toss with olive oil and Cajun seasoning; divide between two greased 15x10x1-in. pans.
2. Roast potatoes until tender, 30-45 minutes, turning once. Meanwhile, mix dip ingredients; serve with potatoes.
PER SERVING 1 wedge: 322 cal., 26g fat (4g sat. fat), 10mg chol., 600mg sodium, 22g carb. (9g sugars, 3g fiber), 2g pro.

⑤ INGREDIENTS FAST FIX ▶

CHEESY BACON SPAGHETTI SQUASH

This quick casserole is called cheesy for a reason. Stir in any kind you've got.
—**JEAN WILLIAMS** STILLWATER, OK

START TO FINISH: 30 MIN.
MAKES: 4 SERVINGS

- 1 large spaghetti squash (3½ pounds)
- 4 bacon strips, chopped
- 3 tablespoons butter
- 1 tablespoon brown sugar
- ½ teaspoon salt
- ¼ teaspoon pepper
- ½ cup shredded Swiss cheese

1. Halve squash lengthwise; discard seeds. Place squash on a microwave-safe plate, cut side down; microwave on high until tender, 15-20 minutes. Cool slightly. Separate strands with a fork.
2. In a large skillet, cook bacon over medium heat until crisp, stirring occasionally. With a slotted spoon, remove bacon to paper towels; reserve the drippings.
3. In same pan, heat drippings over medium heat; stir in butter, brown sugar, salt and pepper until blended. Add squash; toss and heat through. Remove from heat; stir in cheese. Top with bacon.
NOTE This recipe was tested in a 1,100-watt microwave.
PER SERVING 1 cup: 381 cal., 26g fat (12g sat. fat), 54mg chol., 627mg sodium, 32g carb. (4g sugars, 6g fiber), 10g pro.

CHEESY BACON
SPAGHETTI SQUASH

GRILLED FIRECRACKER
POTATO SALAD

GRILLED FIRECRACKER POTATO SALAD

I can eat potato salad like crazy. A little spice is nice, so I use cayenne and paprika in this grilled salad that comes with its own fireworks.

—ASHLEY ARMSTRONG KINGSLAND, GA

PREP: 20 MIN. • **GRILL:** 20 MIN. + CHILLING
MAKES: 16 SERVINGS (1 CUP EACH)

- 3 pounds small red potatoes (about 30), quartered
- 2 tablespoons olive oil
- 1 teaspoon salt
- ½ teaspoon pepper

DRESSING
- 1½ cups mayonnaise
- ½ cup finely chopped onion
- ¼ cup Dijon mustard
- 2 tablespoons sweet pickle relish
- ½ teaspoon paprika
- ¼ teaspoon cayenne pepper

SALAD
- 6 hard-cooked large eggs, chopped
- 2 celery ribs, finely chopped
   Minced fresh chives, optional

1. Toss potatoes with oil, salt and pepper; place in a grill wok or basket. Grill, covered, over medium heat 20-25 minutes or until potatoes are tender, stirring occasionally. Transfer potatoes to a large bowl; cool slightly.
2. In a small bowl, mix dressing ingredients. Add dressing, eggs and celery to potatoes; toss to combine. Refrigerate, covered, 1-2 hours or until cold. If desired, sprinkle with chives.
NOTE *If you do not have a grill wok or basket, use a large disposable foil pan and poke holes in the bottom of the pan.*
PER SERVING *1 cup: 265 cal., 20g fat (3g sat. fat), 77mg chol., 398mg sodium, 16g carb. (2g sugars, 2g fiber), 4g pro.*

EAT SMART FAST FIX
SALMON & SPINACH SALAD WITH AVOCADO

We eat a power salad packed with salmon and spinach at least once a week. It's a cinch to make, even after a hard day's work.

—JENNY DAWSON FOND DU LAC, WI

START TO FINISH: 25 MIN.
MAKES: 2 SERVINGS

- 2 salmon fillets (4 ounces each)
- ¼ teaspoon salt
- ⅛ teaspoon pepper
- 1 teaspoon canola oil
- 4 cups fresh baby spinach
- 2 tablespoons balsamic vinaigrette
- ½ medium ripe avocado, peeled and cubed
- 2 tablespoons dried cranberries
- 2 tablespoons sunflower kernels or pepitas (salted pumpkin seeds)
- 2 tablespoons chopped walnuts, toasted, optional

1. Sprinkle salmon with salt and pepper. In a large nonstick skillet coated with cooking spray, heat oil over medium heat. Add fillets, skin side up; cook 4-5 minutes on each side or until fish just begins to flake easily with a fork.
2. In a large bowl, toss spinach with vinaigrette; divide between two plates. Place salmon over spinach; top with remaining ingredients. Serve salad immediately.
NOTE *To toast nuts, bake in a shallow pan in a 350° oven for 5-10 minutes or cook in a skillet over low heat until lightly browned, stirring occasionally.*
PER SERVING *386 cal., 27g fat (4g sat. fat), 57mg chol., 614mg sodium, 15g carb. (7g sugars, 5g fiber), 23g pro. Diabetic Exchanges: 3 lean meat, 3 fat, 2 vegetable.*

CHICKEN TZATZIKI CUCUMBER BOATS

EAT SMART FAST FIX
CHICKEN TZATZIKI CUCUMBER BOATS

I've tended a garden for decades, and these colorful boats made from cucumbers hold my fresh tomatoes, peas and dill. It's absolute garden greatness.

—RONNA FARLEY ROCKVILLE, MD

START TO FINISH: 15 MIN.
MAKES: 2 SERVINGS

- 2 medium cucumbers
- ½ cup fat-free plain Greek yogurt
- 2 tablespoons mayonnaise
- ½ teaspoon garlic salt
- 3 teaspoons snipped fresh dill, divided
- 1 cup chopped cooked chicken breast
- 1 cup chopped seeded tomato (about 1 large), divided
- ½ cup fresh or frozen peas, thawed

1. Cut each cucumber lengthwise in half; scoop out pulp, leaving a ¼-in. shell. In a medium bowl, mix yogurt, mayonnaise, garlic salt and 1 teaspoon dill; gently stir in chicken, ¾ cup tomato and the peas.
2. Spoon into cucumber shells. Top with the remaining tomato and dill.
NOTE *Skip the peas for a fast and refreshing low-carb lunch or supper.*
PER SERVING *2 filled cucumber halves: 322 cal., 13g fat (2g sat. fat), 59mg chol., 398mg sodium, 18g carb. (10g sugars, 6g fiber), 34g pro. Diabetic Exchanges: 4 lean meat, 2 vegetable, 2 fat, ½ starch.*

HOW-TO
CHOP EGGS WITH EASE

Using a grid-style cooling rack is a faster, less slippery way to "chop" hard-cooked eggs. Set the rack on top of a bowl and smoosh the peeled eggs through.

EAT SMART FAST FIX ▶
STRAWBERRY GARDEN SALAD

When I take this cheery mix of berries, pineapple, red onion and feta to my book club, it's a blockbuster. I add a sprinkle of vanilla sugar almonds on top.
—**DEBORAH LOOP** CLINTON TOWNSHIP, MI

START TO FINISH: 15 MIN.
MAKES: 6 SERVINGS

- 8 **cups spring mix salad greens**
- 2 **cups halved fresh strawberries**
- 1 **cup cubed fresh pineapple**
- ½ **small red onion, thinly sliced**
- ⅓ **cup raspberry vinaigrette**
- ½ **cup crumbled feta cheese**
- ¼ **cup sliced almonds, toasted**

Place greens, fruit and onion in a large bowl. Drizzle with vinaigrette; toss gently to combine. Sprinkle with cheese and almonds. Serve salad immediately.

NOTE *To toast nuts, bake in a shallow pan in a 350° oven for 5-10 minutes or cook in a skillet over low heat until lightly browned, stirring occasionally.*
PER SERVING *1⅓ cups: 106 cal., 4g fat (1g sat. fat), 5mg chol., 164mg sodium, 15g carb. (8g sugars, 4g fiber), 4g pro.* **Diabetic Exchanges:** *1 vegetable, 1 fat, ½ fruit.*

HEALTH TIP *Switch to a baby kale salad blend for more fiber, vitamin C, calcium and iron.*

STRAWBERRY GARDEN SALAD

CITRUS FRUIT SALAD

FAST FIX ▶
CITRUS FRUIT SALAD

Fresh pineapple with yogurt and pecans is a welcome update to the classic ambrosia salad. We stir it up for breakfast, a snack or a cheery side.
—**HEATHER RIVERS** BOISE, ID

START TO FINISH: 25 MIN.
MAKES: 10 SERVINGS

- ½ **cup heavy whipping cream**
- ¾ **cup (6 ounces) vanilla yogurt**
- 1 **medium fresh pineapple, peeled, cored and cubed (about 5 cups)**
- 5 **tangerines, peeled and separated into segments**
- 1 **medium grapefruit, peeled and sectioned**
- ½ **cup chopped pecans, toasted**

1. In a large bowl, beat cream until stiff peaks form. Fold in yogurt.
2. Just before serving, add fruit and stir gently to combine. Sprinkle with toasted pecans.

NOTE *To toast nuts, bake in a shallow pan in a 350° oven for 5-10 minutes or cook in a skillet over low heat until lightly browned, stirring occasionally.*
PER SERVING *¾ cup: 176 cal., 9g fat (3g sat. fat), 17mg chol., 19mg sodium, 25g carb. (19g sugars, 3g fiber), 3g pro.*

EAT SMART FAST FIX ▶
BASIL & HEIRLOOM TOMATO TOSS

I came up with this garden-fresh salad to showcase the heirloom tomatoes and peppers we raised for our stall at the farmers market. Try out other types of basil like lemon, lime, licorice and cinnamon.
—**SUE GRONHOLZ** BEAVER DAM, WI

START TO FINISH: 15 MIN.
MAKES: 4 SERVINGS

- ¼ **cup olive oil**
- 3 **tablespoons red wine vinegar**
- 2 **teaspoons sugar**
- 1 **garlic clove, minced**
- ¾ **teaspoon salt**
- ¼ **teaspoon ground mustard**
- ¼ **teaspoon pepper**
- 2 **large heirloom tomatoes, cut into ½-inch pieces**
- 1 **medium sweet yellow pepper, cut into ½-inch pieces**
- ½ **small red onion, thinly sliced**
- 1 **tablespoon chopped fresh basil**

In a large bowl, whisk the first seven ingredients until blended. Add remaining ingredients; toss gently to combine.
PER SERVING *1 cup: 162 cal., 14g fat (2g sat. fat), 0 chol., 449mg sodium, 10g carb. (5g sugars, 2g fiber), 1g pro.* **Diabetic Exchanges:** *3 fat, 1 vegetable.*

SRIRACHA VEGGIE SLAW

GREEN SALAD WITH BERRIES

SRIRACHA VEGGIE SLAW

I wanted to rev up coleslaw to serve with seafood or pulled pork barbecue. Nothing adds zip like a squirt of Sriracha and a shower of chopped cilantro.

—JULIE PETERSON CROFTON, MD

START TO FINISH: 10 MIN.
MAKES: 6 SERVINGS

- 1 cup mayonnaise
- 3 garlic cloves, minced
- 1 teaspoon Sriracha Asian hot chili sauce
- ¼ teaspoon salt
- ⅛ teaspoon cayenne pepper
- 1 package (14 ounces) coleslaw mix
- ½ cup minced fresh cilantro
- 1 medium ripe avocado, peeled and cubed, optional

In a small bowl, mix the first five ingredients. Place coleslaw mix and cilantro in a large bowl. Add dressing and toss to coat. Refrigerate until serving. If desired, top with avocado.
PER SERVING ⅔ *cup (calculated without avocado): 286 cal., 29g fat (4g sat. fat), 13mg chol., 341mg sodium, 5g carb. (3g sugars, 2g fiber), 1g pro.*

GREEN SALAD WITH BERRIES

For snappy salad that draws a crowd, I do a wonderful combo of spinach, berries and onions. Raise your fork for this one.

—AYSHA SCHURMAN AMMON, ID

START TO FINISH: 15 MIN
MAKES: 4 SERVINGS

- 1 cup torn romaine
- 1 cup fresh baby spinach
- 1 cup sliced fresh strawberries
- ½ cup thinly sliced celery
- ½ small red onion, thinly sliced
- ½ cup coarsely chopped walnuts
- 2 green onions, chopped
- ¼ cup raspberry vinaigrette
- 1 cup fresh raspberries

In a large bowl, combine the first seven ingredients. To serve, drizzle with vinaigrette and toss to combine. Top with raspberries.
PER SERVING *157 cal., 10g fat (1g sat. fat), 0 chol., 50mg sodium, 15g carb. (8g sugars, 5g fiber), 4g pro.* **Diabetic Exchanges:** *2 fat, 1 vegetable, ½ fruit.*
HEALTH TIP *The berries in this salad provide more than half the daily value of vitamin C.*

ROASTED ROSEMARY CAULIFLOWER

Roasting gives cauliflower an amazingly rich and nutty flavor. Sprinkle on the Parmesan to send it over the top.

—JOANN FRITZLER BELEN, NM

START TO FINISH: 30 MIN.
MAKES: 6 SERVINGS

- 1 medium head cauliflower (about 2½ pounds), broken into florets
- 2 tablespoons olive oil
- 2 teaspoons minced fresh rosemary or ¾ teaspoon dried rosemary, crushed
- ½ teaspoon salt

Preheat oven to 450°. Toss all of the ingredients; spread in a greased 15x10x1-in. pan. Roast until tender and lightly browned, 20-25 minutes, stirring occasionally.
PER SERVING ¾ *cup: 44 cal., 3g fat (trace sat. fat), 0 chol., 161mg sodium, 4g carb. (0 sugars, 3g fiber), 2g pro.* **Diabetic Exchanges:** *1 vegetable, ½ fat.*

LEMONY GARBANZO SALAD

BUILD YOUR BOWL

To toss together a salad that satisfies, mix and match these good-for-you ingredients:

LEAFY
Spring greens, arugula, Bibb lettuce, romaine, baby kale, spinach, herbs

HEARTY
Whole wheat orzo, quinoa, chickpeas, black beans, grilled chicken, sauteed shrimp

CRUNCHY
Toasted walnuts or pecans, roasted edamame, pepitas, sunflower kernels

SWEET
Fresh berries, red grapes, mango, dried fruit

CREAMY
Avocado, chopped fresh mozzarella, hard-cooked egg, cottage cheese

BRIGHT
Peppers, purple cabbage, carrots, cucumber, snap peas, radishes, steamed asparagus

TANGY
Citrus juice, Dijon mustard, aged balsamic vinegar

EAT SMART • FAST FIX

LEMONY GARBANZO SALAD

Everybody goes for this super-fresh salad with the cumin-coriander dressing, especially on warm days.

—SONYA LABBE
WEST HOLLYWOOD, CA

START TO FINISH: 15 MIN.
MAKES: 4 SERVINGS

- ¼ cup olive oil
- 3 tablespoons lemon juice
- ¾ teaspoon ground cumin
- ¼ teaspoon salt
- ¼ teaspoon ground coriander
- ¼ teaspoon pepper
- 2 cans (15 ounces each) garbanzo beans or chickpeas, rinsed and drained
- 3 green onions, chopped
- ½ cup plain yogurt
- 1 tablespoon minced fresh parsley
- 1 tablespoon orange marmalade
- 4 cups spring mix salad greens

1. In a large bowl, whisk the first six ingredients until blended. Stir in beans and green onions. In another bowl, mix yogurt, parsley and marmalade.
2. To serve, divide greens among four plates; top with bean mixture. Serve with yogurt sauce.

PER SERVING *363 cal., 19g fat (3g sat. fat), 4mg chol., 478mg sodium, 41g carb. (10g sugars, 10g fiber), 11g pro.*

HEALTH TIP *The garbanzo beans are responsible for most of the 10 grams of fiber in this salad. They also add folate, vitamin B-6, manganese, phosphorous and iron.*

GARDEN-FRESH RAINBOW CHARD

In a 6-quart stockpot, heat 2 tablespoons oil over medium-high heat. Add 1 halved and sliced red onion; cook and stir 2-3 minutes or until tender. Add 3 sliced garlic cloves; cook 1 minute more. Add ¼ cup chicken broth and 2 bunches coarsely chopped rainbow Swiss chard (16 cups); cook and stir 5-6 minutes or until tender. Stir in 2 tablespoons lemon juice, ½ teaspoon salt and ¼ teaspoon pepper.

—TASTE OF HOME TEST KITCHEN

ROASTED
PARMESAN
CARROTS

LOADED BAKED POTATO CASSEROLE

When I bake this for my family, any leftovers are always gone by morning. In the night, people sneak downstairs for a little snack! Stir in broccoli, asparagus or peas if you've got 'em.

—**COLLEEN TRENHOLM** DARTMOUTH, NS

PREP: 10 MIN. ● **BAKE:** 70 MIN. + STANDING
MAKES: 12 SERVINGS

- 2 **pounds potatoes, peeled and thinly sliced (about 6 cups)**
- 1 **large onion, halved and thinly sliced**
- ¼ **cup water**
- ¼ **cup butter, cubed**
- ⅓ **cup all-purpose flour**
- 1 **teaspoon salt**
- 1 **teaspoon ground mustard**
- ½ **teaspoon pepper**
- 2 **cups 2% milk**
- 4 **cups shredded cheddar cheese, divided**
- 4 **cups fresh small broccoli florets**
- 3 **cups cubed fully cooked ham**
- 2 **tablespoons minced fresh chives**

1. Preheat oven to 350°. Place potatoes, onion and water in a microwave-safe bowl. Microwave, covered, on high until potatoes are almost tender, 8-10 minutes; drain.
2. Meanwhile, in a small saucepan, melt butter over medium heat. Stir in flour and seasonings until smooth; cook and stir until lightly browned, 2-3 minutes. Gradually whisk in milk. Bring to a boil, stirring constantly; cook and stir until thickened, about 1-2 minutes. Stir in 3 cups cheese until melted. Remove from heat.
3. To assemble, layer potato mixture, broccoli and ham in a greased 13x9-in. baking dish. Pour the sauce over the top; sprinkle with remaining cheese.
4. Bake, covered, for 45 minutes. Uncover; bake until the potatoes are tender, 25-30 minutes. Sprinkle with chives; let stand 10 minutes.
NOTE *This recipe was tested in a 1,100-watt microwave.*
PER SERVING *343 cal., 19g fat (11g sat. fat), 73mg chol., 922mg sodium, 23g carb. (3g sugars, 2g fiber), 21g pro.*

ROASTED PARMESAN CARROTS

Mom always said eat your carrots to help your eyes. Rich in beta-carotene, carrots support health—and taste amazing when roasted and tossed with Parmesan.

—**TASTE OF HOME TEST KITCHEN**

START TO FINISH: 25 MIN.
MAKES: 4 SERVINGS

- 1 **pound fresh carrots**
- 1 **teaspoon olive oil**
- ½ **teaspoon kosher salt**
- ¼ **teaspoon freshly ground pepper**
- ¼ **teaspoon dried thyme**
- 3 **tablespoons grated Parmesan cheese**

1. Preheat oven to 450°. Cut carrots crosswise in half and then lengthwise into ½-in.-thick sticks. Toss carrots with oil, salt, pepper and thyme; spread evenly in a greased 15x10x10-in. baking pan.
2. Roast 12-15 minutes or until tender and lightly browned, stirring once. Toss with cheese.
PER SERVING *72 cal., 2g fat (1g sat. fat), 3mg chol., 386mg sodium, 11g carb. (5g sugars, 3g fiber), 2g pro. Diabetic Exchanges: 1 vegetable, ½ fat.*

SCALLOPED CORN

My mom got the recipe for this creamy custard from her mother. After this sunny corn has gone around the table, people try to scrape the bowl clean.

—**SANDY JENKINS** ELKHORN, WI

PREP: 10 MIN. ● **BAKE:** 55 MIN.
MAKES: 6 SERVINGS

- 3 **large eggs**
- 1 **cup 2% milk**
- 3 **tablespoons butter, melted**
- 1 **tablespoon sugar**
- 1 **tablespoon finely chopped onion**
- ¼ **teaspoon salt**
- ¼ **teaspoon pepper**
- 4 **cups fresh or frozen corn**
- ¾ **cup crushed saltines (about 23 crackers), divided**

1. Preheat oven to 325°. In a large bowl, whisk the first seven ingredients until blended. Stir in corn and ½ cup crushed saltines.
2. Transfer to a greased 1½-qt. baking dish. Sprinkle with remaining saltines. Bake, uncovered, 55-65 minutes or until golden brown and a knife inserted near the center comes out clean.
PER SERVING *½ cup: 236 cal., 11g fat (5g sat. fat), 112mg chol., 296mg sodium, 29g carb. (10g sugars, 2g fiber), 9g pro.*

FAST FIX ▶
COOL BEANS SALAD

Beans and rice together make a complete protein. So, depending on the serving size, this colorful dish could be a side or a meatless entree. The basmati rice adds a unique flavor and the dressing gives it a bit of a tang.

—**JANELLE LEE** APPLETON, WI

START TO FINISH: 20 MIN.
MAKES: 6 SERVINGS

- 3 cups cooked basmati rice
- 1 can (16 ounces) kidney beans, rinsed and drained
- 1 can (15 ounces) black beans, rinsed and drained
- 1½ cups frozen corn, thawed
- 4 green onions, sliced
- 1 small sweet red pepper, chopped
- ¼ cup minced fresh cilantro

DRESSING
- ½ cup olive oil
- ¼ cup red wine vinegar
- 1 tablespoon sugar
- 1 garlic clove, minced
- 1 teaspoon salt
- 1 teaspoon ground cumin
- 1 teaspoon chili powder
- ¼ teaspoon pepper

In a large bowl, combine the first seven ingredients. In a small bowl, whisk the dressing ingredients; pour over salad and toss to coat. Chill until serving.

PER SERVING *1⅓ cups: 440 cal., 19g fat (3g sat. fat), 0 chol., 659mg sodium, 58g carb. (5g sugars, 8g fiber), 12g pro.*

COOL BEANS SALAD

WHEAT BERRY SALAD

EAT SMART
WHEAT BERRY SALAD

I'm a former junk food fan who discovered the beauty of wheat berries. They're tender yet chewy in this lemony salad tossed with cherries and walnuts.

—**NANCY LANGE** PHOENIX, AZ

PREP: 20 MIN. • **COOK:** 1 HOUR + COOLING
MAKES: 6 SERVINGS

- 1½ cups wheat berries
- 2 celery ribs, finely chopped
- ½ cup dried cherries, chopped
- ½ cup chopped walnuts, toasted
- ¼ cup minced fresh parsley
- 1 green onion, chopped
- 3 tablespoons olive oil
- 2 tablespoons lemon juice
- ¼ teaspoon salt
- ¼ teaspoon pepper
  Mixed salad greens, optional

1. Place wheat berries in a large saucepan; add water to cover by 2 in. Bring to a boil. Reduce heat; simmer, covered, about 1 hour or until tender. Drain; transfer to a large bowl. Cool completely.

2. Add celery, cherries, walnuts, parsley and green onion to wheat berries. In a small bowl, whisk oil, lemon juice, salt and pepper until blended; add to salad and toss to coat. If desired, serve over greens.

NOTE *To toast nuts, bake in a shallow pan in a 350° oven for 5-10 minutes or cook in a skillet over low heat until lightly browned, stirring occasionally.*

PER SERVING *¾ cup (calculated without salad greens): 323 cal., 14g fat (2g sat. fat), 0 chol., 112mg sodium, 45g carb. (7g sugars, 7g fiber), 8g pro.*

TOP TIP
WHEAT BERRIES

Nutritious wheat berries are the whole, unprocessed grain. A quarter cup of dry wheat berries contains a surprising 6 grams of fiber and 6 grams of protein. The berries will slightly more than double in size during cooking.

WARM SQUASH & QUINOA SALAD

When I see butternut squash at the supermarket, I buy it. It's amazing tossed with earthy quinoa, Italian spices and crunchy pine nuts. And don't get me started on the browned butter! Yum.
—CARLY TAYLOR LIBERTYVILLE, IL

START TO FINISH: 30 MIN.
MAKES: 6 SERVINGS

- 2 cups quinoa, rinsed
- 3 teaspoons ground cumin
- 3 cups water
- 2 tablespoons butter
- 3½ cups cubed peeled butternut squash (about ½ medium)
- 1 teaspoon sea salt
- ¾ teaspoon Italian seasoning
- ¼ teaspoon coarsely ground pepper
- ½ cup crumbled feta cheese
  Toasted pine nuts, optional

1. In a large saucepan, combine quinoa, cumin and water; bring to a boil. Reduce heat; simmer, covered, until liquid is absorbed, 10-13 minutes. Remove from heat; keep warm.

2. Meanwhile, in a large skillet, heat butter over medium-low heat until golden brown, 3-5 minutes, stirring constantly. Immediately stir in squash and seasonings; cook, covered, until tender, 10-12 minutes, stirring occasionally. Stir into quinoa. Sprinkle with cheese and, if desired, pine nuts.
PER SERVING *1 cup: 314 cal., 9g fat (4g sat. fat), 15mg chol., 449mg sodium, 49g carb. (2g sugars, 7g fiber), 11g pro.*

ROMAINE WITH WARM RICE & PINTOS

During my undergrad years, my roommate taught me how to cook vegetarian dishes like brown rice with pintos. It's so versatile; you can turn it into a wrap or casserole.
—NATALIE VAN APELDOORN VANCOUVER, BC

START TO FINISH: 30 MIN.
MAKES: 4 SERVINGS

- 1 tablespoon olive oil
- 1 cup frozen corn
- 1 small onion, chopped
- 2 garlic cloves, minced
- 1½ teaspoons chili powder
- 1½ teaspoons ground cumin
- 1 can (15 ounces) pinto beans, rinsed and drained
- 1 package (8.8 ounces) ready-to-serve brown rice
- 1 can (4 ounces) chopped green chilies
- ½ cup salsa
- ¼ cup chopped fresh cilantro
- 1 bunch romaine, quartered lengthwise through the core
- ¼ cup finely shredded cheddar cheese

1. In a large skillet, heat oil over medium-high heat. Add corn and onion; cook and stir 4-5 minutes or until onion is tender. Stir in garlic, chili powder and cumin; cook and stir 1 minute longer.
2. Add beans, rice, green chilies, salsa and cilantro; heat through, stirring occasionally.
3. Serve over romaine wedges. Sprinkle with cheese.
PER SERVING *331 cal., 8g fat (2g sat. fat), 7mg chol., 465mg sodium, 50g carb. (5g sugars, 9g fiber), 12g pro.* **Diabetic Exchanges:** *2½ starch, 2 vegetable, 1 lean meat, ½ fat.*

WARM SQUASH & QUINOA SALAD

**Maria Davis'
Root Stew**
PAGE 38

Soups & Sandwiches

Mix and match these easy dishes to create the ultimate dinnertime pairing. The simple soups, stews, wraps and sandwiches found here are guaranteed to satisfy, and they work great in lunch boxes, too.

Rachel Lewis'
Apple Cider Pulled Pork
PAGE 40

Michelle Beal's
Mexican Cabbage Roll Soup
PAGE 46

Kelley Boyce's
Mighty Hero Sandwich
PAGE 45

SPINACH QUESADILLAS

EAT SMART **FAST FIX** ▶

SPINACH QUESADILLAS

My family reacted to these cheesy quesadillas with oohs and aahs. Remove the spinach from the heat as soon as it wilts so it retains a little bit of crunch.
—**PAM KAISER** MANSFIELD, MO

START TO FINISH: 25 MIN.
MAKES: 4 SERVINGS

- 3 **ounces fresh baby spinach (about 4 cups)**
- 4 **green onions, chopped**
- 1 **small tomato, chopped**
- 2 **tablespoons lemon juice**
- 1 **teaspoon ground cumin**
- ¼ **teaspoon garlic powder**
- 1 **cup shredded reduced-fat Monterey Jack cheese or Mexican cheese blend**
- ¼ **cup reduced-fat ricotta cheese**
- 6 **flour tortillas (6 inches)**
  Reduced-fat sour cream, optional

1. In a large nonstick skillet, cook and stir first six ingredients until spinach is wilted. Remove from heat; stir in cheeses.

2. Top half of each tortilla with spinach mixture; fold other half over filling. Place on a griddle coated with cooking spray; cook over medium heat until golden brown, 1-2 minutes per side. Cut quesadillas in half; if desired, serve with sour cream.
PER SERVING *3 wedges: 281 cal., 12g fat (6g sat. fat), 24mg chol., 585mg sodium, 30g carb. (3g sugars, 4g fiber), 14g pro.* **Diabetic Exchanges:** *2 starch, 1 medium-fat meat, 1 vegetable.*
HEALTH TIP *Use whole wheat tortillas to get almost twice the fiber.*

EAT SMART

ROOT STEW

While cooking up a new comfort food, I made a stew of carrots, turnips, parsnips and rutabaga. When I'm in the mood to change things up, I add potatoes, chicken or beef.
—**MARIA DAVIS** FLOWER MOUND, TX

PREP: 30 MIN. ● **BAKE:** 2 HOURS
MAKES: 8 SERVINGS (2½ QUARTS)

- 2 **tablespoons canola oil, divided**
- 1½ **pounds beef stew meat**
- 1½ **teaspoons salt**
- ½ **teaspoon pepper**
- 1 **medium onion, chopped**
- 6 **garlic cloves, minced**
- 3 **cups reduced-sodium beef broth**
- 2 **bay leaves**
- 1 **teaspoon dried thyme**
- 3 **medium carrots**
- 2 **medium turnips**
- 2 **medium parsnips**
- 1 **small rutabaga**
- 2 **tablespoons cornstarch**
- ¼ **cup cold water**

1. Preheat the oven to 325°. In an ovenproof Dutch oven, heat 1 tablespoon oil over medium heat. Brown beef in batches. Remove from pan; sprinkle with salt and pepper.
2. In same pan, heat remaining oil over medium heat. Add onion; cook and stir 4-6 minutes or until tender. Add garlic; cook 1 minute longer. Stir in broth, bay leaves, thyme and beef; bring to a boil. Bake, covered, 1 hour.
3. Peel and cut remaining vegetables into 1-in. pieces; add to pan. Bake, covered, 1 to 1½ hours longer or until beef and vegetables are tender.
4. In a small bowl, mix cornstarch and water until smooth; stir into stew. Bring to a boil; cook and stir 1-2 minutes or until thickened. Discard bay leaves.
PER SERVING *1¼ cups: 227 cal., 10g fat (3g sat. fat), 55mg chol., 676mg sodium, 16g carb. (6g sugars, 3g fiber), 18g pro.* **Diabetic Exchanges:** *2 lean meat, 1 vegetable, 1 fat, ½ starch.*
HEALTH TIP *Carrots, turnips and rutabagas are all lower-calorie root vegetables. Adding them to soups is a great way to add volume and nutrients while keeping calories in check.*

HOW-TO

QUICKLY PEEL GARLIC

To make a fresh garlic clove easy to peel, gently crush it with the flat side of a large knife blade to loosen the peel. If you don't have a large knife, you can crush the garlic with a small can. The peel will come right off.

TURKEY PESTO SUBS

It was time to change up my usual sandwich rotation. I used pesto with turkey, sweet red pepper and onion to amp up the flavor.

—RUSTY KOLL ELMWOOD, IL

START TO FINISH: 30 MIN.
MAKES: 4 SERVINGS

- 4 teaspoons olive oil, divided
- 1 pound turkey breast tenderloins, cut into thin strips
- 1 medium sweet red pepper, julienned
- 1 medium onion, halved and sliced
- 4 garlic cloves, minced
- ½ cup prepared pesto
- 4 hoagie buns, split partway
- 4 slices provolone cheese, halved

1. Preheat broiler. In a large nonstick skillet, heat 2 teaspoons of oil over medium-high heat. Add turkey; cook and stir 5-6 minutes or until no longer pink. Remove from pan.
2. In same pan, heat remaining oil. Add pepper and onion; cook and stir 3-4 minutes or until tender. Add garlic; cook 1 minute longer. Return turkey to pan; stir in pesto. Remove from heat.

3. Place buns on a baking sheet, cut side up. Top with turkey mixture and cheese. Broil 2-3 in. from heat for 1-2 minutes or until cheese is melted.
PER SERVING *1 sandwich: 579 cal., 27g fat (7g sat. fat), 60mg chol., 958mg sodium, 43g carb. (8g sugars, 3g fiber), 43g pro.*

JALAPENO BURGERS WITH GORGONZOLA

On a whim, we mixed homemade jalapeno jelly into ground beef patties, then topped the burgers with caramelized onions and tangy Gorgonzola cheese. Fabulous!

—BECKY MOLLENKAMP ST. LOUIS, MO

START TO FINISH: 30 MIN.
MAKES: 4 SERVINGS

- 1 tablespoon canola oil
- 1 teaspoon butter
- 1 medium onion, halved and thinly sliced
  Dash salt
  Dash sugar

BURGERS
- ⅓ cup jalapeno pepper jelly
- ½ teaspoon salt
- ¼ teaspoon pepper
- 1 pound ground beef
- 4 hamburger buns, split and toasted
- 2 tablespoons crumbled Gorgonzola cheese
  Thinly sliced jalapeno pepper, optional

1. In a small skillet, heat oil and butter over medium heat. Add onion, salt and sugar; cook and stir 3-4 minutes or until onion is softened. Reduce heat to medium-low; cook 4-6 minutes or until deep golden brown, stirring occasionally.
2. In a large bowl, mix jelly, salt and pepper. Add beef; mix lightly but thoroughly. Shape into four ½-in. thick patties.
3. Grill burgers, covered, over medium heat or broil 4 in. from heat 4-5 minutes on each side or until a thermometer reads 160°. Serve on buns with caramelized onion, cheese and, if desired, sliced jalapeno.
PER SERVING *1 burger: 460 cal., 20g fat (7g sat. fat), 76mg chol., 669mg sodium, 43g carb. (18g sugars, 2g fiber), 25g pro.*

TURKEY PESTO SUBS

FREEZE IT | SLOW COOKER 🍲

APPLE CIDER PULLED PORK

For potlucks and tailgates, we slow-cook pork with cider, onions and spices. These tangy sliders with a side of sweet potato fries make a winning barbecue plate.
—**RACHEL LEWIS** DANVILLE, VA

PREP: 15 MIN. • **COOK:** 8¼ HOURS
MAKES: 12 SERVINGS

- 2 teaspoons seasoned salt
- ½ teaspoon ground mustard
- ½ teaspoon paprika
- ¼ teaspoon ground coriander
- ¼ teaspoon pepper
- 2 medium Granny Smith apples, peeled and coarsely chopped
- 1 medium onion, chopped
- 1 celery rib, chopped
- 1½ cups apple cider or juice
- 1 boneless pork shoulder butt roast (3 pounds)
- 2 tablespoons cornstarch
- 2 tablespoons water
- 24 mini buns, warmed
  Additional apple slices, optional

1. Mix first five ingredients. Place apples, onion, celery and cider in a 5-qt. slow cooker; top with roast. Sprinkle roast with seasoning mixture. Cook, covered, on low until tender, 8-10 hours.
2. Remove roast; shred with two forks. Skim fat from cooking juices. Mix cornstarch and water; stir into cooking juices. Cook, covered, on high until thickened, 10-15 minutes. Stir in pork; serve on buns. If desired, top with apple slices.

FREEZE OPTION *Freeze cooled meat mixture in freezer containers. To use, partially thaw in the refrigerator overnight. Heat through in a saucepan, stirring occasionally and adding a little broth or water if necessary.*

PER SERVING *2 sliders: 375 cal., 15g fat (5g sat. fat), 69mg chol., 563mg sodium, 35g carb. (9g sugars, 2g fiber), 25g pro.*

FAJITA BURGER WRAPS

FAST FIX

FAJITA BURGER WRAPS

This combo gives you a tender burger, crisp veggies and a crunchy shell, plus fajita flavor. Kids love it.
—**ANTONIO SMITH** CANAL WINCHESTER, OH

START TO FINISH: 30 MIN.
MAKES: 4 SERVINGS

- 1 pound lean ground beef (90% lean)
- 2 tablespoons fajita seasoning mix
- 2 teaspoons canola oil
- 1 medium green pepper, cut into thin strips
- 1 medium red sweet pepper, cut into thin strips
- 1 medium onion, halved and sliced
- 4 flour tortillas (10 inches)
- ¾ cup shredded cheddar cheese

1. In a large bowl, combine beef and seasoning mix, mixing lightly but thoroughly. Shape into four ½-in.-thick patties.
2. In a large skillet, heat oil over medium heat. Add the burgers; cook 4 minutes on each side. Remove from pan. In same skillet, add peppers and onion; cook and stir 5-7 minutes or until lightly browned and tender.
3. On the center of each tortilla, place ½ cup pepper mixture, one burger and 3 tablespoons of cheese. Fold sides of tortilla over burger, then fold top and bottom to close, forming a square.
4. Wipe the skillet clean. Place wraps in skillet, seam side down. Cook on medium heat 1-2 minutes on each side or until wraps are golden brown and a thermometer inserted in beef reads 160°.

PER SERVING *1 wrap: 533 cal., 23g fat (9g sat. fat), 92mg chol., 1190mg sodium, 45g carb. (5g sugars, 3g fiber), 34g pro.*

THE ULTIMATE CHICKEN NOODLE SOUP

My first Wisconsin winter was so cold, all I wanted to eat was soup. This recipe is in heavy rotation from November to April and has some devoted fans.

—GINA NISTICO MILWAUKEE, WI

PREP: 15 MIN.
COOK: 45 MIN. + STANDING
MAKES: 10 SERVINGS (3½ QUARTS)

- 2½ pounds bone-in chicken thighs
- 1¼ teaspoons pepper, divided
- ½ teaspoon salt
- 1 tablespoon canola oil
- 1 large onion, chopped
- 1 garlic clove, minced
- 10 cups chicken broth
- 4 celery ribs, chopped
- 4 medium carrots, chopped
- 2 bay leaves
- 1 teaspoon minced fresh thyme or ¼ teaspoon dried thyme
- 3 cups uncooked kluski or other egg noodles (about 8 ounces)
- 1 tablespoon chopped fresh parsley
- 1 tablespoon lemon juice

1. Pat chicken dry with paper towels; sprinkle with ½ teaspoon pepper and salt. In a 6-qt. stockpot, heat oil over medium-high heat. Add the chicken in batches, skin side down; cook for 3-4 minutes or until dark golden brown. Remove chicken from pan; remove and discard skin. Discard drippings, reserving 2 tablespoons.

2. Add onion to the drippings; cook and stir over medium-high heat for 4-5 minutes or until tender. Add the garlic; cook 1 minute longer. Add broth, stirring to loosen browned bits from pan. Bring to a boil. Return chicken to pan. Add celery, carrots, bay leaves and thyme. Reduce heat; simmer, covered, 25-30 minutes or until chicken is tender.

3. Transfer chicken to a plate. Remove soup from the heat. Add noodles; let stand, covered, 20-22 minutes or until noodles are tender.

4. Meanwhile, when chicken is cool enough to handle, remove meat from bones; discard bones. Shred meat into bite-size pieces. Return meat to the stockpot. Stir in parsley and lemon juice. Adjust seasoning with salt and remaining ¾ teaspoon pepper. Remove bay leaves.

PER SERVING *1⅓ cups: 239 cal., 12g fat (3g sat. fat), 68mg chol., 1176mg sodium, 14g carb. (3g sugars, 2g fiber), 18g pro.*

ITALIAN MEATBALL-BEAN SOUP

In North Dakota, it's pretty common for winter temps to fall below zero. Hearty soups like this are a must.

—NOELLE MYERS GRAND FORKS, ND

PREP: 35 MIN. ● **COOK:** 15 MIN.
MAKES: 8 SERVINGS (3 QUARTS)

- 1 large egg, lightly beaten
- ½ cup savory herb or chicken stuffing mix, crushed
- ¼ teaspoon salt
- 1 pound ground chicken

SOUP

- 1 tablespoon olive oil
- 3 celery ribs, chopped
- 2 medium carrots, chopped
- 1 small onion, chopped
- 2 teaspoons Italian seasoning
- 2 garlic cloves, minced
- 3 cans (15 ounces each) cannellini beans, rinsed and drained
- 6 cups reduced-sodium chicken broth
- 1½ teaspoons grated lemon peel
- 5 ounces fresh baby spinach (about 6 cups)
- 2 tablespoons lemon juice

1. Preheat oven to 400°. In a large bowl, combine egg, stuffing mix and salt. Add chicken; mix lightly but thoroughly. Shape into 1¼-in. balls. Place in a greased 15x10x1-in. baking pan. Bake 14-17 minutes or until cooked through.

2. Meanwhile, in a 6-qt stockpot, heat oil over medium heat. Add celery, carrots and onion; cook and stir for 5-7 minutes or until the carrots are softened. Stir in Italian seasoning and garlic; cook 1 minute longer.

3. Add beans, broth and lemon peel; bring to a boil. Reduce heat to low. Stir in the spinach and meatballs; cook just until the spinach is wilted. Stir in the lemon juice.

PER SERVING *1½ cups: 265 cal., 8g fat (2g sat. fat), 61mg chol., 828mg sodium, 30g carb. (2g sugars, 8g fiber), 20g pro.*

THE ULTIMATE
CHICKEN NOODLE SOUP

FAST FIX ▶

MUSHROOM & ONION GRILLED CHEESE SANDWICHES

Take grilled cheese up a notch with baby portobello mushrooms, bacon and cheddar. For weeknight comfort food, it's good to the last crumb.

—**BLAIR LONERGAN** ROCHELLE, VA

START TO FINISH: 25 MIN.
MAKES: 4 SERVINGS

- 3 **tablespoons butter, softened, divided**
- 8 **ounces sliced baby portobello mushrooms**
- 1 **small onion, halved and thinly sliced**
- 8 **thin slices cheddar cheese (about 3 ounces)**
- 8 **slices Texas toast**
- 4 **bacon strips, cooked and crumbled**

1. In a large nonstick skillet coated with cooking spray, heat 1 tablespoon butter over medium-high heat. Add mushrooms and onion; cook and stir 4-5 minutes or until tender. Remove from pan. Wipe skillet clean.

2. Place one slice cheese on each of four bread slices. Top with mushroom mixture, bacon and the remaining cheese and bread. Lightly spread outsides of sandwiches with remaining butter.

3. In same skillet, toast sandwiches in batches over medium heat for 45-60 seconds on each side or until golden brown and cheese is melted.

PER SERVING *1 sandwich: 406 cal., 21g fat (11g sat. fat), 54mg chol., 729mg sodium, 39g carb. (5g sugars, 2g fiber), 16g pro.*

EAT SMART **⑤INGREDIENTS** **FAST FIX** ▶

SPINACH & WHITE BEAN SOUP

For me, soup is love, comfort, happiness and memories. With all its veggies and beans, this one appeals to my kitchen sink style of cooking.

—**ANNETTE PALERMO** BEACH HAVEN, NJ

START TO FINISH: 30 MIN.
MAKES: 6 SERVINGS

- 2 **teaspoons olive oil**
- 3 **garlic cloves, minced**
- 3 **cans (15 ounces each) cannellini beans, rinsed and drained, divided**
- ¼ **teaspoon pepper**
- 1 **carton (32 ounces) vegetable or reduced-sodium chicken broth**
- 4 **cups chopped fresh spinach (about 3 ounces)**
- ¼ **cup thinly sliced fresh basil**
  Shredded Parmesan cheese, optional

1. In a large saucepan, heat oil over medium heat. Add garlic; cook and stir 30-45 seconds or until tender. Stir in two cans of beans, pepper and broth.

2. Puree mixture using an immersion blender. Or, puree in a blender and return to pan. Stir in remaining can of beans; bring to a boil. Reduce heat; simmer, covered, 15 minutes, stirring occasionally.

3. Stir in the spinach and basil; cook, uncovered, for 2-4 minutes or until spinach is wilted. If desired, serve with Parmesan cheese.

PER SERVING *1¼ cups (calculated without cheese): 192 cal., 2g fat (0 sat. fat), 0 chol., 886mg sodium, 33g carb. (1g sugars, 9g fiber), 9g pro.*

HEALTH TIP *As an alternative to reduced-sodium vegetable broth, which can be hard to find, try organic versions of big-brand veggie broths. These are typically lower in sodium than conventional versions.*

MUSHROOM & ONION
GRILLED CHEESE SANDWICHES

ITALIAN-STYLE LENTIL SOUP

CAROLINA SHRIMP SOUP

CAROLINA SHRIMP SOUP

Fresh shrimp from the Carolina coast is one of our favorite foods. We add kale, garlic, red peppers and black-eyed peas to complete this wholesome, filling soup.
—**MARY MARLOWE LEVERETTE** COLUMBIA, SC

START TO FINISH: 25 MIN.
MAKES: 6 SERVINGS

- 4 teaspoons olive oil, divided
- 1 pound uncooked shrimp (31-40 per pound), peeled and deveined
- 5 garlic cloves, minced
- 1 bunch kale, trimmed and coarsely chopped (about 16 cups)
- 1 medium sweet red pepper, cut into ¾-inch pieces
- 3 cups reduced-sodium chicken broth
- 1 can (15½ ounces) black-eyed peas, rinsed and drained
- ¼ teaspoon salt
- ¼ teaspoon pepper
  Minced fresh chives, optional

1. In a 6-qt. stockpot, heat 2 teaspoons oil over medium-high heat. Add the shrimp; cook and stir 2 minutes. Add garlic; cook 1-2 minutes longer or just until shrimp turns pink. Remove from the pot.

2. In same pot, heat remaining oil over medium-high heat. Stir in kale and red pepper; cook, covered, 8-10 minutes or until the kale is tender, stirring occasionally. Add broth; bring to a boil. Stir in peas, salt, pepper and shrimp; heat through. If desired, sprinkle servings with chives.

PER SERVING *1 cup: 188 cal., 5g fat (1g sat. fat), 92mg chol., 585mg sodium, 18g carb. (2g sugars, 3g fiber), 19g pro.* **Diabetic Exchanges:** *2 lean meat, 2 vegetable, ½ starch, ½ fat.*

HEALTH TIP *Aim for lots of color when planning meals. This soup's colorful mix of veggies means you're getting a good variety of nutrients.*

ITALIAN-STYLE LENTIL SOUP

I like to serve lentils often because they're healthy, versatile and inexpensive. This hearty, flavorful soup is among my favorites.
—**RACHEL L KELLER** ROANOKE, VA

PREP: 20 MIN. • **COOK:** 40 MIN.
MAKES: 6 SERVINGS

- 2 teaspoons olive oil
- 2 medium onions, chopped
- 2 celery ribs, thinly sliced
- 1 medium carrot, chopped
- 1 cup dried lentils, rinsed
- ¼ cup minced fresh parsley
- 1 tablespoon reduced-sodium beef bouillon granules
- ½ teaspoon pepper
- 5¼ cups water
- 1 can (6 ounces) tomato paste
- 2 tablespoons white vinegar
- 2 teaspoons brown sugar
- ½ teaspoon salt
- 2 tablespoons shredded Parmesan cheese

1. In a large saucepan coated with cooking spray, heat oil over medium heat. Add onions, celery and carrot; cook and stir until crisp-tender.

2. Stir in lentils, parsley, bouillon, pepper and water; bring to a boil. Reduce heat; simmer, covered, for 20-25 minutes or until lentils are tender, stirring occasionally.

3. Stir in tomato paste, vinegar, brown sugar and salt; heat through. Serve with cheese.

FREEZE OPTION *Freeze cooled soup in freezer containers. To use, partially thaw in refrigerator overnight. Heat through in a saucepan, stirring occasionally and adding a little water if necessary.*

HEALTH TIP *Unlike dried beans, lentils don't have to be soaked before using. They are a quick-to-cook source of iron, most B vitamins and fiber.*

PER SERVING *1 cup: 122 cal., 2g fat (1g sat. fat), 1mg chol., 420mg sodium, 21g carb. (11g sugars, 6g fiber), 6g pro.* **Diabetic Exchanges:** *2 vegetable, 1 starch.*

SPLIT PEA SOUP
WITH HAM

CURRIED CHICKEN
CORN CHOWDER

Here's the ultimate breezy-day chowder.
It's my version of a family recipe.

—**KENDRA DOSS** COLORADO SPRINGS, CO

PREP: 15 MIN. • **COOK:** 30 MIN.
MAKES: 8 SERVINGS (2 QUARTS)

- 1 **tablespoon butter**
- 2 **medium onions, chopped**
- 2 **celery ribs, chopped**
- 2 **teaspoons curry powder**
- ¼ **teaspoon salt**
- ¼ **teaspoon pepper**
  Dash cayenne pepper
- 5 **cups frozen corn (about 25 ounces)**
- 3 **cans (14½ ounces each) reduced-sodium chicken broth**
- ½ **cup all-purpose flour**
- ½ **cup 2% milk**
- 3 **cups cubed cooked chicken breast**
- ⅓ **cup minced fresh cilantro**

1. In a Dutch oven, heat butter over medium heat. Add onions and celery; cook and stir until tender. Stir in seasonings; cook 30 seconds longer.
2. Stir in corn and broth; bring to a boil. Reduce heat; simmer, covered, 15 minutes.
3. In a small bowl, whisk flour and milk until smooth; stir into soup. Bring to a boil; cook and stir 2 minutes or until thickened. Stir in chicken and cilantro; heat through.
PER SERVING *1 cup: 229 cal., 4g fat (2g sat. fat), 45mg chol., 582mg sodium, 28g carb. (5g sugars, 3g fiber), 22g pro. Diabetic Exchanges: 2 starch, 2 lean meat.*

HEALTH TIP *In place of heavy whipping cream, the recipe for this homey soup calls for 2% milk and flour to achieve a thick and creamy texture (a trade secret for lighter soups).*

SPLIT PEA SOUP
WITH HAM

To liven up pea soup, I load mine with potatoes and veggies. It's peppery rather than smoky, and I pass it around with warm corn bread.

—**BARBARA LINK** ALTA LOMA, CA

PREP: 15 MIN. • **COOK:** 1¼ HOURS
MAKES: 12 SERVINGS (3 QUARTS)

- 1 **package (16 ounces) dried green split peas**
- 8 **cups water**
- ¾ **pound potatoes (about 2 medium), cubed**
- 2 **large onions, chopped**
- 2 **medium carrots, chopped**
- 2 **cups cubed fully cooked ham (about 10 ounces)**
- 1 **celery rib, chopped**
- 5 **teaspoons reduced-sodium chicken bouillon granules**
- 1 **teaspoon dried marjoram**
- 1 **teaspoon poultry seasoning**
- 1 **teaspoon rubbed sage**
- ½ **to 1 teaspoon pepper**
- ½ **teaspoon dried basil**

Place all ingredients in a Dutch oven; bring to a boil. Reduce heat; simmer, covered, 1¼ to 1½ hours or until peas and vegetables are tender, stirring occasionally.
PER SERVING *1 cup: 202 cal., 2g fat (trace sat. fat), 14mg chol., 396mg sodium, 33g carb. (5g sugars, 11g fiber), 15g pro. Diabetic Exchanges: 2 starch, 1 lean meat.*

HEALTH TIP *Using only 2 cups of ham adds tons of flavor, but keeps the sodium under 400 milligrams.*

POULTRY SEASONING SUBSTITUTE

If you don't have poultry seasoning on hand, make an easy substitute for the 1 teaspoon called for by increasing the sage by ¾ teaspoon and the marjoram by ¼ teaspoon. Or, use ¼ teaspoon of dried thyme instead of marjoram.

SLIDERS WITH SPICY BERRY SAUCE

For patriotic food, you can't beat a burger. My sliders include red tomatoes, white cheddar and blueberry sauce. For extra pop, I mix in ginger beer and chipotle.

—CRYSTAL SCHLUETER NORTHGLENN, CO

PREP: 40 MIN. • **GRILL:** 10 MIN./BATCH
MAKES: 2 DOZEN

- 2 cups fresh blueberries
- 1 cup ginger beer or ginger ale
- ½ cup balsamic ketchup
- 2 tablespoons steak sauce
- 2 tablespoons honey
- 1 to 2 tablespoons finely chopped chipotle peppers in adobo sauce
- ¼ teaspoon salt
- ¼ teaspoon pepper

SLIDERS

- 2 packages (12 ounces each) Hawaiian sweet rolls
- 3 tablespoons butter, softened
- 3 pounds ground beef
- 1½ teaspoons salt
- ¾ teaspoon pepper
- 6 slices sharp white cheddar or provolone cheese, quartered

- 1 medium red onion, halved and thinly sliced
- 3 plum tomatoes, thinly sliced

1. In a saucepan, combine the first eight ingredients; bring to a boil. Reduce heat; simmer, uncovered, 15-20 minutes or until thickened, stirring occasionally. Cool slightly. Transfer to a food processor; process until pureed. Reserve ¼ cup sauce for brushing burgers.

2. For sliders, split rolls horizontally in half. Spread bottoms with butter. In a large bowl, combine beef, salt and pepper, mixing lightly but thoroughly. Shape into twenty-four ½-in.-thick patties, pressing an indentation in the center of each.

3. In two batches, grill burgers, covered, over medium heat for 3-4 minutes on each side or until a thermometer reads 160°, brushing tops with reserved sauce after turning. Top with cheese; grill, covered, 15-30 seconds longer or until melted. Serve on rolls with onion, tomatoes and remaining sauce.

PER SERVING *1 slider with about 2 teaspoons sauce: 272 cal., 13g fat (6g sat. fat), 62mg chol., 422mg sodium, 23g carb. (11g sugars, 2g fiber), 16g pro.*

MIGHTY HERO SANDWICH

My friend Valerie is a gracious hostess who once served us this Dagwood sandwich. It's easy and colorful, and the marinated veggies give it all kinds of oomph.

—KELLEY BOYCE TULSA, OK

START TO FINISH: 30 MIN.
MAKES: 8 SERVINGS

- ¼ cup balsamic vinegar
- 1 tablespoon minced fresh parsley
- 1 tablespoon olive oil
- 2 garlic cloves, minced
- ¼ teaspoon dried oregano
- ¼ teaspoon pepper
- 1 large tomato, halved and sliced
- 1 cup sliced fresh mushrooms
- 2 thin slices red onion, separated into rings
- 1 round loaf (1 pound) sourdough bread
- 1 small zucchini, shredded
- ½ pound sliced deli turkey
- 6 slices part-skim mozzarella cheese

1. In a large bowl, whisk the first six ingredients until blended. Add tomato, mushrooms and onion; toss gently to coat. Let stand 15 minutes.

2. Meanwhile, cut loaf horizontally in half. Hollow out both parts, leaving a ½-in.-thick shell (save removed bread for another use).

3. Drain marinated vegetables, reserving marinade. Brush marinade over inside of bread halves. Top bottom half with zucchini. Layer with half of the marinated vegetables, ¼ pound turkey and 3 slices cheese; repeat layers. Replace top of loaf. Cut into wedges.

PER SERVING *1 piece: 233 cal., 7g fat (3g sat. fat), 24mg chol., 636mg sodium, 26g carb. (6g sugars, 1g fiber), 16g pro.* **Diabetic Exchanges:** *2 starch, 2 lean meat, ½ fat.*

SLIDERS WITH SPICY BERRY SAUCE

CORN QUESADILLAS

CORN QUESADILLAS

My cheesy corn quesadillas take only minutes to prepare. Leftovers make a great brown-bag lunch.
—**DARLENE BRENDEN** SALEM, OR

START TO FINISH: 15 MIN.
MAKES: 4 SERVINGS

- 1½ cups shredded Monterey Jack or pepper jack cheese
- 1 cup fresh or frozen corn
- 3 green onions, thinly sliced
- ¼ cup chopped fresh cilantro
- 2 tablespoons sour cream
- 1 tablespoon minced chipotle peppers in adobo sauce
- 4 flour tortillas (8 inches)
- 1 teaspoon canola oil
  Guacamole, optional

1. Place the first six ingredients in a large bowl; toss to combine. To assemble, lightly brush the tops of two tortillas with ½ teaspoon oil; turn over. Top with cheese mixture and remaining tortillas. Brush tops with remaining oil.
2. Place a large nonstick skillet over medium heat. In two batches, cook quesadillas 1-2 minutes on each side or until golden brown and cheese is melted. Cut each quesadilla into six wedges. If desired, serve with guacamole.
PER SERVING *3 wedges (calculated without guacamole): 380 cal., 19g fat (10g sat. fat), 43mg chol., 524mg sodium, 36g carb. (3g sugars, 3g fiber), 16g pro.*

MEXICAN CABBAGE ROLL SOUP

I love sharing this humble and hearty soup made with beef, cabbage and green chilies. A blast of minced fresh cilantro gives it a sunshiny finish.
—**MICHELLE BEAL** POWELL, TN

START TO FINISH: 30 MIN.
MAKES: 6 SERVINGS (2 QUARTS)

- 1 pound lean ground beef (90% lean)
- ½ teaspoon salt
- ¾ teaspoon garlic powder
- ¼ teaspoon pepper
- 1 tablespoon olive oil
- 1 medium onion, chopped
- 6 cups chopped cabbage (about 1 small head)
- 3 cans (4 ounces each) chopped green chilies
- 2 cups water
- 1 can (14½ ounces) reduced-sodium beef broth
- 2 tablespoons minced fresh cilantro
  Pico de gallo and reduced-fat sour cream, optional

1. In a large saucepan, cook and crumble beef with seasonings over medium-high heat until no longer pink, 5-7 minutes. Remove from pan.
2. In same pan, heat oil over medium-high heat; saute onion and cabbage 4-6 minutes. Stir in beef, chilies, water and broth; bring to a boil. Reduce the heat; simmer, covered, to allow flavors to blend, about 10 minutes. Stir in the cilantro. If desired, top servings with pico de gallo and sour cream.
FREEZE OPTION *Freeze cooled soup in freezer containers. To use, partially thaw in refrigerator overnight. Heat through in a saucepan, stirring occasionally.*
PER SERVING *1⅓ cups: 186 cal., 9g fat (3g sat. fat), 49mg chol., 604mg sodium, 10g carb. (4g sugars, 4g fiber), 17g pro.* **Diabetic Exchanges:** *2 lean meat, 2 vegetable, ½ fat.*

BALSAMIC BEEF HOAGIES

All my boys (big and small) like sandwiches, and balsamic beef is a welcome change from pulled barbecue chicken. Leftovers go well in quesadillas, on pizza or with rice.
—**BLAIR LONERGAN** ROCHELLE, VA

PREP: 25 MIN. • **COOK:** 5 HOURS
MAKES: 8 SERVINGS

- 1 cup beef broth
- ½ cup balsamic vinegar
- 2 tablespoons brown sugar
- 2 tablespoons Worcestershire sauce
- 4 garlic cloves, minced
- 1 boneless beef chuck roast (2 pounds)

SANDWICHES
- ½ cup mayonnaise
- 8 hoagie buns, split and toasted
- 4 medium tomatoes, sliced
- ½ cup thinly sliced fresh basil

1. In a small bowl, mix the first five ingredients. Place roast in a 4- or 5-qt. slow cooker. Pour broth mixture over top. Cook, covered, on low 5-6 hours or until meat is tender.
2. Remove roast; shred beef with two forks. Skim fat from cooking juices. Return beef and cooking juices to slow cooker; heat through.
3. Spread mayonnaise on buns. Using tongs, place beef on buns; top with tomatoes and basil.

FREEZE OPTION *Freeze cooled meat mixture in freezer containers. To use, partially thaw in the refrigerator overnight. Heat through in a saucepan, stirring occasionally and adding a little broth if necessary.*
PER SERVING *1 sandwich: 549 cal., 26g fat (7g sat. fat), 79mg chol., 669mg sodium, 46g carb. (14g sugars, 2g fiber), 31g pro.*

SOUTHWEST CHICKEN BARLEY CHOWDER

Mashed winter squash helps make this chowder hearty, and this recipe is my favorite way to get barley on the table. My kids even ask for the leftovers.
—**PAMELA CLEGHORN** CAMPBELLSBURG, IN

START TO FINISH: 30 MIN.
MAKES: 8 SERVINGS (2½ QUARTS)

- 2 tablespoons olive oil
- 1 pound boneless skinless chicken breasts, cut into ¾-inch pieces
- 1 small onion, finely chopped
- 1 package (12 ounces) frozen mashed winter squash, thawed (about 1⅓ cups)
- ¾ cup quick-cooking barley
- 2 teaspoons reduced-sodium taco seasoning
- ½ teaspoon salt
- ¼ teaspoon pepper
- 1 carton (32 ounces) reduced-sodium chicken broth
- 1 can (15 ounces) black beans, rinsed and drained
- 2 cups frozen corn
- 1 cup half-and-half cream
- ½ cup salsa
- ½ cup chopped fresh cilantro Diced avocado and chopped tomatoes, optional

1. In a 6-qt. stockpot, heat oil over medium-high heat. Add chicken and onion; cook and stir 2-3 minutes or just until onion is tender.
2. Stir in squash, barley, seasonings and broth; bring to a boil. Reduce heat; simmer, covered, 10-12 minutes or until barley is tender.
3. Add beans, corn, cream, salsa and cilantro; heat chowder through, stirring occasionally. If desired, serve with avocado and tomatoes.

FREEZE OPTION *Freeze cooled soup in freezer containers. To use, partially thaw in refrigerator overnight. Heat through in a saucepan, stirring occasionally and adding a little broth or milk if necessary.*
PER SERVING *1¼ cups: 298 cal., 8g fat (3g sat. fat), 46mg chol., 681mg sodium, 35g carb. (4g sugars, 7g fiber), 20g pro.* **Diabetic Exchanges: 2 starch, 2 lean meat, 1 fat.**

BALSAMIC BEEF HOAGIES

> My husband didn't like sloppy joes until he tried my rendition with its smoky heat. If you need to dial down the fiery zip, reduce the peppers.
> —**BRITTANY ALLYN** MESA, AZ

CHIPOTLE CHILI SLOPPY JOES

EAT SMART **FREEZE IT**

CHIPOTLE CHILI SLOPPY JOES

PREP: 15 MIN. • **COOK:** 20 MIN.
MAKES: 6 SERVINGS

- 1 **pound lean ground beef (90% lean)**
- 1 **cup finely chopped sweet onion**
- ½ **cup finely chopped green pepper**
- 1 **jalapeno pepper, seeded and finely chopped, optional**
- ½ **cup chili sauce**
- ½ **cup water**
- 1 **to 2 chipotle peppers in adobo sauce, finely chopped**
- 1 **tablespoon packed brown sugar**
- 1 **teaspoon yellow mustard**
- 6 **kaiser rolls or hamburger buns, split**
- 2 **tablespoons butter, softened Pickle slices, optional**

1. Preheat broiler. In a large skillet, cook beef, onion, green pepper and, if desired, jalapeno over medium heat for 5-7 minutes or until beef is no longer pink, breaking up beef into crumbles; drain.

2. Stir in chili sauce, water, chipotle peppers, brown sugar and mustard; bring to a boil. Simmer, uncovered, for 8-10 minutes or until slightly thickened, stirring occasionally.

3. Lightly spread cut sides of rolls with butter; arrange on a baking sheet, buttered side up. Broil 3-4 in. from heat until lightly toasted, about 30 seconds. Fill with beef mixture and, if desired, pickles.

FREEZE OPTION *Freeze cooled meat mixture in freezer containers. To use, partially thaw in the refrigerator overnight. Heat through in a saucepan, stirring occasionally and adding a little water if necessary.*

PER SERVING *1 sandwich: 313 cal., 12g fat (5g sat. fat), 57mg chol., 615mg sodium, 32g carb. (11g sugars, 2g fiber), 19g pro.* **Diabetic Exchanges:** *2 starch, 2 lean meat, 1 fat.*

FAST FIX

SAUSAGE BEAN SOUP

Canned beans and quick-cooking sausage make this tasty soup a snap to prepare. It takes just minutes to simmer.
—**MARLENE MUCKENHIRN** DELANO, MN

START TO FINISH: 25 MIN.
MAKES: 6 SERVINGS

- ¾ **pound bulk Italian sausage**
- ½ **cup chopped onion**
- 1 **garlic clove, minced**
- 1 **can (16 ounces) butter beans, rinsed and drained**
- 1 **can (15 ounces) black beans, rinsed and drained**
- 1 **can (14½ ounces) diced tomatoes, undrained**
- 1 **tablespoon minced fresh basil or 1 teaspoon dried basil**
- 1 **can (14½ ounces) reduced-sodium beef broth**
- 2 **tablespoons shredded Parmesan cheese**

1. In a large saucepan, cook and crumble sausage with onion and garlic over medium heat until no longer pink, 5-7 minutes; drain.

2. Stir in beans, tomatoes, basil and broth; bring to a boil. Reduce heat; simmer, covered, 10 minutes. Serve with cheese.

PER SERVING *1 cup: 268 cal., 13g fat (4g sat. fat), 33mg chol., 908mg sodium, 27g carb. (4g sugars, 7g fiber), 15g pro.*

HEALTH TIP *Switch to no-salt-added diced tomatoes and skip the Parmesan cheese to cut about 130 milligrams of sodium. Use no-salt-added beans and save almost 300 milligrams more.*

SAUSAGE BEAN SOUP

ASIAN CHICKEN
CRUNCH WRAPS

FAST FIX ▶

ASIAN CHICKEN CRUNCH WRAPS

My kids love all kinds of wraps and Asian foods. This is an easy go-to in our house that works for everyone.
—MARY LOU TIMPSON COLORADO CITY, AZ

START TO FINISH: 25 MIN.
MAKES: 4 SERVINGS

- 8 frozen breaded chicken tenders (about 10 ounces)
- 2 cups coleslaw mix
- ½ cup sweet chili sauce
- 2 green onions, chopped
- 2 tablespoons chopped fresh cilantro
- 1 teaspoon soy sauce
- 4 flour tortillas (8 inches), warmed
- ½ cup dry roasted peanuts, chopped

1. Bake chicken tenders according to package directions. Meanwhile, in a large bowl, toss coleslaw mix with chili sauce, green onions, chopped cilantro and soy sauce.

2. Arrange chicken down center of each tortilla; top with coleslaw mixture and peanuts. Fold sides of tortillas over filling and roll up. Cut each diagonally in half.
PER SERVING *1 wrap: 519 cal., 21g fat (3g sat. fat), 13mg chol., 1250mg sodium, 66g carb. (19g sugars, 7g fiber), 19g pro.*

EAT SMART

COLD-DAY CHICKEN NOODLE SOUP

When I was sick, my mom would stir up a heartwarming chicken noodle soup. It's so soothing for colds and cold weather days.
—ANTHONY GRAHAM OTTAWA, IL

PREP: 15 MIN. ● **COOK:** 25 MIN.
MAKES: 8 SERVINGS (3 QUARTS)

- 1 tablespoon canola oil
- 2 celery ribs, chopped
- 2 medium carrots, chopped
- 1 medium onion, chopped
- 8 cups reduced-sodium chicken broth
- ½ teaspoon dried basil
- ¼ teaspoon pepper
- 3 cups uncooked whole wheat egg noodles (about 4 ounces)
- 3 cups coarsely chopped rotisserie chicken
- 1 tablespoon minced fresh parsley

1. In a 6-qt. stockpot, heat oil over medium-high heat. Add celery, carrots and onion; cook and stir 5-7 minutes or until tender.
2. Add broth, basil and pepper; bring to a boil. Stir in noodles; cook for 12-14 minutes or until al dente. Stir in chicken and parsley; heat through.
PER SERVING *1½ cups: 195 cal., 6g fat (1g sat. fat), 47mg chol., 639mg sodium, 16g carb. (2g sugars, 3g fiber), 21g pro. Diabetic Exchanges: 2 lean meat, 1 starch, ½ fat.*
HEALTH TIP *Using reduced-sodium chicken broth in this recipe saves 410 milligrams sodium per serving.*

What a Burger!

South Dakota home cook Susan Harju knows that the simplest recipe can most definitely be the best. Her family knows it, too, thanks to these juicy burgers.

MUST-HAVE BURGERS

MAKE THE BEST BURGERS

1. **MIX** Grab a big bowl. Combine chopped green onions, Worcestershire sauce and seasonings. Add the ground beef; hand-mix lightly but thoroughly.

2. **SHAPE** For uniform burgers, make a disc with the beef mixture and cut it into quarters. Pat each portion into a ¾-in.-thick patty.

3. **GRILL** Clean off your grill grate. Then grill the patties, covered, over medium heat, about 6 minutes per side.

4. **TEMP & TOP** When the burgers reach 160°, top with cheese; grill, covered, up to a minute more or until the cheese melts. Pop on buns and serve with your favorite fixings.

FAST FIX

MUST-HAVE BURGERS

My family thinks these juicy cheeseburgers are deluxe, with or without a bun. Customize them with mushrooms, onion, bacon or a shot of hot chili sauce.

—**SUSAN HARJU** SIOUX FALLS, SD

START TO FINISH: 25 MIN.
MAKES: 4 SERVINGS

- 2 **green onions,** chopped
- 1 **tablespoon Worcestershire sauce**
- 1 **teaspoon Montreal steak seasoning**
- ¼ **teaspoon seasoned salt**
- 1⅓ **pounds ground beef**
- 4 **slices cheddar cheese**
- 4 **brioche or other hamburger buns,** split and toasted
  Optional toppings: lettuce leaves, sliced tomato and onion slices

PER SERVING *1 burger (calculated without toppings): 550 cal., 31g fat (13g sat. fat), 153mg chol., 811mg sodium, 28g carb. (7g sugars, 2g fiber), 39g pro.*

PICO DE GALLO BLACK BEAN SOUP

Everyone at my table goes for this feel-good soup. It's great when you're pressed for time and beats fast food, hands down.

—**DARLIS WILFER** WEST BEND, WI

START TO FINISH: 20 MIN.
MAKES: 6 SERVINGS

- 4 **cans (15 ounces each) black beans, rinsed and drained**
- 2 **cups vegetable broth**
- 2 **cups pico de gallo**
- ½ **cup water**
- 2 **teaspoons ground cumin**

TOPPINGS
 Chopped fresh cilantro
 Additional pico de gallo, optional

1. In a Dutch oven, combine the first five ingredients; bring to a boil over medium heat, stirring occasionally. Reduce heat; simmer, uncovered, for 5-7 minutes or until the vegetables in the pico de gallo are softened, stirring occasionally.

2. Puree soup using an immersion blender. Or, cool soup slightly and puree in batches in a blender; return to pan and heat through. Serve with toppings as desired.

 FREEZE OPTION *Freeze cooled soup in freezer containers. To use, partially thaw in refrigerator overnight. Heat through in a saucepan, stirring occasionally and adding a little broth or water if necessary. Top as desired. Black beans are naturally low in fat and high in fiber, protein and folate.*

 PER SERVING *1¼ cups (calculated without additional pico de gallo): 241 cal., 0 fat (0 sat. fat), 0 chol., 856mg sodium, 44g carb. (4g sugars, 12g fiber), 14g pro.*

CRISPY PORK TENDERLOIN SANDWICHES

This breaded tenderloin rekindles memories of a sandwich shop in my Ohio hometown. Even though we've moved away, I'm happy to say my family can still enjoy them thanks to this recipe.

—**ERIN FITCH** SHERRILLS FORD, NC

START TO FINISH: 25 MIN.
MAKES: 4 SERVINGS

- 2 **tablespoons all-purpose flour**
- ½ **teaspoon salt**
- ¼ **teaspoon pepper**
- 1 **large egg, lightly beaten**
- ½ **cup seasoned bread crumbs**
- 3 **tablespoons panko (Japanese) bread crumbs**
- ½ **pound pork tenderloin**
- 2 **tablespoons canola oil**
- 4 **hamburger buns or kaiser rolls, split**
  Optional toppings: lettuce leaves, tomato and pickle slices and mayonnaise

1. In a shallow bowl, mix flour, salt and pepper. Place the egg and the combined bread crumbs into two separate shallow bowls.

2. Cut tenderloin crosswise into four slices; pound each with a meat mallet to ¼-in. thickness. Dip in the flour mixture to coat both sides; shake off excess. Dip in egg, then in crumb mixture, patting to help adhere.

3. In a large skillet, heat oil over medium heat. Cook pork 2-3 minutes on each side or until golden brown. Remove from pan; drain on paper towels. Serve in buns with toppings as desired.

 PER SERVING *1 sandwich (calculated without toppings): 289 cal., 11g fat (2g sat. fat), 43mg chol., 506mg sodium, 29g carb. (3g sugars, 1g fiber), 17g pro. Diabetic Exchanges: 2 starch, 2 lean meat, 1½ fat.*

 HEALTH TIP *Keep carbs to about 10 grams per serving by skipping the bun and serving the pork on grilled portobello mushrooms or eggplant slices instead.*

ITALIAN VEGGIE
BEEF SOUP

PEPPERY PHILLY STEAKS

We love using fresh peppers in these simple sandwiches. Ease is important; we live in a small mountain cabin and often cook on a wood stove.

—**EDIE FITCH** CLIFTON, AZ

START TO FINISH: 30 MIN.
MAKES: 6 SERVINGS

- 3 **tablespoons canola oil, divided**
- 1 **medium green pepper, julienned**
- 1 **medium sweet red pepper, julienned**
- 1 **large onion, halved and thinly sliced**
- 1½ **pounds beef top sirloin steak, cut into ¼-inch strips**
- ½ **teaspoon salt**
- 2 **cans (4 ounces each) whole green chilies, drained and sliced**
- 2 **tablespoons butter, softened**
- 6 **French or Italian sandwich rolls, split**
- 6 **slices Swiss cheese**

1. Preheat oven to 350°. In a large skillet, heat 1 tablespoon canola oil over medium heat. Add peppers and onion; cook and stir until crisp-tender. Remove from pan.
2. In same pan, heat remaining oil over medium-high heat. Add beef; cook and stir 2-3 minutes or until no longer pink. Stir in salt, chilies and pepper mixture; heat through.
3. Spread butter over cut sides of rolls. On roll bottoms, layer steak mixture and cheese; replace tops. Place in a 15x10x1-in. baking pan; cover tightly with foil. Bake 10-12 minutes or until cheese is melted.
PER SERVING *1 sandwich: 473 cal., 21g fat (7g sat. fat), 66mg chol., 650mg sodium, 36g carb. (4g sugars, 2g fiber), 34g pro.*

FREEZE IT EAT SMART **FAST FIX** ›
ITALIAN VEGGIE BEEF SOUP

My father-in-law, Pop Pop, would bring this chunky soup to our house when we were under the weather. We like it so well, we take it to our own friends who need comfort. Always does the trick.

—**SUE WEBB** REISTERSTOWN, MD

START TO FINISH: 30 MIN.
MAKES: 12 SERVINGS (4 QUARTS)

- 1½ **pounds lean ground beef (90% lean)**
- 2 **medium onions, chopped**
- 4 **cups chopped cabbage**
- 1 **package (16 ounces) frozen mixed vegetables**
- 1 **can (28 ounces) crushed tomatoes**
- 1 **bay leaf**
- 3 **teaspoons Italian seasoning**
- 1 **teaspoon salt**
- ½ **teaspoon pepper**
- 2 **cartons (32 ounces each) reduced-sodium beef broth**

1. In a 6-qt. stockpot, cook ground beef and onions over medium-high heat 6-8 minutes or until beef is no longer pink, breaking up beef into crumbles; drain.
2. Add cabbage, mixed vegetables, tomatoes, seasonings and broth; bring to a boil. Reduce heat and simmer, uncovered, 10-15 minutes or until cabbage is crisp-tender. Remove the bay leaf.
FREEZE OPTION *Freeze cooled soup in freezer containers. To use, partially thaw in refrigerator overnight. Heat through in a saucepan, stirring occasionally and adding a little broth if necessary.*
PER SERVING *1⅓ cups: 159 cal., 5g fat (2g sat. fat), 38mg chol., 646mg sodium, 14g carb. (6g sugars, 4g fiber), 15g pro.* **Diabetic Exchanges:** *2 lean meat, 1 vegetable, ½ starch.*

CHICKEN SAUSAGE PITA POCKETS

Chicken sausage comes in many flavors, so I try different ones when I make pitas with fresh basil and veggies. The sandwich is inspired by the Greek gyro.

—CHRISTINA PRICE PITTSBURGH, PA

START TO FINISH: 25 MIN.
MAKES: 4 SERVINGS

- 6 **teaspoons olive oil, divided**
- 1 **package (12 ounces) fully cooked roasted garlic chicken sausage links or flavor of your choice, sliced**
- 1 **cup sliced fresh mushrooms**
- 1 **small onion, halved and sliced**
- 1 **medium zucchini, halved lengthwise and sliced**
- 1 **medium yellow summer squash, halved lengthwise and sliced**
- 3 **tablespoons chopped fresh basil**
- 8 **whole wheat pita pocket halves, warmed**
  Sliced tomato and plain Greek yogurt, optional

1. In a large nonstick skillet, heat 2 teaspoons oil over medium-high heat. Add sausage; cook and stir for 4-6 minutes or until lightly browned. Remove from pan.

2. In same skillet, heat 2 teaspoons oil over medium-high heat. Add sliced mushrooms and onion; cook and stir 4-6 minutes or until tender. Remove from pan.

3. Add remaining oil to pan. Add the zucchini and yellow squash; cook and stir 3-5 minutes or until tender. Stir in the basil, sausage and mushroom mixture; heat through. Serve in pitas. If desired, add tomato and yogurt.

PER SERVING *2 filled pita halves (calculated without tomato and yogurt): 376 cal., 16g fat (3g sat. fat), 70mg chol., 736mg sodium, 39g carb. (5g sugars, 6g fiber), 22g pro.*
Diabetic Exchanges: 3 lean meat, 2 starch, 1½ fat, 1 vegetable.

CHICKEN SAUSAGE PITA POCKETS

PUMPKIN SLOPPY JOES

Cook 2 pounds of ground beef and 1 finely chopped onion over medium-high heat until meat is no longer pink; drain. Stir in 1 teaspoon chili powder, ¾ teaspoon salt, ¼ teaspoon each nutmeg, cloves and pepper, 1 cup ketchup and ½ cup tomato juice; bring to a boil. Add 1 can (15 ounces) pumpkin. Cover and simmer 15 minutes. Serve on buns. Makes 8 servings.

—DONNA MUSSER PEARL CITY, IL

FAST FIX

SHORTCUT SAUSAGE MINESTRONE

I'm convinced this soup has superpowers. It's incredibly soothing—my daughter-in-law asks for it whenever she's feeling under the weather.

—MARTA SMITH CLAREMONT, PA

START TO FINISH: 25 MIN.
MAKES: 6 SERVINGS (2 QUARTS)

- ¾ pound Italian turkey sausage links, casings removed
- 1 small green pepper, chopped
- 1 small onion, chopped
- 2 cups cut fresh green beans or frozen cut green beans
- 2 cups water
- 1 can (16 ounces) kidney beans, rinsed and drained
- 1 can (14½ ounces) diced tomatoes with basil, oregano and garlic, undrained
- 1 can (14½ ounces) reduced-sodium chicken broth
- ¾ cup uncooked ditalini or other small pasta

1. In a 6-qt. stockpot, cook sausage, pepper and onion over medium heat 5-7 minutes or until sausage is no longer pink, breaking up sausage into crumbles; drain.

2. Add green beans, water, kidney beans, tomatoes and broth; bring to a boil. Stir in ditalini; cook, uncovered, 10-11 minutes or until pasta is tender, stirring occasionally.

PER SERVING *1⅓ cups: 232 cal., 4g fat (1g sat. fat), 21mg chol., 773mg sodium, 34g carb. (6g sugars, 7g fiber), 16g pro.*

SHORTCUT SAUSAGE MINESTRONE

TURKEY & DUMPLING SOUP

FAST FIX

TURKEY & DUMPLING SOUP

To show some love at a family gathering, I fill a stockpot with this rich turkey soup brimming with veggies, potatoes and dumplings.

—LEA LIDEL LEANDER, TX

START TO FINISH: 30 MIN.
MAKES: 8 SERVINGS

- 1 tablespoon olive oil
- 2 celery ribs, chopped
- ½ cup chopped onion
- 1½ pounds red potatoes (about 5 medium), cut into ½-inch cubes
- 3½ cups frozen mixed vegetables (about 16 ounces)
- ½ teaspoon pepper
- ½ teaspoon dried thyme
- 2 cartons (32 ounces each) reduced-sodium chicken broth
- 2½ cups coarsely shredded cooked turkey or chicken
- 2 cups biscuit/baking mix
- ⅔ cup 2% milk

1. In a 6-qt. stockpot, heat oil over medium heat; saute celery and onion until tender, 3-4 minutes. Stir in potatoes, mixed vegetables, seasonings and broth; bring to a boil. Reduce heat; cook, covered, until potatoes are almost tender, 8-10 minutes. Add turkey; bring mixture to a simmer.

2. Meanwhile, stir baking mix and milk until a soft dough forms; drop by tablespoonfuls on top of simmering soup. Cook, covered, on low heat until a toothpick inserted in dumplings comes out clean, 8-10 minutes.

PER SERVING *1¾ cups: 350 cal., 8g fat (2g sat. fat), 46mg chol., 1036mg sodium, 47g carb. (7g sugars, 6g fiber), 23g pro.*

BEEF STEW WITH PASTA

I have happy memories of my mother's tomato-y beef stew, so I combined her recipe with a bunch of fall veggies I needed to use. This makes a magnificent stick-to-the-ribs dinner.

—**KRISTEN HEIGL** STATEN ISLAND, NY

PREP: 25 MIN. • **COOK:** 2¼ HOURS
MAKES: 12 SERVINGS (5 QUARTS)

- 3 **tablespoons olive oil, divided**
- 2 **pounds beef stew meat**
- 4 **medium carrots, cut into 1-inch pieces**
- 1 **large onion, chopped**
- 4 **garlic cloves, minced**
- 1 **can (14½ ounces) diced tomatoes, drained**
- 1 **can (12 ounces) tomato paste**
- ¾ **teaspoon salt**
- ½ **teaspoon pepper**
- 2 **cartons (32 ounces each) chicken broth**
- 2 **tablespoons minced fresh parsley, optional**
- 2 **pounds potatoes (about 4 medium), peeled and cubed**
- 1 **can (15 ounces) cannellini beans, rinsed and drained**
- ¼ **cup grated Parmesan cheese**
- 1½ **cups uncooked ditalini or other small pasta**
- 2 **cups chopped fresh spinach**

1. In a 7-qt. Dutch oven, heat 1 tablespoon oil over medium-high heat; brown half of the beef. Remove from pan. Repeat with additional oil and remaining beef.
2. In same pan, saute carrots and onion in remaining oil until onion is tender, 2-3 minutes. Add garlic; cook 1 minute. Stir in tomatoes, tomato paste, salt, pepper, broth, beef and, if desired, parsley; bring to a boil. Reduce heat; simmer, covered, for 1½ hours.
3. Stir in potatoes, beans and cheese; bring to a boil. Stir in ditalini. Reduce the heat; simmer, uncovered, until beef and vegetables are tender, about 15-20 minutes, stirring occasionally. Stir in spinach until wilted.
PER SERVING 1⅔ cups: 342 cal., 10g fat (3g sat. fat), 52mg chol., 999mg sodium, 40g carb. (7g sugars, 5g fiber), 23g pro.

---

⑤ INGREDIENTS
WILD RICE AND MUSHROOM SOUP

Frequently requested at get-togethers, this rich and hearty soup is ready in a flash. Cooking for a vegetarian? Swap in vegetable stock for the beef broth.

—**DANIELLE NOBLE** FORT THOMAS, KY

PREP: 10 MIN. • **COOK:** 35 MIN.
MAKES: 8 SERVINGS (2 QUARTS)

- 1 **pound baby portobello mushrooms, chopped**
- 2 **tablespoons olive oil**
- 2 **packages (6 ounces each) long grain and wild rice mix**
- 1 **carton (32 ounces) reduced-sodium beef broth**
- ½ **cup water**
- 2 **cups heavy whipping cream**

In a Dutch oven, saute mushrooms in oil until tender. Add the rice with contents of seasoning packets, broth and water. Bring to a boil. Reduce heat; cover and simmer for 25 minutes. Add cream and heat through.
PER SERVING 1 cup: 399 cal., 26g fat (14g sat. fat), 84mg chol., 803mg sodium, 35g carb. (2g sugars, 1g fiber), 8g pro.

> **READER RAVE**
>
> This soup was super good, quick and easy. I added a little parsley and basil, and swapped the cream with 30-calorie almond milk for a lower-calorie soup. It was delicious.
>
> **-SAMPIERSON** TASTEOFHOME.COM

WILD RICE AND MUSHROOM SOUP

**Lorraine Caland's
One-Pot Saucy Beef Rotini**
PAGE 63

30-Minute Menus

Every delicious entree, sandwich or main-dish salad on the following pages includes a quick complementary side. And because each menu is table-ready in just 30 minutes or less, weeknight dinners just got a whole lot easier!

Sarah Campbell's Chicken with Red Wine Cream Sauce *PAGE 76*

Kelly Reynolds' Waffle Monte Cristos *PAGE 73*

Edie Farm's Crunchy Tuna Wraps *PAGE 62*

CASHEW TURKEY
SALAD SANDWICHES

EAT SMART **FAST FIX**
CASHEW TURKEY SALAD SANDWICHES

An unsung hero of the holidays is a top-notch sandwich. I love to serve turkey, apricots and cashews tucked into slices of pumpernickel.

—MARY WILHELM SPARTA, WI

START TO FINISH: 15 MIN.
MAKES: 4 SERVINGS

- ¼ cup reduced-fat mayonnaise
- 2 tablespoons reduced-fat plain yogurt
- 1 green onion, chopped
- ¼ teaspoon salt
- ¼ teaspoon pepper
- 1½ cups cubed cooked turkey breast
- ¼ cup thinly sliced celery
- 2 tablespoons chopped dried apricots
- 2 tablespoons chopped unsalted cashews
- 8 slices pumpernickel bread
- 4 lettuce leaves

1. In a bowl, mix the first five ingredients. Stir in turkey, celery, apricots and cashews.

2. Line half of the bread slices with lettuce. Top with turkey mixture and remaining bread.

PER SERVING *1 sandwich: 298 cal., 9g fat (2g sat. fat), 51mg chol., 664mg sodium, 32g carb. (4g sugars, 4g fiber), 22g pro.* **Diabetic Exchanges:** *2 starch, 2 lean meat, 1½ fat.*

ON THE SIDE
SPICED-UP SWEET POTATO FRIES

Preheat oven to 425°. Peel 3 medium sweet potatoes and cut into 1-in. wedges. Combine potatoes and 2 tablespoons olive oil. Coat with 1 teaspoon Cajun seasoning, ½ teaspoon kosher salt and ½ teaspoon pepper. Arrange on a greased 15x10x1-in. baking pan. Bake 20-25 minutes or until golden, turning occasionally. Makes 4 servings.

—DEBRA HUMPHRIES CHANHASSEN, MN

SEARED BALSAMIC SALMON

A friend gave me this quick and easy approach to salmon. It has a mildly sweet sauce and is such a hit, I've passed it to other fish fans.

—TRISH HORTON COLORADO SPRINGS, CO

START TO FINISH: 30 MIN.
MAKES: 4 SERVINGS

- 4 **salmon fillets (4 ounces each)**
- ½ **teaspoon salt**
- 2 **teaspoons canola oil**
- ¼ **cup water**
- ¼ **cup balsamic vinegar**
- 4 **teaspoons lemon juice**
- 4 **teaspoons brown sugar**
  Coarsely ground pepper

1. Sprinkle salmon with salt. In a large nonstick skillet coated with cooking spray, heat oil over medium heat. Place salmon in skillet, skin side up; cook for 4-5 minutes on each side or until fish just begins to flake easily with a fork. Remove from pan; keep warm.

2. In same skillet, combine water, vinegar, lemon juice and brown sugar. Bring to a boil; cook until liquid is reduced to about ⅓ cup, stirring occasionally. Serve salmon with sauce; sprinkle with pepper.

PER SERVING *1 fillet with about 1 tablespoon sauce: 231 cal., 13g fat (2g sat. fat), 57mg chol., 353mg sodium, 9g carb. (9g sugars, trace fiber), 19g pro.* **Diabetic Exchanges:** *3 lean meat, ½ starch, ½ fat.*

ON THE SIDE
LEMON-BUTTER NEW POTATOES

Boil 12 small red potatoes in water for 15-20 minutes or just until tender; drain. Stir in ⅓ cup melted butter, 3 tablespoons lemon juice, 1 teaspoon each salt and grated lemon peel, ¼ teaspoon pepper and ⅛ teaspoon ground nutmeg. Sprinkle with 2 tablespoons minced fresh parsley. Makes 4 servings.

—SANDY MCKENZIE BRAHAM, MN

SEARED BALSAMIC SALMON

LEMON-PEPPER TILAPIA

LEMON-PEPPER TILAPIA

I usually have the ingredients on hand for this lemony dish that's ready in a jiff. I use tilapia, but this method peps up any white fish you like.

—JILL THOMAS WASHINGTON, IN

START TO FINISH: 20 MIN.
MAKES: 6 SERVINGS

- 6 tilapia fillets (6 ounces each)
- 2 tablespoons butter
- 2 teaspoons grated lemon peel
- 1 tablespoon lemon juice
- 1 teaspoon garlic salt
- 1 teaspoon paprika
- ½ teaspoon freshly ground pepper
- ¼ cup minced fresh parsley

1. Preheat oven to 425°. Place tilapia in a 15x10x1-in. baking pan. In a microwave, melt butter; stir in lemon peel and juice. Drizzle over fish fillets; sprinkle with the garlic salt, paprika and pepper.

2. Bake, uncovered, 10-12 minutes or until fish just begins to flake easily with a fork. Sprinkle with parsley.
PER SERVING *1 fillet: 177 cal., 5g fat (3g sat. fat), 93mg chol., 254mg sodium, 1g carb. (0 sugars, 0 fiber), 32g pro. Diabetic Exchanges: 5 lean meat, 1 fat.*

ON THE SIDE
CREAMY GARLIC MASHED POTATOES

In a saucepan, place 5 peeled and cubed potatoes, 15 peeled and halved garlic cloves and 1 teaspoon salt; cover with water. Bring to a boil. Reduce heat; cover and cook for 10-15 minutes or until tender. Drain. Transfer to a bowl; mash. Add ½ cup each butter and heavy cream and 1 teaspoon salt; beat until smooth. Serves 6.

—MYRA INNES AUBURN, KS

SESAME CHICKEN SLAW SALAD

I tasted many types of Asian chicken salad in California. When I moved back to Georgia, I wanted more. Here's a gingery-sweet recipe using wonton strips.

—MICHELLE MULRAIN EVANS, GA

START TO FINISH: 20 MIN.
MAKES: 6 SERVINGS

- 1 package (14 ounces) coleslaw mix
- 4 cups torn romaine
- 3 cups shredded rotisserie chicken
- 1 large sweet red pepper, julienned
- 1 small red onion, halved and thinly sliced
- ¾ cup reduced-fat Asian toasted sesame salad dressing
- 1 medium ripe avocado, peeled and sliced
- 1 can (11 ounces) mandarin oranges, drained
- ¾ cup crunchy garlic ginger or plain wonton strips

1. In a large bowl, combine the first five ingredients. Drizzle with dressing and toss to coat.
2. Top with remaining ingredients. Serve immediately.
NOTE *This recipe was tested with Fresh Gourmet Wonton Strips; look for them in the produce section.*
PER SERVING *2 cups: 309 cal., 13g fat (2g sat. fat), 62mg chol., 414mg sodium, 26g carb. (15g sugars, 5g fiber), 25g pro. Diabetic Exchanges: 3 lean meat, 2 vegetable, 2 fat, 1 starch.*

ON THE SIDE
HERBED PITA CHIPS

Place 4 pita breads on an ungreased baking sheet; brush with 1 tablespoon melted butter. Combine ½ teaspoon each dried basil and thyme; sprinkle over pitas. Cut each into eight wedges. Bake at 400° for 8-10 minutes or until crisp. Makes 6 servings.

—*TASTE OF HOME* TEST KITCHEN

SESAME CHICKEN
SLAW SALAD

BASIL BLTS

CRUNCHY TUNA WRAPS

We love tuna salad wraps loaded with lots of crunchy veggies. It's a great way to shake up standard tuna salad.

—**EDIE FARM** FARMINGTON, NM

START TO FINISH: 10 MIN.
MAKES: 2 SERVINGS

- 1 pouch (6.4 ounces) light tuna in water
- ¼ cup finely chopped celery
- ¼ cup chopped green onions
- ¼ cup sliced water chestnuts, chopped
- 3 tablespoons chopped sweet red pepper
- 2 tablespoons reduced-fat mayonnaise
- 2 teaspoons prepared mustard
- 2 spinach tortillas (8 inches), room temperature
- 1 cup shredded lettuce

In a small bowl, mix the first seven ingredients until blended. Spread over tortillas; sprinkle with lettuce. Roll up tightly jelly-roll style.
PER SERVING *1 wrap: 312 cal., 10g fat (2g sat. fat), 38mg chol., 628mg sodium, 34g carb. (2g sugars, 3g fiber), 23g pro.* **Diabetic Exchanges:** *3 lean meat, 2 starch, ½ fat.*

ON THE SIDE
WATERMELON-BLUEBERRY SALAD

Combine 1 tablespoon honey, ¾ teaspoon lemon juice and ½ teaspoon of minced fresh mint. Add 1 cup seeded chopped watermelon and ½ cup fresh blueberries. Makes 2 servings.

—**JENNI SHARP** MILWAUKEE, WI

FAST FIX ▶
BASIL BLTS

Everybody goes for the bacon in this impressive sandwich. If you've got a garden, harvest your fresh tomatoes and basil, and pile them on.

—**ALISA LEWIS** VERADALE, WA

START TO FINISH: 15 MIN.
MAKES: 4 SERVINGS

- ¼ cup mayonnaise or plain Greek yogurt
- 2 tablespoons minced fresh basil
- 1 teaspoon lemon juice
- ¼ teaspoon salt
- ⅛ teaspoon garlic powder
- 8 thick slices French bread (diagonally cut), toasted
- 4 lettuce leaves
- 2 medium tomatoes, each cut into four slices
- 8 cooked bacon strips

In a small bowl, mix the first five ingredients. Spread over four slices of bread; top with lettuce, tomatoes, bacon and remaining bread.
PER SERVING *1 sandwich: 319 cal., 20g fat (5g sat. fat), 28mg chol., 833mg sodium, 22g carb. (2g sugars, 2g fiber), 12g pro.*

HEALTH TIP *Cut 100 calories and 10 grams fat by switching from mayonnaise to nonfat Greek yogurt.*

ON THE SIDE
FRESH PEACH SALSA

In a food processor, coarsely chop 2 peeled and pitted peaches, 1 seeded tomato, ⅓ cup chopped sweet onion, ¼ cup cilantro and 1 sliced garlic clove. Add 1 can (4 ounces) chopped green chilies, 2 teaspoons cider vinegar, ½ teaspoon lime juice and ⅛ teaspoon pepper; pulse until blended. Serve with tortilla chips. Serves 8.

—**SHAWNA LAUFER** FORT MYERS, FL

CRUNCHY TUNA WRAPS

ONE-POT SAUCY BEEF ROTINI

My husband loves pasta; I cringe over the messy dishes. On Spaghetti Day, as he calls it, I make a one-pot saucy rotini that keeps everyone happy.
—**LORRAINE CALAND** SHUNIAH, ON

START TO FINISH: 30 MIN.
MAKES: 4 SERVINGS

- ¾ **pound lean ground beef (90% lean)**
- 2 **cups sliced fresh mushrooms**
- 1 **medium onion, chopped**
- 3 **garlic cloves, minced**
- ¾ **teaspoon Italian seasoning**
- 2 **cups tomato basil pasta sauce**
- ¼ **teaspoon salt**
- 2½ **cups water**
- 3 **cups uncooked whole wheat rotini (about 8 ounces)**
- ¼ **cup grated Parmesan cheese**

1. In a 6-qt. stockpot, cook the first five ingredients over medium-high heat 6-8 minutes or until beef is no longer pink, breaking up beef into crumbles; drain.

2. Add pasta sauce, salt and water; bring to a boil. Stir in rotini; return to a boil. Reduce heat; simmer, covered, 8-10 minutes or until pasta is al dente, stirring occasionally. Serve with Parmesan cheese.

PER SERVING *1½ cups: 414 cal., 11g fat (4g sat. fat), 57mg chol., 806mg sodium, 49g carb. (12g sugars, 8g fiber), 28g pro.*

ON THE SIDE
FABULOUS GREEN BEANS

Trim 1 pound green beans. Steam beans for 8-10 minutes or until crisp-tender; transfer to serving bowl. Meanwhile, heat ¼ cup cubed butter, 1 tablespoon olive oil, ½ teaspoon each salt, Italian seasoning and lemon juice and ¼ teaspoon grated lemon peel until butter is melted; toss with beans. Makes 4 servings.
—**LORI DANIELS** BEVERLY, WV

ONE-POT SAUCY
BEEF ROTINI

GRILLED
SALMON WRAPS

GRILLED SALMON WRAPS

We eat fish on Fridays, so I like to experiment with different types. I pulled salmon, spinach and avocado from the fridge for these wraps. My kids loved them, and I love them, too, because they're delicious and they contain all four food groups right in one hand-held meal.
—**JENNIFER KREY** CLARENCE, NY

START TO FINISH: 25 MIN.
MAKES: 4 SERVINGS

- 1 **pound salmon fillet (about 1 inch thick)**
- ½ **teaspoon salt**
- ¼ **teaspoon pepper**
- ½ **cup salsa verde**
- 4 **whole wheat tortillas (8 inches), warmed**
- 1 **cup chopped fresh spinach**
- 1 **medium tomato, seeded and chopped**
- ½ **cup shredded Monterey Jack cheese**
- ½ **medium ripe avocado, peeled and thinly sliced**

1. Sprinkle salmon with salt and pepper; place on an oiled grill rack over medium heat, skin side down. Grill, covered, 8-10 minutes or until fish just begins to flake easily with a fork.
2. Remove from grill. Break salmon into bite-size pieces, removing skin if desired. Toss gently with salsa; serve in tortillas. Top with the remaining ingredients.
PER SERVING *1 wrap: 380 cal., 18g fat (5g sat. fat), 69mg chol., 745mg sodium, 27g carb. (2g sugars, 5g fiber), 27g pro. Diabetic Exchanges: 3 lean meat, 2 starch, 2 fat.*

ON THE SIDE
BLACK BEAN SALAD

Combine 1 can (15 ounces) black beans (rinsed and drained), ¾ cup pico de gallo and 1 tablespoon minced fresh cilantro. Chill for 15 minutes. Serves 4.
—**PEG KENKEL-THOMSEN** IOWA CITY, IA

SPICE-RUBBED
CHICKEN THIGHS

SPICE-RUBBED CHICKEN THIGHS

Our go-to meal has always been baked chicken thighs. This easy grilled version takes the cooking outside with a zesty rub of turmeric, paprika and chili powder.
—**BILL STALEY** MONROEVILLE, PA

START TO FINISH: 20 MIN.
MAKES: 6 SERVINGS

- 1 **teaspoon salt**
- 1 **teaspoon garlic powder**
- 1 **teaspoon onion powder**
- 1 **teaspoon dried oregano**
- ½ **teaspoon ground turmeric**
- ½ **teaspoon paprika**
- ¼ **teaspoon chili powder**
- ¼ **teaspoon pepper**
- 6 **boneless skinless chicken thighs (about 1½ pounds)**

1. In a small bowl, mix the first eight ingredients. Sprinkle over both sides of chicken.

2. Moisten a paper towel with cooking oil; using long-handled tongs, rub on grill rack to coat lightly. Grill chicken, covered, over medium heat or broil 4 in. from heat 6-8 minutes on each side or until a thermometer reads 170°.
PER SERVING *169 cal., 8g fat (2g sat. fat), 76mg chol., 460mg sodium, 1g carb. (0 sugars, 0 fiber), 21g pro. Diabetic Exchanges: 3 lean meat.*

ON THE SIDE
GRILLED POTATOES WITH RANCH

Mix 2 tablespoons olive oil, 1 tablespoon barbecue seasoning, 2 minced garlic cloves and 2 teaspoons lemon juice. Toss with 1¾ pounds quartered red potatoes. Seal in a double thickness of heavy-duty foil. Grill, covered, over medium heat 20-25 minutes. Mix ⅔ cup ranch dressing, 4 teaspoon bacon bits, 2 teaspoons minced chives and a dash of hot sauce. Serve with potatoes. Serves 6.
—**CRAIG CARPENTER** CORAOPOLIS, PA

SAUSAGE
ZUCCHINI
SKILLET

EAT SMART **FAST FIX**

SAUSAGE ZUCCHINI SKILLET

This Italian skillet dish started as a side for grilled salmon. Then I transformed it with sausage and rice to give it a new identity.
—**DEBBY ABEL** FLAT ROCK, NC

START TO FINISH: 25 MIN.
MAKES: 4 SERVINGS

- 1 **pound Italian turkey sausage links, casings removed**
- 2 **large zucchini, cut into ½-in. pieces**
- 1 **large sweet onion, chopped**
- 2 **garlic cloves, minced**
- 1 **can (14½ ounces) no-salt-added diced tomatoes, undrained**
- ¼ **teaspoon pepper**
- 2 **cups hot cooked brown rice**

1. In a large nonstick skillet coated with cooking spray, cook sausage, zucchini and onion over medium-high heat 6-8 minutes or until sausage is no longer pink, breaking up sausage into crumbles. Add garlic; cook 1 minute longer. Drain.

2. Stir in tomatoes and pepper; bring to a boil. Reduce heat; simmer, uncovered, 4-5 minutes or until liquid is evaporated, stirring occasionally. Serve with rice.

PER SERVING *1¼ cups sausage mixture with ½ cup cooked rice: 262 cal., 8g fat (2g sat. fat), 42mg chol., 483mg sodium, 33g carb. (7g sugars, 3g fiber), 15g pro.* **Diabetic Exchanges:** *2 lean meat, 2 vegetable, 1 starch..*

ON THE SIDE
SWIRLED DILL ROLLS

Unwrap an 8-ounce tube of refrigerated crescent rolls; do not unroll. Cut into eight slices. Place cut side down on an ungreased baking sheet. Bake at 375° for 11-13 minutes. Combine 2 tablespoons softened butter, ¼ teaspoon onion powder and ¼ teaspoon snipped fresh dill. Spread over warm rolls. Makes 8 rolls.
—**TASTE OF HOME** TEST KITCHEN

BARBECUE CHICKEN QUESADILLAS

When my kids were small, I'd stuff leftover chicken into these oven-baked quesadillas. I often grab rotisserie chicken instead.

—PAM MARTIN CANANDAIGUA, NY

START TO FINISH: 25 MIN.
MAKES: 6 SERVINGS

- 3 cups shredded cooked chicken
- 1 can (4 ounces) chopped green chilies
- ½ cup salsa
- ⅓ cup barbecue sauce
- ¼ cup taco sauce
- 8 flour tortillas (8 inches)
- ¾ cup shredded sharp cheddar cheese
  Sour cream and additional salsa, optional

1. Preheat oven to 450°. In a large bowl, combine the first five ingredients; toss to combine.
2. Divide four tortillas between two baking sheets; spread with chicken mixture. Sprinkle with cheese and top with remaining tortillas.
3. Bake 6-8 minutes or until lightly browned and cheese is melted. Cut each quesadilla into six wedges. If desired, serve with sour cream and additional salsa.

PER SERVING *4 wedges (calculated without sour cream and additional salsa): 446 cal., 15g fat (5g sat. fat), 77mg chol., 814mg sodium, 46g carb. (6g sugars, 3g fiber), 30g pro.*

ON THE SIDE
COLORFUL AVOCADO SALAD

Combine 3 medium tomatoes cut into eighths, 1 large peeled and thinly sliced cucumber, 1 large halved and thinly sliced red onion and 1 medium julienned green pepper. Stir in ⅓ cup Italian salad dressing. Gently add 3 peeled and cubed avocados. Makes 6 servings.

—BEV LEHRMAN JIJOCA, BRAZIL

BARBECUE CHICKEN QUESADILLAS

PEPPER & SALSA COD

MEXICAN HOT DOGS

My stepmom was born in Mexico and introduced us to hot dogs with avocado and bacon. We were instantly hooked. Now our whole family makes them.
—AMANDA BRANDENBURG HAMILTON, OH

START TO FINISH: 20 MIN.
MAKES: 6 SERVINGS

- ½   medium ripe avocado, peeled
- 1   tablespoon lime juice
- ¼   teaspoon salt
- ⅛   teaspoon pepper
- 6   hot dogs
- 6   hot dog buns, split
- 1   small tomato, chopped
- 3   tablespoons finely chopped red onion
- 3   bacon strips, cooked and crumbled

1. In a small bowl, mash avocado with a fork, stirring in lime juice, salt and pepper. Grill hot dogs, covered, over medium heat 7-9 minutes or until heated through, turning occasionally.
2. Serve in buns. Top with avocado mixture, tomato, onion and bacon.
PER SERVING *310 cal., 19g fat (7g sat. fat), 29mg chol., 844mg sodium, 25g carb. (4g sugars, 2g fiber), 11g pro.*

ON THE SIDE
CILANTRO-LIME FRUIT SALAD

Combine 2 cups cantaloupe balls, 2 peeled and finely chopped mangoes, 2 peeled and sliced kiwi fruit and 1 sliced banana. In a small bowl, combine 3 tablespoons minced fresh cilantro, 2 tablespoons lime juice, 1 tablespoon honey and ⅛ teaspoon salt. Toss with fruit. Serves 6.
—DENETTE BRENTS PORTERVILLE, CA

EAT SMART FAST FIX
PEPPER & SALSA COD

After tasting a similar dish at the grocery store, my husband figured out how to make this awesome cod topped with salsa and two kinds of peppers.
—ROBYN GALLAGHER YORKTOWN, VA

START TO FINISH: 30 MIN.
MAKES: 2 SERVINGS

- 2   cod or haddock fillets (6 ounces each)
- 1   teaspoon olive oil
- ¼   teaspoon salt
      Dash pepper
- ⅓   cup orange juice
- ¼   cup salsa
- ⅓   cup julienned green pepper
- ⅓   cup julienned sweet red pepper
      Hot cooked rice

1. Preheat oven to 350°. Brush both sides of fillets with oil; place in a greased 11x7-in. baking dish. Sprinkle with salt and pepper. Pour orange juice over fish; top with salsa and peppers.
2. Bake, covered, 17-20 minutes or until fish just begins to flake easily with a fork. Serve with rice.
PER SERVING *(calculated without rice): 183 cal., 3g fat (1g sat. fat), 65mg chol., 512mg sodium, 9g carb. (6g sugars, 1g fiber), 27g pro.* **Diabetic Exchanges:** *4 lean meat, 1 vegetable, ½ fat.*

ON THE SIDE
TANGY BUTTERED GREEN BEANS

Simmer 1¼ cups trimmed green beans in water for 10 minutes or until tender; drain. Combine 2 tablespoons melted butter, 1 tablespoon cider vinegar, 1 teaspoon sugar, 1 teaspoon lemon juice, ½ teaspoon prepared mustard and ¼ teaspoon salt; stir into beans. Makes 2 servings.
—BETH ALLARD BELMONT, NH

SMOKY ESPRESSO STEAK

This juicy steak rubbed with espresso, cocoa and pumpkin pie spice is one of my husband's favorites. We usually grill it, but broiling works in the chilly months.

—**DEBORAH BIGGS** OMAHA, NE

START TO FINISH: 30 MIN.
MAKES: 4 SERVINGS

- 3 **teaspoons instant espresso powder**
- 2 **teaspoons brown sugar**
- 1½ **teaspoons smoked or regular paprika**
- 1 **teaspoon salt**
- 1 **teaspoon baking cocoa**
- ¼ **teaspoon pumpkin pie spice**
- ¼ **teaspoon pepper**
- 1 **pound beef flat iron or top sirloin steak (¾ inch thick)**

1. Preheat broiler. In a small bowl, mix the first seven ingredients; rub over both sides of steak. Place steak on a broiler pan; let stand 10 minutes.
2. Broil steak 3-4 in. from heat 4-6 minutes on each side or until meat reaches desired doneness (for medium-rare, a thermometer should read 145°; medium, 160°). Let stand 5 minutes before slicing.

PER SERVING *3 ounces cooked beef: 216 cal., 12g fat (5g sat. fat), 73mg chol., 661mg sodium, 4g carb. (2g sugars, 0g fiber), 22g pro.* **Diabetic Exchanges:** *3 lean meat.*

ON THE SIDE
GARLIC BROCCOLI PASTA

Cook 1¾ cups rigatoni according to package directions, adding 2 cups fresh broccoli florets during the last 5 minutes of cooking. In a saucepan saute 3 minced garlic cloves in 4½ teaspoon olive oil until tender. Drain pasta mixture; add to saucepan and toss to coat. Add ¼ cup shredded Parmesan cheese, ½ teaspoon salt and ⅛ teaspoon pepper; toss to combine. Makes 4 servings.

—**MICHELE THOMPSON** SANTA CLARITA, CA

SMOKY ESPRESSO STEAK

GREEK-STYLE RAVIOLI

CUBAN PORK WRAPS

Hot, juicy pork with Swiss, ham and pickles—those are the makings of a classic Cuban sandwich. These wraps pile on all the best-loved flavor, but they're quick to prepare.

—AIMEE BACHMANN NORTH BEND, WA

START TO FINISH: 20 MIN.
MAKES: 4 SERVINGS

- ¾ pound thin boneless pork loin chops, cut into strips
- 1 tablespoon canola oil
- ⅛ teaspoon pepper
- 1 tablespoon Dijon mustard
- 4 multigrain tortillas (10 inches)
- 8 ounces sliced deli ham
- 8 slices Swiss cheese
- 4 thin sandwich pickle slices
- ¼ cup thinly sliced red onion

1. Preheat oven to 350°. In a bowl, toss pork with oil and pepper. Place a large skillet over medium-high heat. Add pork; cook and stir 2-3 minutes or until browned. Remove from heat.
2. Spread mustard onto center of tortillas; layer with ham, cheese, pickle, onion and pork. Fold bottom and sides of tortillas over filling and roll up. Place on an ungreased baking sheet; bake 4-6 minutes or until hot.
PER SERVING *501 cal., 22g fat (8g sat. fat), 86mg chol., 1230mg sodium, 37g carb. (5g sugars, 7g fiber), 39g pro.*

ON THE SIDE
SIMPLE CABBAGE SLAW

Combine 3 cups coleslaw mix, ½ cup finely chopped red pepper, ¼ cup each sugar and cider vinegar, 3 tablespoons water, ¼ teaspoon salt and dash pepper. Chill. Makes 4 servings.

—SANDRA LAMPE MUSCATINE, IA

GREEK-STYLE RAVIOLI

I took an Italian dish and gave it a Greek twist with spinach, olives and feta. I like serving this easy weeknight ravioli with garlic cheese toast.

—HETTI WILLIAMS RAPID CITY, SD

START TO FINISH: 25 MIN.
MAKES: 2 SERVINGS

- 12 frozen cheese ravioli
- ⅓ pound lean ground beef (90% lean)
- 1 cup canned diced tomatoes with basil, oregano and garlic
- 1 cup fresh baby spinach
- ¼ cup sliced ripe olives
- ¼ cup crumbled feta cheese

1. Cook ravioli according to package directions; drain. Meanwhile, in a skillet, cook beef over medium heat 4-6 minutes or until no longer pink; drain. Stir in tomatoes; bring to a boil. Reduce heat; simmer, uncovered, for 10 minutes, stirring occasionally.
2. Add ravioli, spinach and olives; heat through, stirring gently to combine. Sprinkle with cheese.
PER SERVING *1¼ cups: 333 cal., 12g fat (5g sat. fat), 61mg chol., 851mg sodium, 28g carb. (5g sugars, 4g fiber), 23g pro.* **Diabetic Exchanges:** *3 lean meat, 2 starch, ½ fat.*

ON THE SIDE
TOSSED SALAD WITH SIMPLE VINAIGRETTE

Combine 1½ cups torn leaf lettuce, ⅓ cup sliced cucumber, ¼ cup chopped tomato, 2 chopped fresh basil leaves and 1 sliced green onion. Whisk 2 teaspoons rice vinegar, 1½ teaspoon olive oil and dash each salt and pepper. Add to salad. Makes 2 servings.

—MARTHA ATWELL ALAMOGORDO, NM

CUBAN PORK WRAPS

O'BRIEN
SAUSAGE
SKILLET

FAST FIX ▶
O'BRIEN SAUSAGE SKILLET

Inspiration hit one night when I was in a time crunch. This was so satisfying and easy to make, many friends now serve it, too.
—**LINDA HARRIS** WICHITA, KS

START TO FINISH: 20 MIN.
MAKES: 6 SERVINGS

- 1 **package (28 ounces) frozen O'Brien potatoes**
- ¼ **cup plus 2 teaspoons canola oil, divided**
- 1 **package (14 ounces) smoked turkey kielbasa, sliced**
- 2 **medium tart apples, peeled and chopped**
- 1 **medium onion, chopped**
- 1 **cup (4 ounces) shredded cheddar cheese**

1. In a large nonstick skillet, prepare potatoes according to package directions, using ¼ cup oil. In another skillet, heat remaining oil over medium-high heat. Add kielbasa, apples and onion; cook and stir 8-10 minutes or until onion is tender.

2. Spoon sausage mixture over potatoes; sprinkle with cheese. Cook, covered, 3-4 minutes longer or until cheese is melted.

PER SERVING *377 cal., 21g fat (6g sat. fat), 61mg chol., 803mg sodium, 29g carb. (8g sugars, 4g fiber), 17g pro.*

ON THE SIDE
SAVORY GREEN BEANS

Saute ¾ cup chopped sweet red pepper in 1 tablespoon canola oil for 2-3 minutes or until tender. Add 1 minced garlic clove; cook 1 minute longer. Stir in 1½ pounds fresh green beans (trimmed and cut into 2-in. pieces), ½ cup water, 2 tablespoons minced fresh savory, 1½ teaspoon minced chives and ½ teaspoon salt. Cover and simmer 8-10 minutes or until beans are crisp-tender.
—**PEG KENKEL-THOMSEN** IOWA CITY, IA

FAST FIX ▶
WAFFLE MONTE CRISTOS

Waffles packed with turkey, ham, bacon and apricot preserves have so much sweet, smoky love going on. I use frozen waffles to save time, but have at it if you want to put your waffle iron to good use.
—**KELLY REYNOLDS** URBANA, IL

START TO FINISH: 20 MIN.
MAKES: 4 SERVINGS

- ½ **cup apricot preserves**
- 8 **frozen waffles**
- 4 **slices deli turkey**
- 4 **slices deli ham**
- 4 **slices Havarti cheese (about 3 ounces)**
- 4 **bacon strips, cooked**
- 2 **tablespoons butter, softened Maple syrup**

1. Preheat griddle over medium heat. Spread preserves over four waffles. Layer with turkey, ham, cheese and bacon; top with remaining waffles. Lightly spread outsides of waffles with butter.

2. Place on griddle; cook 4-5 minutes on each side or until golden brown and heated through. Serve with maple syrup for dipping.

PER SERVING *1 sandwich (calculated without syrup): 511 cal., 23g fat (10g sat. fat), 70mg chol., 1163mg sodium, 57g carb. (22g sugars, 2g fiber), 21g pro.*

HEALTH TIP *Yep, this is one decadent sandwich. Use cooking spray instead of butter and cut the bacon and cheese in half to save 130 calories, 7 grams saturated fat and almost 300 milligrams sodium.*

ON THE SIDE
POPPY SEED FRUIT SALAD

Combine 1 sliced medium banana, 1 cup each fresh blueberries, raspberries and the sliced strawberries. Combine 2 tablespoons honey, ½ teaspoon lemon juice and ¼ teaspoon poppy seeds. Pour over fruit; toss to coat. Makes 4 servings.
—**DOROTHY DINNEAN** HARRISON, AR

LEMON SALMON
WITH BASIL

EAT SMART **⑤INGREDIENTS** **FAST FIX**

LEMON SALMON WITH BASIL

At our house we opt for healthy foods, and this lemony salmon with basil is a knockout in the good-for-you category. We have it with asparagus or zucchini.

—**SHANNA BELZ** PRINEVILLE, OR

START TO FINISH: 25 MIN.
MAKES: 4 SERVINGS

- 4 **salmon fillets (6 ounces each)**
- 2 **teaspoons olive oil**
- 1 **tablespoon grated lemon peel**
- ½ **teaspoon salt**
- ¼ **teaspoon pepper**
- 2 **tablespoons thinly sliced fresh basil**
- 2 **medium lemons, thinly sliced**
  Additional fresh basil

1. Preheat oven to 375°. Place salmon in a greased 15x10x1-in. baking pan. Drizzle with oil; sprinkle with lemon peel, salt, pepper and 2 tablespoons basil; top with lemon slices.
2. Bake 15-20 minutes or until fish just begins to flake easily with a fork. If desired, top with additional basil.
PER SERVING *1 salmon fillet: 294 cal., 18g fat (3g sat. fat), 85mg chol., 381mg sodium, 3g carb. (1g sugars, 1g fiber), 29g pro. Diabetic Exchanges: 5 lean meat, ½ fat.*

ON THE SIDE
GRILLED ZUCCHINI WITH ONIONS

Drizzle 6 small zucchini (halved lengthwise) with 2 teaspoons olive oil. Grill, covered, over medium heat for 8-10 minutes or until zucchini is tender, turning once. Place in a large bowl. Add 2 thinly sliced green onions, 2 tablespoons lemon juice, 2 teaspoons olive oil, ½ teaspoon salt, and ⅛ teaspoon crushed red pepper flakes. Makes 4 servings.

—**ALIA SHUTTLEWORTH** AUBURN, CA

SPINACH & TORTELLINI SOUP

My tomato-y broth is perfect for cheese tortellini and fresh spinach. Add extra garlic, oregano and basil to suit your taste.

—**DEBBIE WILSON** BURLINGTON, NC

START TO FINISH: 20 MIN.
MAKES: 6 SERVINGS

- 1 **teaspoon olive oil**
- 2 **garlic cloves, minced**
- 1 **can (14½ ounces) no-salt-added diced tomatoes, undrained**
- 3 **cans (14½ ounces each) vegetable broth**
- 2 **teaspoons Italian seasoning**
- 1 **package (9 ounces) refrigerated cheese tortellini**
- 4 **cups fresh baby spinach**
  Shredded Parmesan cheese and freshly ground pepper

1. In a large saucepan, heat oil over medium heat. Add garlic; cook and stir 1 minute. Stir in tomatoes, broth and Italian seasoning; bring to a boil. Add tortellini; bring to a gentle boil. Cook, uncovered, 7-9 minutes or just until tortellini are tender.

2. Stir in spinach. Sprinkle servings with cheese and pepper.

PER SERVING *1⅓ cups (calculated without cheese): 162 cal., 5g fat (2g sat. fat), 18mg chol., 998mg sodium, 25g carb. (4g sugars, 2g fiber), 6g pro.*

ON THE SIDE
GREENS WITH ORANGE VINAIGRETTE

Whisk 2 tablespoons each olive oil and orange juice, 1 tablespoon cider vinegar, 1 teaspoon grated orange peel, and a dash each of salt and pepper. Place 1 package (5 ounces) spring mix salad greens in a large bowl. Drizzle with vinaigrette; toss to coat. Makes 6 servings.

—**KRISTIN BATAILLE** STAMFORD, CT

SPINACH & TORTELLINI SOUP

CHICKEN WITH RED WINE CREAM SAUCE

CHICKEN WITH RED WINE CREAM SAUCE

My creamy chicken tastes like a five-star restaurant dish but takes only minutes and few ingredients to make. Use fresh rosemary. Trust me.

—**SARAH CAMPBELL** TERRE HAUTE, IN

START TO FINISH: 30 MIN.
MAKES: 4 SERVINGS

- 1 tablespoon butter
- 4 bone-in chicken thighs (1½ pounds)
- ½ teaspoon salt
- ¼ teaspoon pepper
- ⅓ cup dry red wine
- 1 garlic clove, minced
- ½ cup heavy whipping cream
- 1 tablespoon minced fresh rosemary

1. In a large skillet, heat butter over medium-high heat. Brown chicken on both sides; season with salt and pepper. Reduce heat to medium; cook, covered, 10-12 minutes or until a thermometer reads 170°-175°. Remove chicken to a serving plate; keep warm.

2. Pour drippings from pan (do not wipe skillet clean); add wine and garlic. Bring to a boil, stirring to loosen browned bits from pan; cook 1-2 minutes or until wine is reduced by half. Stir in cream and rosemary. Return to a boil; cook 1-2 minutes or until slightly thickened. Serve with the chicken.

PER SERVING *1 chicken thigh with 2 tablespoons sauce: 361 cal., 28g fat (13g sat. fat), 130mg chol., 398mg sodium, 1g carb. (1g sugars, 0 fiber), 23g pro.*

ON THE SIDE
RICE PILAF

Combine 2½ cups of chicken broth, 1 teaspoon dried parsley flakes and 2 tablespoons butter in a saucepan; bring to boil. Stir in 1 cup uncooked long grain rice; cover. Reduce heat; simmer for 20 minutes. Makes 4 servings.

—**BARIANNE WILSON** FALFURRIAS, TX

MEATBALL PIZZA

I always keep meatballs and pizza crusts in the freezer to make this specialty at the spur of the moment. Add a tossed salad, and you have a delicious dinner.

—**MARY HUMENIUK-SMITH** PERRY HALL, MD

START TO FINISH: 25 MIN.
MAKES: 8 SLICES

- 1 prebaked 12-inch pizza crust
- 1 can (8 ounces) pizza sauce
- 1 teaspoon garlic powder
- 1 teaspoon Italian seasoning
- ¼ cup grated Parmesan cheese
- 1 small onion, halved and sliced
- 12 frozen fully cooked Italian meatballs (½ ounce each), thawed and halved
- 1 cup (4 ounces) shredded part-skim mozzarella cheese
- 1 cup (4 ounces) shredded cheddar cheese

1. Preheat oven to 350°. Place crust on an ungreased 12-in. pizza pan or baking sheet.

2. Spread sauce over crust; sprinkle with garlic powder, Italian seasoning and Parmesan cheese. Top with onion and meatballs; sprinkle with the remaining cheeses. Bake for 12-17 minutes or until cheese is melted.

PER SERVING *1 slice: 321 cal., 16g fat (8g sat. fat), 36mg chol., 755mg sodium, 28g carb. (3g sugars, 2g fiber), 17g pro.*

ON THE SIDE
LEMONY CAESAR SALAD

In a blender, combine ¾ cup olive oil, 3 tablespoons lemon juice, 2 peeled garlic cloves, ¾ teaspoon salt, ¾ teaspoon ground mustard, ¾ teaspoon Worcestershire sauce and ¼ teaspoon pepper; cover and process until blended. Place 8-12 cups torn romaine in a salad bowl. Add dressing and 1½ cups shredded Parmesan cheese; toss to coat. Makes 8 servings.

—**NORMA HARDER** WEYAKWIN, SK

MEATBALL PIZZA

HAM & SWISS
STROMBOLI

HAM & SWISS STROMBOLI

This is great food to take to someone for dinner. It's also easy to change up the recipe with your favorite meats or cheeses.

—**TRICIA BIBB** HARTSELLE, AL

START TO FINISH: 30 MIN.
MAKES: 6 SERVINGS

- 1 tube (11 ounces) refrigerated crusty French loaf
- 6 ounces sliced deli ham
- ¼ cup finely chopped onion
- 8 bacon strips, cooked and crumbled
- 6 ounces sliced Swiss cheese
  Honey mustard, optional

1. Preheat oven to 375°. Unroll dough on a baking sheet. Place ham down center third of dough to within 1 in. of the ends; top with onion, bacon and cheese. Fold long sides of dough over filling, pinching seam and ends to seal; tuck ends under. Cut several slits in the top.

2. Bake 20-25 minutes or until golden brown. Cut into slices. If desired, serve with honey mustard.

FREEZE OPTION *Securely wrap and freeze cooled unsliced stromboli in heavy-duty foil. To use, reheat stromboli on an ungreased baking sheet in a preheated 375° oven until heated through and a thermometer inserted in center reads 165°.*

PER SERVING *1 slice: 272 cal., 11g fat (5g sat. fat), 40mg chol., 795mg sodium, 26g carb. (3g sugars, 1g fiber), 18g pro.*

ON THE SIDE
PEANUT BUTTER APPLE DIP

In a bowl, combine 8 ounces softened cream cheese, 1 cup peanut butter, 1 cup packed brown sugar and ¼ cup 2% milk; mix well. Serve with apple wedges. Makes 20 servings (2⅔ cups dip).

—**KIM VAN RHEENEN** MENDOTA, IL

BUSY-DAY PORK CHOPS

I created this recipe one day when I needed a simple way to make pork chops. It was so easy and the response was a rave review! They're crispy outside, even though the preparation technique uses less fat.

—**DEE MALTBY** WAYNE, OH

START TO FINISH: 25 MIN.
MAKES: 4 SERVINGS

- ¼ **cup fat-free milk**
- ¼ **cup seasoned bread crumbs**
- ¼ **cup grated Parmesan cheese**
- ¼ **teaspoon each salt, garlic powder and pepper**
- 4 **boneless pork loin chops (4 ounces each)**
   Cooking spray

1. Preheat oven to 375°. Place milk in a shallow bowl. In another shallow bowl, toss crumbs with cheese and the seasonings.
2. Dip pork chops in milk, then coat with crumb mixture. Place on a baking sheet coated with cooking spray; lightly spritz chops with cooking spray.
3. Bake 8-10 minutes on each side or until a thermometer reads 145°. Let stand 5 minutes before serving.

PER SERVING *1 pork chop: 178 cal., 7g fat (3g sat. fat), 57mg chol., 207mg sodium, 3g carb. (0 sugars, 0 fiber), 23g pro.* **Diabetic Exchanges:** *3 lean meat.*

ON THE SIDE
LEMON-THYME ASPARAGUS

In a large skillet, saute 1 pound fresh asparagus (trimmed and cut into 1-in. pieces) and ½ pound sliced fresh mushrooms in 1 tablespoon butter and 1 teaspoon olive oil until tender. Stir in 1½ teaspoons minced fresh thyme, 1 teaspoon grated lemon peel, ½ teaspoon each salt and lemon juice and ¼ teaspoon pepper. Makes 4 servings.

—**SARAH REID** OSHAWA, ON

BUSY-DAY PORK CHOPS

SLOPPY JOE
BISCUIT CUPS

SLOPPY JOE BISCUIT CUPS

I'm a busy teacher and mom, so weekday meals with shortcuts are a huge help. I always have to share the recipe for these when I take them to school.

—**JULIE AHERN** WAUKEGAN, IL

START TO FINISH: 30 MIN.
MAKES: 5 SERVINGS

- 1 **pound lean ground beef (90% lean)**
- ¼ **cup each finely chopped celery, onion and green pepper**
- ½ **cup barbecue sauce**
- 1 **tube (12 ounces) refrigerated biscuits (10 count)**
- ½ **cup shredded cheddar cheese**

1. Heat oven to 400°. In a large skillet, cook beef and vegetables over medium heat 5-7 minutes or until beef is no longer pink, breaking up beef into crumbles; drain. Stir in barbecue sauce; bring to a boil. Reduce heat; simmer, uncovered, 2 minutes, stirring occasionally.
2. Separate dough into 10 biscuits; flatten to 5-in. circles. Press onto bottom and up sides of greased muffin cups. Fill with beef mixture.
3. Bake 9-11 minutes or until biscuits are golden brown. Sprinkle with cheese; bake 1-2 minutes longer or until cheese is melted.

PER SERVING *2 biscuit cups: 463 cal., 22g fat (8g sat. fat), 68mg chol., 1050mg sodium, 41g carb. (16g sugars, 1g fiber), 25g pro.*

ON THE SIDE
FRESH GRAPE BROCCOLI SALAD

Mix ½ cup mayo, 3 tablespoons sugar and 1½ teaspoons cider vinegar. Toss it with 3 cups fresh broccoli, 3 chopped green onions, 1 cup grapes and ½ cup diced celery. Stir in 5 cooked, crumbled bacon strips and ½ cup slivered almonds. Serves 6.
—**M.L. HARTEL** WILLISTON, ND.

CHEESY HAM & POTATO PACKET

(5)INGREDIENTS FAST FIX ▶

CHEESY HAM & POTATO PACKET

I found the technique for grilling ham, potatoes and cheese in foil packets and changed up some ingredients to suit our tastes. I love that this great meal doesn't heat up the kitchen!

—**MOLLY BISHOP** MCCLURE, PA

START TO FINISH: 30 MIN.
MAKES: 4 SERVINGS

- 1½ **pounds medium red potatoes, halved and thinly sliced**
- 1 **medium green pepper, chopped**
- 1 **medium onion, chopped**
- ¼ **teaspoon pepper**
- 2 **cups cubed deli ham**
- 1 **cup shredded cheddar cheese**

1. Toss potatoes with green pepper, onion and pepper; place in center of a greased 24x18-in. piece of heavy-duty foil. Fold foil around vegetables and crimp edges to seal.
2. Grill, covered, over medium heat 15-20 minutes or until potatoes are tender. Remove from grill. Open foil carefully to allow steam to escape. Add ham; sprinkle with cheese. Grill opened packet, covered, 2-4 minutes longer or until cheese is melted.

PER SERVING *1½ cups: 341 cal., 13g fat (6g sat. fat), 70mg chol., 1040mg sodium, 32g carb. (4g sugars, 4g fiber), 26g pro.*

ON THE SIDE
SUMMER SQUASH SAUTE

In a skillet, cook 1 diced bacon strip until crisp. Stir in 1 tablespoon each finely chopped onion, green pepper, sweet red pepper and yellow pepper and ½ teaspoon minced garlic; cook for 2 minutes or until tender. Add 1 chopped summer squash; cover and cook over medium heat for 3-4 minutes or until tender. Serves 2.
—**MAXINE LYNCH** BOISE CITY, OK

RASPBERRY PECAN
CHICKEN SALAD

EAT SMART **FAST FIX**

RASPBERRY PECAN CHICKEN SALAD

I gave this sweet-savory chicken salad a little zip with Chinese five-spice powder, which tastes a bit like pumpkin pie spice. Sprinkle some on roasted carrots for an awesome meal.

—LISA RENSHAW KANSAS CITY, MO

START TO FINISH: 15 MIN.
MAKES: 6 SERVINGS

- 1 **carton (6 ounces) orange yogurt**
- ½ **cup mayonnaise**
- ¼ **teaspoon Chinese five-spice powder**
- 3 **cups cubed cooked chicken**
- 2 **green onions, chopped**
- ¼ **cup sliced celery**
- ¼ **cup chopped pecans, toasted**
- 1 **cup fresh raspberries**
- 12 **slices multigrain bread**

In a large bowl, mix the yogurt, mayonnaise and five-spice powder. Stir in chicken, green onions, celery and pecans. Gently stir in raspberries. Serve on bread.

NOTE *To toast nuts, cook in a skillet over low heat until lightly browned, stirring occasionally.*

PER SERVING *477 cal., 26g fat (4g sat. fat), 70mg chol., 378mg sodium, 31g carb. (10g sugars, 6g fiber), 29g pro.*

ON THE SIDE
BROCCOLI COLESLAW

Combine 6 cups broccoli coleslaw mix and ½ cup chopped green onions. In a jar with a tight fitting lid, combine ⅓ cup canola oil, ¼ cup cider vinegar, 2 tablespoons sugar, 1 teaspoon seasoned salt, ½ teaspoon dill weed, ¼ teaspoon celery seed and ¼ teaspoon pepper; shake well. Drizzle over coleslaw; toss to coat. Makes 6 servings.

—***TASTE OF HOME*** **TEST KITCHEN**

CHEESY SUMMER SQUASH FLATBREADS

When you want a meatless meal with Mediterranean style, these flatbreads smothered with squash, hummus and mozzarella deliver the goods.

—**MATTHEW HASS** FRANKLIN, WI

START TO FINISH: 30 MIN.
MAKES: 4 SERVINGS

- 3 **small yellow summer squash, sliced ¼-inch thick**
- 1 **tablespoon olive oil**
- ½ **teaspoon salt**
- 2 **cups fresh baby spinach, coarsely chopped**
- 2 **naan flatbreads**
- ⅓ **cup roasted red pepper hummus**
- 1 **carton (8 ounces) fresh mozzarella cheese pearls**
  Pepper

1. Preheat oven to 425°. Toss squash with oil and salt; spread evenly in a 15x10x1-in. baking pan. Roast for 8-10 minutes or until tender. Transfer to a bowl; stir in spinach.

2. Place naan on a baking sheet and spread with hummus. Top with squash mixture and cheese. Bake on a lower oven rack for 4-6 minutes or just until the cheese is melted. Sprinkle with pepper.

PER SERVING ½ topped flatbread: 332 cal., 20g fat (9g sat. fat), 47mg chol., 737mg sodium, 24g carb. (7g sugars, 3g fiber), 15g pro.

ON THE SIDE
TOMATOES WITH VINAIGRETTE

In a jar with a tight-fitting lid, combine ⅓ cup vinegar, ⅓ cup canola oil, ¼ cup sugar, 2 teaspoons seasoned salt and a dash of pepper; shake well. Serve over 4 tomatoes (cut into wedges) and leaf lettuce. Serves 4.

—**JOANNE SHEWCHUK** ST. BENEDICT, SK

CHEESY SUMMER
SQUASH FLATBREADS

SWEET & SPICY
PORK CHOPS

EAT SMART **FAST FIX**
LEMON SHRIMP LINGUINE

I like recipes with elegant taste and easy technique like this lemony shrimp pasta. Bring on the grated Parmesan cheese and a sprinkle of red pepper flakes.

—**PATTY WALKER** WEST DES MOINES, IA

START TO FINISH: 25 MIN.
MAKES: 6 SERVINGS

- 12 **ounces uncooked linguine**
- 2 **tablespoons butter**
- 2 **tablespoons olive oil**
- 3 **garlic cloves, minced**
- 1½ **pounds uncooked shrimp (31-40 per pound), peeled and deveined**
- ¼ **teaspoon salt**
- ¼ **teaspoon coarsely ground pepper**
- 1 **teaspoon grated lemon peel**
- ¼ **cup lemon juice**
- 1 **small lemon, halved and sliced, optional**
- 2 **tablespoons minced fresh parsley**

1. Cook linguine according to package directions. Drain and return to pot.
2. Meanwhile, in a large skillet, heat butter and oil over medium-high heat. Add garlic; cook and stir 15 seconds. Add shrimp, salt and pepper; cook and stir 2-3 minutes or until shrimp turn pink. Stir in lemon peel, lemon juice and, if desired, lemon slices.
3. Add to linguine. Sprinkle with parsley and toss to combine.
PER SERVING *1⅓ cups: 378 cal., 11g fat (4g sat. fat), 148mg chol., 267mg sodium, 43g carb. (2g sugars, 2g fiber), 26g pro. Diabetic Exchanges: 3 starch, 3 lean meat, 2 fat.*

ON THE SIDE
LIME-BUTTERED BROCCOLI

Steam 6 cups fresh broccoli florets for 3-4 minutes or until crisp-tender. Combine 2 tablespoons melted butter, 2 teaspoons lime juice and dash each salt and pepper; toss with broccoli. Makes 6 servings.

—**DENISE ALBERS** FREEBURG, IL

EAT SMART **FAST FIX**
SWEET & SPICY PORK CHOPS

My husband used to come home from work before I did, and one night he threw together these amazing chops. We've followed his recipe ever since.

—**KATHY KIRKLAND** DENHAM SPRINGS, LA

START TO FINISH: 20 MIN.
MAKES: 2 SERVINGS

- 2 **tablespoons brown sugar**
- 1 **tablespoon finely chopped onion**
- 1 **to 1½ teaspoons chili powder**
- ½ **teaspoon garlic powder**
- ½ **teaspoon prepared mustard**
- 2 **boneless pork loin chops (4 ounces each)**
  Dash salt and pepper

1. Preheat broiler. In a small bowl, mix the first five ingredients.
2. Place chops on a broiler pan; sprinkle with salt and pepper. Broil 4 in. from heat 5 minutes. Turn; top with brown sugar mixture. Broil 4-5 minutes longer or until a thermometer reads 145°. Let pork chops stand for 5 minutes before serving.
PER SERVING *1 pork chop: 212 cal., 7g fat (2g sat. fat), 55mg chol., 137mg sodium, 15g carb. (14g sugars, 1g fiber), 22g pro. Diabetic Exchanges: 4 lean meat, 1 starch.*

ON THE SIDE
ASIAN CABBAGE SLAW

Combine 1½ cups shredded napa cabbage, segments from 1 orange and ½ cup julienned jicama. Whisk 1 tablespoon each canola oil and rice vinegar, 1 teaspoon sugar, ¼ teaspoon each grated fresh gingerroot and reduced-sodium soy sauce and a dash of pepper. Add to cabbage mixture. Serves 2.

—**LILY JULOW** LAWRENCEVILLE, GA

LEMON SHRIMP LINGUINE

CRANBERRY, BRIE & TURKEY PIZZA

While traveling in New Zealand, my husband and I discovered turkey pizza. We came up with our own version for a creative way to use holiday leftovers.

—KRISTIN STONE LITTLE ELM, TX

START TO FINISH: 25 MIN.
MAKES: 6 SERVINGS

- 1 **prebaked 12-inch pizza crust**
- 1 **cup whole-berry cranberry sauce**
- 1 **teaspoon grated orange peel**
- 2 **cups (8 ounces) shredded part-skim mozzarella cheese**
- 1 **cup coarsely shredded cooked turkey**
- ½ **small red onion, thinly sliced**
- 4 **ounces Brie cheese, cubed**
- 1 **tablespoon minced fresh rosemary**

1. Preheat oven to 450°. Place crust on an ungreased baking sheet.
2. In a small bowl, mix cranberry sauce and orange peel; spread over crust. Top with mozzarella cheese, turkey, onion and Brie cheese; sprinkle with rosemary. Bake 10-12 minutes or until cheese is melted.

PER SERVING *1 slice: 456 cal., 17g fat (9g sat. fat), 67mg chol., 768mg sodium, 49g carb. (14g sugars, 2g fiber), 27g pro.*

ON THE SIDE
ORANGE & ONION SALAD

Separate 1 head Boston lettuce into leaves, thinly slice 1 medium red onion and drain 1 can (11 ounces) mandarin oranges; arrange on salad plates. Top with sliced almonds and serve with poppy seed dressing. Makes 6 servings.

—JEAN ANN PERKINS NEWBURYPORT, MD

CRANBERRY, BRIE
& TURKEY PIZZA

PARMESAN CHICKEN BITES

For tailgates and after-game parties, try dipping these crisp, tender chicken bites in marinara, ranch salad dressing, honey mustard or barbecue sauce. They're all winning combinations.

—**LYNNE NEVRIVY** MALTA, MT

START TO FINISH: 30 MIN.
MAKES: 6 SERVINGS

- 1 **cup crushed Ritz crackers (about 25 crackers)**
- ½ **cup grated Parmesan cheese**
- ¼ **cup finely chopped walnuts**
- 1 **teaspoon dried thyme**
- 1 **teaspoon dried basil**
- ½ **teaspoon seasoned salt**
- ¼ **teaspoon pepper**
- 1 **pound boneless skinless chicken breasts**
- ¼ **cup butter, melted**
  Warm marinara sauce, optional

1. Preheat oven to 400°. Line a baking sheet with foil; grease foil.
2. In a shallow bowl, mix the first seven ingredients.
3. Cut chicken into 1½-in. pieces. Dip in melted butter, then in cracker mixture, patting firmly to adhere. Place on prepared pan.
4. Bake 20-25 minutes or until golden brown and chicken is no longer pink. If desired, serve with sauce.
PER SERVING *289 cal., 18g fat (7g sat. fat), 68mg chol., 469mg sodium, 12g carb. (1g sugars, 1g fiber), 19g pro.*

ON THE SIDE
CORN & PEPPER ORZO

Cook ¾ cup orzo pasta according to package directions. Meanwhile, saute 1 chopped sweet red pepper and 1 chopped onion in 1 tablespoon olive oil for 2 minutes. Add 2 cups thawed frozen corn, 2 teaspoons Italian seasoning and ⅛ tsp. each salt and pepper; cook and stir until tender. Add drained pasta. Serves 6.
—**ANGELA HANKS** CHARLESTON, WV

MEDITERRANEAN MEATBALL SANDWICHES

⑤ INGREDIENTS | **FAST FIX** ▶

MEDITERRANEAN MEATBALL SANDWICHES

I grow onions, garlic and herbs, and I use them all in these saucy sandwiches. You can also shape the meat mixture into traditional meatballs and fry them.

—**ALYSHA BRAUN** ST. CATHARINES, ON

START TO FINISH: 25 MIN.
MAKES: 4 SERVINGS

- 1 **small onion, finely chopped**
- ¼ **cup minced fresh parsley**
- ½ **teaspoon salt**
- ¼ **teaspoon pepper**
- 1 **pound ground beef**
- 4 **whole pita breads, warmed**
  Refrigerated tzatziki sauce
  Optional toppings: sliced tomato, chopped red onion and shredded lettuce

1. In a large bowl, combine onion, parsley, salt and pepper. Add beef; mix lightly but thoroughly. Shape into four 4x2-in. oblong patties.
2. Grill patties, covered, over medium heat or broil 4 in. from heat 4-6 minutes on each side or until a thermometer reads 160°. Serve on pitas with tzatziki sauce and toppings as desired.
PER SERVING *(calculated without sauce and toppings): 379 cal., 14g fat (5g sat. fat), 70mg chol., 682mg sodium, 35g carb. (2g sugars, 2g fiber), 26g pro.*

ON THE SIDE
LEMON-BASIL BOW TIES

Cook 4 cups bow tie pasta. Saute 1 minced garlic clove in 1 teaspoon olive oil for 1 minute. Add 1 tablespoon of lemon juice, 1 teaspoon grated lemon peel, ½ teaspoon salt and ¼ teaspoon pepper. Stir in drained pasta and ½ cup sliced fresh basil. Sprinkle with ¼ cup shredded Parmesan cheese. Makes 4 servings.
—**MICHELLE HARBOUR** LEBANON, TN

CAJUN BAKED CATFISH

CAJUN BAKED CATFISH

This well-seasoned fish gets compliments from family and friends whenever I serve it. It's moist and flaky, and the coating is crispy, crunchy and flecked with paprika.

—**JIM GALES** MILWAUKEE, WI

START TO FINISH: 25 MIN.
MAKES: 2 SERVINGS

- 2 **tablespoons yellow cornmeal**
- 2 **teaspoons Cajun or blackened seasoning**
- ½ **teaspoon dried thyme**
- ½ **teaspoon dried basil**
- ¼ **teaspoon garlic powder**
- ¼ **teaspoon lemon-pepper seasoning**
- 2 **catfish or tilapia fillets (6 ounces each)**
- ¼ **teaspoon paprika**

1. Preheat oven to 400°. In a shallow bowl, mix the first six ingredients.
2. Dip fillets in cornmeal mixture to coat both sides. Place on a baking sheet coated with cooking spray. Sprinkle with paprika.
3. Bake 20-25 minutes or until fish just begins to flake easily with a fork.
PER SERVING *1 fillet: 242 cal., 10g fat (2g sat. fat), 94mg chol., 748mg sodium, 8g carb. (trace sugars, 1g fiber), 27g pro.* **Diabetic Exchanges:** *4 lean meat, ½ starch.*

ON THE SIDE
HERBED POTATO WEDGES

Combine 3 tablespoons grated Parmesan cheese, 1 tablespoon dried basil, ¼ teaspoon salt and ¼ teaspoon pepper. Cut 1 large unpeeled baking potato into wedges. Brush cut sides with 2 teaspoons canola oil; dip into cheese mixture. Place in a greased 8-in. square pan. Bake, uncovered, at 400° for 20-25 minutes or until tender. Makes 2 servings.

—**R. V. TAIBBI** HONOLULU, HI

APPLE-WHITE CHEDDAR GRILLED CHEESE

⑤ INGREDIENTS FAST FIX ▶

APPLE-WHITE CHEDDAR GRILLED CHEESE

On rainy days when we need comfort food in a hurry, I toast sandwiches of cinnamon raisin bread with white cheddar, apple and red onion. They also taste great made with olive oil and vegan cheese!

—**KATHY PATALSKY** NEW YORK, NY

START TO FINISH: 20 MIN.
MAKES: 2 SERVINGS

- 4 **slices whole wheat cinnamon-raisin bread**
- 4 **slices sharp white cheddar cheese (3 ounces)**
- 1 **small apple, thinly sliced**
- 1 **thin slice red onion, separated into rings**
- ¼ **teaspoon crushed red pepper flakes, optional**
- 1 **tablespoon butter, softened**

1. Layer each of two bread slices with one slice cheese. Top with apple and onion. If desired, sprinkle with pepper flakes. Top with the remaining cheese and bread. Spread outsides of the sandwiches with butter.
2. In a large skillet, toast sandwiches over medium-low heat 3-5 minutes on each side or until golden brown and cheese is melted.
PER SERVING *1 sandwich: 456 cal., 27g fat (14g sat. fat), 75mg chol., 616mg sodium, 37g carb. (13g sugars, 5g fiber), 20g pro.*

ON THE SIDE
DILL VEGETABLE DIP

Blend ½ cup sour cream, ¼ cup mayo, 1½ teaspoons finely chopped onion, 1 teaspoon dried parsley flakes and ½ teaspoon each dill weed and seasoned salt. Serves 6.

—**KAREN GARDINER** EUTAW, AL

BERRY TURKEY SANDWICH

EAT SMART FAST FIX

BERRY TURKEY SANDWICH

My turkey sandwich with strawberries, cream cheese and Swiss gets a big thumbs-up. Make it with whole wheat, oatmeal or sunflower seed bread.

—EDWARD MEYER ARNOLD, MO

START TO FINISH: 10 MIN.
MAKES: 2 SERVINGS

- 2 **tablespoons reduced-fat spreadable cream cheese**
- 2 **teaspoons finely chopped pecans**
- 4 **slices whole wheat bread**
- 2 **lettuce leaves**
- 2 **slices reduced-fat Swiss cheese**
- ¼ **pound thinly sliced deli turkey breast**
- 4 **fresh strawberries, sliced**

In a small bow, mix cream cheese and pecans. Spread over two slices of bread; top with lettuce, cheese, turkey, strawberries and remaining bread.

PER SERVING *1 sandwich: 319 cal., 12g fat (5g sat. fat), 45mg chol., 847mg sodium, 32g carb. (5g sugars, 4g fiber), 26g pro.* **Diabetic Exchanges:** *3 lean meat, 2 starch, ½ fat.*

ON THE SIDE
GRILLED BALSAMIC-LIME SWEET POTATOES

Peel and cut 1 large sweet potato into 10 wedges; toss with 2 teaspoons olive oil, ¼ teaspoon salt and dash pepper. Grill on a greased rack, covered, over medium heat for 8-10 minutes or until tender, turning occasionally. Mix 1 tablespoon each minced fresh cilantro, brown sugar and lime juice with 2 teaspoons balsamic glaze; toss with potato wedges. Serves 2.

—RAQUEL PERAZZO WEST NEW YORK, NJ

JOIN THE CLUB

Everyone's into this no-fuss, no-bread riff on a classic. Grab a juicy plum tomato and slice it partway through. Then shimmy your favorite sandwich fixin's between the layers. So cool!

GARDEN VEGETABLE GNOCCHI

When we choose to go meatless, we toss gnocchi (my husband's favorite) with veggies and a dab of pesto. It makes a hearty, satisfying dinner, even without the meat.

—ELISABETH LARSEN PLEASANT GROVE, UT

START TO FINISH: 30 MIN.
MAKES: 4 SERVINGS

- 2 **medium yellow summer squash, sliced**
- 1 **medium sweet red pepper, chopped**
- 8 **ounces sliced fresh mushrooms**
- 1 **tablespoon olive oil**
- ¼ **teaspoon salt**
- ¼ **teaspoon pepper**
- 1 **package (16 ounces) potato gnocchi**
- ½ **cup Alfredo sauce**
- ¼ **cup prepared pesto**
  Chopped fresh basil, optional

1. Preheat oven to 450°. In a greased 15x10x1-in. baking pan, toss vegetables with oil, salt and pepper. Roast 18-22 minutes or until tender, stirring once.

2. Meanwhile, in a large saucepan, cook gnocchi according to package directions. Drain and return to pan.

3. Stir in roasted vegetables, Alfredo sauce and pesto. If desired, sprinkle with basil.

PER SERVING *1½ cups: 402 cal., 14g fat (4g sat. fat), 17mg chol., 955mg sodium, 57g carb. (12g sugars, 5g fiber), 13g pro.*

ON THE SIDE
SIMPLE ITALIAN SPINACH SALAD

Toss 6 ounces fresh baby spinach, 1 sliced green onion, 1 chopped hard-cooked egg and 3 cooked and crumbled bacon strips. In a microwave, heat 3 tablespoons Italian salad dressing until warm; add to salad. Sprinkle with 2 tablespoons shredded Parmesan cheese.

—JUDY BERNACKI LAS VEGAS, NV

GARDEN VEGETABLE
GNOCCHI

CHICKEN RANCH
FLATBREADS

FAST FIX ▶

CHICKEN RANCH FLATBREADS

To get my son to try new things, I revamped this mini pizza. Mr. Picky ate it, so it's definitely family-friendly.
—JENNY DUBINSKY INWOOD, WV

START TO FINISH: 25 MIN.
MAKES: 4 SERVINGS

- **4 whole wheat or white pita breads (6 inches)**
- **2 cups chopped cooked chicken breast**
- **¼ cup reduced-fat ranch salad dressing**
- **2 plum tomatoes, thinly sliced**
- **1 cup (4 ounces) shredded part-skim mozzarella cheese**
- **4 bacon strips, cooked and crumbled**
- **1 teaspoon dried oregano**

1. Preheat oven to 400°. Place pita breads on a large baking sheet; bake 10-12 minutes or until lightly browned. Meanwhile, in a bowl, toss chicken with dressing.
Top pitas with tomatoes and chicken mixture; sprinkle with cheese, bacon and oregano. Bake 8-10 minutes or until cheese is melted.
PER SERVING *1 pita pizza: 448 cal., 16g fat (6g sat. fat), 86mg chol., 888mg sodium, 42g carb. (3g sugars, 5g fiber), 37g pro.*

ON THE SIDE
CREAMY CUCUMBER SALAD

Combine 1 diced cucumber, 2 diced plum tomatoes, 4 sliced green onions, ½ cup sour cream, ¼ teaspoon celery salt and ⅛ teaspoon pepper. Refrigerate until serving. Serves 4.
—RHONDA EGLER MOORESVILLE, IN

FAST FIX ▶

HERB GARDEN FRITTATA

I use pickled peppers and fresh herbs like chives, parsley and basil in this recipe. It's a popular standby for lunch or breakfast.
—KRISTIN CUMMINS MOGADORE, OH

START TO FINISH: 30 MIN.
MAKES: 6 SERVINGS

- **12 large eggs**
- **2 tablespoons minced fresh chives**
- **2 tablespoons minced fresh parsley**
- **2 teaspoons minced fresh basil or ½ teaspoon dried basil**
- **2 teaspoons minced fresh oregano or ½ teaspoon dried oregano**
- **1 teaspoon salt**
- **¼ teaspoon pepper**
- **3 tablespoons olive oil**
- **½ cup sliced pickled peppers**
- **½ cup crumbled goat cheese**

1. Preheat broiler. In a large bowl, whisk the eggs, herbs, salt and pepper until blended.
2. In a 10-in. broiler-safe skillet, heat oil over medium-low heat. Pour in egg mixture. Cook, covered, 10-12 minutes or until nearly set. Top with pickled peppers and cheese.
3. Broil 4-5 in. from heat 3-4 minutes or until eggs are completely set. Let stand 5 minutes. Cut into wedges.
PER SERVING *1 wedge: 234 cal., 19g fat (6g sat. fat), 384mg chol., 708mg sodium, 2g carb. (0 sugars, 1g fiber), 14g pro.*
HEALTH TIP *For all those years, experts were wrong about cholesterol. in food. Turns out, in many people it doesn't negatively affect blood cholesterol the way that they thought.*

ON THE SIDE
HONEY-MELON SALAD WITH BASIL

Combine 3 cups each cubed cantaloupe and honeydew. Whisk 2 tablespoons honey, 1 tablespoon lemon juice, ¼ teaspoon each salt, paprika and pepper. Add to melon. Stir in 2 tablespoons minced fresh basil. Serves 6.
—KHURSHID SHAIK OMAHA, NE

HERB GARDEN FRITTATA

APPLE-GLAZED
CHICKEN THIGHS

EAT SMART ⑤**INGREDIENTS** **FAST FIX**

APPLE-GLAZED CHICKEN THIGHS

My pickatarian child is choosy but willing to eat this chicken glazed with apple juice and thyme. I dish it up with mashed potatoes and green beans.
—**KERRY PICARD** SPOKANE, WA

START TO FINISH: 25 MIN.
MAKES: 6 SERVINGS

- **6 boneless skinless chicken thighs (1½ pounds)**
- **¾ teaspoon seasoned salt**
- **¼ teaspoon pepper**
- **1 tablespoon canola oil**
- **1 cup unsweetened apple juice**
- **1 teaspoon minced fresh thyme or ¼ teaspoon dried thyme**

1. Sprinkle chicken with seasoned salt and pepper. In a large skillet, heat oil over medium-high heat. Brown chicken on both sides. Remove from the pan.

2. Add juice and thyme to skillet. Bring to a boil, stirring to loosen browned bits from pan; cook until liquid is reduced by half. Return chicken to pan; cook, covered, over medium heat 3-4 minutes longer or until a thermometer inserted in chicken reads 170°.

PER SERVING *1 chicken thigh with about 1 tablespoon glaze: 204 cal., 11g fat (2g sat. fat), 76mg chol., 255mg sodium, 5g carb. (4g sugars, trace fiber), 21g pro. **Diabetic Exchanges:** 3 lean meat, ½ fat.*

ON THE SIDE
BACON BRUSSELS SPROUTS

In a large skillet, saute 1 pound halved Brussels sprouts in ¼ cup butter until tender. Add 6 cooked and crumbled bacon strips, ⅔ cup chopped walnuts and 3 minced garlic cloves; cook 1-2 minutes longer or until heated through. Makes 6 servings.
—**LISA DANIELL** LOVELAND, CO

HONEY THYME
GRILLED CHICKEN

HONEY THYME GRILLED CHICKEN

For grilling chicken, I wanted a marinade different from barbecue sauce, so I pulled out some honey and thyme. If you have time, let the chicken marinate awhile to boost flavor.
—**NOEL BIGELOW** ALEXANDRIA, VA

START TO FINISH: 25 MIN.
MAKES: 4 SERVINGS

- ¼ **cup olive oil**
- ¼ **cup honey**
- 1 **garlic clove, minced**
- 8 **chicken drumsticks (about 2 pounds)**
- 1 **teaspoon dried thyme**
- ¾ **teaspoon salt**
- ¼ **teaspoon pepper**

1. In a small bowl, whisk oil, honey and garlic until blended. Sprinkle drumsticks with seasonings.
2. Moisten a paper towel with cooking oil; using long-handled tongs, rub on grill rack to coat lightly. Grill chicken, covered, over medium heat 15-20 minutes or until a thermometer reads 170°-175°, turning occasionally and brushing generously with honey mixture during the last 5 minutes.

PER SERVING *2 chicken drumsticks: 418 cal., 26g fat (5g sat. fat), 95mg chol., 531mg sodium, 18g carb. (17g sugars, 0 fiber), 29g pro.*

ON THE SIDE
PEA 'N' PEANUT SALAD

Combine 10 ounces frozen peas (thawed), 1 cup each dry roasted peanuts and chopped celery, 6 cooked and crumbled bacon strips and ¼ cup chopped red onion. Combine ½ cup mayonnaise and ¼ cup zesty Italian salad dressing; stir into salad. Makes 4 servings.
—**LAURINDA NELSON** PHOENIX, AZ

SAUSAGE & PEPPER
PIEROGI SKILLET

SAUSAGE & PEPPER PIEROGI SKILLET

A package of pierogies lets me serve this skillet meal in a hurry. The whole family goes for it.
—**MOLLY FLESSNER** BLOOMINGTON, IL

START TO FINISH: 20 MIN.
MAKES: 6 SERVINGS

- 1 **package (12.84 ounces) frozen mini four-cheese pierogies**
- 2 **tablespoons olive oil, divided**
- 1 **pound smoked turkey kielbasa, halved lengthwise and sliced diagonally**
- 1 **large sweet red pepper, cut into strips**
- 1 **medium onion, halved and sliced**

1. Boil pierogies according to package directions; drain. Meanwhile, in a large skillet, heat 1 tablespoon oil over medium heat. Add kielbasa, pepper and onion; cook and stir 10-12 minutes or until sausage is browned and onion is tender. Remove from pan.
2. In same skillet, heat remaining oil over medium heat. Add pierogies; cook and stir 1-2 minutes or until lightly browned. Return kielbasa mixture to pan; heat through.

PER SERVING *257 cal., 10g fat (2g sat. fat), 52mg chol., 968mg sodium, 24g carb. (7g sugars, 2g fiber), 16g pro.*

ON THE SIDE
GREEN BEANS WITH BASIL

Trim 1 pound fresh beans. Cook, covered, in ¼ cup boiling water 7-9 minutes or until crisp-tender. Drain; add 2 tablespoons butter, ½ cup chopped onion, ¼ cup chopped celery, 1 minced garlic clove, ½ teaspoon each crushed dried rosemary and dried basil. Cover and cook 4 minutes longer or until vegetables are tender. Makes 6 servings.
—**LAUREL LESLIE** SONORA, CA

**Maggie Schimmel's
Peanut Butter Cookies**
PAGE 111

Give Me 5 or Fewer

Each delicious dish in this chapter uses just five ingredients or less (plus staples like salt, pepper and cooking oil). Choose from crowd-pleasing snacks, beautiful brunch dishes, quick weeknight meals and even heavenly sweets! They're all short on ingredients but big on taste.

Shana Lewis' Italian Smothered Pork Chops *PAGE 101*

Jennifer Eggert's Creamy Tomato Tortellini with Sausage *PAGE 113*

Barbara Carlucci's Macaroon Ice Cream Torte *PAGE 112*

SAGE-RUBBED SALMON

2. Transfer to a greased 13-in. x 9-in. baking dish. Sprinkle with the remaining cheese. Bake, uncovered, at 350° for 20-25 minutes or until heated through.

PER SERVING *311 cal., 14g fat (8g sat. fat), 68mg chol., 579mg sodium, 23g carb. (3g sugars, 1g fiber), 21g pro.*

EAT SMART (5) INGREDIENTS FAST FIX

BALSAMIC-SEASONED STEAK

START TO FINISH: 25 MIN.
MAKES: 4 SERVINGS

- 1 **beef top sirloin steak (¾ inch thick and 1 pound)**
- ¼ **teaspoon coarsely ground pepper**
- 2 **tablespoons balsamic vinegar**
- 2 **teaspoons steak sauce**
- 2 **ounces sliced reduced-fat Swiss cheese, cut into thin strips**

1. Preheat broiler. Place steak on a broiler pan; sprinkle with pepper. Broil 4 in. from heat 7 minutes. Meanwhile, in a small bowl, mix vinegar and steak sauce.

2. Turn the steak; drizzle with 1 tablespoon vinegar mixture. Broil 4-6 minutes longer or just until meat reaches desired doneness (for medium-rare, a thermometer should read 145°; medium, 160°; well-done, 170°).

3. Remove steak to a cutting board; let stand 5 minutes. Cut steak into ¼-in. slices; return to broiler pan, arranging slices close together. Drizzle slices with remaining vinegar mixture; top with cheese. Broil 30-60 seconds longer or just until cheese is melted.

PER SERVING *3 ounces cooked beef with ½ ounce cheese: 188 cal., 8g fat (3g sat. fat), 70mg chol., 116mg sodium, 2g carb. (1g sugars, trace fiber), 26g pro.* **Diabetic Exchanges:** *3 lean meat, ½ fat.*

EAT SMART (5) INGREDIENTS FAST FIX

SAGE-RUBBED SALMON

If you've always thought of sage with turkey, try it with salmon for a little taste of heaven. We serve this with rice, salad and sauteed green beans.
—**NICOLE RASKOPF** BEACON, NY

START TO FINISH: 20 MIN.
MAKES: 6 SERVINGS

- 2 **tablespoons minced fresh sage**
- 1 **teaspoon garlic powder**
- 1 **teaspoon kosher salt**
- 1 **teaspoon freshly ground pepper**
- 1 **skin-on salmon fillet (1½ pounds)**
- 2 **tablespoons olive oil**

1. Preheat oven to 375°. Mix the first four ingredients; rub onto flesh side of salmon. Cut into six portions.

2. In a large cast-iron skillet, heat oil over medium heat. Add salmon, skin side down; cook 5 minutes. Transfer skillet to oven; bake just until fish flakes easily with a fork, for about 10 minutes.

PER SERVING *3 ounces cooked fish: 220 cal., 15g fat (3g sat. fat), 57mg chol., 377mg sodium, 1g carb. (0 sugars, 0 fiber), 19g pro.* **Diabetic Exchanges:** *3 lean meat.*

(5) INGREDIENTS

CHEDDAR CHICKEN SPAGHETTI

My son Charlie was a picky eater when he was young, so I put together some of the things he likes. To this day, he says it's his favorite dish! Children will be proud helping mix up this family favorite.
—**ANN ROBINSON** DAUPHIN ISLAND, AL

PREP: 15 MIN. • **BAKE:** 20 MIN.
MAKES: 6-8 SERVINGS

- 1 **package (7 ounces) spaghetti, broken**
- 2 **cups cubed cooked chicken**
- 2 **cups (8 ounces) shredded cheddar cheese, divided**
- 1 **can (10¾ ounces) condensed cream of chicken soup, undiluted**
- 1 **cup milk**
- 1 **tablespoon diced pimientos, optional**
- ¼ **teaspoon salt**
- ¼ **teaspoon pepper**

1. Cook spaghetti according to package directions. Meanwhile, in a large bowl, combine the chicken, 1 cup cheese, soup, milk, pimientos if desired, salt and pepper. Drain the spaghetti; add to the chicken mixture and toss to coat.

With this recipe, you get a tender steak without a long marinade time. Balsamic vinegar and steak sauce are a great team, and you can't go wrong with melty Swiss on top. —**PEGGY WOODWARD** SHULLSBURG, WI

BALSAMIC-SEASONED STEAK

(5) INGREDIENTS FAST FIX ▶

ARTICHOKE BLUE CHEESE FETTUCCINE

When I'm in a rush, I use jarred Alfredo sauce to speed along my blue-cheesy noodles with mushrooms. Refrigerated fettuccine can get it done even faster.
—**JOLANTHE ERB** HARRISONBURG, VA

START TO FINISH: 20 MIN.
MAKES: 4 SERVINGS

- 1 **package (12 ounces) fettuccine**
- 1 **cup sliced fresh mushrooms**
- 1 **can (14 ounces) water-packed artichoke hearts, drained and chopped**
- 1½ **cups Alfredo sauce**
- ¼ **cup crumbled blue cheese**

1. Cook fettuccine according to package directions.
2. Meanwhile, place a large nonstick skillet coated with cooking spray over medium-high heat. Add mushrooms and artichoke hearts; cook and stir until mushrooms are tender. Stir in Alfredo sauce; bring to a boil over medium heat. Reduce heat; simmer, uncovered, 5 minutes, stirring occasionally.
3. Drain fettuccine, reserving ⅓ cup pasta water. Add fettuccine to the artichoke mixture; toss to combine, adding reserved pasta water if desired. Sprinkle with blue cheese.
PER SERVING *1 cup: 499 cal., 14g fat (9g sat. fat), 33mg chol., 770mg sodium, 74g carb. (6g sugars, 4g fiber), 21g pro.*

ARTICHOKE BLUE
CHEESE FETTUCCINE

SAUSAGE POTATO
SUPPER

(5) INGREDIENTS FAST FIX ▶

SAUSAGE POTATO SUPPER

One Saturday night, I cooked sausage with potatoes and zucchini—the ingredients I had on hand. This spur-of-the-moment supper has been a hit with all six of us ever since.
—**NANCY RUSSELL** ENGLEWOOD, CO

START TO FINISH: 25 MIN.
MAKES: 2 SERVINGS

- 2 **small red potatoes, cubed**
- 1 **tablespoon butter**
- 1 **small zucchini, cut into ¼-inch slices**
- ⅛ **teaspoon garlic salt**
- ½ **pound smoked sausage, cut into ½-inch slices**
- ⅛ **to ¼ teaspoon pepper**
  Grated Parmesan cheese, optional

1. In a small saucepan, combine potatoes and enough water to cover; bring to a boil. Reduce heat; cook, uncovered, until tender, for 15-20 minutes.
2. In a large skillet, heat butter over medium-high heat; saute zucchini with garlic salt until crisp-tender. Add sausage; cook and stir until browned.
3. Drain potatoes; stir into zucchini mixture. Sprinkle with pepper and, if desired, cheese.

PER SERVING *2 cups: 448 cal., 37g fat (17g sat. fat), 91mg chol., 1396mg sodium, 12g carb. (5g sugars, 1g fiber), 18g pro.*

EAT SMART (5) INGREDIENTS

COCONUT MACAROONS

These cookies are my husband's favorites, so I always have to make a few batches if I make them to give away. I also like that it makes a small enough batch for the two of us to nibble on.
—**PENNY ANN HABECK** SHAWANO, WI

PREP: 10 MIN. ● **BAKE:** 20 MIN. + COOLING
MAKES: ABOUT 1½ DOZEN

- 1⅓ **cups flaked coconut**
- ⅓ **cup sugar**
- 2 **tablespoons all-purpose flour**
- ⅛ **teaspoon salt**
- 2 **large egg whites**
- ½ **teaspoon vanilla extract**

1. In a small bowl, combine the coconut, sugar, flour and salt. Add egg whites and vanilla; mix well.
2. Drop by rounded teaspoonfuls onto greased baking sheets. Bake at 325° for 18-20 minutes or until golden brown. Cool on a wire rack.
PER SERVING *1 cookie: 54 cal., 2g fat (2g sat. fat), 0 chol., 41mg sodium, 8g carb. (7g sugars, trace fiber), 1g pro.* **Diabetic Exchanges:** *½ starch, ½ fat.*

ITALIAN SMOTHERED PORK CHOPS

My brother and I come from an Italian family, and we designed these pork chops to include Italian staples like fresh mozzarella, sweet red peppers and green broccoli rabe.

—SHANA LEWIS TOTOWA, NJ

START TO FINISH: 30 MIN.
MAKES: 4 SERVINGS

- ½ **pound broccoli rabe**
- 4 **boneless pork loin chops (¾ inch thick and 6 ounces each)**
- 1 **teaspoon salt**
- 1 **teaspoon garlic powder**
- ½ **teaspoon pepper**
- 1 **tablespoon canola oil**
- ½ **cup sliced roasted sweet red pepper**
- 4 **ounces fresh mozzarella cheese, sliced**

1. Preheat broiler. Trim ½ in. off ends of broccoli rabe; discard any coarse leaves.

2. In a large saucepan, bring 4 cups of water to a boil. Add the broccoli rabe; cook, uncovered, 4-5 minutes or just until crisp-tender. Remove and immediately drop into ice water. Drain and pat dry.

3. Sprinkle the pork chops with seasonings. In a broiler-safe skillet, heat oil over medium-high heat. Add pork chops; cook 3-4 minutes on each side or until a thermometer reads 145°. Remove from heat.

4. Layer chops with the red pepper, broccoli rabe and cheese. Broil 4 in. from heat 1-2 minutes or until cheese is melted.

PER SERVING *365 cal., 20g fat (8g sat. fat), 104mg chol., 808mg sodium, 4g carb. (2g sugars, 2g fiber), 40g pro.*

STRAWBERRY CAKE

Garnish the top with strawberries to hint at the fresh-tasting flavor of this pretty pink cake before you cut it—or let it be a surprise!

—PAM ANDERSON BILLINGS, MT

PREP: 25 MIN. • **BAKE:** 25 MIN. + COOLING
MAKES: 12-16 SERVINGS

- 1 **package white cake mix (regular size)**
- 1 **package (3 ounces) strawberry gelatin**
- 1 **cup water**
- ½ **cup canola oil**
- 4 **large egg whites**
- ½ **cup mashed unsweetened strawberries**
  Whipped cream or frosting of your choice

1. Preheat oven to 350°. In a large bowl, combine dry cake mix, gelatin powder, water and oil. Beat on low speed 1 minute or until moistened; beat on medium 4 minutes.

2. In a small bowl with clean beaters, beat egg whites on high speed until stiff peaks form. Fold egg whites and mashed strawberries into cake batter.

3. Pour into three greased and floured 8-in. round baking pans. Bake 25-30 minutes or until a toothpick comes out clean. Cool for 10 minutes before removing from pans to wire racks to cool completely.

4. Spread whipped cream or frosting between layers and over top and sides of cake. If frosted with whipped cream, store in the refrigerator.

PER SERVING *1 slice: 222 cal., 10g fat (2g sat. fat), 0 chol., 231mg sodium, 31g carb. (19g sugars, 1g fiber), 3g pro.*

SAUTEED SPICED SALMON

My husband and friends love this flavorful salmon. You'll love that it's rich in heart-healthy omega-3 fatty acids—and so easy and delicious!

—KATHY GARRISON FORT WORTH, TX

START TO FINISH: 15 MIN.
MAKES: 4 SERVINGS

- 2 **teaspoons dill weed**
- 2 **teaspoons chili powder**
- 1 **teaspoon salt-free lemon-pepper seasoning**
- ½ **teaspoon ground cumin**
- 4 **salmon fillets (4 ounces each), skin removed**
- 1 **tablespoon canola oil**
  Lemon wedges, optional

1. Combine the dill, chili powder, lemon-pepper and cumin; rub over the fillets.

2. In a large nonstick skillet coated with cooking spray, cook salmon in oil over medium-high heat 5-6 minutes on each side or until fish flakes easily with a fork. Serve with lemon wedges if desired.

PER SERVING *1 fillet: 246 cal., 16g fat (3g sat. fat), 67mg chol., 82mg sodium, 2g carb. (trace sugars, 1g fiber), 23g pro.* **Diabetic Exchanges:** *3 lean meat, 1½ fat.*

ITALIAN SMOTHERED
PORK CHOPS

BROCCOLI &
CHIVE-STUFFED
MINI PEPPERS

PORTOBELLO
& ONION TART

(5) INGREDIENTS FAST FIX

BROCCOLI & CHIVE-STUFFED MINI PEPPERS

Crunchy peppers perfectly balance the creamy filling in these party appetizers. Fresh chives help them stand out.

—JEAN MCKENZIE VANCOUVER, WA

START TO FINISH: 30 MIN.
MAKES: 2 DOZEN

- 12 **miniature sweet peppers**
- 1 **package (8 ounces) cream cheese, softened**
- ⅓ **cup minced fresh chives**
- ⅛ **teaspoon salt**
- ⅛ **teaspoon pepper**
- ⅔ **cup finely chopped fresh broccoli**
- ⅔ **cup shredded cheddar cheese**

1. Preheat oven to 400°. Cut peppers lengthwise in half; remove seeds. In a bowl, mix cream cheese, chives, salt and pepper; stir in broccoli. Spoon into pepper halves.

2. Place on a foil-lined baking sheet; bake 9-11 minutes or until heated through. Sprinkle with cheddar cheese. Bake 3-4 minutes longer or until cheese is melted. Cool slightly before serving.

PER SERVING *1 stuffed pepper half: 48 cal., 4g fat (2g sat. fat), 14mg chol., 68mg sodium, 1g carb. (1g sugars, 0 fiber), 1g pro.*

(5) INGREDIENTS FAST FIX

PORTOBELLO & ONION TART

This buttery tart is comfort with a capital "C," and fragrant with fresh herbs on top. We pair it with a salad for dinner or an egg for breakfast.

—ROBIN WAGGANER SAN JOSE, CA

START TO FINISH: 30 MIN.
MAKES: 4 SERVINGS

- 1 **sheet frozen puff pastry, thawed**
- 2 **tablespoons olive oil, divided**
- ½ **pound sliced baby portobello mushrooms**
- 1 **large onion, halved and thinly sliced**
- ¼ **teaspoon salt**
- 2 **large eggs**
- 1 **cup (4 ounces) crumbled goat cheese or Gorgonzola cheese**
- 2 **teaspoons minced fresh rosemary, optional**

1. Preheat oven to 400°. Unfold puff pastry onto a parchment paper-lined baking sheet. Using a sharp knife, score a ½-in. border along edges of pastry. Within border, prick pastry with a fork. Bake 8-10 minutes or until golden brown. Remove from oven. If center has puffed, flatten pastry gently with a spatula.

2. Meanwhile, in a large skillet, heat 1 tablespoon oil over medium-high heat. Add mushrooms; cook and stir 4-5 minutes or until lightly browned. Remove from pan. To same pan, add remaining oil and the onion; cook and stir 2-3 minutes or until lightly browned. Return mushrooms to pan; stir in salt.

3. In a small bowl, whisk eggs until blended; stir in cheese. Pour into crust. Top evenly with mushroom mixture. Bake 13-15 minutes or just until cheese mixture is set. If desired, sprinkle with minced rosemary.

PER SERVING *503 cal., 33g fat (10g sat. fat), 128mg chol., 525mg sodium, 41g carb. (3g sugars, 7g fiber), 15g pro.*

CUKE CANOES

Scoop out the seeds and fill fresh cucumbers with whatever floats your boat.

MUFFULETTA

Giardiniera + provolone + salami

BLT

Cream cheese + bacon + lettuce + tomatoes

COUNTRY CLUB

Chicken salad + grapes + pecans

HOISIN-PINEAPPLE SALMON

⑤INGREDIENTS FAST FIX

CHORIZO PUMPKIN PASTA

I'm a busy student, and this spicy-sweet pasta makes a perfect quick dinner. Even better, it works on a bigger scale to feed a bunch of friends.

—CHRISTINE YANG SYRACUSE, NY

START TO FINISH: 30 MIN.
MAKES: 6 SERVINGS

- 3 **cups uncooked gemelli or spiral pasta (about 12 ounces)**
- 1 **package (12 ounces) fully cooked chorizo chicken sausage links or flavor of choice, sliced**
- 1 **cup canned pumpkin**
- 1 **cup half-and-half cream**
- ¾ **teaspoon salt**
- ¼ **teaspoon pepper**
- 1½ **cups shredded Manchego or Monterey Jack cheese**
  Minced fresh cilantro, optional

1. Cook pasta according to package directions. Drain, reserving ¾ cup pasta water.
2. Meanwhile, in a large skillet, saute sausage over medium heat until lightly browned; reduce heat to medium-low. Add pumpkin, cream, salt and pepper; cook and stir until heated through. Toss with pasta and enough pasta water to moisten; stir in cheese. If desired, sprinkle with cilantro.
PER SERVING *1⅓ cups: 471 cal., 20g fat (11g sat. fat), 92mg chol., 847mg sodium, 48g carb. (7g sugars, 3g fiber), 26g pro.*

EAT SMART ⑤INGREDIENTS FAST FIX

HOISIN-PINEAPPLE SALMON

My mouth waters when I think of this sweet and tangy glaze. It's a tropical treat at any time of year.

—NAYLET LAROCHELLE MIAMI, FL

START TO FINISH: 20 MIN.
MAKES: 4 SERVINGS

- 4 **salmon fillets (6 ounces each)**
- 2 **tablespoons hoisin sauce**
- ¼ **teaspoon pepper**
- ½ **cup unsweetened crushed pineapple**
- ¼ **cup orange marmalade**
- 2 **tablespoons chopped fresh cilantro**

1. Preheat oven to 400°. Spread salmon with hoisin sauce; sprinkle with pepper. Place on a greased foil-lined baking sheet, skin side down. Bake 12-15 minutes or until fish begins to flake easily with a fork.
2. Meanwhile, in a small saucepan, combine pineapple and marmalade. Bring to a boil, stirring occasionally; cook and stir 4-6 minutes or until slightly thickened. Spoon over salmon; sprinkle with cilantro.
PER SERVING *1 salmon fillet with 2 tablespoons sauce: 349 cal., 16g fat (3g sat. fat), 86mg chol., 226mg sodium, 21g carb. (18g sugars, 1g fiber), 29g pro.* **Diabetic Exchanges:** *4 lean meat, 1½ starch.*

CHORIZO PUMPKIN PASTA

BUFFALO CHICKEN POCKETS

FREEZE IT (5)INGREDIENTS FAST FIX

BUFFALO CHICKEN POCKETS

Here's my idea of pub food made easy: biscuits flavored with Buffalo wing sauce and blue cheese. They're my Friday night favorite.

—**MARIA REGAKIS** SAUGUS, MA

START TO FINISH: 30 MIN.
MAKES: 8 SERVINGS

- ¾ pound ground chicken
- ⅓ cup Buffalo wing sauce
- 1 tube (16.3 ounces) large refrigerated buttermilk biscuits
- ½ cup shredded cheddar cheese
  Blue cheese salad dressing, optional

1. Preheat oven to 375°. In a large skillet, cook chicken over medium heat 5-7 minutes or until no longer pink, breaking into crumbles; drain. Remove from heat; stir in wing sauce.
2. On a lightly floured surface, roll each biscuit into a 6-in. circle; top each with ¼ cup chicken mixture and 2 tablespoons cheese. Fold dough over filling; pinch edge to seal.
3. Transfer to an ungreased baking sheet. Bake 12-14 minutes or until golden brown. If desired, serve with blue cheese dressing.
FREEZE OPTION *Freeze cooled pockets in a resealable plastic freezer bag. To use, reheat pockets on an ungreased baking sheet in a preheated 375° oven until heated through.*
PER SERVING *1 pocket (calculated without blue cheese dressing): 258 cal., 12g fat (5g sat. fat), 35mg chol., 987mg sodium, 25g carb. (3g sugars, 1g fiber), 12g pro.*

EAT SMART (5)INGREDIENTS FAST FIX

CRUNCHY ONION BARBECUE CHICKEN

I threw this easy dish together and was thrilled with how tasty it turned out. The crispy fried onions and baked-on barbecue sauce add flavor and texture to regular chicken breasts.

—**JANE HOLEY** CLAYTON, MI

PREP: 10 MIN. ● **BAKE:** 25 MIN.
MAKES: 4 SERVINGS

- ½ cup barbecue sauce
- 1⅓ cups french-fried onions, crushed
- ¼ cup grated Parmesan cheese
- ½ teaspoon pepper
- 4 boneless skinless chicken breast halves (6 ounces each)

1. Place barbecue sauce in a shallow bowl. In another shallow bowl, combine the onions, cheese and pepper. Dip both sides of chicken in barbecue sauce, then dip one side in onion mixture.
2. Place the chicken, crumb side up, on a baking sheet coated with cooking spray. Bake at 400° for 22-27 minutes or until a meat thermometer reads 170°.
PER SERVING *286 cal., 10g fat (3g sat. fat), 97mg chol., 498mg sodium, 9g carb. (4g sugars, trace fiber), 36g pro.* **Diabetic Exchanges:** *5 lean meat, 1 fat, ½ starch.*

(5)INGREDIENTS FAST FIX

SAGE & BROWNED BUTTER RAVIOLI

After enjoying a similar dish in Italy, we came home and planted sage in our garden to be sure we could recreate it. Such a quick and easy weeknight supper using the fruits of our labor, and it always brings back fond memories of our trip.

—**RHONDA HAMILTON** PORTSMOUTH, OH

START TO FINISH: 30 MIN.
MAKES: 4 SERVINGS

- 1 package (20 ounces) refrigerated cheese ravioli or 2 packages (9 ounces each) mushroom agnolotti
- ½ cup butter, cubed
- ½ cup coarsely chopped fresh sage
- ½ teaspoon salt
- 2 tablespoons lemon juice
- ¼ cup shredded Parmesan cheese

1. Cook ravioli according to package directions. In a large heavy saucepan, melt butter over medium heat. Heat 5-7 minutes or until golden brown, stirring constantly. Immediately stir in sage and salt; remove from heat.
2. Drain the ravioli, reserving 2 tablespoons of pasta water. Add the ravioli, pasta water and lemon juice to the butter mixture; gently toss to coat. Serve with cheese.
PER SERVING *1 cup: 621 cal., 34g fat (21g sat. fat), 120mg chol., 1103mg sodium, 58g carb. (2g sugars, 3g fiber), 23g pro.*

SPAGHETTI SQUASH
& SAUSAGE EASY MEAL

FREEZE IT   (5)INGREDIENTS   FAST FIX

HAM & BRIE PASTRIES

Growing up, I loved pocket pastries. Now with a busy family, I need quick bites, and my spin on the classic ham and cheese delivers at snack or supper time.

—**JENN TIDWELL** FAIR OAKS, CA

START TO FINISH: 30 MIN.
MAKES: 16 PASTRIES

1   **sheet frozen puff pastry, thawed**
⅓   **cup apricot preserves**
4   **slices deli ham, quartered**
8   **ounces Brie cheese, cut into 16 pieces**

1. Preheat oven to 400°. On a lightly floured surface, unfold puff pastry. Roll pastry to a 12-in. square; cut into sixteen 3-in. squares. Place 1 teaspoon preserves in center of each square; top with ham, folding as necessary, and cheese. Overlap two opposite corners of pastry over the filling; pinch tightly to seal.
2. Place on a parchment paper-lined baking sheet. Bake 15-20 minutes or until golden brown. Cool on pan for 5 minutes before serving.
FREEZE OPTION *Freeze cooled pastries in a freezer container, separating layers with waxed paper. To use, reheat pastries on a baking sheet in a preheated 400° oven until heated through.*
PER SERVING *1 appetizer: 144 cal., 8g fat (3g sat. fat), 17mg chol., 192mg sodium, 13g carb. (3g sugars, 1g fiber), 5g pro.*

---

(5)INGREDIENTS   FAST FIX

SPAGHETTI SQUASH & SAUSAGE EASY MEAL

I first created this recipe—now my son's favorite dish—using homegrown squash, kielbasa and salsa. It's so simple and good.
—**PAM MASCARENAS** TAYLORSVILLE, UT

START TO FINISH: 30 MIN.
MAKES: 6 SERVINGS

1   **medium spaghetti squash**
1   **tablespoon olive oil**
1   **package (14 ounces) smoked sausage, halved lengthwise and sliced**
1   **cup pico de gallo**
¼   **teaspoon salt**
⅛   **teaspoon pepper**

1. Cut squash lengthwise in half; discard seeds. Place halves on a microwave-safe plate, cut side down.
Microwave, uncovered, on high for 15-20 minutes or until tender.
2. Meanwhile, in a large skillet, heat oil over medium heat. Add sausage; cook and stir 4-5 minutes or until lightly browned.
3. When squash is cool enough to handle, use a fork to separate strands. Add squash, pico de gallo, salt and pepper to sausage; heat through, tossing to combine.
NOTE *This recipe was tested in a 1,100-watt microwave.*
PER SERVING *1 cup: 326 cal., 22g fat (8g sat. fat), 44mg chol., 901mg sodium, 24g carb. (2g sugars, 5g fiber), 12g pro.*
HEALTH TIP *Eating lower carb, but still want a homey, satisfying dinner? One cup cooked spaghetti squash has about 10 grams carbs versus 45 grams for regular spaghetti.*

TOP TIP

BRIE

With a buttery texture and an edible, slightly salty rind, Brie cheese is ideal for pairing with sweet, fruity preserves. Although Brie originates in France, you will probably find American versions (which are more affordable) to be widely available in grocery stores.

HAM & BRIE
PASTRIES

⑤ INGREDIENTS

MAPLE TOAST AND EGGS

I live in the country, right next door to my sister and brother-in-law. They and their two children all enjoy this dish each time I serve it as a special evening meal—although it's just as good when you make it for breakfast or lunch.

—**SUSAN BUTTEL** PLATTSBURGH, NY

PREP: 20 MIN. • **BAKE:** 20 MIN.
MAKES: 12 CUPS

- 12 **bacon strips, diced**
- ½ **cup maple syrup**
- ¼ **cup butter**
- 12 **slices firm-textured white bread**
- 12 **large eggs**
  Salt and pepper to taste

1. In a large skillet, cook bacon over medium heat until crisp. Using a slotted spoon, remove to paper towels to drain. In a small saucepan, heat syrup and butter until butter is melted; set aside.

2. Trim crust from bread; flatten slices with a rolling pin. Brush one side generously with syrup mixture; press each slice into a greased muffin cup with syrup side down. Divide bacon among muffin cups.

3. Carefully break one egg into each cup. Sprinkle with salt and pepper. Cover with foil. Bake at 400° for 18-20 minutes or until the egg whites are completely set and the yolks begin to thicken but are not hard. Serve immediately,

PER SERVING *2 each: 671 cal., 46g fat (18g sat. fat), 476mg chol., 805mg sodium, 44g carb. (20g sugars, 1g fiber), 21g pro.*

MAPLE TOAST AND EGGS

ASPARAGUS NICOISE SALAD

EAT SMART ⑤**INGREDIENTS** **FAST FIX** ▶

ASPARAGUS NICOISE SALAD

I've used my Nicoise as an appetizer or main-dish salad, and it's a winner every time I put it on the table. Here's to a colorful, do-ahead sure thing.

—**JAN MEYER** ST. PAUL, MN

START TO FINISH: 20 MIN.
MAKES: 4 SERVINGS

- 1 **pound small red potatoes (about 10), halved**
- 1 **pound fresh asparagus, trimmed and halved crosswise**
- 3 **pouches (2½ ounces each) albacore white tuna in water**
- ½ **cup pitted Greek olives, halved, optional**
- ½ **cup zesty Italian salad dressing**

1. Place potatoes in a large saucepan; add water to cover by 2 inches. Bring to a boil. Reduce heat; cook, uncovered, 10-12 minutes or until tender, adding asparagus during the last 2-4 minutes of cooking. Drain the potatoes and asparagus; immediately drop into ice water.

2. To serve, drain potatoes and asparagus; pat dry and divide among four plates. Add tuna and, if desired, olives. Drizzle with dressing.

PER SERVING *233 cal., 8g fat (trace sat. fat), 22mg chol., 583mg sodium, 23g carb. (4g sugars, 3g fiber), 16g pro.* **Diabetic Exchanges:** *2 lean meat, 1½ starch, 1½ fat, 1 vegetable.*

CHICKEN ENCHILADA BAKE

FREEZE IT ⑤ **INGREDIENTS**

CHICKEN ENCHILADA BAKE

Good thing the recipe makes a lot, because your family won't want to stop eating this cheesy Southwestern casserole. The green enchilada sauce brightens it right up.
—**MELANIE BURNS** PUEBLO WEST, CO

PREP: 20 MIN. ● **BAKE:** 50 MIN. + STANDING
MAKES: 10 SERVINGS

4½ cups shredded rotisserie chicken
1 can (28 ounces) green enchilada sauce
1¼ cups (10 ounces) sour cream
9 corn tortillas (6 inches), cut into 1½-inch pieces
4 cups shredded Monterey Jack cheese

1. Preheat oven to 375°. In a greased 13x9-in. baking dish, layer half of each of the following: chicken, enchilada sauce, sour cream, tortillas and cheese. Repeat layers.
2. Bake, covered, for 40 minutes. Uncover; bake until bubbly, for about 10 minutes. Let stand for 15 minutes before serving.
FREEZE OPTION *Cover and freeze unbaked casserole. To use, partially thaw in refrigerator overnight. Remove from refrigerator 30 minutes before baking. Preheat oven to 375°. Bake the casserole as directed, increasing time as necessary to heat through and for a thermometer inserted in the center to read 165°.*

PER SERVING *1 cup: 469 cal., 29g fat (14g sat. fat), 113mg chol., 1077mg sodium, 16g carb. (3g sugars, 1g fiber), 34g pro.*

TOP TIP

ENCHILADA SAUCE
Enchilada sauce is a blend of tomatoes, oil and spices thickened with a little flour or cornstarch. Green enchilada sauce is made from tomatillos instead of tomatoes.

BACON AND
SPINACH PIZZA

BACON AND SPINACH PIZZA

Our go-to pizza is a snap to make using packaged pizza crust and ready-to-serve bacon. The kids don't even mind the spinach on top!

—**ANNETTE RIVA** NAPERVILLE, IL

START TO FINISH: 20 MIN.
MAKES: 6 SERVINGS

- 1 prebaked 12-inch pizza crust
- ⅓ cup pizza sauce
- 1 cup shaved Parmesan cheese
- 2 cups fresh baby spinach, thinly sliced
- 8 ready-to-serve fully cooked bacon strips, cut into 1-inch pieces

Preheat oven to 450°. Place crust on an ungreased baking sheet. Spread with sauce; top with ½ cup cheese, spinach and bacon. Sprinkle with remaining cheese. Bake until cheese is melted, 8-10 minutes.

PER SERVING *1 slice: 269 cal., 10g fat (4g sat. fat), 10mg chol., 726mg sodium, 31g carb. (2g sugars, 2g fiber), 15g pro.* **Diabetic Exchanges:** *2 starch, 2 medium-fat meat.*

PEANUT BUTTER COOKIES

It is amazing how much flavor these simple cookies have. I make them often because I always have the ingredients on hand. It's nice that the recipe makes a little batch.

—**MAGGIE SCHIMMEL** WAUWATOSA, WI

START TO FINISH: 30 MIN.
MAKES: 2 DOZEN

- 1 large egg, beaten
- 1 cup sugar
- 1 cup creamy peanut butter

1. In a large bowl, mix all ingredients. Scoop level tablespoonfuls and roll into balls. Place on ungreased baking sheets and flatten with a fork.

2. Bake at 350° for about 18 minutes or until set. Remove to wire racks to cool.

NOTE *This recipe does not contain flour.*

PER SERVING *2 each: 197 cal., 11g fat (2g sat. fat), 18mg chol., 105mg sodium, 21g carb. (18g sugars, 1g fiber), 6g pro.*

BAKED OMELET ROLL

BAKED OMELET ROLL

This hands-off omelet bakes in the oven, so you don't have to keep a constant eye on it like eggs you cook on the stovetop. And it looks fancy.

—**SUSAN HUDON** FORT WAYNE, IN

START TO FINISH: 30 MIN.
MAKES: 6 SERVINGS

- 6 large eggs
- 1 cup milk
- ½ cup all-purpose flour
- ½ teaspoon salt
- ¼ teaspoon pepper
- 1 cup (4 ounces) shredded cheddar cheese
  Thinly sliced green onions, optional

1. Place eggs and milk in a blender. Add the flour, salt and pepper; cover and process until smooth. Pour into a greased 13x9-in. baking pan. Bake at 375° for 20-25 minutes or until eggs are set.

2. Sprinkle with cheese. Roll up omelet in pan, starting with a short side. Place with seam side down on a serving platter. Cut into ¾-in. slices. If desired, sprinkle with green onions.

PER SERVING *2 slice: 204 cal., 12g fat (6g sat. fat), 238mg chol., 393mg sodium, 11g carb. (3g sugars, 0 fiber), 13g pro.*

RED PEPPER & PARMESAN TILAPIA

My husband and I are always looking for light fish recipes because of their health benefits. This one's a hit with us both, and we've tried it at dinner parties, too. It's a staple in our house.

—**MICHELLE MARTIN** DURHAM, NC

START TO FINISH: 20 MIN.
MAKES: 4 SERVINGS

- ¼ cup egg substitute
- ½ cup grated Parmesan cheese
- 1 teaspoon Italian seasoning
- ½ to 1 teaspoon crushed red pepper flakes
- ½ teaspoon pepper
- 4 tilapia fillets (6 ounces each)

1. Place egg substitute in a shallow bowl. In another shallow bowl, combine the cheese, Italian seasoning, pepper flakes and pepper. Dip fillets in egg substitute, then cheese mixture.

2. Place in a 15-in. x 10-in. x 1-in. baking pan coated with cooking spray. Bake at 425° for 10-15 minutes or until fish flakes easily with a fork.

PER SERVING *1 fillet: 179 cal., 4g fat (2g sat. fat), 89mg chol., 191mg sodium, 1g carb. (trace sugars, trace fiber), 35g pro.* **Diabetic Exchanges:** *5 lean meat.*

SPAGHETTI WITH FRESH
TOMATO SAUCE

MACAROON ICE CREAM TORTE

My family loves frozen treats. With chocolate four ways, this one is so beautiful, people think it came from an ice cream shop.

—**BARBARA CARLUCCI** ORANGE PARK, FL

PREP: 20 MIN. + FREEZING
MAKES: 16 SERVINGS

- 30 **chocolate or plain macaroon cookies, crumbled**
- 1 **quart coffee ice cream, softened if necessary**
- 1 **quart chocolate ice cream, softened if necessary**
- 1 **cup milk chocolate toffee bits or 4 (1.4-ounce) Heath candy bars, coarsely chopped**
  Hot fudge topping, warmed

1. Sprinkle a third of the cookies into an ungreased 9-in. springform pan. Layer with 2 cups coffee ice cream, another third of the cookies, 2 cups chocolate ice cream and ½ cup toffee bits; repeat layers.
2. Freeze, covered, until firm. May be frozen up to 2 months. Remove torte from freezer 10 minutes before slicing. Serve with fudge topping.
PER SERVING *1 slice (calculated without fudge topping): 341 cal., 20g fat (11g sat. fat), 36mg chol., 110mg sodium, 37g carb. (35g sugars, 2g fiber), 4g pro.*

MACAROON ICE CREAM TORTE

EAT SMART **(5) INGREDIENTS** **FREEZE IT**

SPAGHETTI WITH FRESH TOMATO SAUCE

When my mom made spaghetti sauce, the house would smell so good that I'd open the windows to torture the neighbors. It tastes even more wonderful the next day, when the flavors have really melded.

—**VERA SCHULZE** HOLBROOK, NY

PREP: 15 MIN. • **COOK:** 30 MIN.
MAKES: 4 SERVINGS

- 2 **tablespoons olive oil**
- 1 **large onion, finely chopped**
- 2 **pounds plum tomatoes, chopped (about 5 cups)**
- 1 **teaspoon salt**
- ¼ **teaspoon pepper**
- 8 **ounces uncooked spaghetti**
- ¼ **cup thinly sliced fresh basil**
- 1 **teaspoon sugar, optional**
  Grated Romano cheese and additional basil

1. In a 6-qt. stockpot, heat oil over medium heat. Add onion; cook and stir 4-6 minutes or until tender. Stir in tomatoes, salt and pepper; bring to a boil. Reduce heat; simmer, uncovered, 20-25 minutes or until thickened. Meanwhile, cook spaghetti according to package directions.
2. Stir ¼ cup basil and, if desired, sugar into sauce. Serve with spaghetti. Top with cheese and additional basil.
FREEZE OPTION *Freeze cooled sauce in freezer containers. To use, partially thaw in refrigerator overnight. Heat through in a saucepan, stirring occasionally.*
PER SERVING *1 cup spaghetti with ¾ cup sauce (calculated without cheese): 327 cal., 8g fat (1g sat. fat), 0 chol., 607mg sodium, 55g carb. (9g sugars, 5g fiber), 10g pro.*

BLUE CHEESE-CRUSTED SIRLOIN STEAKS

CREAMY TOMATO TORTELLINI WITH SAUSAGE

No one will believe that just three ingredients make up this tomato sauce that tastes like it bubbled away all day on top of the stove. It's that good.

—**JENNIFER EGGERT** SCOTTSDALE, AZ

START TO FINISH: 25 MIN.
MAKES: 6 SERVINGS

- 1 **package (19 ounces) frozen cheese tortellini**
- 2 **fully cooked Italian chicken sausage links (3 ounces each), sliced**
- 1 **can (14½ ounces) diced tomatoes with garlic and onion, undrained**
- 1 **package (6 ounces) fresh baby spinach**
- 4 **ounces reduced-fat cream cheese**

1. Cook tortellini according to package directions. Meanwhile, in a large nonstick skillet coated with cooking spray, cook and stir sausage over medium-high heat 4-5 minutes or until browned. Add the tomatoes and spinach; cook and stir just until the spinach is wilted. Stir in cream cheese until melted.

2. Drain tortellini; add to sausage mixture. Toss to combine.

TORTELLINI SPINACH SALAD *Cook tortellini as directed; drain and rinse with cold water. Toss with spinach and ⅔ cup poppy seed salad dressing and ½ cup shredded Parmesan cheese.*

PER SERVING *1⅓ cups: 298 cal., 13g fat (6g sat. fat), 49mg chol., 824mg sodium, 31g carb. (5g sugars, 2g fiber), 17g pro.*

BLUE CHEESE-CRUSTED SIRLOIN STEAKS

According to my wife, this smothered steak is my specialty. I like to make it for her on Friday nights to say goodbye to a long week.

—**MICHAEL ROUSE** MINOT, ND

START TO FINISH: 30 MIN.
MAKES: 4 SERVINGS

- 2 **tablespoons butter, divided**
- 1 **medium onion, chopped**
- ⅓ **cup crumbled blue cheese**
- 2 **tablespoons soft bread crumbs**
- 1 **beef top sirloin steak (1 inch thick and 1½ pounds)**
- ¾ **teaspoon salt**
- ½ **teaspoon pepper**

1. Preheat broiler. In a large broil-safe skillet, heat 1 tablespoon butter over medium heat; saute the onion until tender. Transfer to a bowl; stir in the cheese and bread crumbs.

2. Cut steak into four pieces; sprinkle with salt and pepper. In same pan, heat remaining butter over medium heat; cook steaks until desired doneness (for medium-rare, a thermometer should read 145°; medium, 160°), 4-5 minutes per side.

3. Spread onion mixture over steaks. Broil 4-6 in. from heat until lightly browned, 2-3 minutes.

DRESSED-UP SIRLOIN STEAK *Mix 1 tablespoon olive oil, 1½ teaspoons minced garlic, 1 teaspoon dried oregano and 1 teaspoon pepper. Rub over both sides of steak. Brush with ¼ cup Catalina salad dressing. Do not brown steaks; broil as directed for 5-7 minutes on each side or until desired doneness. Serve with additional Catalina if desired.*

NOTE *To make soft bread crumbs, tear bread into pieces and place in a food processor or blender. Cover and pulse until crumbs form. One slice of bread yields ½ to ¾ cup crumbs.*

PER SERVING *326 cal., 16g fat (8g sat. fat), 92mg chol., 726mg sodium, 5g carb. (2g sugars, 1g fiber), 39g pro.*

TOP TIP

BABY SPINACH

Using baby spinach saves prep time because you don't have to remove the tough stems as you do with mature spinach. And some people prefer the tender texture of baby spinach in salads.

Candace Havely's Rosemary Shrimp with Spaghetti *PAGE 129*

Express Entrees

Every delicious entree in this chapter is table-ready in half an hour or less. From seared scallops and lettuce wraps to pork chops and chicken pasta, you'll find dozens of quick-cooking favorites here.

**Stacy Mullens'
Bean & Bacon Griddle
Burritos** *PAGE 117*

**Donna Lindecamp's
Dijon Beef Tenderloin**
PAGE 125

**Cathryn Eckley's
Chicken with Pear &
Sweet Potato** *PAGE 133*

BACON-GARLIC CHICKEN

EAT SMART **FAST FIX**
SPICY MANGO SCALLOPS

Warm up your whole family with this spicy-sweet dish. If you prepare the recipe with smaller scallops, be sure to decrease the cooking time.

—**NICOLE FILIZETTI** STEVENS POINT, WI

START TO FINISH: 30 MIN.
MAKES: 4 SERVINGS

- 12 **sea scallops (1½ pounds)**
- 1 **tablespoon peanut or canola oil**
- 1 **medium red onion, chopped**
- 1 **garlic clove, minced**
- ¼ **to ½ teaspoon crushed red pepper flakes**
- ½ **cup unsweetened pineapple juice**
- ¼ **cup mango chutney**
- 2 **cups hot cooked basmati rice**
   Minced fresh cilantro

1. Pat scallops dry with paper towels. In a large skillet, heat oil over medium-high heat. Add scallops; cook for 1-2 minutes on each side or until golden brown and firm. Remove from pan.
2. Add onion to same pan; cook and stir until tender. Add garlic and pepper flakes; cook 1 minute longer. Stir in pineapple juice. Bring to a boil; cook until liquid is reduced by half. Stir in the chutney.
3. Return scallops to the pan; heat through, stirring gently to coat. Serve with rice; sprinkle with cilantro.
PER SERVING *3 scallops with ½ cup rice and 2 tablespoons sauce: 371 cal., 5g fat (1g sat. fat), 56mg chol., 447mg sodium, 47g carb. (13g sugars, 1g fiber), 31g pro. Diabetic Exchanges: 4 lean meat, 3 starch, ½ fat.*

SPICY MANGO SCALLOPS

EAT SMART **FAST FIX**
BACON-GARLIC CHICKEN

Help yourself to my recipe for wonderful Italian stovetop chicken. It can be thrown together in minutes but tastes like a much bigger production.

—**YVONNE STARLIN** WESTMORELAND, TN

START TO FINISH: 30 MIN.
MAKES: 4 SERVINGS

- 4 **boneless skinless chicken breast halves (5 ounces each)**
- ¼ **teaspoon salt**
- ½ **teaspoon pepper**
- ¼ **cup all-purpose flour**
- 3 **bacon strips, chopped**
- 1 **tablespoon butter**
- 4 **garlic cloves, thinly sliced**
- 2 **teaspoons minced fresh rosemary or ¾ teaspoon dried rosemary, crushed**
- ⅛ **teaspoon crushed red pepper flakes**
- 1 **cup reduced-sodium chicken broth**
- 1 **tablespoon lemon juice**

1. Pound chicken with a meat mallet to ½-in. thickness; sprinkle with salt and pepper. Lightly coat both sides with flour; shake off excess.
2. In a nonstick skillet, cook bacon over medium-high heat until crisp, stirring occasionally. With a slotted spoon, remove bacon to paper towels; reserve 1 teaspoon drippings.
3. In same pan, heat butter and drippings over medium heat. Add the chicken; cook until no longer pink, 4-6 minutes per side. Remove from pan.
4. Add garlic, rosemary and pepper flakes to pan; cook and stir until garlic begins to color, 1-2 minutes. Stir in broth and lemon juice; bring to a boil, stirring to loosen browned bits from pan. Cook until slightly thickened, about 3-4 minutes.
5. Return chicken and bacon to pan; heat through, turning chicken a few times to coat.
PER SERVING *232 cal., 9g fat (4g sat. fat), 88mg chol., 488mg sodium, 5g carb. (0 sugars, 0 fiber), 30g pro. Diabetic Exchanges: 4 lean meat, 1 fat.*

SPICY TURKEY LETTUCE WRAPS

My go-to meal after an evening run is this satisfying turkey wrap with jicama, a potato-like root veggie used often in Mexican cooking.

—**CHRISTIE ARP** BLUE RIDGE, GA

START TO FINISH: 20 MIN.
MAKES: 2 SERVINGS

- ½ pound lean ground turkey
- ½ cup chopped peeled jicama or celery
- ¼ cup chopped onion
- 2 tablespoons reduced-sodium soy sauce
- 2 teaspoons minced fresh gingerroot
- 1 garlic clove, minced
- ⅛ teaspoon cayenne pepper
- ⅛ teaspoon pepper
- ¼ cup julienned carrot
- 6 Bibb lettuce leaves
  Hot mustard, optional

1. In a large skillet, cook turkey, jicama and onion over medium heat 4-6 minutes or until turkey is no longer pink, breaking up turkey into crumbles. Stir in soy sauce, ginger, garlic and peppers. Add carrot; cook and stir 1-2 minutes longer or until liquid is absorbed.
2. Serve in lettuce. If desired, serve with mustard.
PER SERVING 3 wraps (*calculated without mustard*): 212 cal., 9g fat (2g sat. fat), 78mg chol., 655mg sodium,

9g carb. (*2g sugars, 3g fiber*), 24g pro.
Diabetic Exchanges: 3 lean meat, 1 vegetable.

APPLE-CHERRY PORK MEDALLIONS

If you're too busy to cook, my pork medallions with tangy apple-cherry sauce, fresh rosemary and thyme deliver the goods in a hurry.

—**GLORIA BRADLEY** NAPERVILLE, IL

START TO FINISH: 30 MIN.
MAKES: 4 SERVINGS

- 1 pork tenderloin (1 pound)
- 1 teaspoon minced fresh rosemary or ¼ teaspoon dried rosemary, crushed
- 1 teaspoon minced fresh thyme or ¼ teaspoon dried thyme
- ½ teaspoon celery salt
- 1 tablespoon olive oil
- 1 large apple, sliced
- ⅔ cup unsweetened apple juice
- 3 tablespoons dried tart cherries
- 1 tablespoon honey
- 1 tablespoon cider vinegar
- 1 package (8.8 ounces) ready-to-serve brown rice

1. Cut tenderloin crosswise into 12 slices; sprinkle with rosemary, thyme and celery salt. In a large nonstick skillet, heat the oil over medium-high heat. Brown pork on both sides; remove from pan.
2. In same skillet, combine apple, apple juice, cherries, honey and vinegar. Bring to a boil, stirring to

loosen browned bits from pan. Reduce heat; simmer, uncovered, 3-4 minutes or just until apple is tender.
3. Return pork to pan, turning to coat with sauce; cook, covered, 3-4 minutes or until pork is tender. Meanwhile, prepare rice according to package directions; serve with pork mixture.
PER SERVING 3 ounces cooked pork with ⅓ cup rice and ¼ cup apple mixture: 349 cal., 9g fat (2g sat. fat), 64mg chol., 179mg sodium, 37g carb. (*16g sugars, 4g fiber*), 25g pro.
Diabetic Exchanges: 3 lean meat, 2½ starch.

FAST FIX ## BEAN & BACON GRIDDLE BURRITOS

These griddle burritos with bacon and veggies make an awesome casual meal. I use fresh pico de gallo when I can, but a jar of salsa works if that's what you've got.

—**STACY MULLENS** GRESHAM, OR

START TO FINISH: 20 MIN.
MAKES: 4 SERVINGS

- 1 can (16 ounces) fat-free refried beans
- ½ cup salsa, divided
- 4 flour tortillas (8 inches)
- ½ cup crumbled cotija cheese or shredded Monterey Jack cheese
- 3 bacon strips, cooked and coarsely chopped
- 2 cups shredded lettuce

1. In a small bowl, mix beans and ¼ cup salsa until blended. Place tortillas on a griddle; cook over medium heat 1 minute, then turn over. Place bean mixture, cheese and bacon onto centers of tortillas; cook 1-2 minutes longer or until tortillas begin to crisp.
2. Remove from griddle; immediately top with lettuce and remaining salsa. To serve, fold bottom and sides of tortilla over filling.
PER SERVING 1 burrito: 375 cal., 10g fat (4g sat. fat), 21mg chol., 1133mg sodium, 52g carb. (*1g sugars, 8g fiber*), 18g pro.
HEALTH TIP *Use Amy's Organic Light In Sodium Refried Beans or Eden Foods Lightly Salted Refried Beans and save almost 300 milligrams of sodium per serving.*

SPICY TURKEY LETTUCE WRAPS

CHICKEN STIR-FRY
WITH NOODLES

EAT SMART **FAST FIX**

CHICKEN STIR-FRY WITH NOODLES

A noodle stir-fry on a cooking show caught my eye. I ran with the idea and loaded it with veggies. Now it's our favorite healthy hurry-up meal.
—**BEVERLY NORRIS** EVANSTON, WY

START TO FINISH: 30 MIN.
MAKES: 4 SERVINGS

- 8 **ounces uncooked whole wheat spaghetti**
- ½ **head bok choy (about 1 pound)**
- 2 **tablespoons canola oil, divided**
- 1 **pound boneless skinless chicken breasts, cubed**
- 1 **celery rib, sliced**
- ½ **cup coarsely chopped green pepper**
- ½ **cup coarsely chopped sweet red pepper**
- ⅓ **cup coarsely chopped onion**
- 6 **tablespoons reduced-sodium teriyaki sauce**

1. Cook spaghetti according to package directions; drain. Meanwhile, trim and discard root end of bok choy. Cut stalks into 1-in. pieces. Coarsely chop leaves.
2. In a large skillet, heat 1 tablespoon oil over medium-high heat. Add chicken; stir-fry 5-7 minutes or until no longer pink. Remove from pan.
3. Stir-fry bok choy stalks, celery, peppers and onion in remaining oil 4 minutes. Add bok choy leaves; stir-fry 3-5 minutes longer or until leaves are tender. Stir in teriyaki sauce. Add spaghetti and chicken; heat through, tossing to combine.
PER SERVING *1½ cups: 434 cal., 11g fat (1g sat. fat), 63mg chol., 623mg sodium, 53g carb. (10g sugars, 9g fiber), 35g pro.*

EAT SMART **FAST FIX**

ASIAN PORK MEDALLIONS

When I stepped up my nutrition game, my kids missed the Chinese food I'd often grabbed. I created this tasty Asian-style pork, and now nobody asks for takeout.
—**DIANNE LUEHRING** EDMOND, OK

START TO FINISH: 25 MIN.
MAKES: 4 SERVINGS

- ¼ **cup dry sherry or reduced-sodium chicken broth**
- 3 **tablespoons reduced-sodium soy sauce**
- 1 **tablespoon brown sugar**
- 1 **tablespoon hoisin sauce**
- 1 **garlic clove, minced**
- ⅛ **teaspoon cayenne pepper**
- 1 **tablespoon sesame oil**
- 1 **pound pork tenderloin, cut into ½-in. slices**
  Hot cooked brown rice, optional
  Sliced green onions, optional

1. In a small bowl, mix the first six ingredients until blended.
2. In a large skillet, heat oil over medium-high heat. In batches, cook pork 3-4 minutes on each side or until tender; remove from pan.
3. In same skillet, bring sauce mixture to a boil; cook and stir 1-2 minutes or until thickened. Return pork to pan; heat through, turning to coat. If desired, serve with rice and top with green onions.
PER SERVING *½ cup (calculated without rice): 202 cal., 7g fat (2g sat. fat), 63mg chol., 566mg sodium, 6g carb. (4g sugars, 0 fiber), 23g pro.*
Diabetic Exchanges: *3 lean meat, 2½ starch.*

ASIAN PORK MEDALLIONS

CAULIFLOWER
& TOFU CURRY

LEMONY CHICKPEAS

These saucy chickpeas add just a little heat to meatless Mondays. They're especially good over hot, fluffy brown rice.
—**APRIL STREVELL** RED BANK, NJ

START TO FINISH: 30 MIN.
MAKES: 4 SERVINGS

- 2 **cups uncooked instant brown rice**
- 1 **tablespoon olive oil**
- 1 **medium onion, chopped**
- 2 **cans (15 ounces each) chickpeas, rinsed and drained**
- 1 **can (14 ounces) diced tomatoes, undrained**
- 1 **cup vegetable broth**
- ¼ **teaspoon crushed red pepper flakes**
- ¼ **teaspoon pepper**
- ½ **teaspoon grated lemon peel**
- 3 **tablespoons lemon juice**

1. Cook rice according to package directions. Meanwhile, in a large skillet, heat oil over medium heat. Add onion; cook and stir 3-4 minutes or until tender.
2. Stir in chickpeas, tomatoes, broth, pepper flakes and pepper; bring to a boil. Reduce heat; simmer, covered, for 10 minutes to allow flavors to blend. Uncover; simmer 4-5 minutes or until liquid is slightly reduced, stirring occasionally. Stir in lemon peel and lemon juice. Serve with rice.
FREEZE OPTION *Do not prepare rice until later. Freeze cooled chickpea mixture in freezer containers. To use, partially thaw in refrigerator overnight. Heat through in a saucepan, stirring occasionally and adding a little broth if necessary. Serve with rice.*
PER SERVING *1 cup chickpea mixture with 1 cup rice: 433 cal., 9g fat (0 sat. fat), 0 chol., 679mg sodium, 76g carb. (10g sugars, 12g fiber), 13g pro.*

CAULIFLOWER
& TOFU CURRY

Cauliflower, garbanzo beans and tofu are subtle on their own, but together they make an awesome curry. We have this recipe weekly because one of us is always craving it.
—**PATRICK MCGILVRAY** CINCINNATI, OH

START TO FINISH: 30 MIN.
MAKES: 6 SERVINGS

- 1 **tablespoon olive oil**
- 2 **medium carrots, sliced**
- 1 **medium onion, chopped**
- 3 **teaspoons curry powder**
- ¼ **teaspoon salt**
- ¼ **teaspoon pepper**
- 1 **small head cauliflower, broken into florets (about 3 cups)**
- 1 **can (14½ ounces) fire-roasted crushed tomatoes**
- 1 **package (14 ounces) extra-firm tofu, drained and cut into ½-inch cubes**
- 1 **cup vegetable broth**
- 1 **can (15 ounces) garbanzo beans or chickpeas, rinsed and drained**
- 1 **can (13.66 ounces) coconut milk**
- 1 **cup frozen peas**
  Hot cooked rice
  Chopped fresh cilantro

1. In a 6-qt. stockpot, heat oil over medium-high heat. Add carrots and onion; cook and stir 4-5 minutes or until onion is tender. Stir in curry, salt and pepper.
2. Add cauliflower, tomatoes, tofu and broth; bring to a boil. Reduce heat; simmer, covered, 10 minutes. Stir in the garbanzo beans, coconut milk and peas; return to a boil. Reduce heat to medium; cook, uncovered, for 5-7 minutes or until mixture is slightly thickened and cauliflower is tender, stirring occasionally.
3. Serve with rice. Sprinkle with chopped cilantro.
PER SERVING *1⅓ cups (calculated without rice) equals 338 cal., 21g fat (13g sat. fat), 0 chol., 528mg sodium, 29g carb., 7g fiber, 13g pro.*
HEALTH TIP *Just one-half cup cooked cauliflower provides nearly half the daily value for vitamin C, not to mention sulfur-containing compounds that may help protect against certain cancers.*

WHITE BEANS
& BOW TIES

MARRAKESH CHICKEN & COUSCOUS

I love to make fast dinners with boxed grains. They already have a flavor packet, and the sky's the limit on their possibilities. Here, I transformed couscous into a one-pot delight that transports you to a faraway land of exotic flavor. My family loves this recipe.

—**DEVON DELANEY** WESTPORT, CT

START TO FINISH: 30 MIN.
MAKES: 6 SERVINGS

- 1 **tablespoon olive oil**
- 1 **pound boneless skinless chicken thighs, cut into 1¼-inch pieces**
- 1 **can (14½ ounces) diced tomatoes, undrained**
- 1 **jar (7½ ounces) marinated quartered artichoke hearts, drained**
- ¼ **cup lemon juice**
- 2 **tablespoons apricot preserves**
- ½ **teaspoon salt**
- ½ **teaspoon ground cumin**
- ¼ **teaspoon crushed red pepper flakes**
- ⅛ **teaspoon ground cinnamon**
- 1 **package (5.8 ounces) roasted garlic and olive oil couscous**
  Chopped smoked almonds, optional

1. In a 6-qt. stockpot, heat oil over medium-high heat. Brown chicken on both sides. Stir in tomatoes, artichoke hearts, lemon juice, preserves, salt, spices and seasoning packet from couscous; bring to a boil. Reduce heat; simmer, covered, 10 minutes to allow flavors to develop and for chicken to cook through.

2. Stir in couscous; remove from heat. Let stand, covered, 5 minutes. If desired, sprinkle with almonds.

PER SERVING *1⅓ cups: 326 cal., 14g fat (3g sat. fat), 50mg chol., 751mg sodium, 30g carb. (8g sugars, 2g fiber), 19g pro. Diabetic Exchanges: 3 lean meat, 2 starch, ½ fat.*

WHITE BEANS & BOW TIES

When we have fresh veggies, we toss them with pasta shapes like penne or bow tie. For add-ins, think heirloom tomatoes, onion and garlic.

—**ANGELA BUCHANAN** LONGMONT, CO

START TO FINISH: 25 MIN.
MAKES: 4 SERVINGS

- 2½ **cups uncooked whole wheat bow tie pasta (about 6 ounces)**
- 1 **tablespoon olive oil**
- 1 **medium zucchini, sliced**
- 2 **garlic cloves, minced**
- 2 **large tomatoes, chopped**
- 1 **can (15 ounces) cannellini beans, rinsed and drained**
- 1 **can (2¼ ounces) sliced ripe olives, drained**
- ¾ **teaspoon freshly ground pepper**
- ½ **cup crumbled feta cheese**

1. Cook pasta according to package directions. Drain, reserving ½ cup pasta water.

2. Meanwhile, in a large skillet, heat oil over medium-high heat. Add the zucchini; cook and stir 2-4 minutes or until crisp-tender. Add garlic; cook 30 seconds longer. Stir in tomatoes, beans, olives and pepper; bring to a boil. Reduce heat; simmer, uncovered, 3-5 minutes or until tomatoes are softened, stirring occasionally.

3. Add pasta; toss to combine, adding enough pasta water to moisten. Stir in feta cheese.

PER SERVING *1½ cups: 348 cal., 9g fat (2g sat. fat), 8mg chol., 394mg sodium, 52g carb. (4g sugars, 11g fiber), 15g pro.*

HEALTH TIP *Boost protein in meatless pasta dishes by using whole wheat noodles, adding white beans or stirring in a little cheese—or all three!*

SOUTHERN PORK & RICE

At our house, we're big on healthy eating. These ultra-tender chops with colorful rice and black-eyed peas make a healthy meal that's fancy enough for a dinner party.

—**ANNIE HOLMES** MURFREESBORO, TN

START TO FINISH: 25 MIN.
MAKES: 4 SERVINGS

- 4 **boneless pork loin chops (6 ounces each)**
- 1 **teaspoon seafood seasoning, divided**
- 1 **tablespoon olive oil**
- 1 **medium sweet red pepper, chopped**
- 1 **medium onion, chopped**
- 2 **teaspoons Worcestershire sauce**
- 1 **can (15½ ounces) black-eyed peas, rinsed and drained**
- 1 **can (14½ ounces) diced tomatoes with mild green chilies**
- 1 **cup uncooked instant rice**
- 1 **cup reduced-sodium chicken broth**

1. Sprinkle pork with ¾ teaspoon seafood seasoning. In a large skillet, heat oil over medium heat; brown chops on both sides. Remove from pan.
2. Add pepper and onion to skillet; cook and stir until tender, 4-5 minutes. Stir in remaining seafood seasoning, Worcestershire sauce, peas, tomatoes, rice and broth. Bring to a boil. Place chops over top. Reduce heat; simmer, covered, until a thermometer inserted in pork reads 145°, 2-3 minutes. Let stand, covered, 5 minutes before serving.

PER SERVING *1 pork chop with 1¼ cups rice mixture: 484 cal., 13g fat (4g sat. fat), 82mg chol., 764mg sodium, 45g carb. (7g sugars, 6g fiber), 42g pro.* **Diabetic Exchanges:** *5 lean meat, 3 starch, ½ fat.*

HEALTH TIP *Make this meal gluten-free by using gluten-free broth and Worcestershire sauce.*

THAI CHICKEN PASTA SKILLET

This gorgeous Bangkok-style pasta has been a faithful standby for many years and always gets loads of praise. For a potluck, we increase the recipe and make it ahead.

—**SUSAN TEN PAS** MYRTLE CREEK, OR

START TO FINISH: 30 MIN.
MAKES: 6 SERVINGS

- 6 **ounces uncooked whole wheat spaghetti**
- 2 **teaspoons canola oil**
- 1 **package (10 ounces) fresh sugar snap peas, trimmed and cut diagonally into thin strips**
- 2 **cups julienned carrots (about 8 ounces)**
- 2 **cups shredded cooked chicken**
- 1 **cup Thai peanut sauce**
- 1 **medium cucumber, halved lengthwise, seeded and sliced diagonally**
  Chopped fresh cilantro, optional

1. Cook spaghetti according to package directions; drain.
2. Meanwhile, in a large skillet, heat oil over medium-high heat. Add snap peas and carrots; stir-fry 6-8 minutes or until crisp-tender. Add chicken, peanut sauce and spaghetti; heat through, tossing to combine.
3. Transfer to a serving plate. Top with cucumber and, if desired, cilantro.

PER SERVING *1⅓ cups: 403 cal., 15g fat (3g sat. fat), 42mg chol., 432mg sodium, 43g carb. (15g sugars, 6g fiber), 25g pro.* **Diabetic Exchanges:** *3 lean meat, 2½ starch, 2 fat, 1 vegetable.*

HEALTH TIP *Fruits are typically associated with the antioxidant vitamin C, but sugar snap peas are an excellent source as well.*

SOUTHERN PORK & RICE

TOMATO-GARLIC
LENTIL BOWLS

TOMATO-GARLIC LENTIL BOWLS

An Ethiopian recipe inspired this feel-good dinner that's tangy, creamy and packed with hearty comfort.

—**RACHAEL CUSHING** PORTLAND, OR

START TO FINISH: 30 MIN.
MAKES: 6 SERVINGS

- 1 tablespoon olive oil
- 2 medium onions, chopped
- 4 garlic cloves, minced
- 2 cups dried lentils, rinsed
- 1 teaspoon salt
- ½ teaspoon ground ginger
- ½ teaspoon paprika
- ¼ teaspoon pepper
- 3 cups water
- ¼ cup lemon juice
- 3 tablespoons tomato paste
- ¾ cup fat-free plain Greek yogurt
  Chopped tomatoes and minced fresh cilantro, optional

1. In a large saucepan, heat oil over medium-high heat; saute onions for 2 minutes. Add garlic; cook 1 minute. Stir in lentils, seasonings and water; bring to a boil. Reduce heat; simmer, covered, until the lentils are tender, 25-30 minutes.

2. Stir in lemon juice and tomato paste; heat through. Serve with yogurt and, if desired, tomatoes and cilantro.

PER SERVING *¾ cup: 294 cal., 3g fat (trace sat. fat), 0 chol., 419mg sodium, 49g carb. (5g sugars, 8g fiber), 21g pro.* **Diabetic Exchanges:** *3 starch, 2 lean meat, ½ fat.*

HEALTH TIP *Lentils have twice as much protein and iron as quinoa.*

STICKY ASIAN CHICKEN

STICKY ASIAN CHICKEN

As a working mom with three children, I need dishes that hit the spot and come together fast. I double this Asian-style chicken because leftovers are awesome.

—**JENNIFER CARNEGIE** LAKE OSWEGO, OR

START TO FINISH: 25 MIN.
MAKES: 6 SERVINGS

- 1 tablespoon canola oil
- 6 boneless skinless chicken thighs (about 1½ pounds)
- ⅓ cup soy sauce
- ⅓ cup white wine or reduced-sodium chicken broth
- 3 tablespoons sugar
- 3 garlic cloves, minced
- 1 tablespoon cornstarch
- 3 tablespoons water

1. In a large skillet, heat the oil over medium-high heat. Brown the chicken on both sides.

2. In a small bowl, mix soy sauce, wine, sugar and garlic; pour over chicken. Bring to a boil. Reduce heat; simmer, covered, 5-7 minutes or until a thermometer inserted in chicken reads 170°. Remove the chicken and keep warm.

3. Remove cooking juices from pan; skim fat and return juices to pan. In a small bowl, mix cornstarch and water until smooth; stir into juices. Bring to a boil, stirring constantly; cook and stir 1-2 minutes or until thickened. Serve with chicken.

PER SERVING *1 chicken thigh with 1 tablespoon sauce: 229 cal., 11g fat (2g sat. fat), 76mg chol., 881mg sodium, 8g carb. (6g sugars, 0 fiber), 23g pro.*

HAM PASTA TOSS

Cook 12 ounces whole wheat spaghetti according to package directions; drain. In a large skillet, saute 2 cups shredded or cubed ham in 3 tablespoons butter for 2-4 minutes or until browned. Add 2 minced garlic cloves; cook 1 minute longer. Stir in spaghetti, 3 cups thawed frozen peas and 2 tablespoons minced fresh parsley; heat through. Stir in ¼ cup grated Parmesan cheese. Makes 6 servings.

—**SHARON GERST** NORTH LIBERTY, IA

EAT SMART **FAST FIX** ▶

GARLIC-MUSHROOM TURKEY

My daughter is a choosy eater, and even she approves of this simple weeknight turkey.
—**RICK FLEISHMAN** BEVERLY HILLS, CA

START TO FINISH: 30 MIN.
MAKES: 4 SERVINGS

- ½ cup all-purpose flour
- ½ teaspoon dried oregano
- ½ teaspoon paprika
- ¾ teaspoon salt, divided
- ¼ teaspoon pepper, divided
- 1 tablespoon olive oil
- 1 package (17.6 ounces) turkey breast cutlets
- ½ pound sliced fresh mushrooms
- ¾ cup reduced-sodium chicken broth
- ¼ cup dry white wine or additional broth
- 2 garlic cloves, minced

1. In a large shallow dish, mix flour, oregano, paprika, ½ teaspoon salt and ⅛ teaspoon pepper. Dip cutlets in flour mixture to coat both sides; shake off excess.
2. In a large nonstick skillet, heat oil over medium heat. In batches, add turkey and cook 1-2 minutes on each side or until no longer pink; remove from pan.
3. Add remaining ingredients to skillet; stir in the remaining salt and pepper. Cook, uncovered, 4-6 minutes or until the mushrooms are tender, stirring occasionally. Return turkey to pan; heat through, turning to coat.
PER SERVING *218 cal., 4g fat (1g sat. fat), 77mg chol., 440mg sodium, 8g carb. (1g sugars, 1g fiber), 34g pro. Diabetic Exchanges: 4 lean meat, ½ starch, ½ fat.*

TOP TIP

OREGANO

Oregano comes in two types. The sweet Mediterranean one is often simply labeled oregano. It belongs to the mint family. Mexican oregano, a member of the verbena family, has a more intense flavor and citrusy notes.

CURRY TURKEY STIR-FRY

EAT SMART **FAST FIX** ▶

CURRY TURKEY STIR-FRY

Just open the fridge and go to town making this simple throw-together curry. We prefer turkey, but if you like chicken, shrimp or even bean sprouts and carrots, by all means, add them.
—**LAUREN RUSH** CLARK, NJ

START TO FINISH: 20 MIN.
MAKES: 4 SERVINGS

- ½ teaspoon cornstarch
- 2 tablespoons reduced-sodium soy sauce
- 1 tablespoon minced fresh cilantro
- 1 tablespoon honey
- 1 teaspoon curry powder
- 1 teaspoon sesame or canola oil
- 1 garlic clove, minced
- ⅛ teaspoon crushed red pepper flakes, optional
- 1 tablespoon canola oil
- 1 large sweet red pepper, julienned
- 3 green onions, cut into 2-inch pieces
- 2 cups cubed cooked turkey breast
- 2 cups hot cooked brown rice

1. Mix first seven ingredients and, if desired, pepper flakes. In a large skillet, heat 1 tablespoon canola oil over medium-high heat; stir-fry red pepper until crisp-tender, about 2 minutes. Add green onions; stir-fry until tender, 1-2 minutes.
2. Stir cornstarch mixture and add to pan. Bring to a boil; cook and stir until thickened, 1-2 minutes. Stir in turkey; heat through. Serve with rice.
PER SERVING *¾ cup turkey mixture with ½ cup rice: 287 cal., 7g fat (1g sat. fat), 60mg chol., 351mg sodium, 31g carb. (7g sugars, 3g fiber), 25g pro. Diabetic Exchanges: 3 lean meat, 2 starch, 1 fat.*

CHICKEN WITH FIRE-ROASTED TOMATOES

My skillet chicken has the colors and flavors of Italy and is so easy. The fire-roasted tomatoes sound complicated, but all you have to do is open a can.

—**MARGARET WILSON** SAN BERNARDINO, CA

START TO FINISH: 30 MIN.
MAKES: 4 SERVINGS

- **2** tablespoons salt-free garlic herb seasoning blend
- **½** teaspoon salt
- **¼** teaspoon Italian seasoning
- **¼** teaspoon pepper
- **⅛** teaspoon crushed red pepper flakes, optional
- **4** boneless skinless chicken breast halves (6 ounces each)
- **1** tablespoon olive oil
- **1** can (14½ ounces) fire-roasted diced tomatoes, undrained
- **¾** pound fresh green beans, trimmed
- **2** tablespoons water
- **1** tablespoon butter
  Hot cooked pasta, optional

1. Mix the first five ingredients; sprinkle over both sides of chicken breasts. In a large skillet, heat oil over medium heat. Brown chicken on both sides. Add tomatoes; bring to a boil. Reduce heat; simmer, covered, for 10-12 minutes or until a thermometer inserted in chicken reads 165°.
2. Meanwhile, in a 2-qt. microwave-safe dish, combine green beans and water; microwave, covered, on high for 3-4 minutes or just until tender. Drain.
3. Remove chicken from skillet; keep warm. Stir butter and beans into the tomato mixture. Serve with chicken and, if desired, pasta.

PER SERVING *1 chicken breast half with 1 cup bean mixture: 294 cal., 10g fat (3g sat. fat), 102mg chol., 681mg sodium, 12g carb. (5g sugars, 4g fiber), 37g pro.* **Diabetic Exchanges:** *5 lean meat, 1 vegetable, 1 fat.*

DIJON BEEF TENDERLOIN

I like having an ace recipe up my sleeve, and this tenderloin with Dijon is my go-to for birthdays, buffets and holidays.

—**DONNA LINDECAMP** MORGANTON, NC

START TO FINISH: 20 MIN.
MAKES: 4 SERVINGS

- **4** beef tenderloin steaks (1 inch thick and 4 ounces each)
- **½** teaspoon salt
- **¼** teaspoon pepper
- **5** tablespoons butter, divided
- **1** large onion, halved and thinly sliced
- **1** cup beef stock
- **1** tablespoon Dijon mustard

1. Sprinkle steaks with salt and pepper. In a large skillet, heat 2 tablespoons butter over medium-high heat. Add steaks; cook for 4-6 minutes on each side or until meat reaches desired doneness (for medium-rare, a thermometer should read 145°; medium, 160°; well-done, 170°). Remove from pan; keep warm.
2. In same pan, heat 1 tablespoon butter over medium heat. Add onion; cook and stir 4-6 minutes or until tender. Stir in stock; bring to a boil. Cook 1-2 minutes or until liquid is reduced by half. Stir in mustard; remove from heat. Cube remaining butter; stir into sauce just until blended. Serve with steaks.

PER SERVING *3 ounces cooked beef with ¼ cup sauce: 317 cal., 21g fat (12g sat. fat), 88mg chol., 626mg sodium, 5g carb. (2g sugars, 1g fiber), 26g pro.*

CHICKEN WITH FIRE-ROASTED TOMATOES

CILANTRO BEEF TACOS

EAT SMART (5) INGREDIENTS FAST FIX ▶

PAN-SEARED COD

Cod has a soft, buttery appeal that goes great with cilantro, onions and crunchy pine nuts. This is the easiest, tastiest cod preparation I've found.
—**LUCY LU WANG** SEATTLE, WA

START TO FINISH: 25 MIN.
MAKES: 2 SERVINGS

- 2 **cod fillets (6 ounces each)**
- ½ **teaspoon salt**
- ¼ **teaspoon pepper**
- 3 **tablespoons olive oil, divided**
- ½ **large sweet onion, thinly sliced**
- ½ **cup dry white wine**
- ¼ **cup coarsely chopped fresh cilantro**
- 1 **tablespoon pine nuts or sliced almonds**

1. Pat the cod dry with paper towels and sprinkle with salt and pepper. In a large nonstick skillet, heat 2 tablespoons oil over medium-high heat. Brown fillets lightly on both sides; remove from pan.
2. In same skillet, heat remaining oil over medium heat. Add onion; cook and stir 4-5 minutes or until softened. Stir in wine; cook 3-4 minutes longer or until onion is lightly browned, stirring occasionally. Return cod to pan. Reduce heat to low; cook, covered, 2-3 minutes or until fish just begins to flake easily with a fork.
3. Remove cod from pan. Add cilantro and pine nuts to onion; serve with fish.
PER SERVING *1 fillet with ¼ cup onion mixture: 378 cal., 24g fat (3g sat. fat), 65mg chol., 691mg sodium, 8g carb. (5g sugars, 1g fiber), 28g pro.*

PAN-SEARED COD

FAST FIX ▶

CILANTRO BEEF TACOS

When I have leftover steak, it's time to make tacos. Set out bowls of toppings like lettuce, tomatoes, sour cream, avocado and salsa. That's a fiesta.
—**PATTI ROSE** TINLEY PARK, IL

START TO FINISH: 30 MIN.
MAKES: 4 SERVINGS

- 1 **beef flank steak (1 pound)**
- ½ **teaspoon salt**
- ¼ **teaspoon pepper**
- 4 **teaspoons olive oil, divided**
- 1 **medium onion, halved and sliced**
- 1 **jalapeno pepper, seeded and finely chopped**
- 1 **garlic clove, minced**
- ½ **cup salsa**
- ¼ **cup minced fresh cilantro**
- 2 **teaspoons lime juice**
  Dash hot pepper sauce
- 8 **flour tortillas (6 inches), warmed**
  Optional toppings: salsa, cilantro, shredded lettuce and sour cream

1. Sprinkle steak with salt and pepper. In a large skillet, heat 2 teaspoons oil over medium-high heat. Add steak; cook 5-7 minutes on each side or until meat reaches desired doneness (for medium-rare, a thermometer should read 145°; medium, 160°; well-done, 170°). Remove from pan.
2. In the same skillet, heat remaining oil over medium heat. Add the onion; cook and stir 4-5 minutes or until tender. Add jalapeno and garlic; cook 2 minutes longer. Stir in the salsa, cilantro, lime juice and pepper sauce; heat through.
3. Thinly slice steak across the grain; stir into onion mixture. Serve in tortillas; top as desired.
NOTE *Wear disposable gloves when cutting hot peppers; the oils can burn skin. Avoid touching your face.*
PER SERVING *2 tacos (calculated without toppings): 451 cal., 20g fat (7g sat. fat), 54mg chol., 884mg sodium, 38g carb. (3g sugars, 4g fiber), 27g pro.*

APPLE & SWEET
POTATO QUINOA

APPLE & SWEET POTATO QUINOA

When feeding three hungry boys, I rely on quick, filling and tasty meals. My boys aren't big quinoa fans, but the sweet potatoes and apples won them over.

—**CHERYL BEADLE** PLYMOUTH, MI

START TO FINISH: 30 MIN.
MAKES: 6 SERVINGS

- 2¼ cups chicken or vegetable stock
- 1 cup quinoa, rinsed
- 2 tablespoons canola oil
- 2 pounds sweet potatoes (about 3 medium), peeled and cut into ½-inch pieces
- 2 shallots, finely chopped
- 3 medium Gala or Honeycrisp apples, cut into ¼-inch slices
- ½ cup white wine or additional stock
- ½ teaspoon salt
- 1 can (15 ounces) black beans, rinsed and drained

1. In a large saucepan, combine stock and quinoa; bring to a boil. Reduce heat; simmer, covered, 15-20 minutes or until liquid is almost absorbed. Remove from heat.
2. Meanwhile, in a 6-qt. stockpot, heat oil over medium heat. Add sweet potatoes and shallots; cook and stir 5 minutes. Add apples; cook and stir 6-8

minutes longer until potatoes and apples are tender.
3. Stir in wine and salt. Bring to a boil; cook, uncovered, until wine is evaporated, about 1 minute. Stir in black beans and quinoa; heat through.
PER SERVING 1⅓ cups: 423 cal., 7g fat (1g sat. fat), 0 chol., 541mg sodium, 76g carb. (23g sugars, 10g fiber), 12g pro.

HEALTH TIP *Quinoa is one of the only plant foods that has all of the amino acids we need. Cook it up with gluten-free vegetable stock for a meatless meal that's also gluten-free.*

SUN-DRIED TOMATO LINGUINE

We call this Gus's Special Pasta because my oldest child claimed it as his own. It's cheesy, garlicky goodness and quick to fix.

—**COURTNEY GAYLORD** COLUMBUS, IN

START TO FINISH: 25 MIN.
MAKES: 6 SERVINGS

- 1 package (16 ounces) linguine
- 1 jar (7 ounces) julienned oil-packed sun-dried tomatoes
- 6 garlic cloves, minced
- 1 tablespoon lemon juice
- ½ cup minced fresh parsley
- 1½ cups crumbled feta cheese
- 1½ cups grated Parmesan cheese

1. In a 6-qt. stockpot, cook linguine according to package directions for al dente. Drain, reserving ½ cup pasta water; return linguine to pot.
2. Meanwhile, drain the tomatoes, reserving 2 tablespoons oil. In a small microwave-safe bowl, combine garlic and reserved oil; microwave on high for 45 seconds. Stir in the drained tomatoes and lemon juice.
3. Add tomato mixture to linguine. Toss with parsley, cheeses and enough pasta water to moisten.
PER SERVING 1⅓ cups: 542 cal., 21g fat (8g sat. fat), 32mg chol., 726mg sodium, 68g carb. (3g sugars, 6g fiber), 23g pro.

BLACK BEAN CHICKEN WITH RICE

This Tex-Mex dish is a snap to make, and now that my kids have grown, I can add a drizzle of hot sauce to boost the heat.

—**MOLLY NEWMAN** PORTLAND, OR

PREP/TOTAL: 25 MIN.
MAKES: 4 SERVINGS

- 3 teaspoons chili powder
- 1 teaspoon ground cumin
- 1 teaspoon pepper
- ¼ teaspoon salt
- 4 boneless skinless chicken breast halves (4 ounces each)
- 2 teaspoons canola oil
- 1 can (15 ounces) black beans, rinsed and drained
- 1 cup frozen corn
- 1 cup salsa
- 2 cups hot cooked brown rice

1. In a small bowl, mix seasonings; sprinkle over both sides of chicken. In a large nonstick skillet coated with cooking spray, heat oil over medium heat. Brown chicken on both sides.
2. Add beans, corn and salsa to skillet; cook, covered, 10-15 minutes or until a thermometer inserted in chicken reads 165°. Remove chicken from pan; cut into slices. Serve with the bean mixture and rice.
PER SERVING 1 chicken breast half with ¾ cup bean mixture and ½ cup cooked rice: 400 cal., 7g fat (1g sat. fat), 63mg chol., 670mg sodium, 52g carb. (4g sugars, 8g fiber), 32g pro.

COD WITH HEARTY
TOMATO SAUCE

ASIAN GLAZED CHICKEN THIGHS

Everyone goes for this super moist, garlicky chicken, including my fussy kids. For your holiday buffet or family gathering, serve it with rice or noodles.
—**CAROLE LOTITO** HILLSDALE, NJ

START TO FINISH: 25 MIN.
MAKES: 4 SERVINGS

- ¼ cup rice vinegar
- 3 tablespoons reduced-sodium soy sauce
- 2 tablespoons honey
- 2 teaspoons canola oil
- 4 boneless skinless chicken thighs (about 1 pound)
- 3 garlic cloves, minced
- 1 teaspoon minced fresh gingerroot or ½ teaspoon ground ginger
  Toasted sesame seeds, optional

1. In a small bowl, whisk vinegar, soy sauce and honey until blended. In a large nonstick skillet, heat oil over medium-high heat. Brown chicken on both sides.
2. Add garlic and ginger to skillet; cook and stir 1 minute (do not allow garlic to brown). Stir in the vinegar mixture; bring to a boil. Reduce heat; simmer, covered, 8-10 minutes or until a thermometer inserted in chicken reads 170°.
3. Uncover and simmer 1-2 minutes longer or until the sauce is slightly thickened. If desired, cut into bite-size pieces and sprinkle with sesame seeds before serving.
PER SERVING (*calculated without seeds*): *247 cal., 11g fat (2g sat. fat), 76mg chol., 735mg sodium, 15g carb. (14g sugars, 0 fiber), 22g pro.* **Diabetic Exchanges:** *3 lean meat, 1 starch, ½ fat.*

COD WITH HEARTY TOMATO SAUCE

 My father made up this sweet, flavorful recipe for my mother when he would cook for the night. We serve it with whole wheat pasta or brown rice.
—**ANN MARIE EBERHART** GIG HARBOR, WA

START TO FINISH: 30 MIN.
MAKES: 4 SERVINGS

- 2 cans (14½ ounces each) diced tomatoes with basil, oregano and garlic, undrained
- 4 cod fillets (6 ounces each)
- 2 tablespoons olive oil, divided
- 2 medium onions, halved and thinly sliced (about 1½ cups)
- ½ teaspoon dried oregano
- ¼ teaspoon pepper
- ¼ teaspoon crushed red pepper flakes
  Hot cooked whole wheat pasta
  Minced fresh parsley, optional

1. Place tomatoes in a blender. Cover and process until pureed.
2. Pat fish dry with paper towels. In a large skillet, heat 1 tablespoon oil over medium-high heat. Add cod fillets; cook 2-4 minutes on each side or until surface of fish begins to color. Remove from pan.
3. In same skillet, heat remaining oil over medium-high heat. Add onions; cook and stir 2-4 minutes or until tender. Stir in seasonings and pureed tomatoes; bring to a boil. Add cod; return just to a boil, spooning sauce over tops. Reduce heat; simmer, uncovered, 5-7 minutes or until fish just begins to flake easily with a fork. Serve with pasta. If desired, sprinkle with parsley.
PER SERVING *1 fillet with ¾ cup sauce: 271 cal., 8g fat (1g sat. fat), 65mg chol., 746mg sodium, 17g carb. (9g sugars, 4g fiber), 29g pro.* **Diabetic Exchanges:** *3 lean meat, 2 vegetable, 1½ fat.*

ASIAN GLAZED CHICKEN THIGHS

CHORIZO BURRITO BOWLS

FAST FIX

CHORIZO BURRITO BOWLS

I'm always on the hunt for fast and filling meals. Chicken sausage makes an awesome one-dish dinner by itself or served with brown rice in a burrito.
—**ELISABETH LARSEN** PLEASANT GROVE, UT

START TO FINISH: 25 MIN.
MAKES: 4 SERVINGS

- 2 teaspoons canola oil
- 1 package (12 ounces) fully cooked jalapeno or chorizo chicken sausage links, sliced
- 1 medium onion, chopped
- 1 can (15 ounces) no-salt-added black beans, rinsed and drained
- 1 can (10 ounces) diced tomatoes and green chilies, undrained
- 1 cup fresh or frozen corn
- 1 package (8.8 ounces) ready-to-serve brown rice
- 2 cups fresh baby spinach
- ¼ cup crumbled queso fresco or shredded Monterey Jack cheese
  Chopped fresh cilantro

1. In a large skillet, heat oil over medium heat. Add sausage; cook and stir until lightly browned. Remove from pan.
2. Add onion to same skillet; cook and stir 3-5 minutes or until tender. Stir in beans, tomatoes, corn and sausage; bring to a boil. Reduce heat; simmer, uncovered, 5 minutes. Stir in rice and spinach; cook 2-3 minutes or until heated through and spinach is wilted. Sprinkle with cheese and cilantro.
PER SERVING 1⅓ cups: 425 cal., 14g fat (3g sat. fat), 70mg chol., 1275mg sodium, 52g carb. (7g sugars, 8g fiber), 27g pro.

EAT SMART FAST FIX

ROSEMARY SHRIMP WITH SPAGHETTI

Shrimp, garlic and rosemary make a top-notch flavor combo. Serve this pasta with slices of garlic bread to scoop up every last bit of goodness.
—**CANDACE HAVELY** STERLING, CO

START TO FINISH: 30 MIN.
MAKES: 4 SERVINGS

- 8 ounces uncooked white fiber or whole wheat spaghetti
- 1 tablespoon olive oil
- 1 pound uncooked shrimp (31-40 per pound), peeled and deveined
- 2 garlic cloves, minced
- 1½ teaspoons minced fresh rosemary or ½ teaspoon dried rosemary, crushed
- 2 cups fresh baby spinach
- 2 tablespoons lemon juice
- ¼ teaspoon salt
- ¼ teaspoon pepper
- ¼ cup crumbled feta cheese

1. Cook spaghetti according to package directions. Drain, reserving ½ cup pasta water.
2. Meanwhile, in a large skillet, heat oil over medium heat. Add shrimp, garlic and rosemary; cook and stir for 3-4 minutes or just until shrimp turn pink. Stir in spinach; cook, covered, until slightly wilted.
3. Add spaghetti, lemon juice, salt and pepper; toss to combine, adding reserved pasta water as desired. Sprinkle with cheese. Remove from heat; let stand, covered, until cheese is softened.
PER SERVING 1½ cups: 349 cal., 7g fat (2g sat. fat), 142mg chol., 366mg sodium, 46g carb. (2g sugars, 8g fiber), 29g pro. **Diabetic Exchanges:** 3 starch, 3 lean meat, ½ fat.

EAT SMART FAST FIX

MEDITERRANEAN CHICKPEAS

Add this to your meatless Monday lineup. Top the finished dish with feta cheese—and don't skimp on it!
—**ELAINE OBER** BROOKLINE, MA

START TO FINISH: 25 MIN.
MAKES: 4 SERVINGS

- 1 cup water
- ¾ cup uncooked whole wheat couscous
- 1 tablespoon olive oil
- 1 medium onion, chopped
- 2 garlic cloves, minced
- 1 can (15 ounces) chickpeas or garbanzo beans, rinsed and drained
- 1 can (14½ ounces) no-salt-added stewed tomatoes, cut up
- 1 can (14 ounces) water-packed artichoke hearts, rinsed, drained and chopped
- ½ cup pitted Greek olives, coarsely chopped
- 1 tablespoon lemon juice
- ½ teaspoon dried oregano
  Dash pepper
  Dash cayenne pepper

1. In a small saucepan, bring water to a boil. Stir in couscous. Remove from heat; let stand, covered, 5-10 minutes or until water is absorbed. Fluff with a fork.
2. Meanwhile, in a large nonstick skillet, heat oil over medium-high heat. Add onion; cook and stir until tender. Add garlic; cook 1 minute longer. Sir in remaining ingredients; heat through, stirring occasionally. Serve with couscous.
PER SERVING 1 cup chickpea mixture with ⅔ cup couscous: 340 cal., 10g fat (1g sat. fat), 0 chol., 677mg sodium, 51g carb. (9g sugars, 9g fiber), 11g pro.

TOP TIP

FETA CHEESE

This salty, crumbly Greek-style cheese is traditionally made with sheep's or goat's milk, but most American brands are made with cow's milk. Not fond of feta? Substitute ricotta salata, which is sharper and not as salty, or queso blanco, which is milky and mild.

FETA SHRIMP TACOS

FETA SHRIMP TACOS

A unique combination of taco seasoning and feta cheese works remarkably well in these refreshing tacos. It's a good thing you get two per serving, because you won't want to stop at one!
—**ATHENA RUSSELL** GREENVILLE, SC

START TO FINISH: 30 MIN.
MAKES: 4 SERVINGS

- ¼ **cup Miracle Whip Light or reduced-fat mayonnaise**
- 1 **tablespoon cider vinegar**
- 1 **tablespoon stone-ground mustard**
- ¼ **teaspoon pepper**
- 2 **cups shredded red cabbage**
- ¼ **cup finely chopped sweet onion**
- 1 **banana pepper, finely chopped**
- 1 **pound uncooked shrimp (31-40 per pound), peeled and deveined**
- 1 **tablespoon reduced-sodium taco seasoning**
- 1 **tablespoon olive oil**
- 8 **whole wheat tortillas (8 inches), warmed**
- ½ **cup crumbled feta cheese**
  Sliced avocado, optional

1. In a bowl, mix Miracle Whip, vinegar, mustard and pepper. Add cabbage, onion and banana pepper; toss to coat. Refrigerate until serving.
2. Toss shrimp with taco seasoning. In a large nonstick skillet, heat oil over medium-high heat. Add shrimp; cook and stir 3-4 minutes or until shrimp turn pink. Serve in tortillas; top with slaw, cheese and, if desired, avocado.

PER SERVING *2 tacos (calculated without avocado): 443 cal., 12g fat (2g sat. fat), 150mg chol., 882mg sodium, 55g carb. (5g sugars, 8g fiber), 30g pro.*

HEALTH TIP *Using reduced-sodium taco seasoning instead of regular saves more than 80 milligrams of sodium per serving. You can save 125 milligrams more with salt-free Southwest chipotle seasoning or your own salt-free blend.*

GARLIC TILAPIA
WITH SPICY KALE

GARLIC TILAPIA WITH SPICY KALE

We make this main dish and side together, and adjust the heat from the red pepper flakes depending on who's at the table.
—**TARA CRUZ** KERSEY, CO

START TO FINISH: 30 MIN.
MAKES: 4 SERVINGS

- 3 **tablespoons olive oil, divided**
- 2 **garlic cloves, minced**
- 1 **teaspoon fennel seed**
- ½ **teaspoon crushed red pepper flakes**
- 1 **bunch kale, trimmed and coarsely chopped (about 16 cups)**
- ⅔ **cup water**
- 4 **tilapia fillets (6 ounces each)**
- ¾ **teaspoon pepper, divided**
- ½ **teaspoon garlic salt**
- 1 **can (15 ounces) cannellini beans, rinsed and drained**
- ½ **teaspoon salt**

1. In a 6-qt. stockpot, heat 1 tablespoon oil over medium heat. Add garlic, fennel and pepper flakes; cook and stir 1 minute. Add kale and water; bring to a boil. Reduce heat; simmer, covered, 10-12 minutes or until kale is tender.
2. Meanwhile, sprinkle tilapia with ½ teaspoon pepper and garlic salt. In a large skillet, heat remaining oil over medium heat. Add tilapia; cook for 3-4 minutes on each side or until fish just begins to flake easily with a fork.
3. Add beans, salt and remaining pepper to kale; heat through, stirring occasionally. Serve with tilapia.

PER SERVING *1 fillet with 1 cup kale mixture: 359 cal., 13g fat (2g sat. fat), 83mg chol., 645mg sodium, 24g carb. (0 sugars, 6g fiber), 39g pro.* **Diabetic Exchanges:** *5 lean meat, 2 fat, 1½ starch.*

HEALTH TIP *Almost half of all Americans don't get enough vitamin A. One serving of this dish gives you three times the daily recommendation for this immune-boosting vitamin.*

PORK PANCIT

EAT SMART FAST FIX

PORK PANCIT

A dear friend gave me a pork recipe so tempting, we never have leftovers. Try it with other meats, like chicken or sausage.
—**PRISCILLA GILBERT**
INDIAN HARBOUR BEACH, FL

START TO FINISH: 30 MIN.
MAKES: 6 SERVINGS

- 8 **ounces uncooked vermicelli or angel hair pasta**
- 1 **pound boneless pork loin chops (½ inch thick), cut into thin strips**
- 3 **tablespoons canola oil, divided**
- 4 **garlic cloves, minced**
- 1½ **teaspoons salt, divided**
- 1 **medium onion, halved and thinly sliced**
- 2½ **cups shredded cabbage**
- 1 **medium carrot, julienned**
- 1 **cup fresh snow peas**
- ¼ **teaspoon pepper**

1. Break vermicelli in half; cook according to package directions. Drain.

2. Meanwhile, in a bowl, toss pork with 2 tablespoons oil, garlic and ½ teaspoon salt. Place a large skillet over medium-high heat. Add half of the pork mixture; stir-fry 2-3 minutes or until browned. Remove from pan. Repeat with remaining pork mixture.

3. In same skillet, heat remaining oil over medium-high heat. Add onion; stir-fry 1-2 minutes or until tender. Add remaining vegetables; stir-fry for 3-5 minutes or until crisp-tender. Stir in pepper and remaining salt. Return pork to pan. Add vermicelli; heat through, tossing to combine.

PER SERVING *1⅓ cups: 326 cal., 12g fat (2g sat. fat), 36mg chol., 627mg sodium, 34g carb. (3g sugars, 3g fiber), 21g pro.* **Diabetic Exchanges:** *2 starch, 2 lean meat, 1 vegetable, 1 fat.*

FAST FIX

TURKEY SALTIMBOCCA

I kept prosciutto and sage in this Italian classic, but instead of veal I added turkey. This saltimbocca is so divine, you won't believe how quick and easy it is.
—**DEIRDRE COX** KANSAS CITY, MO

START TO FINISH: 30 MIN.
MAKES: 2 SERVINGS

- ¼ **cup all-purpose flour**
- 1 **turkey breast tenderloin (8 ounces)**
- ⅛ **teaspoon pepper**
- 1½ **teaspoons olive oil**
- 2 **tablespoons butter, divided**
- 1 **thin slice prosciutto or deli ham, cut into thin strips**
- 2 **tablespoons minced fresh sage**
- ¼ **cup white wine or chicken broth**

1. Place flour in a large shallow bowl. Cut tenderloin horizontally in half; flatten each half with a meat mallet to ½-in. thickness. Sprinkle with pepper. Dip in flour to coat both sides; shake off excess.

2. In a large skillet, heat the oil and 1 tablespoon butter over medium heat. Add turkey; cook 3-4 minutes on each side or until no longer pink. Remove from pan; keep warm.

3. In same pan, heat 1½ teaspoons butter over medium-high heat. Add prosciutto and sage; cook and stir until slightly crisp. Add wine or broth to pan; increase heat to medium-high. Cook until liquid is slightly reduced, stirring to loosen browned bits from pan. Remove from heat; stir in the remaining 1½ teaspoons butter. Serve with turkey.

PER SERVING *300 cal., 17g fat (8g sat. fat), 92mg chol., 279mg sodium, 4g carb. (0 sugars, 0 fiber), 29g pro.*

CUMIN CHICKEN

My zesty chicken spiced with cumin and oregano comes together fast when weeknights get crazy busy. We add picante sauce for extra kick.

—MARGARET ALLEN ABINGDON, VA

START TO FINISH: 30 MIN.
MAKES: 4 SERVINGS

- 2 **teaspoons ground cumin, divided**
- ½ **teaspoon dried oregano**
- ¼ **teaspoon garlic salt**
- 1 **tablespoon canola oil**
- 4 **boneless skinless chicken breast halves (4 ounces each)**
- ½ **cup picante sauce**
- ¼ **cup water**
- 1 **teaspoon reduced-sodium chicken bouillon granules**

1. Mix 1 teaspoon cumin, oregano and garlic salt; sprinkle over both sides of chicken. In a large nonstick skillet, heat oil over medium heat. Brown chicken on both sides.

2. In a small bowl, mix picante sauce, water, bouillon and remaining cumin; pour over the chicken. Bring to a boil. Reduce heat; simmer, covered, for 8-12 minutes or until a thermometer inserted in chicken reads 165°.

3. Remove chicken from pan; keep warm. Bring sauce to a boil; cook, uncovered, for 3-4 minutes or until thickened, stirring occasionally. Serve with chicken.

PER SERVING *1 chicken breast half with 3 tablespoons sauce: 170 cal., 6g fat (1g sat. fat), 63mg chol., 377mg sodium, 3g carb. (1g sugars, 0 fiber), 23g pro.* **Diabetic Exchanges:** *3 lean meat, 1 fat.*

CUMIN CHICKEN

QUICK SHRIMP CREOLE

My mother made shrimp Creole when I was growing up, so I've carried on the family tradition. For extra heat, bring on the Louisiana hot sauce.

—GINA NORTON WONDER LAKE, IL

START TO FINISH: 30 MIN.
MAKES: 6 SERVINGS

- 3 **cups uncooked instant brown rice**
- 3 **tablespoons canola oil**
- 2 **medium onions, halved and sliced**
- 1 **medium sweet red pepper, coarsely chopped**
- 1 **medium green pepper, coarsely chopped**
- ½ **cup chopped celery**
- 2 **tablespoons all-purpose flour**
- 1 **teaspoon dried oregano**
- ¾ **teaspoon pepper**
- ½ **teaspoon salt**
- 1 **can (14½ ounces) diced tomatoes, undrained**
- 1 **can (8 ounces) tomato sauce**
- 1 **pound uncooked shrimp (31-40 per pound), peeled and deveined**
  Louisiana-style hot sauce, optional

1. Cook rice according to package directions. Meanwhile, in a large skillet, heat oil over medium-high heat. Add the onions, peppers and celery; cook and stir 6-8 minutes or until tender.

2. Stir in flour, oregano, pepper and salt until blended. Stir in tomatoes and tomato sauce. Bring to a boil, stirring constantly; cook and stir until thickened. Reduce heat; simmer, covered, 5-8 minutes or until flavors are blended, stirring occasionally.

3. Add shrimp; cook, covered, 4-5 minutes longer or until shrimp turn pink, stirring occasionally. Serve with rice and, if desired, hot sauce.

PER SERVING *1 cup shrimp mixture with ⅔ cup rice (calculated without hot sauce): 356 cal., 10g fat (1g sat. fat), 92mg chol., 588mg sodium, 48g carb. (6g sugars, 5g fiber), 19g pro.* **Diabetic Exchanges:** *2½ starch, 2 lean meat, 1½ fat, 1 vegetable.*

CHICKEN WITH PEAR & SWEET POTATO

When my husband was deployed to Iraq, a girlfriend shared this yummy chicken. I served it when he returned home, and now it's a tradition at our house.

—CATHRYN ECKLEY FORT MEADE, MD

START TO FINISH: 30 MIN.
MAKES: 4 SERVINGS

- 4 **boneless skinless chicken breast halves (5 ounces each)**
- ¼ **teaspoon pepper**
- ¾ **teaspoon salt, divided**
- 1 **tablespoon canola oil**
- 1 **medium sweet potato (about ¾ pound), peeled and cut into ½-inch pieces**
- ½ **cup plus 3 tablespoons water, divided**
- 1 **medium ripe pear, cut into ½-inch pieces**
- 1 **tablespoon red wine vinegar**
- 1 **tablespoon Dijon mustard**
- 1 **teaspoon minced fresh tarragon or ¼ teaspoon dried tarragon**

1. Pound chicken breasts with a meat mallet to ½-in. thickness; sprinkle with pepper and ½ teaspoon salt.

2. In a large nonstick skillet, heat oil over medium heat. Add chicken; cook 3-4 minutes on each side or until no longer pink. Remove from pan; keep warm.

3. In same pan, combine the sweet potato and ½ cup water; bring to a boil. Reduce heat; simmer, covered, 5 minutes. Stir in pear; cook, covered, 4-5 minutes longer or until potato is tender. Add vinegar, mustard and tarragon; stir in remaining water and heat through. Serve with chicken.

PER SERVING *4 ounces cooked chicken with ¾ cup potato mixture: 301 cal., 7g fat (1g sat. fat), 78mg chol., 610mg sodium, 28g carb. (13g sugars, 4g fiber), 30g pro.* **Diabetic Exchanges:** *4 lean meat, 1½ starch, ½ fat.*

CHARD & BACON LINGUINE

¼ teaspoon seasoned salt
¼ teaspoon pepper
½ pound ground beef
½ pound bulk pork sausage
¼ cup plus 2 tablespoons all-purpose flour, divided
2½ cups reduced-sodium beef broth, divided
   Hot mashed potatoes
   Minced fresh parsley, optional

1. Mix the first four ingredients. Add the beef and sausage; mix lightly but thoroughly. Shape into 1-in. balls; toss with ¼ cup flour, coating lightly.
2. In a large skillet, brown meatballs over medium-high heat. Add 2 cups broth; bring to a boil. Reduce heat; simmer, covered, until meatballs are cooked through, 5-6 minutes.
3. Remove meatballs with a slotted spoon. Mix the remaining flour into broth until smooth. Bring to a boil; cook and stir until thickened, 1-2 minutes. Return meatballs to pan; heat through. Serve with mashed potatoes. If desired, sprinkle with parsley.
PER SERVING (*calculated without mashed potatoes*): *348 cal., 21g fat (7g sat. fat), 115mg chol., 846mg sodium, 17g carb. (1g sugars, 1g fiber), 21g pro.*

GRANDMA'S SWEDISH MEATBALLS

EAT SMART **FAST FIX** ▸
CHARD & BACON LINGUINE

I use Swiss chard every way I can, and that includes stirring it into this breezy linguine. When you're short on time, this dish keeps life simple.
—**DIANE NEMITZ** LUDINGTON, MI

START TO FINISH: 30 MIN.
MAKES: 4 SERVINGS

8 ounces uncooked whole wheat linguine
4 bacon strips, chopped
4 garlic cloves, minced
½ cup reduced-sodium chicken broth
½ cup dry white wine or additional chicken broth
¼ teaspoon salt
6 cups chopped Swiss chard (about 6 ounces)
⅓ cup shredded Parmesan cheese

1. Cook linguine according to package directions; drain. Meanwhile, in a large skillet, cook bacon over medium heat until crisp, stirring occasionally. Add garlic; cook 1 minute longer.
2. Add broth, wine, salt and Swiss chard to skillet; bring to a boil. Cook and stir 4-5 minutes or until chard is tender.
3. Add linguine; heat through, tossing to combine. Sprinkle with cheese.
PER SERVING *1 cup: 353 cal., 14g fat (5g sat. fat), 23mg chol., 633mg sodium, 47g carb. (2g sugars, 7g fiber), 14g pro.* **Diabetic Exchanges:** *3 starch, 1 medium-fat meat, 1 vegetable.*
HEALTH TIP *The dark green color of Swiss chard is a clue that it's an excellent source of immune-boosting vitamin A.*

FAST FIX ▸
GRANDMA'S SWEDISH MEATBALLS

My mother made these hearty meatballs when we were growing up, and now my kids love them, too. My daughter likes to help shake the meatballs in flour.
—**KARIN NESS** BIG LAKE, MN

START TO FINISH: 30 MIN.
MAKES: 4 SERVINGS

1 large egg, lightly beaten
½ cup crushed saltines (about 10 crackers)

APPLE CHICKEN CURRY

2 teaspoons olive oil
1 small onion, chopped
2 garlic cloves, minced
1 can (15 ounces) black beans,
  rinsed and drained
1½ teaspoons ground cumin
½ teaspoon onion powder
½ teaspoon pepper
¼ teaspoon cayenne pepper
¼ teaspoon salt
8 corn tortillas (6 inches)
  Cooking spray
1 cup shredded Monterey Jack
  cheese
  Shredded lettuce, optional

1. Preheat broiler. Place sweet potato in a microwave-safe bowl; microwave, covered, on high until tender, 2-3 minutes. For sauce, mix mayonnaise, lime juice and chipotle pepper.

2. In a large saucepan, heat oil over medium heat; saute onion until tender, 3-4 minutes. Add garlic; cook 1 minute. Stir in beans and seasonings; heat through. Stir in sweet potato; keep warm.

3. In two batches, spritz tortillas with cooking spray and place on a baking sheet; broil 4-5 in. from heat until crisp and lightly browned, about 1 minute per side. Sprinkle immediately with cheese. To serve, top tortillas with sauce, bean mixture and, if desired, shredded lettuce.

NOTE *This recipe was tested in an 1,100-watt microwave.*

PER SERVING *2 tostadas: 407 cal., 15g fat (6g sat. fat), 27mg chol., 676mg sodium, 54g carb. (8g sugars, 10g fiber), 16g pro.*

APPLE CHICKEN CURRY

When she was in college, my daughter introduced me to curry dishes. Now we love the aroma of apples simmering with chicken, curry and coconut milk.
—**DAWN ELLIOTT** GREENVILLE, MI

START TO FINISH: 30 MIN.
MAKES: 4 SERVINGS

4 boneless skinless chicken thighs
  (about 1 pound)
¾ teaspoon salt, divided
¼ teaspoon pepper
1 tablespoon olive oil
1 medium sweet red pepper,
  julienned
1 small onion, halved and thinly
  sliced
3 teaspoons curry powder
2 garlic cloves, minced
2 medium Granny Smith apples, cut
  into ¾-inch pieces
1 cup frozen peas
1 cup light coconut milk
2 cups cooked brown rice

1. Sprinkle chicken with ½ teaspoon salt and pepper. In a large skillet, heat oil over medium-high heat. Brown chicken on both sides; remove from the pan.

2. Add red pepper and onion to skillet; cook and stir 5 minutes. Stir in curry powder and garlic; cook 1 minute longer. Stir in apples, peas, coconut milk and remaining salt.

3. Return chicken to pan; bring to a boil. Reduce heat; simmer, covered, 8-10 minutes or until a thermometer inserted in chicken reads 170°. Serve with rice.

PER SERVING *435 cal., 17g fat (6g sat. fat), 76mg chol., 550mg sodium, 43g carb. (13g sugars, 7g fiber), 26g pro.* **Diabetic Exchanges:** *3 lean meat, 2½ starch, 2 fat, ½ fruit.*

HEALTH TIP *Long grain and instant brown rice are nutritionally similar, so go ahead and take the shortcut.*

BLACK BEAN & SWEET POTATO TOSTADAS

These veggie-packed tostadas won over my meat-loving husband. To make them even faster, shop for baked tostada shells.
—**LAUREN DELANEY-WALLACE**
GLEN CARBON, IL

START TO FINISH: 30 MIN.
MAKES: 4 SERVINGS

1 medium sweet potato, peeled and
  cut into ½-in. cubes
¼ cup fat-free mayonnaise
2 teaspoons lime juice
1 to 3 teaspoons minced chipotle
  pepper in adobo sauce

BLACK BEAN & SWEET
POTATO TOSTADAS

HONEY-PECAN
CHICKEN BREASTS

EAT SMART FAST FIX ▸

ONE-POT CHICKEN PESTO PASTA

When my garden basil goes nuts, I make pesto and keep it frozen in small containers for the right opportunity, like this saucy one-pot chicken with pasta.

—**KIMBERLY FENWICK** HOBART, IN

START TO FINISH: 30 MIN.
MAKES: 4 SERVINGS

- 1 **pound boneless skinless chicken thighs, cut into 1-inch pieces**
- 1 **teaspoon salt-free seasoning blend**
- 2 **teaspoons olive oil**
- 1 **can (14½ ounces) reduced-sodium chicken broth**
- 2 **tablespoons lemon juice**
- 1 **cup uncooked gemelli or spiral pasta**
- 2 **cups fresh broccoli florets**
- 1 **cup frozen peas**
- ⅓ **cup prepared pesto**

1. Toss chicken with seasoning blend. In a large nonstick skillet, heat oil over medium-high heat. Add chicken and brown evenly; remove from pan.

2. In same pan, combine broth and lemon juice; bring to a boil, stirring to loosen browned bits from pan. Stir in pasta; return to a boil. Reduce heat; simmer, covered, 10 minutes.

3. Add broccoli; cook, covered, for 5 minutes. Return chicken to pan; cook, covered, 2-3 minutes longer or until pasta is tender and chicken is no longer pink, stirring occasionally. Add peas; heat through. Stir in pesto.

PER SERVING *1 cup: 404 cal., 18g fat (4g sat. fat), 76mg chol., 646mg sodium, 29g carb. (4g sugars, 4g fiber), 30g pro.* ***Diabetic Exchanges:*** *3 lean meat, 2 starch, 2 fat.*

FAST FIX ▸

HONEY-PECAN CHICKEN BREASTS

We're big on entertaining and, when we do, this sweet and spicy chicken is often on the menu. The pecans add a touch of crunch and fill the house with an awesome aroma when they're toasting.

—**PENNY DAVIS** NEWMAN LAKE, WA

START TO FINISH: 25 MIN.
MAKES: 2 SERVINGS

- 2 **boneless skinless chicken breast halves (6 ounces each)**
- ¼ **teaspoon salt**
- ¼ **teaspoon garlic powder**
- ⅛ **teaspoon pepper**
- ⅛ **to ¼ teaspoon cayenne pepper**
- 1 **tablespoon butter**
- 3 **tablespoons honey**
- 2 **tablespoons finely chopped pecans**

1. Pound chicken with a meat mallet to ½-in. thickness. Sprinkle with seasonings.

2. In a large nonstick skillet, heat butter over medium heat; brown chicken on both sides. Cook, covered, until chicken is no longer pink, 6-8 minutes, turning once. Drizzle with honey and sprinkle with pecans. Cook, covered, until the chicken is glazed, 2-3 minutes.

PER SERVING *1 chicken breast half: 382 cal., 15g fat (5g sat. fat), 109mg chol., 436mg sodium, 27g carb. (25g sugars, 1g fiber), 35g pro.*

EAT SMART FAST FIX ▸

GARLIC LEMON SHRIMP

This shrimp is amazingly quick. Serve it with crusty bread so you can soak up the luscious garlic lemon sauce.

—**ATHENA RUSSELL** GREENVILLE, SC

START TO FINISH: 20 MIN.
MAKES: 4 SERVINGS

- 2 **tablespoons olive oil**
- 1 **pound uncooked shrimp (26-30 per pound), peeled and deveined**
- 3 **garlic cloves, thinly sliced**
- 1 **tablespoon lemon juice**
- 1 **teaspoon ground cumin**
- ¼ **teaspoon salt**
- 2 **tablespoons minced fresh parsley**
  Hot cooked pasta or rice

In a large skillet, heat oil over medium-high heat; saute shrimp 3 minutes. Add garlic, lemon juice, cumin and salt; cook and stir until shrimp turn pink. Stir in parsley. Serve with pasta.

PER SERVING *163 cal., 8g fat (1g sat. fat), 138mg chol., 284mg sodium, 2g carb. (trace sugars, trace fiber), 19g pro.* ***Diabetic Exchanges:*** *3 lean meat, 1½ fat.*

HEALTH TIP *Cooking the shrimp in olive oil instead of butter saves about 3 grams of saturated fat per serving.*

ONE-POT CHICKEN
PESTO PASTA

SPAGHETTI SQUASH LO MEIN

SPAGHETTI SQUASH LO MEIN

My colorful lo mein is a lighter version of the classic Chinese dish that everyone at our table loves. Try it with a squirt of spicy Sriracha.
—**LOANNE CHIU** FORT WORTH, TX

START TO FINISH: 30 MIN.
MAKES: 4 SERVINGS

- 1 **small spaghetti squash (about 2 pounds)**
- 2 **tablespoons sesame oil, divided**
- 1 **package (12 ounces) fully cooked roasted garlic chicken sausage links or flavor of choice, sliced**
- 2½ **cups julienned carrots**
- 2½ **cups shredded red cabbage**
- ¼ **teaspoon salt**
- ⅛ **teaspoon pepper**
- ¼ **cup chopped fresh cilantro Reduced-sodium soy sauce and Sriracha Asian hot chili sauce, optional**

1. Halve squash lengthwise; discard seeds. Place squash on a microwave-safe plate, cut side down; microwave on high until tender, 13-16 minutes. Cool slightly. Separate strands with a fork.
2. In a large skillet, heat 1 teaspoon oil over medium-high heat; saute sausage until browned, 4-6 minutes. Remove from pan.
3. In same pan, heat 2 teaspoons oil over medium-high heat; saute carrots and cabbage until crisp-tender, 4-6 minutes. Stir in salt and pepper. Add squash, sausage and remaining oil; toss and heat through. Sprinkle with cilantro. If desired, serve with soy sauce and chili sauce.
NOTE *This recipe was tested in an 1,100-watt microwave.*
PER SERVING *1½ cups: 316 cal., 15g fat (3g sat. fat), 70mg chol., 731mg sodium, 29g carb. (6g sugars, 7g fiber), 18g pro.* **Diabetic Exchanges:** *2 lean meat, 1½ starch, 1½ fat, 1 vegetable.*

FETTUCCINE WITH SEA SCALLOPS

When we decided to lose weight, my husband and I tried this recipe and loved it so much we had it every Tuesday. He'd fix it on the nights I was running late.
—**DONNA THOMPSON** LARAMIE, WY

START TO FINISH: 30 MIN.
MAKES: 2 SERVINGS

- 4 **ounces uncooked fettuccine**
- 1 **tablespoon olive oil**
- ½ **medium sweet red pepper, julienned**
- 1 **garlic clove, minced**
- ½ **teaspoon grated lemon peel**
- ¼ **teaspoon crushed red pepper flakes**
- ½ **cup reduced-sodium chicken broth**
- ¼ **cup white wine or additional broth**
- 1 **tablespoon lemon juice**
- 6 **sea scallops (about ¾ pound)**
- 2 **teaspoons grated Parmesan cheese**

1. Cook fettuccine according to package directions; drain.
2. Meanwhile, in a large skillet, heat oil over medium-high heat. Add red pepper, garlic, lemon peel and pepper flakes; cook and stir 2 minutes. Stir in broth, wine and lemon juice. Bring to a boil. Reduce heat; simmer, uncovered, for 5-6 minutes or until the liquid is reduced by half.
3. Cut each scallop horizontally in half; add to pan. Cook, covered, for 4-5 minutes or until scallops are firm and opaque, stirring occasionally. Serve with fettuccine. Sprinkle with cheese.
PER SERVING *421 cal., 10g fat (2g sat. fat), 42mg chol., 861mg sodium, 49g carb. (4g sugars, 3g fiber), 30g pro.*

> **TOP TIP**
>
> ## FARMED SCALLOPS
> Because scallops are filter-feeders that live on plankton, they don't require feeding. Their low environmental impact makes farmed scallops a green choice. They're getting more common in stores.

**Sherri Melotik's
Ham & Veggie Casserole**
PAGE 146

Casseroles & Oven Dishes

You're going to love discovering these casseroles, pizzas, roasted meats and one-dish dinners. Fresh and hot from the oven, these cool-weather classics are the very definition of simple comfort food.

**Ashli Kottwitz's
Chicken Reuben Roll-Ups**
PAGE 144

**Mary Marlowe Leverette's
Mozzarella Corn Bread Pizza**
PAGE 153

**Hiroko Miles'
Artichoke Cod with Sun-Dried
Tomatoes** *PAGE 147*

FREEZE IT

BACON-COLBY LASAGNA

My grandmother loaded her cheesy lasagna with bacon, something she borrowed from carbonara-style pasta. Learning by her side taught me so much.

—**CATHY MCCARTNEY** DAVENPORT, IA

PREP: 30 MIN. • **BAKE:** 45 MIN. + STANDING
MAKES: 2 LASAGNAS (12 SERVINGS EACH)

- 24 uncooked lasagna noodles
- 2 pounds lean ground beef (90% lean)
- 2 medium onions, chopped
- 1½ pounds bacon strips, cooked and crumbled
- 2 cans (15 ounces each) tomato sauce
- 2 cans (14½ ounces each) diced tomatoes, undrained
- 2 tablespoons sugar
- 1 teaspoon salt
- 8 cups shredded Colby-Monterey Jack cheese

1. Preheat oven to 350°. Cook noodles according to package directions for al dente; drain.

2. In a 6-qt. stockpot, cook beef and onions over medium-high heat 10-12 minutes or until beef is no longer pink, breaking up beef into crumbles; drain. Stir in bacon, tomato sauce, tomatoes, sugar and salt; heat through.

3. Spread 1 cup sauce into each of two greased 13x9-in. baking dishes. Layer each dish with four noodles, 1⅔ cups sauce and 1⅓ cups cheese. Repeat layers twice.

4. Bake, covered, for 40 minutes. Uncover; bake 5-10 minutes longer or until bubbly. Let stand 15 minutes before serving.

FREEZE OPTION *Cool unbaked lasagnas; cover and freeze. To use, partially thaw in the refrigerator overnight. Remove from refrigerator 30 minutes before baking. Preheat oven to 350°. Bake the lasagna as directed, increasing time as necessary to heat through and for a thermometer inserted in center to read 165°.*

PER SERVING *1 piece: 357 cal., 18g fat (11g sat. fat), 67mg chol., 744mg sodium, 25g carb. (4g sugars, 2g fiber), 23g pro.*

BUFFALO BLUE CHEESE MEAT LOAF

BUFFALO BLUE CHEESE MEAT LOAF

I made meat loaf with wing sauce for my guy, who prefers food with big flavors. He went crazy for it, and now likes it even more than traditional Buffalo wings!

—**LATESHA HARRIS** BEAVERTON, OR

PREP: 20 MIN. • **BAKE:** 40 MIN.
MAKES: 4 SERVINGS

- 1 large egg, lightly beaten
- 1 small onion, finely chopped
- ¼ cup panko (Japanese) bread crumbs
- ¼ cup Buffalo wing sauce
- 1 teaspoon dried oregano
- ½ teaspoon pepper
- 1 pound ground beef

TOPPING
- ¼ cup Buffalo wing sauce
- ¼ cup crumbled blue cheese

1. Preheat oven to 350°. In a large bowl, combine the first six ingredients. Add beef; mix lightly but thoroughly. Shape into an 8x4-in. loaf in a greased 11x7-in. baking dish.

2. Bake 20 minutes. Spread wing sauce over top; sprinkle with cheese. Bake 20-30 minutes longer or until a thermometer reads 160°. Let stand 5 minutes before slicing.

PER SERVING *1 slice: 286 cal., 17g fat (7g sat. fat), 123mg chol., 1093mg sodium, 7g carb. (1g sugars, 1g fiber), 24g pro.*

EAT SMART **FAST FIX** ▶

GREEK FISH BAKE

As a military spouse living overseas, I got the chance to try many styles of cooking. Here's a Mediterranean-inspired recipe that we still love today.

—**STACEY BOYD** SPRINGFIELD, VA

START TO FINISH: 30 MIN.
MAKES: 4 SERVINGS

- 4 cod fillets (6 ounces each)
- 2 tablespoons olive oil
- ¼ teaspoon salt
- ⅛ teaspoon pepper
- 1 small green pepper, cut into thin strips
- ½ small red onion, thinly sliced
- ¼ cup pitted Greek olives, sliced
- 1 can (8 ounces) tomato sauce
- ¼ cup crumbled feta cheese

1. Preheat oven to 400°. Place cod in a greased 13x9-in. baking dish. Brush with oil; sprinkle with salt and pepper. Top with green pepper, onion and Greek olives.

2. Pour tomato sauce over the top; sprinkle with cheese. Bake until fish just begins to flake easily with a fork, 15-20 minutes.

PER SERVING *1 fillet with toppings: 246 cal., 12g fat (2g sat. fat), 68mg chol., 706mg sodium, 6g carb. (2g sugars, 2g fiber), 29g pro.* **Diabetic Exchanges:** *4 lean meat, 1½ fat, 1 vegetable.*

STUFFED IOWA CHOPS

TARRAGON-DIJON PORK CHOPS

For my smoky chops, I add tarragon for a hint of herbal flavor. If you like a lot of sauce, double or triple those ingredients.

—JULIE DANLER BEL AIRE, KS

START TO FINISH: 30 MIN.
MAKES: 4 SERVINGS

- 4 boneless pork loin chops (¾ inch thick and 6 ounces each)
- ½ teaspoon garlic powder
- ¼ teaspoon pepper
- 2 tablespoons olive oil, divided
- 1 pound sliced fresh mushrooms
- 4 green onions, chopped
- ¼ cup Dijon mustard
- 1 to 1½ teaspoons chipotle or other hot pepper sauce
- 1 tablespoon red wine, optional
- 1 tablespoon minced fresh tarragon

1. Preheat oven to 400°. Sprinkle chops with garlic powder and pepper. In a large ovenproof skillet, heat 1 tablespoon oil over medium heat. Brown chops on both sides; remove from pan.

2. In same pan, heat remaining oil over medium-high. Add mushrooms and onions; cook and stir 3 minutes. Place chops over mushroom mixture. Bake, uncovered, 8-10 minutes or until a thermometer in pork reads 145°.

3. In a small bowl, mix the mustard, pepper sauce and, if desired, wine; spread over chops. Bake 2 minutes longer. Sprinkle with tarragon.

PER SERVING *1 pork chop with ⅓ cup mushroom mixture: 334 cal., 17g fat (5g sat. fat), 82mg chol., 417mg sodium, 8g carb. (3g sugars, 2g fiber), 37g pro.* **Diabetic Exchanges:** *5 lean meat, 1½ fat, ½ starch.*

TOP TIP

OLIVE OIL

Common olive oil works better for cooking at high heat than virgin or extra-virgin oil. These higher grades have full flavor for cold foods, but they smoke at lower temperatures.

STUFFED IOWA CHOPS

These hearty chops satisfy big appetites at our house. If the meat is too thin to stuff, shingle the chops and place stuffing in between before baking.

—JUDITH SMITH DES MOINES, IA

PREP: 20 MIN. ● **BAKE:** 50 MIN.
MAKES: 4 SERVINGS

- 4 bone-in pork loin chops (1½ inches thick and 8 ounces each)
- 1 tablespoon canola oil
- 1 tablespoon finely chopped onion
- 1 tablespoon minced fresh parsley
- 1 tablespoon 2% milk
- ¼ teaspoon salt
- ¼ teaspoon rubbed sage
- ¼ teaspoon pepper
- 1 cup chopped peeled apple
- 1 cup whole kernel corn
- 1 cup dry bread crumbs

SAUCE
- ⅓ cup honey
- 3 to 4 tablespoons Dijon mustard
- ¾ teaspoon minced fresh rosemary or ⅛ teaspoon dried rosemary, crushed

1. Preheat oven to 350°. Cut a pocket in each pork chop by slicing almost to the bone. In a large skillet, heat oil over medium heat. Brown chops on each side; cool slightly.

2. In a bowl, mix onion, parsley, milk and seasonings. Add apple, corn and bread crumbs; toss to combine. Spoon into pork chops; place in a greased 13x9-in. baking dish.

3. In a small bowl, mix the sauce ingredients; reserve half of the sauce for brushing. Pour remaining sauce over pork chops. Bake, uncovered, 50-60 minutes or until a thermometer inserted in stuffing reads 165°, brushing occasionally with reserved sauce during the last 20 minutes.

PER SERVING *1 stuffed pork chop: 601 cal., 24g fat (8g sat. fat), 112mg chol., 875mg sodium, 54g carb. (31g sugars, 3g fiber), 41g pro.*

Oh My, Potpie!

Nick Iverson, our Test Kitchen's lead test cook, shows you how to make an amazing potpie on the fly. Even the gorgeous crust is easy!

**PUFF PASTRY
CHICKEN POTPIE**

PUFF PASTRY CHICKEN POTPIE

When my wife is craving comfort food, I whip up my chicken potpie. It's easy to make, sticks to your ribs and delivers soul-satisfying flavor.

—**NICK IVERSON** MILWAUKEE, WI

PREP: 45 MIN. • **BAKE:** 45 MIN. + STANDING
MAKES: 8 SERVINGS

- 1 **package (17.3 ounces) frozen puff pastry, thawed**
- 2 **pounds boneless skinless chicken breasts, cut into 1-inch pieces**
- 1 **teaspoon salt, divided**
- 1 **teaspoon pepper, divided**
- 4 **tablespoons butter, divided**
- 1 **large onion, chopped**
- 2 **garlic cloves, minced**
- 1 **teaspoon minced fresh thyme or ¼ teaspoon dried thyme**
- 1 **teaspoon fresh sage or ¼ teaspoon rubbed sage**
- ½ **cup all-purpose flour**
- 2 **cups chicken broth**
- 1 **cup plus 1 tablespoon half-and-half cream, divided**
- 2 **cups frozen mixed vegetables (about 10 ounces)**
- 1 **tablespoon lemon juice**
- 1 **large egg yolk**

PER SERVING *1 piece: 523 cal., 25g fat (10g sat. fat), 118mg chol., 829mg sodium, 42g carb. (4g sugars, 6g fiber), 30g pro.*

MAKE PERFECT POTPIE

1. **CUT** Roll each pastry sheet into a 12x10-in. rectangle. Cut one sheet crosswise into six 2-in. strips; cut the remaining sheet lengthwise into five 2-in. strips. On a baking sheet, closely weave strips to make a lattice. Freeze while making filling.

2. **SEAR** Toss chicken with ½ teaspoon each salt and pepper. In a large skillet over medium-high heat, brown chicken in 1 tablespoon butter, 5-7 minutes. Remove from pan.

3. **SAUTE** In same skillet, heat the remaining butter over medium-high; saute onion 5-7 minutes. Add garlic and herbs; cook 1 minute. Add flour; cook 1 minute. Stir in broth and 1 cup cream. Bring to a boil, stirring constantly; cook 2 minutes. Add the vegetables, lemon juice, chicken and remaining salt and pepper; return mixture to a boil.

4. **BAKE** Transfer to greased 2-qt. oblong baking dish. Top with lattice; trim to fit. Whisk yolk and remaining cream; brush over top. Bake at 400° for 45-55 minutes.

CHICKEN TAMALE BAKE

When I serve this Mexican-style casserole, everyone scrapes their plates clean. Offer fresh toppings like green onions, tomatoes and avocado.

—JENNIFER STOWELL MONTEZUMA, IA

PREP: 10 MIN. • **BAKE:** 25 MIN. + STANDING
MAKES: 8 SERVINGS

- 1 large egg, lightly beaten
- 1 can (14¾ ounces) cream-style corn
- 1 package (8½ ounces) corn bread/muffin mix
- 1 can (4 ounces) chopped green chilies
- ⅓ cup 2% milk
- ¼ cup shredded Mexican cheese blend

TOPPING

- 2 cups coarsely shredded cooked chicken
- 1 can (10 ounces) enchilada sauce
- 1 teaspoon ground cumin
- ½ teaspoon onion powder
- 1¾ cups shredded Mexican cheese blend
  Chopped green onions, tomatoes and avocado, optional

1. Preheat oven to 400°. In a large bowl, combine the first six ingredients; stir just until the dry ingredients are moistened. Transfer to a greased 13x9-in. baking dish. Bake 15-18 minutes or until light golden brown and a toothpick inserted in center comes out clean.
2. In a large skillet, combine chicken, enchilada sauce, cumin and onion powder; bring to a boil, stirring occasionally. Reduce heat; simmer, uncovered, 5 minutes. Spread over corn bread layer; sprinkle with cheese.
3. Bake 10-12 minutes longer or until cheese is melted. Let stand 10 minutes before serving. If desired, top with green onions, tomatoes and avocado.
PER SERVING *1 piece (calculated without optional toppings): 364 cal., 17g fat (7g sat. fat), 81mg chol., 851mg sodium, 35g carb. (9g sugars, 4g fiber), 21g pro.*

HOISIN PORK TENDERLOIN

HOISIN PORK TENDERLOIN

Ramen noodles are anything but college-casual when they're served with saucy pork tenderloin. Our guests go nuts when we sit down to this Asian-style meal.

—CONNIE KELLER LAKE OZARK, MO

START TO FINISH: 30 MIN.
MAKES: 4 SERVINGS

- ⅓ cup hoisin sauce
- 3 tablespoons reduced-sodium soy sauce
- 3 tablespoons sugar
- 3 garlic cloves, minced
  Dash crushed red pepper flakes
- 1 pork tenderloin (1 pound)
- ¼ cup water
- 2 tablespoons butter
- 2 packages (3 ounces each) ramen noodles or 2 cups hot cooked rice
  Sliced green onions

1. Preheat oven to 475°. Off the heat, mix first five ingredients in a small saucepan. Place tenderloin on a greased rack in a foil-lined 15x10x1-in. pan; brush with ¼ cup hoisin mixture. Roast until a thermometer reads 145°, 15-20 minutes.
2. Stir water into remaining hoisin mixture; bring to a boil. Reduce heat; simmer, uncovered, to allow flavors to blend, about 5 minutes, stirring occasionally. Remove from heat; stir in butter. Keep warm.
3. Remove pork from oven; let stand for 5 minutes before slicing. Cook the noodles according to package directions, omitting the seasoning packets; drain. Serve with pork; top with sauce and green onions.
PER SERVING *3 ounces cooked pork with ½ cup noodles and 2 tablespoons sauce: 458 cal., 17g fat (9g sat. fat), 80mg chol., 1010mg sodium, 45g carb. (15g sugars, 1g fiber), 28g pro.*

PASTA FAGIOLI AL FORNO

CHICKEN REUBEN ROLL-UPS

My husband loves Reuben sandwiches and anything with chicken, so I combined his two favorites into a fun roll-up.

—**ASHLI KOTTWITZ** HERMITAGE, TN

START TO FINISH: 30 MIN.
MAKES: 2 SERVINGS

- 2 **slices swirled rye and pumpernickel bread**
- 2 **boneless skinless chicken breast halves (4 ounces each)**
- ¼ **teaspoon garlic salt**
- ¼ **teaspoon pepper**
- 2 **slices Swiss cheese**
- 2 **slices deli corned beef**
- 2 **tablespoons Thousand Island salad dressing**
  Additional Thousand Island salad dressing, optional

1. Preheat oven to 425°. Tear bread into 2-in. pieces; place in a blender. Cover and pulse to form coarse crumbs; transfer to a shallow bowl.
2. Pound chicken breasts with a meat mallet to ¼-in. thickness; sprinkle with garlic salt and pepper. Top with cheese and corned beef. Roll up the chicken from a short side; secure with toothpicks. Brush outsides with salad dressing; roll in bread crumbs.
3. Place roll-ups on a greased baking sheet, seam side down. Bake 20-25 minutes or until chicken is no longer pink. Discard toothpicks; if desired, serve with additional dressing.

PER SERVING *1 roll-up (calculated without additional dressing): 326 cal., 13g fat (4g sat. fat), 89mg chol., 790mg sodium, 18g carb. (3g sugars, 2g fiber), 32g pro.*

HEALTH TIP *A traditional Reuben sandwich can be upwards of 700 calories, 40 grams of fat and nearly 3,000 milligrams of sodium. This roll-up has all the flavor without requiring a post-dinner workout.*

PASTA FAGIOLI AL FORNO

The name of this Italian-inspired dish means baked pasta with beans. But my busy family translates it as "super-satisfying dinner."
—**CINDY PRELLER** GRAYSLAKE, IL

PREP: 35 MIN. • **BAKE:** 30 MIN. + STANDING
MAKES: 8 SERVINGS

- 3 **cups uncooked penne pasta (about 12 ounces)**
- 1 **can (28 ounces) whole plum tomatoes**
- 1 **pound bulk Italian sausage**
- 1 **medium onion, chopped**
- 1 **medium carrot, chopped**
- 1 **celery rib, chopped**
- 4 **garlic cloves, minced**
- 2 **tablespoons tomato paste**
- 1 **teaspoon dried oregano**
- ½ **teaspoon salt**
- ½ **teaspoon dried basil**
- ¼ **teaspoon crushed red pepper flakes**
- ¼ **teaspoon pepper**
- 1 **can (15 ounces) cannellini beans, rinsed and drained**
- ½ **cup grated Parmesan cheese, divided**
- ½ **cup minced fresh parsley, divided**
- 2 **cups shredded fontina or provolone cheese**

1. Preheat oven to 350°. Cook pasta according to package directions for al dente; drain.

2. Meanwhile, drain the tomatoes, reserving the juices; coarsely chop tomatoes. In a 6-qt. stockpot, cook and crumble sausage with onion, carrot, celery and garlic over medium-high heat until no longer pink, 6-8 minutes; drain. Stir in tomato paste, seasonings, chopped tomatoes and reserved juices; bring to a boil. Reduce heat; simmer, uncovered, 10 minutes.
3. Stir in beans and ¼ cup each Parmesan cheese and parsley. Stir in pasta. Transfer to a greased 13x9-in. baking dish; sprinkle with fontina cheese and remaining Parmesan.
4. Bake, covered, 20 minutes. Uncover; bake until cheese is melted, 10-15 minutes. Sprinkle with remaining parsley.

FREEZE OPTION *Cool unbaked casserole; cover and freeze. To use, partially thaw in the refrigerator overnight. Remove from refrigerator 30 minutes before baking. Preheat the oven to 350°. Bake as directed, increasing time as necessary to heat through and for a thermometer inserted in center to read 165°.*

PER SERVING *440 cal., 23g fat (10g sat. fat), 66mg chol., 1029mg sodium, 37g carb. (5g sugars, 6g fiber), 22g pro.*

QUINOA & BLACK BEAN-
STUFFED PEPPERS

QUINOA & BLACK BEAN-STUFFED PEPPERS

If you're thinking about a meatless meal, give these no-fuss peppers a try. They come together with a just few ingredients and put a tasty spin on low-fat dinner.

—CINDY REAMS PHILIPSBURG, PA

START TO FINISH: 30 MIN.
MAKES: 4 SERVINGS

- 1½ cups water
- 1 cup quinoa, rinsed
- 4 large green peppers
- 1 jar (16 ounces) chunky salsa, divided
- 1 can (15 ounces) black beans, rinsed and drained
- ½ cup reduced-fat ricotta cheese
- ½ cup shredded Monterey Jack cheese, divided

1. Preheat oven to 400°. In a small saucepan, bring water to a boil. Add quinoa. Reduce heat; simmer, covered, 10-12 minutes or until the water is absorbed.
2. Meanwhile, cut and discard tops from peppers; remove seeds. Place in a greased 8-in. square baking dish, cut side down. Microwave, uncovered, on high 3-4 minutes or until crisp-tender. Turn peppers cut side up.
3. Reserve ⅓ cup salsa; add remaining salsa to quinoa. Stir in beans, ricotta cheese and ¼ cup Jack cheese. Spoon mixture into peppers; sprinkle with remaining cheese. Bake, uncovered, 10-15 minutes or until filling is heated through. Top with reserved salsa.
PER SERVING 1 stuffed pepper: 393 cal., 8g fat (4g sat. fat), 20mg chol., 774mg sodium, 59g carb. (10g sugars, 10g fiber), 18g pro.

GARLIC & HERB STEAK PIZZA

We crave pizza that's fast, cheesy and original. This one with steak and veggies is perfect for folks who like their pie loaded with toppings.

—JADE FEARS GRAND RIDGE, FL

START TO FINISH: 30 MIN.
MAKES: 6 SERVINGS

- 1 beef top sirloin steak (¾ inch thick and 1 pound)
- ¾ teaspoon salt
- ¾ teaspoon pepper
- 1 tablespoon olive oil
- 1 prebaked 12-inch thin pizza crust
- ½ cup garlic-herb spreadable cheese (about 3 ounces)
- 2 cups chopped fresh spinach
- 1 cup sliced red onion
- 1 cup sliced fresh mushrooms
- 1½ cups shredded part-skim mozzarella cheese

1. Preheat oven to 450°. Season steak with salt and pepper. In a large skillet, heat oil over medium heat. Add the steak; cook 5-6 minutes on each side or until a thermometer reads 145° for medium-rare doneness. Remove from the pan.
2. Meanwhile, place pizza crust on an ungreased baking sheet; spread with garlic-herb cheese. Top with spinach and onion.
3. Cut steak into slices; arrange on pizza. Top with mushrooms and cheese. Bake 8-10 minutes or until cheese is melted. Cut into 12 pieces.
PER SERVING 2 pieces: 440 cal., 23g fat (11g sat. fat), 72mg chol., 926mg sodium, 29g carb. (3g sugars, 2g fiber), 30g pro.

PUMPKIN SEED BAKED CHICKEN

For a new coating on baked chicken, I use pumpkin seeds and cheese crackers to make it crunchy on the outside and tender on the inside.

—NANCY HEISHMAN LAS VEGAS, NV

PREP: 20 MIN. ● **BAKE:** 30 MIN.
MAKES: 4 SERVINGS

- ½ cup finely crushed cheese crackers (about 1 cup whole)
- 2 teaspoons paprika
- ½ teaspoon salt
- ½ teaspoon garlic powder
- ¼ teaspoon pepper
- ⅔ cup salted pumpkin seeds or pepitas, divided
- 1 large egg
- 3 tablespoons honey
- 2 tablespoons lemon juice
- 4 boneless skinless chicken breast halves (6 ounces each)

1. Preheat oven to 350°. Place first five ingredients and 3 tablespoons of the pumpkin seeds in a shallow bowl. Finely chop remaining pumpkin seeds; stir into cracker mixture. In another shallow bowl, whisk together egg, honey and lemon juice. Dip both sides of chicken in egg mixture, then in crumb mixture, patting to adhere.
2. Bake on a greased baking sheet until a thermometer reads 165°, 30-35 minutes.
PER SERVING 1 chicken breast half: 378 cal., 16g fat (4g sat. fat), 118mg chol., 525mg sodium, 16g carb. (7g sugars, 2g fiber), 42g pro.

FAST FIX ▶

HAM & VEGGIE CASSEROLE

I've paired ham with broccoli and cauliflower for years. To complete this casserole dinner, I serve it with warm dinner rolls.

—**SHERRI MELOTIK** OAK CREEK, WI

START TO FINISH: 30 MIN.
MAKES: 4 SERVINGS

- 1 package (16 ounces) frozen broccoli florets
- 1 package (16 ounces) frozen cauliflower
- 2 teaspoons plus 2 tablespoons butter, divided
- ¼ cup seasoned bread crumbs
- 2 tablespoons all-purpose flour
- 1½ cups 2% milk
- ¾ cup shredded sharp cheddar cheese
- ½ cup grated Parmesan cheese
- 1½ cups cubed fully cooked ham (about 8 ounces)
- ¼ teaspoon pepper

1. Preheat oven to 425°. Cook the broccoli and cauliflower according to package directions; drain.
2. Meanwhile, in a small skillet, melt 2 teaspoons butter. Add bread crumbs; cook and stir over medium heat 2-3 minutes or until lightly toasted. Remove from heat.
3. In a large saucepan, melt remaining butter over medium heat. Stir in flour until smooth; gradually whisk in milk. Bring to a boil, stirring constantly; cook and stir 1-2 minutes or until thickened. Remove from heat; stir in cheeses until blended. Stir in ham, pepper and vegetables.
4. Transfer to a greased 8-in. square baking dish. Sprinkle with toasted crumbs. Bake, uncovered, 10-15 minutes or until heated through.
PER SERVING *1½ cups: 420 cal., 23g fat (13g sat. fat), 89mg chol., 1233mg sodium, 25g carb. (10g sugars, 6g fiber), 28g pro.*

SPINACH & CHICKEN PHYLLO PIE

SPINACH & CHICKEN PHYLLO PIE

For a showstopping lunch, I make chicken pie with phyllo and spinach. Even our kids go for it. It's so delicious served with a minty fruit salad.

—**KATIE FERRIER** HOUSTON, TX

PREP: 35 MIN. • **BAKE:** 35 MIN.
MAKES: 8 SERVINGS

- 2 pounds ground chicken
- 1 large onion, chopped
- 1 teaspoon pepper
- 1 teaspoon dried oregano
- ¾ teaspoon salt
- ½ teaspoon ground nutmeg
- ¼ teaspoon crushed red pepper flakes
- 3 packages (10 ounces each) frozen chopped spinach, thawed and squeezed dry
- 4 large eggs, lightly beaten
- 3 cups crumbled feta cheese
- 20 sheets phyllo dough (14x9-inch size)
  Cooking spray

1. Preheat oven to 375°. In a large skillet, cook chicken and onion over medium-high heat 7-9 minutes or until chicken is no longer pink, breaking up chicken into crumbles; drain. Stir in seasonings. Add spinach; cook and stir until liquid is evaporated. Transfer to a large bowl; cool slightly. Stir in beaten eggs and cheese.
2. Layer 10 sheets of phyllo dough in a greased 13x9-in. baking dish, spritzing each with cooking spray. (Keep the remaining phyllo covered with plastic wrap and a damp towel to prevent it from drying out.) Spread spinach mixture over phyllo. Top with the remaining sheets of phyllo, spritzing each with cooking spray. Cut into eight rectangles.
3. Bake, uncovered, 35-40 minutes or until golden brown. If necessary, recut rectangles before serving.
PER SERVING *1 piece: 442 cal., 23g fat (8g sat. fat), 191mg chol., 921mg sodium, 25g carb. (3g sugars, 6g fiber), 35g pro.*

ARTICHOKE COD WITH SUN-DRIED TOMATOES

Cod is a great break from really rich dishes around the holidays. I like to serve it over a bed of greens, pasta or quinoa. A squeeze of lemon gives it another layer of freshness.

—HIROKO MILES EL DORADO HILLS, CA

START TO FINISH: 30 MIN.
MAKES: 6 SERVINGS

- 1 can (14 ounces) quartered water-packed artichoke hearts, drained
- ½ cup julienned soft sun-dried tomatoes (not packed in oil)
- 2 green onions, chopped
- 3 tablespoons olive oil
- 1 garlic clove, minced
- 6 cod fillets (6 ounces each)
- 1 teaspoon salt
- ½ teaspoon pepper
  Salad greens and lemon wedges, optional

1. Preheat oven to 400°. In a small bowl, combine first five ingredients; toss to combine.
2. Sprinkle both sides of cod with salt and pepper; place in a 13x9-in. baking dish coated with cooking spray. Top with artichoke mixture.
3. Bake, uncovered, 15-20 minutes or until fish just begins to flake easily with a fork. If desired, serve over greens with lemon wedges.
NOTE *This recipe was tested with sun-dried tomatoes that can be used without soaking. When using other sun-dried tomatoes that are not oil-packed, cover with boiling water and let stand until softened. Drain before using.*
PER SERVING *1 fillet with ⅓ cup artichoke mixture: 231 cal., 8g fat (1g sat. fat), 65mg chol., 665mg sodium, 9g carb. (3g sugars, 2g fiber), 29g pro.*
Diabetic Exchanges: *4 lean meat, 1½ fat, 1 vegetable.*

TRIPLE-STUFFED SWEET POTATOES

My kids love sweet potatoes stuffed with leftover turkey and dressing. We enjoy being in the kitchen together, each of us making our own potato boats.

—ANE BURKE BELLA VISTA, AR

START TO FINISH: 30 MIN.
MAKES: 8 SERVINGS

- 4 medium sweet potatoes (about 2½ pounds)
- 2 tablespoons butter, softened
- 2 tablespoons brown sugar
- ¾ teaspoon salt
- ¼ teaspoon pepper
- ¼ cup whole-berry cranberry sauce
- 3 cups cubed cooked turkey
- ½ cup miniature marshmallows
- ½ cup chopped pecans
- ½ cup flaked coconut

1. Preheat oven to 425°. Scrub and pierce sweet potatoes with a fork; place on a microwave-safe plate. Microwave, uncovered, on high 12-14 minutes or until tender, turning once.
2. When cool enough to handle, cut each potato lengthwise in half. Scoop out pulp, leaving ¼-in.-thick shells. Place potato shells in a 15x10x1-in. baking pan.
3. In a large bowl, mash pulp with butter, brown sugar, salt and pepper; stir in cranberry sauce. Fold in turkey, marshmallows and pecans; spoon into shells. Sprinkle with coconut. Bake 8-10 minutes or until heated through.
NOTE *This recipe was tested in an 1,100-watt microwave.*
PER SERVING *1 stuffed sweet potato half: 317 cal., 12g fat (5g sat. fat), 61mg chol., 330mg sodium, 36g carb. (19g sugars, 4g fiber), 18g pro.*

TRIPLE-STUFFED
SWEET POTATOES

ROASTED VEGGIE STRUDEL

FAST FIX ▶

SPINACH & GOUDA-STUFFED PORK CUTLETS

This started as a restaurant copycat dish at home. Cheese just oozes out of the center, and the mustard lends a lot of flavor.
—JOAN OAKLAND TROY, MT

START TO FINISH: 30 MIN.
MAKES: 2 SERVINGS

- 3 tablespoons dry bread crumbs
- 2 tablespoons grated Parmesan cheese
- 2 pork sirloin cutlets (3 ounces each)
- ¼ teaspoon salt
- ⅛ teaspoon pepper
- 2 slices smoked Gouda cheese (about 2 ounces)
- 2 cups fresh baby spinach
- 2 tablespoons horseradish mustard

1. Preheat oven to 400°. In a shallow bowl, mix bread crumbs and Parmesan cheese.
2. Sprinkle tops of cutlets with salt and pepper. Layer one end of each with Gouda cheese and spinach. Fold the cutlets in half, enclosing filling; secure with toothpicks. Brush with mustard; dip in bread crumb mixture, patting to help coating adhere.
3. Place on a greased foil-lined baking sheet. Bake 12-15 minutes or until golden brown and pork is tender. Discard toothpicks before serving.
PER SERVING 1 stuffed cutlet: 299 cal., 16g fat (7g sat. fat), 91mg chol., 898mg sodium, 10g carb. (2g sugars, 2g fiber), 30g pro.

ROASTED VEGGIE STRUDEL

Roasted Brussels sprouts and potatoes go so well with bacon and Brie in my shortcut strudel. I leave the potato skin on for extra flavor and texture.
—CAROLE HOLT MENDOTA HEIGHTS, MN

PREP: 40 MIN. + COOLING • **BAKE:** 20 MIN.
MAKES: 4 SERVINGS

- 2 cups Brussels sprouts, quartered
- 1 small Yukon Gold potato, cut into ½-inch cubes
- 1 tablespoon olive oil
- ½ teaspoon garlic pepper blend
- ¼ teaspoon salt
- ⅓ cup julienned oil-packed sun-dried tomatoes
- 2 green onions, chopped
- 1 tube (8 ounces) refrigerated crescent rolls
- 4 ounces Brie cheese, cut into ½-in. cubes
- 5 bacon strips, cooked and crumbled
- 1 large egg
- 3 tablespoons pine nuts

1. Preheat oven to 425°. Toss the first five ingredients; spread in a greased 15x10x1-in. pan. Roast until tender, about 15 minutes, stirring once.
2. Drain tomatoes, reserving 1 tablespoon oil for egg wash. Add tomatoes and green onions to roasted vegetables; cool. Reduce oven setting to 350°.
3. On a lightly floured surface, unroll the crescent dough into one long rectangle; pinch to seal perforations. Roll dough into a 14x9-in. rectangle; transfer to a large baking sheet. Stir cheese and bacon into vegetables; spoon lengthwise down center third of rectangle. On each long side, cut 1-in. strips at an angle to within ½ inch of filling. Fold one strip from each side over filling, pinching ends to join; repeat. Seal ends of braid.
4. Whisk together egg and reserved oil; brush over strudel. Sprinkle with pine nuts. Bake until golden brown, 20-25 minutes.
PER SERVING 1 piece: 532 cal., 35g fat (12g sat. fat), 62mg chol., 1035mg sodium, 36g carb. (6g sugars, 3g fiber), 18g pro.

SPINACH & GOUDA-STUFFED PORK CUTLETS

OVEN-FRIED
FISH & CHIPS

ROSEMARY-LEMON CHICKEN THIGHS

A cooking show inspired me to create this lemony chicken.

—**JENN TIDWELL** FAIR OAKS, CA

START TO FINISH: 30 MIN.
MAKES: 4 SERVINGS

- 2 **bacon strips, chopped**
- 1 **teaspoon minced fresh rosemary or ¼ teaspoon dried rosemary, crushed**
- 4 **boneless, skin-on chicken thighs**
- ⅛ **teaspoon pepper**
  Dash salt
- ⅓ **cup chicken broth**
- 3 **tablespoons lemon juice**

1. In a large skillet, cook and stir bacon and rosemary over medium heat until bacon is crisp. Using a slotted spoon, remove bacon to paper towels; reserve drippings in pan.
2. Sprinkle chicken with pepper and salt; brown in drippings on both sides. Cook, covered, skin side down, over medium heat 4-6 minutes or until a thermometer reads 170°. Remove from pan; keep warm. Pour off drippings from pan.
3. Add broth and lemon juice to same skillet. Bring to a boil, scraping to loosen browned bits from pan; cook until liquid is reduced by half. Spoon over chicken; sprinkle with bacon.
NOTE *Ask your butcher to remove the bones from your chicken thighs but to leave the skin intact.*
PER SERVING *1 chicken thigh with 1 tablespoon sauce and 2 teaspoons cooked bacon: 286 cal., 20g fat (6g sat. fat), 91mg chol., 279mg sodium, 1g carb. (1g sugars, 0 fiber), 24g pro.*

COOK & FREEZE BACON

I fry 2 pounds or more of bacon at a time, drain the slices well, then freeze them. The slices don't stick together, so it's easy to remove a few from the bag for a sandwich or to crumble for a recipe.

—**SHIRLEY M.** GOLDSBORO, NC

OVEN-FRIED FISH & CHIPS

My baked fish is a shoo-in when you want fish and chips without the frying mess. I dare say they're a little upgrade from the English pub classic.

—**REENI PISANO** WAPPINGERS FALLS, NY

PREP: 15 MIN. • **BAKE:** 55 MIN.
MAKES: 4 SERVINGS

- ⅓ **cup mayonnaise**
- 2 **tablespoons dill pickle relish or chopped dill pickle**
- 2 **teaspoons grated lemon peel**

FISH AND POTATOES

- 1½ **pounds baking potatoes (about 3 medium)**
- 2 **teaspoons olive oil**
- ¾ **teaspoon kosher salt, divided**
- ½ **teaspoon coarsely ground pepper, divided**
- ½ **cup panko (Japanese) bread crumbs**
- ¼ **cup seasoned bread crumbs**
- 4 **cod fillets (4 ounces each)**
- 2 **tablespoons mayonnaise**
- 2 **tablespoons grated Parmesan cheese**
- 2 **teaspoons chopped fresh parsley**
  Malt vinegar, optional

1. For tartar sauce, in a small bowl, mix mayonnaise, relish and lemon peel. Refrigerate until serving.
2. Preheat oven to 400°. Cut potatoes lengthwise into 1-in.-thick wedges; toss with oil, ½ teaspoon salt and ¼ teaspoon pepper. Spread evenly in a greased 15x10x1-in. baking pan. Roast 40-45 minutes or until golden brown, stirring occasionally.
3. Meanwhile, in a small skillet, toast panko bread crumbs over medium-low heat 5-7 minutes or until lightly browned, stirring occasionally. Transfer to a shallow bowl; stir in seasoned bread crumbs.
4. Sprinkle cod with the remaining salt and pepper; spread top and sides of fish with mayonnaise. Dip in crumb mixture to cover mayonnaise, pressing firmly to help adhere. Place in a greased 15x10x1-in. baking pan, crumb side up. Sprinkle with any remaining crumb mixture. Bake 12-15 minutes or until fish just begins to flake easily with a fork.
5. Toss potatoes with cheese and parsley. Serve fish and potatoes with tartar sauce and, if desired, vinegar.
PER SERVING *equals 475 cal., 24g fat (4g sat. fat), 54mg chol., 789mg sodium, 40g carb., 5g fiber, 23g pro.*

My colorful boats with quinoa, chickpeas and pumpkin seeds use delicata squash, a winter squash that's cream-colored with green stripes. In a pinch, acorn squash will do. —**LAUREN KNOELKE** MILWAUKEE, WI

QUINOA-STUFFED SQUASH BOATS

QUINOA-STUFFED SQUASH BOATS

START TO FINISH: 30 MIN.
MAKES: 8 SERVINGS

- 4 delicata squash (about 12 ounces each)
- 3 teaspoons olive oil, divided
- ⅛ teaspoon pepper
- 1 teaspoon salt, divided
- 1½ cups vegetable broth
- 1 cup quinoa, rinsed
- 1 can (15 ounces) chickpeas, rinsed and drained
- ¼ cup dried cranberries
- 1 green onion, thinly sliced
- 1 teaspoon minced fresh sage
- ½ teaspoon grated lemon peel
- 1 teaspoon lemon juice
- ½ cup crumbled goat cheese
- ¼ cup salted pumpkin seeds or pepitas, toasted

1. Preheat oven to 450°. Cut each squash lengthwise in half; remove and discard seeds. Lightly brush cut sides with 1 teaspoon oil; sprinkle with pepper and ½ teaspoon salt. Place on a baking sheet, cut side down. Bake 15-20 minutes or until tender.

2. Meanwhile, in a large saucepan, bring broth and quinoa to a boil. Reduce heat; simmer, covered, 12-15 minutes or until liquid is absorbed.

3. Stir in chickpeas, cranberries, green onion, sage, lemon peel, lemon juice and the remaining oil and salt; spoon into squash. Sprinkle with cheese and pumpkin seeds.

PER SERVING *1 stuffed squash half: 275 cal., 8g fat (2g sat. fat), 9mg chol., 591mg sodium, 46g carb. (9g sugars, 10g fiber), 9g pro.* **Diabetic Exchanges:** *3 starch, 1 lean meat, ½ fat.*

TOP TIP

GET TO KNOW QUINOA

Unlike other grains, quinoa is a complete protein. It's an excellent choice for vegetarian and vegan meals, which tend to be low in protein.

FIESTA BEEF & CHEESE SKILLET COBBLER

FIESTA BEEF & CHEESE SKILLET COBBLER

I tweaked my beefy skillet cobbler until it achieved wow status. I must have gotten it right, as it's become a family tradition. Top it off with lettuce, avocado, cherry tomatoes and a dollop of sour cream.

—**GLORIA BRADLEY** NAPERVILLE, IL

PREP: 40 MIN. ● **BAKE:** 15 MIN. + STANDING
MAKES: 8 SERVINGS

- 1 pound ground beef
- 1 can (15 ounces) black beans, rinsed and drained
- 1 can (14½ ounces) diced tomatoes with mild green chilies
- 1 can (10 ounces) enchilada sauce
- 1 teaspoon ground cumin
- 4 tablespoons chopped fresh cilantro or parsley, divided
- 1½ cups biscuit/baking mix
- 1½ cups shredded Colby-Monterey Jack cheese, divided
- 4 bacon strips, cooked and crumbled
- ⅔ cup 2% milk
- 1 large egg, lightly beaten
  Sour cream, optional

1. Preheat oven to 400°. In a 10-in. ovenproof skillet, cook beef over medium heat 5-7 minutes or until no longer pink, breaking into crumbles; drain. Stir in the beans, tomatoes, enchilada sauce and cumin; bring to a boil. Reduce heat; simmer, uncovered, for 20 minutes to allow flavors to blend, stirring occasionally. Stir in 2 tablespoons cilantro.

2. In a bowl, combine baking mix, ½ cup cheese, bacon and remaining cilantro. Add milk and beaten egg; stir just until a soft dough is formed. Spoon over beef mixture.

3. Bake, uncovered, 13-15 minutes or until golden brown. Sprinkle with remaining cheese; bake 2-3 minutes longer or until cheese is melted. Let stand 10 minutes before serving. If desired, serve with sour cream.

PER SERVING *(calculated without sour cream): 373 cal., 18g fat (9g sat. fat), 83mg chol., 949mg sodium, 30g carb. (4g sugars, 4g fiber), 23g pro.*

SAUSAGE & SPINACH CRESCENT BAKE

SAUSAGE & SPINACH CRESCENT BAKE

A classic Florentine casserole has spinach and cheese. I make a yummy version with mozzarella, mushrooms and sausage. It's gone in the blink of an eye at our house.

—**NOELLE CARLE** BRISTOW, OK

PREP: 20 MIN. • **BAKE:** 25 MIN. + STANDING
MAKES: 8 SERVINGS

- 1 **pound bulk pork sausage**
- 2 **cups sliced fresh mushrooms**
- 1 **medium onion, chopped**
- 2 **garlic cloves, minced**
- 1 **package (10 ounces) frozen chopped spinach, thawed and squeezed dry**
- 1 **cup shredded part-skim mozzarella cheese**
- 4 **ounces cream cheese, softened**
- 1 **cup half-and-half cream**
- 1 **tube (8 ounces) refrigerated crescent rolls**

1. Preheat oven to 350°. In a large skillet, cook sausage, mushrooms, onion and garlic over medium heat 6-8 minutes or until sausage is no longer pink, breaking up sausage into crumbles. Drain.

2. Add spinach, mozzarella cheese, cream cheese and half-and-half cream to sausage mixture; cook and stir until blended. Transfer to a greased 13x9-in. baking dish.

3. Unroll crescent dough into one long rectangle; press perforations to seal. Place over sausage mixture. Bake, covered, 10 minutes. Bake, uncovered, 12-15 minutes longer or until golden brown and filling is bubbly. Let stand 5-10 minutes before cutting.

PER SERVING *1 piece: 401 cal., 29g fat (12g sat. fat), 70mg chol., 758mg sodium, 18g carb. (5g sugars, 1g fiber), 15g pro.*

FAST FIX

MOZZARELLA MUSHROOMS WITH GARLIC TOAST

I came up with this dinner using ingredients I had on hand. It turned out to be so delicious, my wife and I now make it for special occasions.

—**MARC BUSHEE** MOORHEAD, MN

START TO FINISH: 30 MIN.
MAKES: 6 SERVINGS

- 2 **tablespoons butter, softened**
- 1 **tablespoon minced fresh basil**
- 1 **garlic clove, minced**
- 1 **French bread baguette (10½ ounces)**

MUSHROOMS

- 2 **tablespoons butter, softened**
- 1 **pound sliced baby portobello mushrooms**
- 2 **garlic cloves, minced**
- 1 **package (3 ounces) julienned soft sun-dried tomatoes (not packed in oil)**
- ¼ **cup dry red wine**
- 3 **tablespoons chopped fresh basil, divided**
- ¼ **teaspoon salt**
- ⅛ **teaspoon pepper**
- 8 **ounces fresh mozzarella cheese, thinly sliced**

1. Preheat broiler. Mix butter, basil and garlic. Cut baguette horizontally in half; spread with butter mixture. Cut each half into six portions; place on a baking sheet, cut side up.

2. In a broiler-safe skillet, heat 2 tablespoons butter over medium heat; saute mushrooms until tender, 5-7 minutes. Add garlic; cook 1 minute. Stir in tomatoes, wine, 2 tablespoons basil, salt and pepper; cook, uncovered, for 3 minutes, stirring occasionally. Remove from heat; top with cheese. Broil 4-5 in. from heat until cheese is melted, 2-3 minutes; sprinkle with remaining basil.

3. Broil baguette portions until lightly toasted. Serve with mushrooms.

NOTE *This recipe was tested with sun-dried tomatoes that can be used without soaking. When using other sun-dried tomatoes that are not oil-packed, cover with boiling water and let stand until softened. Drain before using.*

PER SERVING *366 cal., 16g fat (10g sat. fat), 50mg chol., 562mg sodium, 39g carb. (9g sugars, 5g fiber), 13g pro.*

MOZZARELLA MUSHROOMS WITH GARLIC TOAST

THAI CHICKEN CASSEROLE

THAI CHICKEN CASSEROLE

Whenever my family goes out, I can count on someone ordering the chicken pad thai. So I decided to create an easy version at home. Top it with a sprinkle of peanuts and minced cilantro.

—SANDRA DOMBEK CAMILLUS, NY

START TO FINISH: 30 MIN.
MAKES: 6 SERVINGS

- 1 bottle (11½ ounces) Thai peanut sauce
- 1 cup chicken broth
- 3 cups shredded rotisserie chicken
- 3 cups coleslaw mix
- 4 green onions, chopped
- 1 package (14 ounces) thick rice noodles
  Chopped peanuts and minced fresh cilantro, optional

1. Preheat oven to 400°. Whisk together peanut sauce and broth; toss with shredded chicken, coleslaw mix and green onions.
2. Prepare noodles according to package directions; drain and toss immediately with chicken mixture. Transfer to a greased 13x9-in. baking dish. Bake, covered, until heated through, 10-15 minutes. If desired, top with peanuts and cilantro.
PER SERVING *1⅓ cups: 578 cal., 17g fat (3g sat. fat), 63mg chol., 784mg sodium, 72g carb. (14g sugars, 2g fiber), 31g pro.*

HEALTH TIP *Bump up the fiber with 100% whole grain brown rice noodles, which are newer to the market. If you can't find them, use whole wheat fettuccine instead.*

MOZZARELLA CORN BREAD PIZZA

My sons like pizza, but not takeout pies. I pull out my trusty baking pan to make a corn bread pizza with veggies in the crust and fresh herbs and peppers on top.

—MARY MARLOWE LEVERETTE COLUMBIA, SC

PREP: 15 MIN. + STANDING ● **BAKE:** 20 MIN.
MAKES: 10 SERVINGS

- 3 cups shredded zucchini
- 1 teaspoon salt, divided
- 2 packages (8½ ounces each) corn bread/muffin mix
- 3 large eggs, lightly beaten
- ¼ teaspoon pepper

TOPPINGS

- 1 jar (14 ounces) pizza sauce
- ¾ cup chopped sweet red or green pepper
- 1 can (2¼ ounces) sliced ripe olives, drained
- 4 green onions, chopped
- ⅓ cup coarsely chopped fresh basil
- 1 tablespoon minced fresh oregano or 1 teaspoon dried oregano
- 3 cups shredded part-skim mozzarella cheese

1. Preheat oven to 450°. Place zucchini in a colander over a bowl; sprinkle with ¾ teaspoon salt and toss. Let stand 15 minutes.
2. Press zucchini and blot dry with paper towels; transfer to a large bowl. Add muffin mixes, eggs, pepper and remaining salt; stir until blended. Spread evenly into a greased 15x10x1-in. baking pan. Bake 8-10 minutes or until lightly browned. Reduce oven setting to 350°.
3. Spread pizza sauce over crust. Top with red pepper, olives and green onions. Sprinkle with herbs and cheese. Bake 12-15 minutes or until cheese is melted.
PER SERVING *1 piece: 366 cal., 15g fat (6g sat. fat), 79mg chol., 912mg sodium, 42g carb. (14g sugars, 5g fiber), 15g pro.*

SPINACH AND FETA
STUFFED CHICKEN

FAST FIX

GLAZED SMOKED CHOPS WITH PEARS

My husband would eat pork chops every day if he could. Luckily, they're good in all sorts of ways, including with pears.

—**LYNN MORETTI** OCONOMOWOC, WI

START TO FINISH: 30 MIN.
MAKES: 4 SERVINGS

- 4 **smoked boneless pork chops**
- 1 **tablespoon olive oil**
- 1 **large sweet onion, cut into thin wedges**
- ½ **cup dry red wine or reduced-sodium chicken broth**
- 2 **tablespoons balsamic vinegar**
- 2 **tablespoons honey**
- 2 **large ripe pears, cut into 1-inch wedges**

1. Preheat oven to 350°. In an ovenproof skillet over medium-high heat, brown pork chops on both sides; remove from pan.
2. In same pan, heat oil over medium heat; saute onion until tender, for 3-5 minutes. Add wine, vinegar and honey; bring to a boil, stirring to loosen browned bits from pan. Reduce heat; simmer, uncovered, until slightly thickened, about 5 minutes, stirring occasionally.
3. Return chops to pan; top with pears. Transfer to oven; bake until pears are tender, 10-15 minutes.
PER SERVING *313 cal., 4g fat (6g sat. fat), 41mg chol., 1056mg sodium, 34g carb. (26g sugars, 4g fiber), 22g pro.*

GLAZED SMOKED
CHOPS WITH
PEARS

FAST FIX

SPINACH AND FETA STUFFED CHICKEN

My chicken bundles are simple and comforting. Serve them with wild rice and green beans for one of our favorite meals.

—**JIM KNEPPER** MOUNT HOLLY SPRINGS, PA

START TO FINISH: 30 MIN.
MAKES: 2 SERVINGS

- 8 **ounces fresh spinach (about 10 cups)**
- 1½ **teaspoons cider vinegar**
- ½ **teaspoon sugar**
- ⅛ **teaspoon pepper**
- 2 **boneless skinless chicken thighs**
- ½ **teaspoon chicken seasoning**
- 3 **tablespoons crumbled feta cheese**
- 1 **teaspoon olive oil**
- ¾ **cup reduced-sodium chicken broth**
- 1 **teaspoon butter**

1. Preheat oven to 375°. In a large skillet, cook and stir spinach over medium-high heat until wilted. Stir in vinegar, sugar and pepper; cool slightly.

2. Pound chicken thighs with a meat mallet to flatten slightly; sprinkle with chicken seasoning. Top chicken with spinach mixture and cheese. Roll up chicken from a long side; tie securely with kitchen string.
3. In an ovenproof skillet, heat oil over medium-high heat; add chicken and brown on all sides. Transfer to oven; roast until a thermometer inserted in chicken reads 170°, 13-15 minutes.
4. Remove chicken from pan; keep warm. On stovetop, add broth and butter to skillet; bring to a boil, stirring to loosen browned bits from pan. Cook until slightly thickened, 3-5 minutes. Serve with chicken.
PER SERVING *1 chicken roll-up with 2 tablespoons sauce: 253 cal., 14g fat (5g sat. fat), 86mg chol., 601mg sodium, 5g carb. (2g sugars, 2g fiber), 26g pro.* **Diabetic Exchanges:** *3 lean meat, 2 vegetable, 1½ fat.*

TRADITIONAL MEAT LOAF

TRADITIONAL MEAT LOAF

Homemade meat loaf is a must-have comfort food and it freezes well, so we increase the recipe and stash a loaf for a crazy day.

—**GAIL GRAHAM** MAPLE RIDGE, BC

PREP: 15 MIN. ● **BAKE:** 1 HOUR + STANDING
MAKES: 6 SERVINGS

- 3 slices bread
- 1 large egg, lightly beaten
- ⅔ cup 2% milk
- 1 cup shredded cheddar cheese
- 1 medium onion, finely chopped
- ½ cup finely shredded carrot
- 1 teaspoon salt
- ¼ teaspoon pepper
- 1½ pounds ground beef

GLAZE

- ¼ cup packed brown sugar
- ¼ cup ketchup
- 1 tablespoon prepared mustard

1. Preheat the oven to 350°. Tear bread into 2-inch pieces; place in a blender. Cover and pulse to form coarse crumbs; transfer to a large bowl. Stir in the egg, milk, cheese, onion, carrot, salt and pepper. Add the beef; mix lightly but thoroughly. Transfer mixture to a greased 9x5-in. loaf pan.

2. In a small bowl, mix the glaze ingredients; spread over loaf. Bake 60-75 minutes or until a thermometer reads 160°. Let stand 10 minutes before slicing.

FREEZE OPTION *Bake meat loaf without glaze. Securely wrap cooled meat loaf in plastic and foil, then freeze. To use, partially thaw meat loaf in refrigerator overnight. Prepare and spread glaze over top; reheat on a greased shallow baking pan in a preheated 350° oven until heated through and a thermometer inserted in center reads 165°.*

SAVORY MEAT LOAF *Omit shredded carrot. Saute ½ cup chopped green pepper with onion in 2 teaspoons canola oil until tender. Add 2 minced garlic cloves and cook 1 minute. Cool slightly. Combine with the bread, egg, milk, cheese, salt and pepper. Add 1 teaspoon crushed dried rosemary. Proceed as recipe directs.*

PER SERVING *1 slice: 394 cal., 21g fat (10g sat. fat), 128mg chol., 843mg sodium, 23g carb. (15g sugars, 1g fiber), 28g pro.*

PIZZA MARGHERITA

This classic pie starts with a chewy homemade crust, then is topped with tomatoes, mozzarella, oregano and fresh basil. It's scrumptious!

—**LORETTA LAWRENCE** MYRTLE BEACH, SC

PREP: 30 MIN. + RISING ● **BAKE:** 15 MIN.
MAKES: 2 PIZZAS (8 SLICES EACH)

- 3 teaspoons active dry yeast
- 1 cup warm water (110° to 115°)
- 2 tablespoons olive oil
- 1 teaspoon sugar
- 1 teaspoon salt
- 3 cups bread flour

TOPPINGS

- 2 cans (14½ ounces each) diced tomatoes, drained
- 20 fresh basil leaves, thinly sliced
- 2 tablespoons minced fresh oregano or 2 teaspoons dried oregano
- 8 cups shredded part-skim mozzarella cheese
- ½ teaspoon crushed red pepper flakes
- ⅛ teaspoon salt
- ⅛ teaspoon pepper
- 2 tablespoons olive oil

1. In a small bowl, dissolve yeast in warm water. In a large bowl, combine the oil, sugar, salt and 1 cup flour; beat until smooth. Stir in enough of the remaining flour to form a soft dough.

2. Turn onto a floured surface; knead until smooth and elastic, 6-8 minutes. Place in a greased bowl, turning once to grease the top. Cover with plastic wrap and let rise in a warm place until doubled, about 1 hour.

3. Punch dough down; divide in half. Roll each portion into a 13-in. circle. Transfer to two greased 14-in. pizza pans; build up edges slightly. Cover with a clean kitchen towel; let rest for 10 minutes.

4. Spoon tomatoes over dough. Top with basil, oregano, cheese, pepper flakes, salt and pepper. Drizzle with oil. Bake at 450° for 15-20 minutes or until crust is golden brown.

PER SERVING *1 slice: 263 cal., 12g fat (6g sat. fat), 33mg chol., 523mg sodium, 21g carb. (3g sugars, 1g fiber), 17g pro.* **Diabetic Exchanges:** *2 lean meat, 1½ starch, 1 fat.*

Kathleen Rappleye's Cream Cheese Chicken Soup
PAGE 162

Cook Once, Eat Twice

Let your cooking do double duty with these cleverly paired recipes. Make extra food one night and then transform the leftovers into an all-new, equally tasty meal later in the week. Win!

Suzette Zara's Chicken with Olives & Artichokes PAGE 164

Mary Ann Lee's Applesauce Mini Muffins PAGE 159

Susan Burkett's Sassy Pot Roast PAGE 165

SLOW-COOKED LEMONY NEW POTATOES

These spuds do a slow simmer with carrots and onion for a comforting side that amps up any entree.

—TASTE OF HOME TEST KITCHEN

PREP: 10 MIN. • **COOK:** 4¼ HOURS
MAKES: 4 SERVINGS PLUS LEFTOVERS

- 4 **medium carrots, halved lengthwise and cut into 1-inch pieces**
- 1 **large sweet onion, coarsely chopped**
- 1½ **pounds baby red potatoes, quartered**
- 3 **tablespoons butter, melted**
- ¾ **teaspoon salt**
- ¼ **teaspoon pepper**
- 1 **cup frozen peas (about 4 ounces)**
- 1 **teaspoon grated lemon peel**
- 2 **tablespoons minced fresh chives**

1. Place carrots and onion in a 4-qt. slow cooker; top with potatoes. Drizzle with melted butter; sprinkle with salt and pepper. Cook, covered, on low 4-5 hours or until vegetables are tender.

2. Add peas to slow cooker. Cook, covered, on high 10-15 minutes or until heated through. Stir in lemon peel.

3. Reserve 3 cups potato mixture for Primavera Chicken Soup. To serve remaining potato mixture, sprinkle with chives.

PER SERVING *¾ cup: 141 cal., 5g fat (3g sat. fat), 11mg chol., 298mg sodium, 23g carb. (5g sugars, 3g fiber), 3g pro.* **Diabetic Exchanges:** *1½ starch, 1 fat.*

PRIMAVERA CHICKEN SOUP

MAKE THIS...

SLOW-COOKED LEMONY NEW POTATOES

...THE THIS

PRIMAVERA CHICKEN SOUP

Get out the ladle and bowls for a soothing, hearty soup that's like a warm hug from the inside out. Slow-cooked potatoes make it so simple.

—TASTE OF HOME TEST KITCHEN

START TO FINISH: 25 MIN.
MAKES: 4 SERVINGS

- 5 **cups reduced-sodium chicken broth**
- ½ **pound fresh asparagus, trimmed, cut into 1-inch pieces**
- 1 **teaspoon minced fresh thyme or ½ teaspoon dried thyme**
- 2 **cups cubed rotisserie chicken**
- 3 **cups Slow-Cooked Lemony New Potatoes (recipe at left)**

In a large saucepan, bring broth to a boil. Add asparagus and thyme; cook, uncovered, for 2-4 minutes or until asparagus is crisp-tender. Stir in the chicken and reserved potato mixture; heat through.

PER SERVING *1⅓ cups: 297 cal., 10g fat (4g sat. fat), 74mg chol., 858mg sodium, 24g carb. (7g sugars, 4g fiber), 28g pro.*

TOP TIP

ASPARAGUS SUBSTITUTION

If asparagus isn't in season, substitute cut fresh green beans in the soup recipe.

HEAVENLY APPLESAUCE

Every year, my husband and I take our two daughters to an orchard to pick apples. Then we make this luscious applesauce. Jars of it are wonderful to share with friends and neighbors.

—**JENNIFER PURCELL** VERMILION, OH

PREP: 25 MIN. • **COOK:** 6 HOURS
MAKES: 8 SERVINGS PLUS LEFTOVERS

- 5 pounds apples, peeled and sliced (about 13 cups)
- ¾ cup packed light brown sugar
- ⅔ cup unsweetened apple juice
- 2 teaspoons ground cinnamon
- 1 teaspoon pumpkin pie spice
- 1 tablespoon vanilla extract

1. In a 5- or 6-qt. slow cooker, combine the first five ingredients. Cook, covered, on low 6-8 hours or until apples are soft.
2. Add vanilla; stir to break up apples. Reserve ¾ cup applesauce for Applesauce Mini Muffins. Serve remaining applesauce warm or refrigerate and serve cold.

FREEZE OPTION *Freeze the cooled applesauce in freezer containers. To use, thaw in refrigerator overnight.*
PER SERVING *⅔ cup: 211 cal., 1g fat (0 sat. fat), 0 chol., 7mg sodium, 54g carb. (48g sugars, 4g fiber), 0 pro.*

APPLESAUCE MINI MUFFINS

Children reach with both hands for these irresistible cinnamon-spiced mini muffins. They're easy to bake up any time because they use pantry ingredients.

—**MARY ANN LEE** CLIFTON PARK, NY

PREP: 25 MIN. • **BAKE:** 10 MIN.
MAKES: ABOUT 3 DOZEN

- ½ cup butter, softened
- ½ cup sugar
- 2 large eggs
- ¾ cup Heavenly Applesauce (recipe at left) or other cinnamon applesauce
- 1 teaspoon vanilla extract
- 1⅔ cups all-purpose flour
- 1 teaspoon baking powder
- ½ teaspoon salt
- ¼ teaspoon ground nutmeg

TOPPING
- ⅓ cup sugar
- ½ teaspoon ground cinnamon
- 3 tablespoons butter, melted

1. Preheat oven to 400°. In a large bowl, cream butter and sugar until light and fluffy. Add eggs, one at a time, beating well after each addition. Gradually beat in applesauce and vanilla. Whisk flour, baking powder, salt and nutmeg. Add to creamed mixture; stir just until moistened.
2. Fill paper-lined mini-muffin cups three-fourths full. Bake 10-12 minutes or until a toothpick comes out clean. Cool 5 minutes before removing from pans to wire racks.
3. For topping, in a small bowl, mix sugar and cinnamon. Dip tops of warm muffins in melted butter, then in cinnamon sugar. Serve warm.
PER SERVING *1 mini muffin: 85 cal., 4g fat (2g sat. fat), 20mg chol., 76mg sodium, 12g carb. (7g sugars, 0 fiber), 1g pro.*

MAKE THIS... HEAVENLY APPLESAUCE

...THEN THIS! APPLESAUCE MINI MUFFINS

MAKE THIS...

HEARTY CHILI
WITHOUT BEANS

4. Reserve 5 cups chili for Layered Enchilada Casserole. Serve the remaining chili with rice or pasta; top as desired.

FREEZE OPTION *Freeze cooled chili in freezer containers. To use, partially thaw in refrigerator overnight. Heat through in a saucepan, stirring occasionally and adding a little water or broth if necessary.*

PER SERVING *1 cup (calculated without rice and toppings): 278 cal., 13g fat (5g sat. fat), 85mg chol., 863mg sodium, 13g carb. (6g sugars, 3g fiber), 29g pro.*

TOP TIP

GREAT IDEAS FOR LEFTOVER CHILI

Taste of Home's Facebook fans shared some of the smart and easy ways they use up leftover chili—when there's any left in the fridge.

Add a package of melted cream cheese to make a dip, and serve with nachos.

—MARY DIKA FISHER
GRANDE PRAIRIE, AB

Chili makes a great omelet filling. Top with avocado, cheese and chopped onions.

—LINDA HENRY RICHARDSON
DENVER, CO

I call it Mexaroni. Mix leftover chili with macaroni and cheese and a drained can of corn. Then put cheddar cheese and crumbled corn chips on top. Bake till heated through.

—JOYCE DYKES
CASSVILLE, MO

There are so many different choices! I like to use it as a juicy burger topping.

—PHILLIS FELICE
WINNSBORO, TX

FREEZE IT **SLOW COOKER**

HEARTY CHILI WITHOUT BEANS

When I prepare this zesty chili, I like to combine everything the night before. Then I load the slow cooker in the morning and come home to a fabulous dinner.

—MOLLY BUTT GRANVILLE, OH

PREP: 25 MIN. ● **COOK:** 6 HOURS
MAKES: 5 SERVINGS PLUS LEFTOVERS

- 2 **teaspoons canola oil**
- 1 **large green pepper, chopped**
- 1 **large onion, chopped**
- 2 **garlic cloves, minced**
- 3 **pounds lean ground beef (90% lean)**
- 2 **cans (14½ ounces each) stewed tomatoes, undrained**
- 2 **cans (8 ounces each) tomato sauce**
- 2 **cans (4 ounces each) chopped green chilies**
- ½ **cup minced fresh parsley**
- 2 **tablespoons chili powder**
- 1¼ **teaspoons salt**
- 1 **teaspoon paprika**
- ½ **teaspoon pepper**
  Hot cooked rice or pasta
  Optional toppings: shredded cheddar cheese, sour cream and sliced green onions

1. In a large skillet, heat oil over medium-high heat. Add the green pepper, onion and garlic; cook and stir 3-4 minutes or until tender. Transfer to a 6-qt. slow cooker.

2. In same skillet, add beef half at a time; cook over medium-high heat for 6-8 minutes or until no longer pink, breaking into crumbles. Using a slotted spoon, transfer to slow cooker.

3. Stir tomatoes, tomato sauce, chilies, parsley and seasonings into beef mixture. Cook, covered, on low for 6-8 hours to allow flavors to blend.

LAYERED ENCHILADA CASSEROLE

LAYERED ENCHILADA CASSEROLE

Here's a heap of cozy comfort. The Taste of Home Test Kitchen took my recipe for chili without beans and turned it into a scrumptious enchilada casserole.
—**MOLLY BUTT** GRANVILLE, OH

PREP: 15 MIN • **BAKE:** 35 MIN. + STANDING
MAKES: 12 SERVINGS

- **5 cups reserved Hearty Chili without Beans (recipe on facing page) or any thick chili without beans**
- **1½ cups frozen corn (about 8 ounces)**
- **1 can (15 ounces) black beans, rinsed and drained**
- **1 can (15 ounces) pinto beans, rinsed and drained**
- **6 flour tortillas (10 inches)**
- **3 cups shredded Mexican cheese blend, divided**
- **1 can (10 ounces) enchilada sauce**
  Shredded lettuce and chopped fresh tomatoes, optional

1. Preheat oven to 375°. In a large bowl, mix reserved chili, corn and beans. Spread 1 cup chili mixture into a greased 13x9-in. baking dish. Layer with two tortillas, 2 cups chili mixture, 1 cup cheese and ½ cup enchilada sauce. Repeat layers. Top with the remaining tortillas and chili mixture.

2. Bake, covered, 20-25 minutes or until heated through. Sprinkle with remaining cheese. Bake, uncovered, 10-15 minutes longer or until cheese is melted. Let stand 10 minutes before cutting. If desired, serve with lettuce and tomatoes.

FREEZE OPTION *Cover and freeze unbaked casserole. To use, partially thaw in refrigerator overnight. Remove from refrigerator 30 minutes before baking. Preheat oven to 375°. Cover casserole with foil; bake as directed, increasing covered time to 40-45 minutes or until a thermometer inserted in center reads 165°. Serve as directed.*

PER SERVING *1 piece (calculated without toppings): 409 cal., 17g fat (7g sat. fat), 60mg chol., 1031mg sodium, 41g carb. (5g sugars, 6g fiber), 25g pro.*

GREEK ROASTED
CHICKEN AND POTATOES

GREEK ROASTED CHICKEN AND POTATOES

This is a nice meal to prepare for company or to serve your family for Sunday dinner. All you need with it is a tossed salad and some crusty French bread.

—PELLA VISNICK DALLAS, TX

PREP: 10 MIN. • **BAKE:** 2 HOURS + STANDING
MAKES: 8-10 SERVINGS

- 1 roasting chicken (6 to 7 pounds)
     Salt and pepper to taste
- 2 to 3 teaspoons dried oregano, divided
- 4 to 6 baking potatoes, peeled and quartered
- ¼ cup butter, melted
- 3 tablespoons lemon juice
- ¾ cup chicken broth

1. Preheat oven to 350°. Place chicken breast side up on a rack in a roasting pan. Sprinkle with salt and pepper and half of the oregano. Arrange potatoes around chicken; sprinkle with salt, pepper and remaining oregano. Pour butter and lemon juice over chicken and potatoes. Add chicken broth to pan.
2. Bake, uncovered, 2-2½ hours or until a thermometer inserted in thigh reads 180°, basting frequently with pan drippings.
3. Remove chicken from oven; tent with foil. Let stand 15 minutes before carving. If desired, skim fat and thicken the pan drippings for gravy. Serve with chicken.

ROSEMARY-LEMON ROAST CHICKEN *Brush the chicken with 1 tablespoon olive oil. Combine*

2 tablespoons each grated lemon peel and minced fresh rosemary with 2 teaspoons each salt and coarsely ground pepper; sprinkle over chicken and potatoes. Add broth to pan and bake as directed.

PER SERVING *(calculated without salt): 425 cal., 24g fat (8g sat. fat), 120mg chol., 214mg sodium, 16g carb. (1g sugars, 2g fiber), 36g pro.*

FAST FIX
CREAM CHEESE CHICKEN SOUP

...THEN THIS!

After tasting a similar soup in a restaurant, I went home and cooked up my own version. It's warmly soothing on a cool night. For a change of pace, try substituting ham or turkey for the chicken.

—KATHLEEN RAPPLEYE MESA, AZ

START TO FINISH: 30 MIN.
MAKES: 8 SERVINGS

- 1 small onion, chopped
- 1 tablespoon butter
- 3 cups chicken broth
- 3 medium carrots, cut into ¼-inch slices
- 2 medium potatoes, peeled and cubed
- 2 cups cubed cooked roasted chicken (from either recipe variation at left)
- 2 tablespoons minced fresh parsley
     Salt and pepper to taste
- ¼ cup all-purpose flour
- 1 cup milk
- 1 package (8 ounces) cream cheese, cubed

1. In a large saucepan, saute onion in butter. Add the broth, carrots and potatoes. Bring to a boil. Reduce heat; cover and simmer for 15 minutes or until vegetables are tender. Add the chicken, parsley, salt and pepper; heat mixture through.
2. Combine flour and milk until smooth; add to the vegetable mixture. Bring to a boil, then cook and stir for 2 minutes or until thickened. Reduce heat. Add cream cheese; cook and stir until melted.

PER SERVING *1 cup: 272 cal., 15g fat (8g sat. fat), 70mg chol., 504mg sodium, 18g carb. (5g sugars, 2g fiber), 16g pro.*

⑤ INGREDIENTS
HARD-COOKED EGGS

MAKE THIS

Here's a foolproof technique for making hard-cooked eggs to eat plain or to use in various recipes.

—TASTE OF HOME TEST KITCHEN

PREP: 20 MIN. + COOLING
MAKES: 12 SERVINGS

- 12 large eggs
      Cold water

1. Place eggs in a single layer in a large saucepan; add enough cold water to cover by 1 in. Cover and quickly bring to a boil. Remove from the heat. Let stand for 15 minutes for large eggs (18 minutes for extra-large eggs and 12 minutes for medium eggs).
2. Rinse eggs in cold water and place in ice water until completely cooled. Drain and refrigerate.

PER SERVING *1 each: 75 cal., 5g fat (2g sat. fat), 213mg chol., 63mg sodium, 1g carb. (1g sugars, 0 fiber), 6g pro.*

FAST FIX
CREAMY EGG SALAD

I love the versatility of egg salad—serve it over mixed greens, piled into a sandwich or alongside your favorite crisp crackers.

—CYNTHIA KOHLBERG SYRACUSE, IN

START TO FINISH: 10 MIN.
MAKES: 3 CUPS

- 3 ounces cream cheese, softened
- ¼ cup mayonnaise
- ½ teaspoon salt
- ⅛ teaspoon pepper
- ¼ cup finely chopped green or sweet red pepper
- ¼ cup finely chopped celery
- ¼ cup sweet pickle relish
- 2 tablespoons minced fresh parsley
- 8 Hard-Cooked Eggs (recipe above), chopped

In a bowl, mix the cream cheese, mayonnaise, salt and pepper until smooth. Stir in green pepper, celery, relish and parsley. Fold in the eggs. Refrigerate, covered, until serving.

PER SERVING *½ cup: 234 cal., 19g fat (6g sat. fat), 268mg chol., 466mg sodium, 5g carb. (4g sugars, 0 fiber), 9g pro.*

...THEN THIS!

CREAMY EGG SALAD

MAKE THIS... →

CHICKEN WITH OLIVES & ARTICHOKES

FAST FIX ▶

CHICKEN & FETA SPINACH SALAD

In my all-purpose salad, you can change up the pasta, nuts and cheese. If you have tomatoes, leftover turkey or a fresh lemon to squeeze, go for it.

—**DONNA BARDOCZ** HOWELL, MI

START TO FINISH: 25 MIN.
MAKES: 6 SERVINGS

- 1½ cups uncooked orzo pasta (about 8 ounces)
- 5 ounces fresh baby spinach (about 6 cups), finely chopped
- 4 reserved chicken thighs from Chicken with Olives & Artichokes (recipe at left), shredded, or 1½ cups any shredded cooked chicken
- 1 cup crumbled feta cheese
- ¾ cup sliced almonds, toasted
- ⅓ cup finely chopped red onion
- ¼ cup chicken broth
- ¼ cup olive oil
- 1 tablespoon minced fresh basil or ¾ teaspoon dried basil
- ¾ teaspoon salt
- ¼ teaspoon white pepper

1. Cook orzo according to package directions for al dente. Drain orzo; rinse with cold water and drain well.
2. In a large bowl, combine spinach, orzo, chicken, feta cheese, almonds and onion. In a small bowl, whisk the remaining ingredients until blended. Add to salad; toss gently to combine.
NOTE *To toast nuts, bake in a shallow pan in a 350° oven for 5-10 minutes or cook in a skillet over low heat until lightly browned, stirring occasionally.*
PER SERVING *1⅓ cups: 531 cal., 26g fat (6g sat. fat), 68mg chol., 627mg sodium, 44g carb. (3g sugars, 4g fiber), 29g pro.*

SLOW COOKER 🍲

CHICKEN WITH OLIVES & ARTICHOKES

My grandmother came from the region around Seville, Spain, where olives and red wine are produced. Those ingredients get starring roles in her scrumptious chicken.

—**SUZETTE ZARA** SCOTTSDALE, AZ

PREP: 30 MIN. • **COOK:** 4 HOURS
MAKES: 4 SERVINGS PLUS LEFTOVERS

- ¼ cup all-purpose flour
- ½ teaspoon garlic salt
- ¼ teaspoon pepper
- 8 bone-in chicken thighs (3 pounds), skin removed if desired
- 1 tablespoon olive oil
- 4 garlic cloves, thinly sliced
- 1 tablespoon grated lemon peel
- 1 teaspoon dried thyme
- ½ teaspoon dried rosemary, crushed
- 1 can (14 ounces) water-packed quartered artichoke hearts, drained
- ½ cup pimiento-stuffed olives
- 1 bay leaf
- 1½ cups orange juice
- ¾ cup chicken broth
- 2 tablespoons honey

GREMOLATA
- ¼ cup minced fresh basil
- 1 teaspoon grated lemon peel
- 1 garlic clove, minced

1. In a shallow bowl, mix flour, garlic salt and pepper. Dip chicken thighs in flour mixture to coat both sides; shake off excess. In a large skillet, heat oil over medium heat. In batches, brown chicken on both sides. Transfer to a 4-qt. slow cooker.
2. Sprinkle garlic, lemon peel, thyme and rosemary over chicken. Top with artichoke hearts, olives and bay leaf. In a bowl, mix orange juice, broth and honey; pour over top. Cook, covered, on low 4-5 hours or until chicken is tender. Remove bay leaf.
3. Reserve four chicken thighs for Chicken & Feta Spinach Salad; cover and refrigerate. To serve remaining chicken, mix gremolata ingredients in a small bowl. Sprinkle over chicken and artichoke mixture.
PER SERVING *1 chicken thigh with ¼ cup artichoke mixture and 1 tablespoon gremolata: 434 cal., 21g fat (4g sat. fat), 81mg chol., 971mg sodium, 34g carb. (17g sugars, 1g fiber), 26g pro.*

...THEN THIS! →

CHICKEN & FETA SPINACH SALAD

SASSY POT ROAST

SUNDAY HERBED POT ROAST SOUP

I love having leftovers. It means less cooking the next day, and I often use the the leftovers to make soup. With this recipe, you could easily substitute roast chicken and chicken broth for the leftover beef and beef broth.

—**DEONNA WEIGHT** KEARNS, UT

PREP: 20 MIN. • **COOK:** 35 MIN.
MAKES: 6 SERVINGS

- 1 **small onion, diced**
- 1 **tablespoon olive oil**
- 3 **medium potatoes, cubed**
- 2 **large carrots, chopped**
- ½ **pound sliced fresh mushrooms**
- 3 **cans (14½ ounces each) reduced-sodium beef broth**
- 4 **teaspoons balsamic vinegar**
- 1 **tablespoon dried parsley flakes**
- ½ **teaspoon garlic powder**
- ½ **teaspoon dried thyme**
- ½ **teaspoon dried rosemary, crushed**
- ¼ **teaspoon pepper**
- ⅛ **teaspoon salt**
- 1½ **cups cubed cooked Sassy Pot Roast (recipe at left)**

1. In a large saucepan, saute onion in oil for 2 minutes. Add potatoes and carrots; cook 2 minutes longer. Add mushrooms; cook for 2-3 minutes or until onion is tender.

2. Stir in the broth, vinegar and seasonings. Bring to a boil. Reduce heat; cover and simmer for 13-18 minutes or until potatoes are tender. Stir in beef; heat through.

PER SERVING *1⅓ cups: 192 cal., 6g fat (1g sat. fat), 23mg chol., 618mg sodium, 25g carb. (8g sugars, 3g fiber), 10g pro.* **Diabetic Exchanges:** *1 starch, 1 lean meat, 1 vegetable, ½ fat.*

MAKE THIS... →

SASSY POT ROAST

We lost this recipe for several years, so it's even more special to us now that we found it again. I love walking into my home after a long day at the office and smelling this lovely pot roast.

—**SUSAN BURKETT** MONROEVILLE, PA

PREP: 15 MIN. • **COOK:** 8 HOURS
MAKES: 8 SERVINGS

- 1 **boneless beef chuck roast (2 pounds)**
- ½ **teaspoon salt**
- ½ **teaspoon pepper**
- 2 **teaspoons olive oil**
- 1 **large onion, chopped**
- 1 **can (8 ounces) tomato sauce**
- ¼ **cup water**
- ¼ **cup lemon juice**
- ¼ **cup cider vinegar**
- ¼ **cup ketchup**
- 2 **tablespoons brown sugar**
- 1 **tablespoon Worcestershire sauce**
- ½ **teaspoon ground mustard**
- ½ **teaspoon paprika**

1. Sprinkle beef with salt and pepper. In a large skillet, brown beef in oil on all sides; drain.

2. Transfer to a 4-qt. slow cooker. Sprinkle with onion. Combine the remaining ingredients; pour over meat. Cover and cook on low for 8-10 hours or until meat is tender. Skim fat. If desired, thicken cooking liquid.

PER SERVING *3 ounces cooked beef: 243 cal., 12g fat (4g sat. fat), 74mg chol., 443mg sodium, 10g carb. (7g sugars, 1g fiber), 23g pro.* **Diabetic Exchanges:** *3 lean meat.*

READER RAVE

"Good recipe for leftover pot roast. I used my own recipe—maybe it tastes better using the *Taste of Home* recipe called for. I like recipes for leftovers like this."

—**CWBUFF2** TASTEOFHOME.COM

**Gina Idone's
Delicious Almond Braids**
PAGE 169

Breads in a Jiffy

Does anything in the world beat oven-fresh bread? We don't think so...and neither will you, after you sample the hearty loaves, savory biscuits and sweet muffins in this chapter.

Maxine Hron's Bohemian Kolaches *PAGE 168*

Katherine Wollgast's Cranberry Chip Monkey Bread *PAGE 175*

Paula Marchesi's Olive & Onion Quick Bread *PAGE 174*

BOHEMIAN KOLACHES

In Eastern Europe, a *kolache* is typically shaped into a circle, which is a symbol of good luck, prosperity and eternity. My mother-in-law gave me this recipe.
—**MAXINE HRON** QUINCY, IL

PREP: 30 MIN. + RISING ● **BAKE:** 10 MIN.
MAKES: ABOUT 28 ROLLS

- 2 packages (¼ ounce each) active dry yeast
- ½ cup sugar, divided
- 2 cups warm 2% milk (110° to 115°)
- 5¾ to 6½ cups all-purpose flour
- 4 large egg yolks
- 1 teaspoon salt
- ¼ cup butter, softened
- 2 cups canned prune, poppy seed, cherry or lemon pie filling
- 1 large egg white, beaten

1. In a small bowl, dissolve yeast and 1 tablespoon sugar in warm milk; let for stand 10 minutes. In a large bowl, combine 2 cups flour, the remaining sugar, egg yolks, salt, butter and yeast mixture. Mix until smooth. Add enough of the remaining flour to make a stiff dough.

2. Turn out onto a floured surface and knead until smooth and elastic, about 6-8 minutes. Add additional flour, if necessary. Place dough in greased bowl, turning once to grease top. Cover; let rise in a warm place until doubled in bulk, about 1 hour.

3. Punch dough down and allow to rise again. Roll out on floured surface to ½-in. thickness. Cut with large glass or 2½-in. cutter. Place on greased baking sheets; let rise until doubled, about 45 minutes.

4. Firmly press indentation in center and fill each roll with a heaping tablespoon of filling. Brush dough with egg white. Bake at 350° 10-15 minutes or until rolls are light golden brown.
PER SERVING *1 kolache: 164 cal., 3g fat (2g sat. fat), 37mg chol., 116mg sodium, 29g carb. (9g sugars, 1g fiber), 4g pro.*

APPLE-ALMOND MUFFINS

EAT SMART **FREEZE IT**
APPLE-ALMOND MUFFINS

I like to snack on apple slices slathered with almond butter. That's the flavor combo that inspired these muffins. Add a dash of almond extract to boost the nuttiness.
—**KELLY ALESSO** CHICAGO, IL

PREP: 15 MIN. ● **BAKE:** 20 MIN.
MAKES: 15 MUFFINS

- 1 cup all-purpose flour
- ¾ cup whole wheat flour
- ¼ cup sugar
- ¼ cup packed brown sugar
- 3 teaspoons baking powder
- ¾ teaspoon ground cinnamon
- ½ teaspoon salt
- 1 large egg
- 1¼ cups 2% milk
- ⅓ cup creamy almond butter
- 2 tablespoons canola oil
- 1 teaspoon vanilla extract
- 1 medium apple, peeled and finely chopped
- ½ cup slivered almonds, divided

1. Preheat oven to 400°. In a large bowl, whisk the first seven ingredients. In another bowl, whisk the egg, milk, almond butter, oil and vanilla until blended. Add to the flour mixture; stir just until moistened. Fold in apple and ¼ cup almonds.

2. Fill 15 greased or paper-lined muffin cups three-fourths full. Sprinkle with remaining almonds.

3. Bake 18-20 minutes or until a toothpick inserted in center comes out clean. Cool 5 minutes before removing from pans to wire racks. Serve warm.
FREEZE OPTION *Freeze cooled muffins in resealable plastic freezer bags. To use, thaw muffins at room temperature or, if desired, microwave each muffin on high for 20-30 seconds or until heated through.*

PER SERVING *1 muffin: 168 cal., 8g fat (1g sat. fat), 16mg chol., 189mg sodium, 22g carb. (9g sugars, 2g fiber), 5g pro.* **Diabetic Exchanges:** *1½ starch, 1 fat.*

BANANA AND NUT BREAD

This bread smells heavenly in the oven and comes out moist and chock-full of banana flavor and crunchy nuts.

—CARLENE JOLLEY FULTON, KY

PREP: 15 MIN. • **BAKE:** 65 MIN. + COOLING
MAKES: 1 LOAF (16 SLICES)

- ½ cup butter, softened
- 1½ cups sugar
- 2 large eggs
- 2 tablespoons 2% milk
- 1 teaspoon vanilla or rum extract
- 2 cups all-purpose flour
- 1 teaspoon baking soda
- ½ teaspoon salt
- 1 cup mashed ripe bananas (2 to 3 medium)
- ¾ cup chopped pecans

1. Preheat oven to 325°. In a large bowl, cream butter and sugar until light and fluffy. Add eggs, one at a time, beating well after each addition. Beat in milk and vanilla. In another bowl, whisk flour, baking soda and salt; add to creamed mixture alternately with bananas, beating well after each addition. Fold in pecans.

2. Transfer to a greased 9x5-in. loaf pan. Bake 65-75 minutes or until a toothpick inserted in center comes out clean. Cool in pan 10 minutes before removing to a wire rack to cool.

FREEZE OPTION *Securely wrap cooled loaf in plastic and foil, then freeze. To use, thaw at room temperature.*

PER SERVING *1 slice: 239 cal., 10g fat (4g sat. fat), 39mg chol., 209mg sodium, 35g carb. (21g sugars, 1g fiber), 3g pro.*

DELICIOUS ALMOND BRAIDS

Similar to an almond crescent, this coffee cake is light and flaky with a rich almond center. It's so versatile you can serve it for dessert, breakfast or brunch. It tastes like it came from a high-end bakery, but puff pastry dough makes it easy.

—GINA IDONE STATEN ISLAND, NY

PREP: 25 MIN. • **BAKE:** 30 MIN. + COOLING
MAKES: 2 BRAIDS (6 SLICES EACH)

- 1 package (7 ounces) almond paste
- ½ cup butter
- ½ cup sugar
- 1 large egg
- 2 tablespoons all-purpose flour
- 1 package (17.3 ounces) frozen puff pastry, thawed

GLAZE
- ¾ cup plus 1 tablespoon confectioners' sugar
- 2 tablespoons 2% milk
- ½ teaspoon almond extract
- ¼ cup sliced almonds, toasted

1. Place the almond paste, butter and sugar in a food processor; cover and pulse until chopped. Add egg and flour; process until smooth.

2. Unfold puff pastry sheets onto a greased baking sheet. Spread half of the filling mixture down the center third of one pastry sheet. On each side, cut eight strips about 3½ in. into the center. Starting at one end, fold alternating strips at an angle across filling. Pinch ends to seal. Repeat with remaining pastry and filling. Bake at 375° for 30-35 minutes or until golden brown. Remove to a wire rack.

3. Combine the confectioners' sugar, milk and almond extract. Drizzle over braids; sprinkle with almonds. Cut into slices.

PER SERVING *1 slice: 430 cal., 25g fat (8g sat. fat), 38mg chol., 197mg sodium, 49g carb. (22g sugars, 4g fiber), 6g pro.*

BANANA AND NUT BREAD

MONKEY BREAD
BISCUITS

ORANGE CORN MUFFINS

This is an old recipe that I decided to improve upon—I thought the topping made the muffin too sweet, so I left it off. I also took out the pecans that were called for. Sometimes, I make lemon corn muffins by substituting lemon peel if I don't have an orange on hand.

—HOPE HUGGINS SANTA CRUZ, CA

PREP: 20 MIN. • **BAKE:** 15 MIN.
MAKES: 1 DOZEN

- 1 **cup yellow cornmeal**
- 1 **cup all-purpose flour**
- ⅓ **cup sugar**
- 4 **teaspoons baking powder**
- ¼ **teaspoon salt**
- 1 **large egg, beaten**
- 1 **cup 2% milk**
- ¼ **cup canola oil**
- 1 **tablespoon grated orange peel**

1. In a bowl, combine the cornmeal, flour, sugar, baking powder and salt. In another bowl, combine egg, milk, oil and orange peel. Stir into cornmeal mixture just until moistened.
2. Fill 12 greased muffin cups two-thirds full. Bake at 425° for 15 minutes or until lightly brown. Cool 5 minutes before removing to wire racks. Serve warm.

PER SERVING *1 muffin: 161 cal., 6g fat (1g sat. fat), 20mg chol., 198mg sodium, 24g carb. (7g sugars, 1g fiber), 3g pro.*

MONKEY BREAD BISCUITS

Classic monkey bread is a sweetly spiced breakfast treat. I came up with an easy dinner version featuring garlic and Italian seasoning the crowd will love.

—DANA JOHNSON SCOTTSDALE, AZ

START TO FINISH: 20 MIN.
MAKES: 1 DOZEN

- 1 **tube (16.3 ounces) large refrigerated flaky biscuits**
- 3 **tablespoons butter, melted**
- 1 **garlic clove, minced**
- ½ **teaspoon Italian seasoning**
- ¼ **cup grated Parmesan cheese**
  Additional Italian seasoning

1. Preheat oven to 425°. Separate biscuits; cut each into six pieces. In a large bowl, combine butter, garlic and Italian seasoning; add biscuit pieces and toss to coat.
2. Place four biscuit pieces in each of 12 greased muffin cups. Sprinkle with the Parmesan and additional Italian seasoning. Bake 8-10 minutes or until golden brown. Serve warm.

PER SERVING *1 biscuit: 159 cal., 9g fat (3g sat. fat), 9mg chol., 418mg sodium, 16g carb. (3g sugars, 1g fiber), 3g pro.*

THREE-GRAIN BREAD

My grandchildren really like this hearty loaf's crunchy crust and chewy inside. I like how nutritious it is, containing more fiber than many other loaves.

—JOHN REED LEES SUMMIT, MO

PREP: 10 MIN. • **BAKE:** 3 HOURS
MAKES: 1 LOAF (2 POUNDS, 20 SLICES)

- 1½ **cups water (70° to 80°)**
- ½ **cup honey**
- 1½ **teaspoons salt**
- 2 **cups bread flour**
- 1 **cup whole wheat flour**
- ¾ **cup rye flour**
- ¾ **cup cornmeal**
- 2¼ **teaspoons active dry yeast**

1. In bread machine pan, place all ingredients in order suggested by manufacturer. Select basic bread setting. Choose crust color and loaf size if available.
2. Bake according to bread machine directions (check dough after 5 minutes of mixing; add 1-2 tablespoons of water or flour if needed).

PER SERVING *1 slice: 132 cal., 1g fat (trace sat. fat), 0 chol., 178mg sodium, 29g carb. (7g sugars, 2g fiber), 3g pro.*
***Diabetic Exchanges:** 2 starch.*

ORANGE CORN MUFFINS

LOUISIANA PECAN BACON BREAD

ORANGE CHOCOLATE CHIP SCONES

My family asks for these scones all the time, but saving this special treat for celebrations makes them feel extra-special.

—LESLIE PARKER AVOCA, IA

PREP: 20 MIN. ● **BAKE:** 15 MIN.
MAKES: 16 SCONES

- 3 cups all-purpose flour
- ⅓ cup sugar
- 2½ teaspoons baking powder
- ½ teaspoon baking soda
- ¼ teaspoon salt
- ¾ cup cold butter, cubed
- 1 cup (6 ounces) semisweet chocolate chips
- 1 cup buttermilk
- 4 teaspoons grated orange peel
- 1 teaspoon orange extract
- 2 tablespoons sugar
- ¼ teaspoon ground cinnamon
- 1 tablespoon heavy whipping cream

1. Preheat oven to 400°. In a large bowl, whisk the first five ingredients. Cut in butter until mixture resembles coarse crumbs. Stir in chocolate chips. In another bowl, mix milk, orange peel and extract until blended; stir into flour mixture just until moistened.
2. Turn dough onto a lightly floured surface; knead gently 10 times. Divide dough in half. Pat each portion into an 8-in. circle and cut each into eight wedges. Place wedges on a greased baking sheet.
3. In a small bowl, mix sugar and cinnamon. Lightly brush scones with cream; sprinkle with cinnamon sugar. Bake 15-17 minutes or until golden brown. Serve warm.
PER SERVING *1 scone: 245 cal., 13g fat (8g sat. fat), 25mg chol., 238mg sodium, 31g carb. (12g sugars, 1g fiber), 3g pro.*

FREEZE IT

LOUISIANA PECAN BACON BREAD

One Christmas, the babysitter brought gifts for my daughter and a basket of goodies, including pecan bread. Whenever I make this bread, I remember that kind soul.

—MARINA CASTLE KELLEY

CANYON COUNTRY, CA

PREP: 20 MIN. ● **BAKE:** 50 MIN. + COOLING
MAKES: 1 LOAF (16 SLICES)

- 6 bacon strips, chopped
- 6 ounces cream cheese, softened
- ⅓ cup sugar
- 1 large egg
- 2 cups all-purpose flour
- 2½ teaspoons baking powder
- ½ teaspoon salt
- ¾ cup 2% milk
- 1 cup chopped pecans
- ¼ cup finely chopped onion
- ¼ cup chopped green pepper

1. Preheat oven to 350°. In a large skillet, cook bacon over medium-low heat until crisp, stirring occasionally. Remove with a slotted spoon; drain on paper towels. Reserve the drippings (about 2 tablespoons); cool slightly.

2. In a large bowl, beat cream cheese, sugar and reserved drippings until smooth. Beat in egg. In another bowl, whisk flour, baking powder and salt; add to the cream cheese mixture alternately with milk, beating well after each addition. Fold in pecans, onion, pepper and bacon. Transfer to a greased 9x5-in. loaf pan.
3. Bake 50-60 minutes or until a toothpick inserted in center comes out clean. Cool in pan 10 minutes before removing to a wire rack to cool.
FREEZE OPTION *Securely wrap cooled loaves in plastic and foil, then freeze. To use, thaw in the refrigerator.*
PER SERVING *1 slice: 198 cal., 12g fat (4g sat. fat), 29mg chol., 242mg sodium, 18g carb. (6g sugars, 1g fiber), 5g pro.*

TOP TIP

CUTTING IN BUTTER

Cutting butter into dry ingredients results in tiny bits of flour-coated butter throughout the dough, creating a bread that is both tender and crumbly at the same time. If you don't have a pastry blender, use two knives to cut in the cold butter.

Holidays and nut breads are made for each other. My spiced quick bread has three of the ingredients I can't resist—eggnog, apricots and macadamia nuts.
—**NANCY HEISHMAN** LAS VEGAS, NV

APRICOT & MACADAMIA EGGNOG BREAD

FREEZE IT
APRICOT & MACADAMIA EGGNOG BREAD

PREP: 20 MIN. • **BAKE:** 50 MIN. + COOLING
MAKES: 2 LOAVES (12 SLICES EACH)

- 4¾ cups all-purpose flour
- ¾ cup sugar
- 2 tablespoons baking powder
- ½ teaspoon salt
- 1 teaspoon ground cinnamon
- 1 teaspoon ground nutmeg
- 2 large eggs
- 2½ cups eggnog
- ½ cup canola oil
- 1 tablespoon grated orange peel
- ¼ cup orange juice
- ¾ cup chopped dried apricots
- ¾ cup chopped macadamia nuts

GLAZE
- ¾ cup confectioners' sugar
- 1 to 2 tablespoons eggnog

1. Preheat oven to 350°. In a large bowl, whisk the first six ingredients. In another bowl, whisk eggs, 2½ cups eggnog, oil, orange peel and orange juice until blended. Add to the flour mixture; stir just until moistened. Fold in apricots and macadamia nuts.
2. Transfer to two greased 8x4-in. loaf pans. Bake 50-60 minutes or until a toothpick inserted in the center comes out clean. Cool in pans for 10 minutes before removing to wire racks to cool completely.
3. For glaze, in a small bowl, mix the confectioners' sugar with enough eggnog to reach drizzling consistency. Spoon over loaves.
FREEZE OPTION *Securely wrap cooled loaves in plastic and foil, then freeze. To use, thaw at room temperature.*
NOTE *This recipe was tested with commercially prepared eggnog.*
PER SERVING *1 slice: 242 cal., 10g fat (2g sat. fat), 32mg chol., 186mg sodium, 35g carb. (15g sugars, 1g fiber), 5g pro.*

HAM & GREEN
ONION BISCUITS

HAM & GREEN ONION BISCUITS

I started with my grandmother's biscuits and added a bit of my personality. When I make these with my kids, it feels like she is with us.
—**AMY CHASE** VANDERHOOF, BC

PREP: 20 MIN. • **BAKE:** 10 MIN.
MAKES: ABOUT 1 DOZEN

- 2 cups all-purpose flour
- 3 teaspoons baking powder
- 1 teaspoon sugar
- ¼ teaspoon garlic salt
  Dash pepper
- 6 tablespoons cold butter, cubed
- 1 cup finely chopped fully cooked ham
- 2 green onions, chopped
- ¾ cup 2% milk

1. Preheat oven to 450°. In a large bowl, whisk the first five ingredients. Cut in butter until mixture resembles coarse crumbs. Stir in ham and green onions. Add the milk; stir just until moistened.
2. Turn dough onto a lightly floured surface; knead gently 8-10 times. Pat or roll dough to ½-in. thickness; cut with a floured 2½-in. biscuit cutter. Place 2 in. apart on an ungreased baking sheet. Bake 10-12 minutes or until golden brown. Serve warm.
PER SERVING *1 biscuit: 151 cal., 7g fat (4g sat. fat), 23mg chol., 315mg sodium, 17g carb. (1g sugars, 1g fiber), 5g pro.*

CHEESE FLATBREAD

The convenience of frozen bread dough and dried herbs makes this treat about as easy as it gets. To boost fiber, you can also use frozen whole wheat bread dough.
—**SHARON DELANEY-CHRONIS**
SOUTH MILWAUKEE, WI

PREP: 5 MIN. + RISING • **BAKE:** 20 MIN.
MAKES: 16 SERVINGS

- 1 loaf (1 pound) frozen bread dough, thawed
- 2 tablespoons butter, softened
- 2 teaspoons paprika
- ½ teaspoon garlic powder
- ½ teaspoon dried oregano
- ½ teaspoon dried basil
- 1 cup shredded part-skim mozzarella cheese

1. On a lightly floured surface, roll the dough into a 16x11-in. rectangle. Transfer to a 15x10x1-in. baking pan coated with cooking spray; build up edges slightly. Spread with softened butter. Sprinkle with paprika, garlic powder, oregano and basil. Prick the dough several times with a fork then sprinkle with cheese. Cover and let rise for 30 minutes.
2. Bake at 375° for 20-25 minutes or until crust is golden brown and cheese is melted. Serve warm.
PER SERVING *1 slice: 111 cal., 4g fat (2g sat. fat), 8mg chol., 202mg sodium, 14g carb. (1g sugars, 1g fiber), 5g pro.* **Diabetic Exchanges:** *1 starch, ½ fat.*

OLIVE & ONION
QUICK BREAD

SURPRISE HERB ROLLS

My mom and I created these rolls for Thanksgiving one year, and they were a big hit with our guests.

—**HANNAH HEINRITZ** MENOMONEE FALLS, WI

PREP: 20 MIN. + RISING ● **BAKE:** 20 MIN.
MAKES: 1 DOZEN

- ½ **cup sour cream**
- ⅛ **teaspoon dried basil**
- ⅛ **teaspoon dried marjoram**
- ⅛ **teaspoon dried oregano**
- ⅛ **teaspoon dried parsley flakes**
- ⅛ **teaspoon dried rosemary, crushed**
- ⅛ **teaspoon dried thyme**
  Dash rubbed sage
- 1 **loaf (1 pound) frozen bread dough, thawed**
- 2 **tablespoons butter, melted**
- 3 **tablespoons grated Parmesan cheese**

1. In a small bowl, mix sour cream and herbs until blended. Divide the dough into 12 portions. On a lightly floured surface, roll each into a 4-in. circle. Top each with 2 teaspoons sour cream mixture; bring edges of dough up over filling and pinch to seal.
2. Place in greased muffin cups, seam side down. Cover rolls with kitchen towels; let rise in a warm place until doubled, about 45 minutes. Preheat the oven to 350°.
3. Brush tops with melted butter; sprinkle with cheese. Bake 18-20 minutes or until golden brown.
PER SERVING *1 roll: 148 cal., 5g fat (3g sat. fat), 13mg chol., 248mg sodium, 19g carb. (2g sugars, 2g fiber), 5g pro.*

OLIVE & ONION QUICK BREAD

I've been baking for over 50 years and never tire of making and creating new recipes for my family, friends and co-workers. Baking actually relaxes me; it makes me feel like an artist creating a masterpiece of love. This savory loaf makes a great gift.

—**PAULA MARCHESI** LENHARTSVILLE, PA

PREP: 15 MIN. ● **BAKE:** 45 MIN. + COOLING
MAKES: 1 LOAF (12 SLICES)

- 1 **tablespoon canola oil**
- 1 **medium onion, finely chopped**
- 2 **cups all-purpose flour**
- 1 **tablespoon minced fresh rosemary**
- 1 **teaspoon baking soda**
- ½ **teaspoon salt**
- 2 **large eggs**
- 1 **cup buttermilk**
- 2 **tablespoons butter, melted**
- ¼ **cup plus 2 tablespoons sharp cheddar cheese, divided**
- ¼ **cup each chopped pitted green and ripe olives**

1. Preheat oven to 350°. In a skillet, heat oil over medium-high heat. Add onion; cook and stir 2-3 minutes or until tender. Remove from heat.
2. In a large bowl, whisk the flour, rosemary, baking soda and salt. In another bowl, whisk eggs, buttermilk and melted butter until blended. Add to the flour mixture; stir just until moistened. Fold in ¼ cup cheese, olives and onion.
3. Transfer to a greased 8x4-in. loaf pan. Bake 40 minutes. Sprinkle the remaining cheese over top. Bake 5-10 minutes longer or until a toothpick inserted in center comes out clean. Cool in pan for 10 minutes before removing to a wire rack to cool.
PER SERVING *1 slice: 150 cal., 6g fat (2g sat. fat), 41mg chol., 373mg sodium, 18g carb. (1g sugars, 1g fiber), 5g pro.*

SURPRISE HERB ROLLS

CRANBERRY CHIP
MONKEY BREAD

BANANA BRICKLE MUFFINS

Toffee bits add a nice unexpected flavor to these delicious banana muffins. Serve them at breakfast, lunch, dinner or as a special snack.

—**ANDRA COGAN** GROSSE POINTE PARK, MI

PREP: 15 MIN. ● **BAKE:** 20 MIN.
MAKES: 1 DOZEN

- 2 cups all-purpose flour
- ½ cup packed brown sugar
- 1 tablespoon baking powder
- 1 cup mashed ripe bananas
- ½ cup 2% milk
- ⅓ cup canola oil
- 1 large egg
- 1 package (8 ounces) brickle toffee bits, divided

1. In a large bowl, combine the flour, brown sugar and baking powder. In a small bowl, combine the bananas, milk, canola oil and egg. Stir into dry ingredients just until moistened. Fold in 1 cup toffee bits.
2. Fill greased muffin cups three-fourths full. Sprinkle with remaining toffee bits. Bake at 350° for 18-20 minutes or until a toothpick inserted near the center comes out clean. Cool for 5 minutes before removing from pan to a wire rack. Serve warm.
PER SERVING *1 muffin: 319 cal., 15g fat (4g sat. fat), 27mg chol., 248mg sodium, 44g carb. (27g sugars, 1g fiber), 3g pro.*

CRANBERRY CHIP MONKEY BREAD

Monkey bread has always been a favorite at our house, but I wanted a holiday version. This one with cranberries and eggnog is a breakfast treat or knockout dessert.

—**KATHERINE WOLLGAST** FLORISSANT, MO

PREP: 15 MIN. ● **BAKE:** 40 MIN.
MAKES: 16 SERVINGS

- ¾ cup sugar, divided
- 4 teaspoons ground cinnamon
- 4 tubes (7½ ounces each) refrigerated buttermilk biscuits
- ½ cup white baking chips
- ½ cup dried cranberries
- ¼ cup chopped walnuts or pecans
- ¼ cup butter, cubed
- ½ cup eggnog

GLAZE
- 1 cup confectioners' sugar
- ½ teaspoon rum or vanilla extract
- 2 to 3 tablespoons eggnog
  Optional toppings: additional dried cranberries, white baking chips and chopped nuts

1. Preheat oven to 350°. In a large bowl, mix ½ cup sugar and cinnamon. Cut each biscuit into quarters; add to sugar mixture and toss to coat.
2. Arrange half the biscuits in a greased 10-in. tube pan. Sprinkle with baking chips, cranberries and walnuts. Top with remaining biscuits.

3. In a microwave, melt butter. Stir in eggnog and remaining sugar until blended; pour over biscuits.
4. Bake 40-45 minutes or until golden brown. Cool in pan 5 minutes before inverting onto a serving plate.
5. For glaze, in a small bowl, mix confectioners' sugar, extract and enough eggnog to reach a drizzling consistency. Spoon over warm bread. Sprinkle with toppings as desired.
NOTE *This recipe was tested with commercially prepared eggnog.*
PER SERVING *(calculated without optional toppings): 310 cal., 13g fat (5g sat. fat), 15mg chol., 596mg sodium, 47g carb. (26g sugars, 1g fiber), 4g pro.*

|||||||||||||||||||||||||||||||||||||||||||||||||||||||||||||

CANDY BAR CROISSANTS

Unroll 1 tube (8 ounces) refrigerated crescent roll dough; separate into triangles. Brush with 1 tablespoon softened butter. Arrange 2 plain milk chocolate candy bars (1.55 ounces each), broken into small pieces, evenly over triangles; roll up from the wide end. Place point side down on a greased baking sheet; curve ends slightly. Brush with 1 lightly beaten large egg; sprinkle with 2 tablespoons sliced almonds. Bake at 375° for 11-13 minutes or until golden brown. Cool on a wire rack.

—**BEVERLY STERLING** GASPORT, NY

**Gilda Lester's
Asparagus & Cheese Frittata**
PAGE 187

Breakfast & Brunch

Mornings will be the most cheerful part of the day when you serve any of these sunny selections. You'll find easy recipes for busy workdays and elegant dishes for company. So use this chapter to make a great start to any day!

Lea Langhoff's Chunky Breakfast Cookies PAGE 180

Julia Huntington's Brunch Buddies Enchiladas PAGE 187

Natalie Hess' Deluxe Ham & Egg Sandwiches PAGE 183

ASPARAGUS & HAM STRATA

For a quick and easy make-ahead breakfast, do all the prep work the night before. The next morning, just pop it in the oven. This casserole version of quiche is so hearty and delicious.

—**ALLA GRAY** ST. THOMAS, PA

PREP: 20 MIN. + CHILLING ● **BAKE:** 1 HOUR.
MAKES: 6 SERVINGS

- 5 **large eggs**
- 2 **cups whole milk**
- ½ **cup half-and-half cream**
- ½ **teaspoon salt**
- ¼ **teaspoon pepper**
- ⅛ **teaspoon ground nutmeg**
- 4 **cups cubed Italian or French bread (about 6 ounces)**
- 1¼ **cups (5 ounces) shredded Monterey Jack cheese, divided**
- 1 **cup cubed deli ham (½ inch)**
- 1 **cup cut fresh asparagus (1-inch pieces)**

1. In a large bowl, whisk the first six ingredients until blended. Stir in bread, 1 cup of the cheese, ham and asparagus. Transfer to a greased 8-in. square baking dish. Refrigerate, covered, several hours or overnight.
2. Preheat oven to 325°. Remove strata from refrigerator while oven heats. Bake, uncovered, 20 minutes. Sprinkle with remaining cheese; bake 40-50 minutes longer or until puffed, golden and a knife inserted in the center comes out clean. Let stand for 5-10 minutes before serving.
FREEZE OPTION *After assembling, cover and freeze the strata. To use, partially thaw strata in refrigerator overnight. Remove from refrigerator 30 minutes before baking. Preheat oven to 325°. Bake strata as directed, increasing time as necessary for a knife inserted in the center to come out clean.*
PER SERVING *1 piece: 320 cal., 18g fat (9g sat. fat), 208mg chol., 839mg sodium, 18g carb. (7g sugars, 1g fiber), 22g pro.*

APPLE-SAGE SAUSAGE PATTIES

APPLE-SAGE SAUSAGE PATTIES

Apple and sausage naturally go together. Add sage, and you've got a standout patty. They're freezer friendly, so I make them ahead and grab when needed.

—**SCARLETT ELROD** NEWNAN, GA

PREP: 35 MIN. + CHILLING
COOK: 10 MIN./BATCH
MAKES: 16 PATTIES

- 1 **large apple**
- 1 **large egg, lightly beaten**
- ½ **cup chopped fresh parsley**
- 3 **to 4 tablespoons minced fresh sage**
- 2 **garlic cloves, minced**
- 1¼ **teaspoons salt**
- ½ **teaspoon pepper**
- ½ **teaspoon crushed red pepper flakes**
- 1¼ **pounds lean ground turkey**
- 6 **teaspoons olive oil, divided**

1. Peel and coarsely shred apple; place the apple in a colander over a plate. Let stand 15 minutes. Squeeze and blot dry with paper towels.
2. In a large bowl, combine the egg, parsley, sage, garlic, seasonings and apple. Add turkey; mix lightly but thoroughly. Shape into sixteen 2-in. patties. Place the patties on waxed paper-lined baking sheets. Refrigerate, covered, 8 hours or overnight.
3. In a large nonstick skillet, heat 2 teaspoons oil over medium heat. In batches, cook patties 3-4 minutes on each side or until golden brown and a thermometer reads 165°, adding additional oil as needed.
FREEZE OPTION *Place uncooked patties on plastic wrap-lined baking sheets; wrap and freeze until firm. Remove from pans and transfer to resealable plastic bags; return to freezer. To use, cook frozen patties as directed, increasing time to 4-5 minutes on each side.*
PER SERVING *1 patty: 79 cal., 5g fat (1g sat. fat), 36mg chol., 211mg sodium, 2g carb. (1g sugars, trace fiber), 8g pro.* **Diabetic Exchanges:** *1 lean meat, ½ fat.*

BLUEBERRY-ORANGE BLINTZES

Blintzes are aces for brunch time because I can make the crepes ahead. They taste so indulgent that guests don't know they're lower in fat and calories.
—**MARY JOHNSON** COLOMA, WI

PREP: 15 MIN. + CHILLING ● **BAKE:** 25 MIN.
MAKES: 6 SERVINGS

- 1 **large egg**
- 1 **cup fat-free milk**
- ¾ **cup all-purpose flour**
- 1 **carton (15 ounces) part-skim ricotta cheese**
- 6 **tablespoons orange marmalade, divided**
- 1 **tablespoon sugar**
- ⅛ **teaspoon ground cinnamon**
- ⅔ **cup reduced-fat sour cream**
- 2 **cups fresh blueberries or raspberries, divided**

1. In a large bowl, whisk the egg, milk and flour until blended. Refrigerate, covered, 1 hour.

2. Preheat oven to 350°. Place a 6-in. nonstick skillet coated with cooking spray over medium heat. Stir batter; fill a ¼-cup measure halfway with batter and pour into center of pan. Quickly lift and tilt pan to coat bottom evenly. Cook until top appears dry; turn crepe over and cook for 15-20 seconds longer or until bottom is cooked. Remove to a wire rack. Repeat with remaining batter.

3. In a small bowl, mix ricotta cheese, 2 tablespoons marmalade, sugar and cinnamon. Spoon about 2 tablespoons mixture onto each crepe; top with about 1 tablespoon blueberries. Fold opposite sides of crepes over filling, forming a rectangular bundle.

4. Place blintzes on a 15x10x1-in. baking pan coated with cooking spray, seam side down. Bake, uncovered, 10-15 minutes or until heated through. Serve with sour cream and remaining marmalade and blueberries.

FREEZE OPTION *Freeze cooled crepes between layers of waxed paper in a resealable plastic freezer bag. To use, thaw overnight in the refrigerator. Proceed as directed.*

HEALTH TIP *Use reduced-fat ricotta instead of part-skim and save 30 calories and 3 grams fat per serving.*

PER SERVING *2 blintzes with toppings: 301 cal., 9g fat (5g sat. fat), 63mg chol., 129mg sodium, 42g carb. (23g sugars, 2g fiber), 14g pro. Diabetic Exchanges: 2 starch, 2 lean meat, ½ fruit.*

HONEYDEW SALAD WITH LIME DRESSING

Green is my favorite color, and grapes, cucumber and kiwi make this refreshing salad green to the max. For more, add green apples and pears.
—**MELISSA MCCABE** VICTOR, NY

START TO FINISH: 20 MIN.
MAKES: 8 SERVINGS

- ¼ **cup lime juice**
- ¼ **cup honey**
- 1 **tablespoon minced fresh mint leaves**
- 4 **cups cubed honeydew (about 1 small)**
- 2 **cups green grapes**
- 4 **medium kiwifruit, peeled, halved lengthwise and sliced**
- 1 **medium cucumber, halved lengthwise and sliced**

For dressing, in a small bowl, whisk lime juice, honey and mint until blended. Place the fruit and cucumber in a large bowl; add dressing and toss to coat. Refrigerate until serving.

PER SERVING *1 cup: 120 cal., 0 fat (0 sat. fat), 0 chol., 22mg sodium, 31g carb. (26g sugars, 3g fiber), 1g pro. Diabetic Exchanges: 1 starch, 1 fruit.*

HEALTH TIP *Swap cantaloupe for honeydew and get a boost of vitamin A. One cup of cantaloupe has a whopping 120% of the daily value, whereas honeydew only provides 2%. Most other nutrient amounts are similar between the melons.*

BLUEBERRY-ORANGE BLINTZES

HONEYDEW SALAD WITH LIME DRESSING

CHICKEN SAUSAGE
& POTATO HASH

FREEZE IT
CHUNKY BREAKFAST COOKIES

Who says cookies aren't for breakfast? We devour these hearty oatmeal cookies, especially on the run. Add any dried fruits and nuts you have on hand.

—**LEA LANGHOFF** ROUND LAKE, IL

PREP: 20 MIN. ● **BAKE:** 15 MIN./BATCH
MAKES: 16 COOKIES

- ⅔ cup butter, softened
- ⅔ cup packed brown sugar
- 1 large egg
- 1 large egg yolk
- 1½ cups old-fashioned oats
- ¾ cup all-purpose flour
- ¾ cup whole wheat flour
- 1 teaspoon baking soda
- ½ teaspoon salt
- 1 cup semisweet chocolate chunks
- 1 cup chopped dates
- ½ cup flaked coconut

1. Preheat oven to 350°. In a large bowl, cream butter and brown sugar until light and fluffy. Beat in egg and egg yolk. In another bowl, mix oats, flours, baking soda and salt; gradually beat into creamed mixture. Stir in remaining ingredients.
2. Shape ¼ cupfuls of dough into balls; flatten to ¾-in. thickness. Place 2 in. apart on ungreased baking sheets.
3. Bake 13-15 minutes or until golden brown. Cool on pans for 2 minutes. Remove to wire racks to cool. Serve warm or at room temperature. To reheat, microwave each cookie on high for 15-20 seconds or just until warmed.
  FREEZE OPTION *Freeze unbaked cookies in a freezer container, separating layers with waxed paper. To use, place dough portions 2 in. apart on ungreased baking sheets; let stand at room temperature 30 minutes before baking. Bake as directed, increasing time by 1-2 minutes.*
PER SERVING *1 cookie: 291 cal., 15g fat (9g sat. fat), 44mg chol., 239mg sodium, 40g carb. (24g sugars, 3g fiber), 4g pro.*

FAST FIX
CHICKEN SAUSAGE & POTATO HASH

This hash is our total comfort food, whether it's for breakfast, lunch or dinner. We like it with fried or poached eggs on top.

—**LISA SPEER** PALM BEACH, FL

START TO FINISH: 30 MIN.
MAKES: 4 SERVINGS

- 3 tablespoons canola oil, divided
- 1 package (12 ounces) fully cooked sun-dried tomato chicken sausage links or flavor of your choice, coarsely chopped
- 1 package (20 ounces) refrigerated diced potatoes with onion
- ½ cup chopped sweet onion
- ¼ teaspoon plus ⅛ teaspoon pepper, divided
- ½ cup chopped roasted sweet red pepper
- 1 tablespoon butter
- 4 large eggs

1. In a large nonstick skillet, heat 1 tablespoon oil over medium-high heat. Add sausage; cook and stir 4-6 minutes or until lightly browned. Remove the sausage from pan.
2. In same pan, heat remaining oil over medium heat. Add potatoes, sweet onion and ¼ teaspoon pepper; cook, covered, 10-12 minutes or until golden brown, turning potatoes every 2 minutes. Stir in the red pepper and sausage; heat through.
3. Meanwhile, in another large nonstick skillet, heat the butter over medium-high heat. Break eggs, one at a time, into pan; immediately reduce heat to low. Cook, covered, for 5-6 minutes or until whites are completely set and yolks just begin to thicken. If desired, carefully turn eggs and cook the second side to desired doneness. Remove from heat; sprinkle with remaining pepper. Serve over hash.
PER SERVING *446 cal., 25g fat (6g sat. fat), 264mg chol., 1045mg sodium, 27g carb. (4g sugars, 2g fiber), 23g pro.*

MUSHROOM-GOUDA QUICHE

BRUNCH BANANA SPLITS

My whole family loves bananas, fruit and granola for breakfast. I topped it all with yogurt, nuts and honey and called it a split. This is perfect to serve on a busy morning or a special one!

—NANCY HEISHMAN LAS VEGAS, NV

START TO FINISH: 10 MIN.
MAKES: 4 SERVINGS

- 4 small bananas, peeled and halved lengthwise
- 2 cups (16 ounces) fat-free vanilla Greek yogurt
- 2 small peaches, sliced
- 1 cup fresh raspberries
- ½ cup granola without raisins
- 2 tablespoons sliced almonds, toasted
- 2 tablespoons sunflower kernels
- 2 tablespoons honey

Divide banana slices among four shallow dishes. Top with remaining ingredients.

PER SERVING *340 cal., 6g fat (1g sat. fat), 0 chol., 88mg sodium, 61g carb. (38g sugars, 9g fiber), 17g pro.*

HEALTH TIP *Yogurt's combination of carbs and protein helps give you long-lasting energy. It's also a rich source of phosphorous, which is vital to energy production and storage.*

MUSHROOM-GOUDA QUICHE

For a laid-back Sunday brunch, we make a quiche in no time using refrigerated pie pastry. Load it up with mushrooms, aromatic arugula and creamy Gouda.

—THOMAS FAGLON SOMERSET, NJ

PREP: 15 MIN. ● **BAKE:** 30 MIN. + STANDING
MAKES: 6 SERVINGS

- 1 sheet refrigerated pie pastry
- 4 large eggs
- 1 cup heavy whipping cream
- ¼ teaspoon salt
- ¼ teaspoon pepper
- 2 cups sliced fresh shiitake mushrooms (about 4 ounces)
- 1 cup (4 ounces) shredded Gouda or Monterey Jack cheese
- 1 cup chopped arugula or fresh baby spinach

1. Preheat oven to 350°. Unroll pastry into a 9-in. pie plate; flute the edge. Refrigerate while preparing filling.
2. In a large bowl, whisk eggs, cream, salt and pepper. Stir in remaining ingredients. Pour into pie shell.
3. Bake on a lower oven rack 30-35 minutes or until crust is golden brown

and a knife inserted near the center comes out clean. Let stand 10 minutes before cutting.

FREEZE OPTION *Cover and freeze unbaked quiche. To use, remove from freezer 30 minutes before baking (do not thaw). Preheat oven to 350°. Place quiche on a baking sheet; cover edge loosely with foil. Bake as directed, increasing time as necessary for a knife inserted in the center to come out clean.*
PER SERVING *1 piece: 422 cal., 33g fat (18g sat. fat), 207mg chol., 452mg sodium, 21g carb. (4g sugars, 1g fiber), 12g pro.*

BAKED PEACH PANCAKE

Combine 2 cups sliced peeled peaches with 4 teaspoons sugar and 1 teaspoon lemon juice; set aside. In a large bowl, beat 3 eggs until fluffy. Beat in ½ cup all-purpose flour, ½ cup whole milk and ½ teaspoon salt until smooth. Melt 2 tablespoons butter in a 10-in. ovenproof skillet in a 400° oven. Immediately pour batter into pan. Bake 20-25 minutes or until puffed. Top with peaches; sprinkle with nutmeg. If desired, serve with sour cream.

—NANCY WILKINSON PRINCETON, NJ

HASH BROWN
QUICHE CUPS

EAT SMART **FAST FIX** ▶

ITALIAN GARDEN FRITTATA

I like to serve this pretty frittata with melon wedges for a delicious breakfast or brunch.

—SALLY MALONEY DALLAS, GA

START TO FINISH: 30 MIN.
MAKES: 4 SERVINGS

- 4 **large eggs**
- 6 **large egg whites**
- ½ **cup grated Romano cheese, divided**
- 1 **tablespoon minced fresh sage**
- ½ **teaspoon salt**
- ¼ **teaspoon pepper**
- 1 **teaspoon olive oil**
- 1 **small zucchini, sliced**
- 2 **green onions, chopped**
- 2 **plum tomatoes, thinly sliced**

1. Preheat broiler. In a large bowl, whisk eggs, egg whites, ¼ cup cheese, sage, salt and pepper until blended.
2. In a 10-in. broiler-safe skillet coated with cooking spray, heat the oil over medium-high heat. Add zucchini and green onions; cook and stir 2 minutes. Reduce heat to medium-low. Pour in egg mixture. Cook, covered, for 4-7 minutes or until eggs are nearly set.
3. Uncover; top with tomatoes and remaining cheese. Broil 3-4 in. from heat 2-3 minutes or until eggs are completely set. Let stand 5 minutes. Cut into wedges.
PER SERVING *1 slice: 183 cal., 11g fat (5g sat. fat), 228mg chol., 655mg sodium, 4g carb. (3g sugars, 1g fiber), 18g pro.* **Diabetic Exchanges:** *2 medium-fat meat, 1 vegetable.*
HEALTH TIP *Using six egg whites, which is equivalent to three whole eggs, saves almost 30 calories and 4 grams fat per serving.*

FREEZE IT EAT SMART **FAST FIX** ▶

HASH BROWN QUICHE CUPS

Quiche cups are my showstopper potluck dish. Hash browns and Asiago cheese make up the crusts. Eggs, spinach and bacon do the rest.

—NICOLE STONE GILBERTVILLE, IA

START TO FINISH: 30 MIN.
MAKES: 4 SERVINGS

- 1 **large egg**
- ¼ **teaspoon salt**
- ⅛ **teaspoon pepper**
- 2 **cups frozen shredded hash brown potatoes, thawed**
- ¼ **cup shredded Asiago cheese**

FILLING

- 3 **large eggs**
- 1 **tablespoon minced fresh chives**
- ⅓ **cup shredded Colby-Monterey Jack cheese**
- ⅓ **cup fresh baby spinach, thinly sliced**
- 2 **bacon strips, cooked and crumbled**

1. Preheat oven to 400°. Grease eight muffin cups.
2. In a bowl, whisk the egg, salt and pepper until blended; stir in potatoes and Asiago cheese. To form crusts, press about ¼ cup potato mixture onto bottom and up sides of each prepared muffin cup. Bake 14-17 minutes or until light golden brown.
3. For filling, in a small bowl, whisk eggs and chives until blended; stir in cheese and spinach. Spoon into crusts; top with bacon. Bake for 6-8 minutes longer or until a knife inserted in the center comes out clean.
PER SERVING *2 mini quiches: 180 cal., 11g fat (5g sat. fat), 205mg chol., 375mg sodium, 8g carb. (1g sugars, 0 fiber), 12g pro.* **Diabetic Exchanges:** *2 medium-fat meat, ½ starch.*

CHORIZO & GRITS BREAKFAST BOWLS

Growing up, I bonded with my dad over chorizo and eggs. My fresh approach combines them with grits and black beans. Add a spoonful of pico de gallo.

—**JENN TIDWELL** FAIR OAKS, CA

START TO FINISH: 30 MIN.
MAKES: 6 SERVINGS

- 2 teaspoons olive oil
- 1 package (12 ounces) fully cooked chorizo chicken sausages or flavor of choice, sliced
- 1 large zucchini, chopped
- 3 cups water
- ¾ cup quick-cooking grits
- 1 can (15 ounces) black beans, rinsed and drained
- ½ cup shredded cheddar cheese
- 6 large eggs
  Pico de gallo and chopped fresh cilantro, optional

1. In a large nonstick skillet, heat oil over medium heat. Add sausage; cook and stir 2-3 minutes or until lightly browned. Add zucchini; cook and stir 4-5 minutes longer or until tender. Remove from pan; keep warm.

2. Meanwhile, in a large saucepan, bring water to a boil. Slowly stir in grits. Reduce heat to medium-low; cook, covered, about 5 minutes or until thickened, stirring occasionally. Stir in the beans and cheese until blended. Remove from heat.

3. Wipe skillet clean; coat with cooking spray and place over medium heat. In batches, break eggs, one at a time, into pan. Immediately reduce heat to low; cook until the whites are completely set and the yolks begin to thicken but are not hard, about 5 minutes.

4. To serve, divide grits mixture among six bowls. Top with chorizo mixture, eggs and, if desired, pico de gallo and cilantro.

PER SERVING *344 cal., 14g fat (5g sat. fat), 239mg chol., 636mg sodium, 30g carb. (4g sugars, 4g fiber), 24g pro.* **Diabetic Exchanges:** *3 medium-fat meat, 2 starch.*

HEALTH TIP *Pulses like black beans are part of the legume family and a rich source of iron, which helps transport oxygen to muscles.*

DELUXE HAM & EGG SANDWICHES

My hearty cheesy breakfast sandwich is packed with provolone on top and Laughing Cow on the bottom. In between, I add ham, spinach and eggs sunny-side up.

—**NATALIE HESS** CEDAR RAPIDS, IA

START TO FINISH: 30 MIN.
MAKES: 4 SERVINGS

- 1 submarine bun, split
- 4 wedges The Laughing Cow garlic and herb Swiss cheese
- 3 ounces thinly sliced fully cooked Black Forest ham
- 3 teaspoons butter, divided
- ½ medium red onion, thinly sliced
- 2 cups fresh baby spinach
- 4 large eggs
- ⅛ teaspoon pepper
- 4 slices provolone cheese

1. Preheat broiler. Cut bun crosswise in half; split each half to separate top and bottom. Spread with the cheese wedges. Place halves on a foil-lined 15x10x1-in. baking pan.

2. Place a large nonstick skillet over medium-high heat; lightly brown ham on each side. Place ham on bread.

3. In same skillet, heat 1 teaspoon butter over medium-high heat. Add onion and spinach; cook and stir for 2-4 minutes or until spinach is wilted. Divide mixture among sandwiches. Wipe skillet clean if necessary.

4. In same skillet, heat remaining butter over medium-high heat. Break eggs and slip into pan, one at a time. Immediately reduce heat to low; cover and cook slowly 5-6 minutes or until egg whites are completely set and yolks begin to thicken but are not hard. Sprinkle with pepper.

5. Place eggs over spinach mixture; top with provolone cheese. Broil sandwiches 4-5 in. from heat for 2-3 minutes or until the cheese is slightly melted.

PER SERVING *1 open-faced sandwich: 293 cal., 17g fat (9g sat. fat), 223mg chol., 768mg sodium, 14g carb. (4g sugars, 1g fiber), 20g pro.*

CHORIZO & GRITS
BREAKFAST BOWLS

Oh My Omelet

Ontario reader Milynne Charlton makes any morning feel Sunday-special by tucking veggies and cheese into fluffy eggs.

MEDITERRANEAN OMELET

PREPARE A TOP-NOTCH OMELET

1. **WHISK & POUR** Whisk the eggs, water, salt and pepper. In a large nonstick skillet, heat the butter on medium-high. When it sizzles, pour in the egg mixture.

2. **COOK** As the eggs set, push the cooked parts toward the center, letting the uncooked eggs flow underneath. (A wide spatula works especially well for this.)

3. **FILL & FOLD** When eggs are cooked, add cheese, tomato and green onion to one side. Slide your spatula under the other half to fold it over.

4. **SLIDE, SLICE & SERVE** Slide the omelet onto a plate or cutting board. Slice it in half and dig in with a friend!

⑤ INGREDIENTS | **FAST FIX ▷**

MEDITERRANEAN OMELET

This fluffy omelet gives us reason to get a move on for breakfast. For extra flair, add some chopped fresh herbs like basil, oregano or tarragon.

—**MILYNNE CHARLTON** SCARBOROUGH, ON

START TO FINISH: 10 MIN.
MAKES: 2 SERVINGS

  4 **large eggs**
  ¼ **cup water**
  ⅛ **teaspoon salt**
      Dash pepper
  1 **tablespoon butter**
  ¼ **cup crumbled feta or goat cheese**
  ¼ **cup chopped tomato**
  1 **green onion, chopped**

PER SERVING *½ omelet: 236 cal., 18g fat (8g sat. fat), 395mg chol., 472mg sodium, 3g carb. (1g sugars, 1g fiber), 15g pro.*

FRITTATA FLORENTINE

EGG-TOPPED BISCUIT WAFFLES

Breakfast for dinner is hot stuff at our house. As a mom, I like transforming an ordinary breakfast sandwich into something magical and kid-friendly.

—AMY LENTS GRAND FORKS, ND

START TO FINISH: 25 MIN.
MAKES: 4 SERVINGS

- 1½ cups biscuit/baking mix
- ¾ cup shredded Swiss cheese
- ⅛ teaspoon pepper
- ½ cup 2% milk
- 4 large eggs
- 4 bacon strips, cooked and crumbled
  Cubed avocado and pico de gallo, optional

1. Preheat a four-square waffle iron. Place baking mix, cheese and pepper in a bowl. Add the milk; stir just until moistened. Transfer to a lightly floured surface; knead gently 4-6 times. Pat or roll dough into an 8-in. square; cut into four 4-in. squares.
2. Generously grease top and bottom grids of the waffle maker. Place one portion of dough on each section of waffle maker, pressing an indentation in each for eggs.
3. Break an egg over each biscuit; sprinkle with bacon. Close lid carefully over eggs; cook until the biscuits are golden brown. If desired, top with the avocado and pico de gallo.
NOTE *Recipe may also be baked in a round waffle maker. Divide biscuit dough into four portions; pat each into a 4½-in. circle. Assemble and cook one serving at a time.*
PER SERVING *(calculated without optional toppings):* 386 cal., 20g fat (8g sat. fat), 215mg chol., 802mg sodium, 33g carb. (3g sugars, 1g fiber), 19g pro.

FRITTATA FLORENTINE

My family is all about brunchy meals like this gorgeous Italian omelet. It's loaded with ingredients we tend to have at the ready.

—JENNY FLAKE NEWPORT BEACH, CA

START TO FINISH: 30 MIN.
MAKES: 4 SERVINGS

- 6 large egg whites
- 3 large eggs
- ½ teaspoon dried oregano
- ¼ teaspoon garlic powder
- ¼ teaspoon salt
- ¼ teaspoon pepper
- 1 tablespoon olive oil
- 1 small onion, finely chopped
- ¼ cup finely chopped sweet red pepper
- 2 turkey bacon strips, chopped
- 1 cup fresh baby spinach
- 3 tablespoons thinly sliced fresh basil leaves
- ½ cup shredded part-skim mozzarella cheese

1. Preheat broiler. In a small bowl, whisk the first six ingredients.
2. In an 8-in. ovenproof skillet, heat oil over medium-high. Add onion, red pepper and bacon; cook 4-5 minutes or until onion is tender. Reduce heat to medium-low; top with spinach.
3. Pour in egg mixture. As eggs set, push cooked portions toward the center, letting uncooked eggs flow underneath; cook until eggs are nearly thickened. Remove from the heat; sprinkle with basil, then cheese.
4. Broil 3-4 in. from heat 2-3 minutes or until eggs are completely set. Let stand 5 minutes. Cut into wedges.

PER SERVING *1 slice: 176 cal., 11g fat (4g sat. fat), 174mg chol., 451mg sodium, 4g carb. (2g sugars, 1g fiber), 15g pro. Diabetic Exchanges: 2 medium-fat meat, ½ fat.*

GOLDEN OAT PANCAKES

My husband's face lights up when I make these country-style flapjacks. Serve them for a weekend breakfast or brunch, or freeze and toast them later.

—RAYMONDE BOURGEOIS SWASTIKA, ON

START TO FINISH: 25 MIN.
MAKES: 10 PANCAKES

- 1 cup old-fashioned oats
- 1⅓ cups 2% milk
- ¾ cup all-purpose flour
- 4 teaspoons baking powder
- 4 teaspoons brown sugar
- ¼ teaspoon salt
- 2 large eggs, lightly beaten
- 3 tablespoons canola oil

1. In a small bowl, mix oats and milk; let stand 5 minutes. In a large bowl, whisk flour, baking powder, brown sugar and salt. Stir eggs and oil into oat mixture. Add to flour mixture; stir just until moistened.
2. Lightly grease a griddle; heat over medium heat. Pour the batter by ¼ cupfuls onto griddle. Cook until bubbles on top begin to pop and the bottoms are golden brown. Turn; cook until second side is golden brown.
PER SERVING: *2 pancakes: 70 cal., 13g fat (2g sat. fat), 80mg chol., 498mg sodium, 30g carb. (7g sugars, 2g fiber), 8g pro.*

BACON, EGG & AVOCADO SANDWICHES

ORANGE DREAM PULL-APART BREAD

My kitchen therapy is to bake treats for friends and co-workers. This pull-apart bread brings on the smiles as they face a busy day.

—**VICKIE FRIDAY MARTIN** SCROGGINS, TX

PREP: 25 MIN. • **BAKE:** 35 MIN.
MAKES: 10 SERVINGS

- 1 **package (8 ounces) cream cheese**
- 2 **tubes (7½ ounces each) small refrigerated buttermilk biscuits (10 count)**
- 1 **cup packed brown sugar**
- 1 **cup chopped pecans**
- 4 **teaspoons grated orange peel**
- ½ **cup butter, melted**

1. Preheat oven to 375°. Cut cream cheese into 20 pieces. Using a small knife, cut a horizontal pocket into the side of each biscuit; fill each with a piece of cream cheese. Pinch opening to seal.

2. In a shallow bowl, mix brown sugar, pecans and orange peel. Dip biscuits in melted butter; roll in brown sugar mixture. Stand biscuits on their side in a greased 10-in. fluted tube pan.

3. Bake 35-40 minutes or until golden brown. Cool in pan 5 minutes before inverting onto a serving plate. Serve bread warm.

PER SERVING *2 filled biscuits: 444 cal., 30g fat (12g sat. fat), 49mg chol., 612mg sodium, 42g carb. (25g sugars, 1g fiber), 5g pro.*

FAST FIX ▶

BACON, EGG & AVOCADO SANDWICHES

My husband wanted bacon and eggs, but I wanted a BLT. We settled our standoff with an irresistible sandwich we've had many times since.

—**PATTI DARWIN** LUBBOCK, TX

START TO FINISH: 25 MIN.
MAKES: 2 SERVINGS

- 2 **bacon strips, halved crosswise**
- 2 **large eggs**
- ⅛ **teaspoon garlic salt**
- ⅛ **teaspoon pepper**
- 2 **tablespoons Miracle Whip or mayonnaise**
- 4 **slices sourdough bread, toasted**
- 2 **teaspoons butter, softened**
- 4 **thin slices tomato**
- ½ **medium ripe avocado, peeled and sliced**
- 2 **slices Gouda cheese, optional**
- 1 **slice red onion, separated into rings, optional**

1. In a large nonstick skillet, cook bacon over medium heat until crisp. Remove to paper towels to drain. Pour off drippings.

2. In same skillet, break eggs, one at a time, into pan; immediately reduce heat to low. Cook until whites are completely set and yolks begin to thicken. Remove from heat; sprinkle with garlic salt and pepper.

3. Spread Miracle Whip over two slices of toast. Top with eggs, bacon, tomato, avocado and, if desired, cheese and onion. Spread butter over the remaining toast; place over top.

PER SERVING *1 sandwich: 448 cal., 23g fat (7g sat. fat), 209mg chol., 864mg sodium, 44g carb. (7g sugars, 4g fiber), 18g pro.*

HEALTH TIP *Avocados are known for their healthy monounsaturated fat, but they are also a good source of vitamins C, K and E plus most B vitamins.*

PUMPKIN PIE SMOOTHIES

In a blender, process 1 can (15 ounces) chilled pumpkin, 1⅓ cups of chilled evaporated milk, 1 cup orange juice, ⅓ cup packed brown sugar, ½ teaspoon pumpkin pie spice, ¼ teaspoon cinnamon and 1 small ripe banana until smooth. Makes 4 servings.

—**KAREN SIKORA** DAYTON, NV

ASPARAGUS &
CHEESE FRITTATA

10 large eggs
2 cups half-and-half cream
2 tablespoons all-purpose flour
½ teaspoon salt
½ teaspoon onion powder
½ teaspoon pepper

TOPPINGS

4 green onions, thinly sliced
½ cup cherry tomatoes, quartered
1 can (2¼ ounces) sliced ripe olives, drained, optional

1. Preheat oven to 350°. Place 2 cups cheese, ham, green pepper, onion and tomato in a large bowl; toss to combine. Place ½ cup mixture off center on each tortilla. Roll up and place in a greased 13x9-in. baking dish, seam side down.
2. In another bowl, whisk eggs, cream, flour and seasonings until blended; pour over enchiladas. Sprinkle with remaining cheese; add toppings.
3. Bake, covered, for 30 minutes. Uncover; bake 10-15 minutes longer or until a knife inserted in egg portion comes out clean. Let stand 10 minutes before serving.

FREEZE OPTION *Cover and freeze unbaked casserole. To use, partially thaw in refrigerator overnight. Remove from refrigerator 30 minutes before baking. Preheat oven to 350°. Cover casserole with foil; bake as directed, increasing uncovered time to 25-35 minutes or until the cheese is melted and a thermometer reads 165°.*

PER SERVING *1 enchilada (calculated without olives): 375 cal., 22g fat (10g sat. fat), 214mg chol., 832mg sodium, 22g carb. (3g sugars, 2g fiber), 21g pro.*

ASPARAGUS & CHEESE FRITTATA

This rich and creamy frittata begins in the skillet and ends in the oven. We like this melty, cheesy happiness with a green salad on the side.
—**GILDA LESTER** MILLSBORO, DE

START TO FINISH: 30 MIN.
MAKES: 4 SERVINGS

5 large eggs
½ cup grated Romano cheese
½ cup vegetable broth
¼ teaspoon salt
¼ teaspoon pepper
2 slices Italian bread (½ inch thick), cubed
2 tablespoons olive oil
2 cups cut fresh asparagus (½-inch pieces)
1 medium onion, finely chopped
½ cup shredded Gruyere cheese

1. Preheat broiler. In a small bowl, whisk the first five ingredients until blended; stir in bread cubes.
2. In an 8-in. ovenproof skillet, heat oil over medium-high heat. Add asparagus and onion; cook and stir 8-10 minutes or until onion is tender.

3. Reduce heat to medium-low; pour in egg mixture. Cook, uncovered, 4-6 minutes or until nearly set. Sprinkle with Gruyere cheese.
4. Broil 3-4 in. from heat 5-7 minutes or until cheese is melted and eggs are completely set. Let stand 5 minutes. Cut into wedges.

PER SERVING *1 wedge: 325 cal., 22g fat (9g sat. fat), 263mg chol., 779mg sodium, 12g carb. (3g sugars, 2g fiber), 21g pro.*

BRUNCH BUDDIES ENCHILADAS

In our women's group, we take turns making brunch. I was tired of the same casseroles so I invented this Mexican-style bake. The recipe requests keep coming.
—**JULIA HUNTINGTON** CHEYENNE, WY

PREP: 40 MIN. • **BAKE:** 40 MIN. + STANDING
MAKES: 12 SERVINGS

3 cups (12 ounces) shredded Mexican cheese blend, divided
2 cups cubed fully cooked ham
1 small green pepper, chopped
1 small onion, chopped
1 medium tomato, chopped
12 flour tortillas (6 inches)

BRUNCH BUDDIES
ENCHILADAS

CALICO SCRAMBLED EGGS

When you're short on time and rushing to get a morning meal on the table, this recipe is eggs-actly what you need. There's a short ingredient list, and cooking is kept to a minimum.

—TASTE OF HOME TEST KITCHEN

START TO FINISH: 20 MIN.
MAKES: 4 SERVINGS

- 8 **large eggs**
- ¼ **cup 2% milk**
- ⅛ to ¼ **teaspoon dill weed**
- ⅛ to ¼ **teaspoon salt**
- ⅛ to ¼ **teaspoon pepper**
- 1 **tablespoon butter**
- ½ **cup chopped green pepper**
- ¼ **cup chopped onion**
- ½ **cup chopped fresh tomato**

1. In a bowl, whisk the first five ingredients until blended. In a 12-in. nonstick skillet, heat the butter over medium-high heat. Add green pepper and onion; cook and stir until tender. Remove from pan.

2. In same pan, pour in egg mixture; cook and stir over medium heat until eggs begin to thicken. Add tomato and pepper mixture; cook until heated through and no liquid egg remains, stirring gently.

PER SERVING *1 cup: 188 cal., 13g fat (5g sat. fat), 381mg chol., 248mg sodium, 4g carb. (3g sugars, 1g fiber), 14g pro.* **Diabetic Exchanges:** *2 medium-fat meat, ½ fat.*

CALICO SCRAMBLED EGGS

MEDITERRANEAN VEGGIE BRUNCH PUFF

MEDITERRANEAN VEGGIE BRUNCH PUFF

I make breakfast casseroles with whatever I have, like spinach, sweet red pepper and cheddar. With this puff, we like the burst of flavor from Greek vinaigrette.

—ANGELA ROBINSON FINDLAY, OH

PREP: 25 MIN. + CHILLING ● **BAKE:** 25 MIN.
MAKES: 8 SERVINGS

- 6 **large eggs**
- 2 **large egg whites**
- 1 **cup whole milk**
- 1 **garlic cloves, minced**
- ½ **teaspoon salt**
- ¼ **teaspoon pepper**
- 5 **cups cubed croissants (about 6 ounces)**
- ¾ **cup chopped roasted sweet red peppers, divided**
- ½ **cup finely chopped sweet onion**
- 1 **package (10 ounces) frozen chopped spinach, thawed and squeezed dry**
- 1 **cup shredded cheddar cheese**
- ½ **cup crumbled feta cheese**
- 3 **tablespoons Greek vinaigrette**

1. In a large bowl, whisk the first six ingredients until blended. Place croissant pieces in a single layer in a greased 11x7-in. baking dish; top with ½ cup red pepper, onion and spinach. Pour egg mixture over top. Sprinkle with the cheeses. Refrigerate mixture, covered, overnight.

2. Finely chop remaining red pepper; place in a jar with a tight-fitting lid. Add vinaigrette; shake to combine and refrigerate until serving.

3. Preheat the oven to 350°. Remove casserole from refrigerator while oven heats. Bake, uncovered, 25-30 minutes or until a knife inserted in the center comes out clean. Let stand for 5-10 minutes before cutting. Serve with vinaigrette mixture.

FREEZE OPTION *Cover and freeze unbaked casserole. To use, partially thaw in refrigerator overnight. Remove from refrigerator 30 minutes before baking. Preheat oven to 350°. Bake casserole as directed, increasing time as necessary to heat through and for a thermometer inserted in center to read 165°.*

PER SERVING *1 piece with 1½ teaspoons vinaigrette mixture: 281 cal., 17g fat (8g sat. fat), 175mg chol., 656mg sodium, 16g carb. (6g sugars, 2g fiber), 14g pro.*

PRETTY CRANBERRY COFFEE CAKE

Cranberries make this coffee cake a beautiful quick bread that's perfect for the holidays. For extra shimmer, we add a drizzle of almond-flavored glaze.

—**DARLENE BRENDEN** SALEM, OR

PREP: 20 MIN. • **BAKE:** 1 HOUR
MAKES: 16 SERVINGS

- 1 cup butter, softened
- 1 cup sugar
- 2 large eggs
- 1 teaspoon almond extract
- 2 cups all-purpose flour
- 1 teaspoon baking powder
- 1 teaspoon baking soda
- ½ teaspoon salt
- 1 cup (8 ounces) sour cream
- 1 can (14 ounces) whole-berry cranberry sauce
- ½ cup chopped walnuts

OPTIONAL GLAZE
- ⅓ cup confectioners' sugar
- ½ teaspoon almond extract
- 2 to 4 teaspoons warm water

1. Preheat oven to 350°. In a large bowl, cream butter and sugar until light and fluffy. Add eggs, one at a time, beating well after each addition. Beat in extract. In another bowl, whisk flour, baking powder, baking soda and salt; add to creamed mixture alternately with sour cream, beating well after each addition.

2. Spoon a third of the batter into a greased 9-in. square baking pan. Top with a third of the cranberry sauce. Repeat layers twice. Sprinkle with the walnuts.

3. Bake 60-65 minutes or until a toothpick inserted in cake portion comes out clean. Cool on a wire rack.

4. For glaze if desired, in a small bowl, mix confectioners' sugar, extract and enough water to reach a drizzling consistency. Spoon over coffee cake.

PER SERVING *1 piece (calculated without glaze): 305 cal., 17g fat (9g sat. fat), 63mg chol., 295mg sodium, 35g carb. (19g sugars, 1g fiber), 4g pro.*

CHEESE & SAUSAGE BREAKFAST PIZZA

My unusual breakfast pizza with salsa and sausage is a crowd pleaser at church events. Try it with a dash of sweet and spicy Tiger Sauce.

—**KELLY BUCKLEY** NORTON, KS

PREP: 25 MIN. • **BAKE:** 25 MIN.
MAKES: 12 SERVINGS

- 1 pound bulk pork sausage
- 1 medium onion, finely chopped
- ¼ cup salsa
- ½ teaspoon onion powder
- ½ teaspoon ground coriander
- ½ teaspoon ground cumin
- 2 tubes (8 ounces each) refrigerated crescent rolls
- 2 cups (8 ounces) shredded cheddar cheese
- 8 large eggs
- ¼ cup grated Parmesan cheese
- ¼ cup 2% milk
- ¼ teaspoon salt
- ¼ teaspoon pepper
  Tiger Sauce, optional

1. Preheat oven to 350°. In a large skillet, cook sausage and onion over medium heat 5-7 minutes or until sausage is no longer pink, breaking up sausage into crumbles; drain. Stir in salsa and seasonings. Remove from the heat.

2. Unroll both tubes of crescent dough and press onto bottom and up sides of an ungreased 15x10x1-in. baking pan. Press perforations to seal. Top with sausage mixture and cheddar cheese. In a bowl, whisk the eggs, Parmesan cheese, milk, salt and pepper until blended; pour over the sausage and cheese.

3. Bake pizza on a lower oven rack 23-28 minutes or until crust is lightly browned and egg mixture is set. If desired, serve with Tiger sauce.

NOTE *This recipe was tested with TryMe brand Tiger Sauce, a sweet and mildly spicy sauce. Look for it in the condiments section.*

PER SERVING *1 piece (calculated without Tiger Sauce): 380 cal., 26g fat (10g sat. fat), 165mg chol., 798mg sodium, 18g carb. (4g sugars, 0 fiber), 16g pro.*

PRETTY CRANBERRY COFFEE CAKE

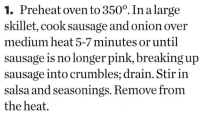

SPICED
BLUEBERRY
QUINOA

SMOKED SAUSAGE BREAKFAST HASH

This hash, full of red potatoes, sweet potatoes and sausage, brightens up any day. We spread the love throughout the week and pile leftovers into burritos and casseroles.

—**JAMIE BURTON** HIGHLANDS RANCH, CO

PREP: 15 MIN. • **BAKE:** 25 MIN
MAKES: 4 SERVINGS

- 1 **pound red potatoes (about 3 medium), cut into ½-inch cubes**
- 1 **medium sweet potato, peeled and cut into ½-inch cubes**
- 1 **medium onion, chopped**
- 1½ **cups sliced smoked turkey sausage (about 8 ounces)**
- 4 **garlic cloves, minced**
- 1 **teaspoon Creole seasoning**
- 2 **cups chopped fresh spinach**
- 1 **tablespoon butter**
- 4 **large eggs**

1. Preheat oven to 425°. In a large bowl, toss together the first six ingredients. Spread evenly in a greased 15x10x1-in. baking pan. Roast 20-25 minutes or until vegetables are tender, stirring once. Stir in spinach; roast 5 minutes longer.
2. Meanwhile, in a large nonstick skillet, heat butter over medium-high heat. Break eggs, one at a time, into pan; immediately reduce heat to low. Cook until whites are completely set and yolks begin to thicken but are not hard, about 5 minutes. Serve eggs over the hash.
PER SERVING *1 egg with 1¼ cups hash: 317 cal., 11g fat (4g sat. fat), 229mg chol., 842mg sodium, 35g carb. (8g sugars, 4g fiber), 19g pro.*

SPICED BLUEBERRY QUINOA

I took up eating quinoa when I found out how much protein it has. It's really an easy dish to experiment with. The first version of this recipe used shredded apples instead of blueberries. And it was just as delicious as this one!

—**SHANNON COPLEY** PICKERINGTON, OH

PREP: 10 MIN. • **COOK:** 30 MIN.
MAKES: 2 SERVINGS

- ½ **cup quinoa, rinsed and well drained**
- 2 **cups unsweetened almond milk**
- 2 **tablespoons honey**
- ½ **teaspoon ground cinnamon**
- ¼ **teaspoon salt**
- 1 **cup fresh or frozen blueberries, thawed**
- ¼ **teaspoon vanilla extract**
- 2 **tablespoons chopped almonds, toasted**

1. In a small saucepan, cook and stir quinoa over medium heat 5-7 minutes or until lightly toasted. Stir in almond milk, honey, cinnamon and salt; bring to a boil. Reduce the heat; simmer, uncovered, 20-25 minutes or until quinoa is tender and liquid is almost absorbed, stirring occasionally.
2. Remove mixture from heat; stir in blueberries and vanilla. Sprinkle with the almonds.
PER SERVING *1 cup: 352 cal., 10g fat (1g sat. fat), 0 chol., 479mg sodium, 59g carb. (25g sugars, 7g fiber), 9g pro.*
HEALTH TIP *Quinoa is a good source of trace minerals that are important in turning carbs into energy, such as manganese and copper.*

SMOKED SAUSAGE
BREAKFAST HASH

SAUSAGE-VEGETABLE
EGG BAKE

EGGS IN PURGATORY

Tomatoes and red pepper flakes add the zing in these saucy eggs. Serve them with toasted bread or sauteed polenta rounds.

—NICK IVERSON MILWAUKEE, WI

START TO FINISH: 30 MIN
MAKES: 4 SERVINGS

- 2 tablespoons canola oil
- 1 medium onion, chopped
- ¼ cup tomato paste
- 2 garlic cloves, minced
- 2 teaspoons smoked paprika
- ½ teaspoon sugar
- ½ teaspoon crushed red pepper flakes
- 2 cans (14½ ounces each) fire-roasted diced tomatoes, undrained
- 4 large eggs
- ¼ cup shredded Manchego or Monterey Jack cheese
- 2 tablespoons minced fresh parsley
- 1 tube (18 ounces) polenta, sliced and warmed, optional

1. In a large skillet, heat oil over medium-high heat. Add onion; cook and stir 6-8 minutes or until tender. Stir in tomato paste, garlic, paprika, sugar and pepper flakes; cook for 2 minutes longer.

2. Stir in tomatoes; bring to a boil. Reduce heat to maintain a simmer. With the back of a spoon, make four wells in sauce. Break an egg into each well. Sprinkle with cheese; cook, covered, 8-10 minutes or until egg whites are completely set and yolks begin to thicken but are not hard. Sprinkle with parsley. If desired, serve with polenta.

PER SERVING (*calculated without bread*): *255 cal., 14g fat (4g sat. fat), 193mg chol., 676mg sodium, 20g carb. (9g sugars, 3g fiber), 11g pro.* **Diabetic Exchanges:** *1½ fat, 1 starch, 1 medium-fat meat.*
HEALTH TIP *Vitamins A and C are important to the immune system, so the tomatoes in this dish will help keep you healthy and feeling good.*

SAUSAGE-VEGETABLE EGG BAKE

When we were kids, our mom tucked homegrown Swiss chard inside this comfy casserole. Now I grow the chard, make the dish and savor the memories.

—CATHY BANKS ENCINITAS, CA

PREP: 25 MIN. • **BAKE:** 1 HOUR
MAKES: 8 SERVINGS

- 1 package (19½ ounces) Italian turkey sausage links, casings removed
- 1 tablespoon butter
- ¾ pound sliced fresh mushrooms
- 3 cups thinly sliced Swiss chard
- ¼ cup white wine
- 3 garlic cloves, minced
- 9 large eggs
- 1¼ cups 2% milk
- ¼ teaspoon salt
- ¼ teaspoon pepper
- 1 cup (4 ounces) shredded part-skim mozzarella cheese
- ¼ cup grated Parmesan or shredded fontina cheese
  Minced fresh parsley

1. Preheat oven to 350°. In a large skillet, cook sausage over medium heat 5-7 minutes or until no longer pink, breaking into crumbles. Using a slotted spoon, transfer sausage to a greased 13x9-in. baking dish, spreading evenly. Remove drippings from pan.

2. In same skillet, heat butter over medium-high heat. Add mushrooms; cook and stir 3-5 minutes or until tender. Add Swiss chard, wine and garlic; cook and stir 1-2 minutes longer or until chard is tender and liquid is almost evaporated. Add to baking dish.

3. In a large bowl, whisk eggs, milk, salt and pepper until blended; pour over vegetable mixture. Sprinkle with mozzarella cheese.

4. Bake, uncovered, for 45 minutes. Sprinkle with Parmesan cheese. Bake 10-15 minutes longer or until a knife inserted near the center comes out clean. Let stand 5 minutes before serving. Sprinkle with parsley.

PER SERVING *1 piece: 248 cal., 15g fat (6g sat. fat), 253mg chol., 640mg sodium, 6g carb. (3g sugars, 1g fiber), 21g pro.*

Heidi Vawdrey's
**Moist & Tender Turkey
Breast** PAGE 201

Slow-Cooked Sensations

Having a home-cooked meal waiting when you return from work or errands is a wonderful welcome! So is waking up to a hot breakfast, cozying up with slow-simmered soups, and making and taking potluck sides with ease. Find all those amazing dishes right here.

Kathleen Murphy's Western Omelet Casserole PAGE 194

Lisa Moriarty's Seafood Cioppino PAGE 195

Loren Martin's Spice-Braised Pot Roast PAGE 197

SLOW COOKER 🍲

CHOCOLATE ESPRESSO LAVA CAKE

When a chocolate craving hits, I whip up this cake that my aunt inspired. It's gooey and saucy but not too sweet. It's also potluck-perfect.

—**LISA RENSHAW** KANSAS CITY, MO

PREP: 15 MIN. • **COOK:** 3 HOURS + STANDING
MAKES: 16 SERVINGS

- 1 **package chocolate fudge cake mix (regular size)**
- 1 **tablespoon instant espresso powder**
- 3 **cups 2% milk**
- 1 **package (3.9 ounces) instant chocolate pudding mix**
- 1 **cup (6 ounces) semisweet chocolate chips**
- 1 **cup white baking chips**

1. Prepare cake mix batter according to package directions, adding espresso powder before mixing. Transfer to a greased 4-qt. slow cooker.
2. In a small bowl, whisk milk and pudding mix for 2 minutes. Let stand 2 minutes or until soft-set. Pour over the batter. Cook, covered, on low for 3-3½ hours or until a toothpick inserted in cake portion comes out with moist crumbs.
3. Sprinkle top with chocolate chips and baking chips. Turn off slow cooker; remove insert. Let stand, uncovered, 15-30 minutes or until chips are softened. Serve warm.
PER SERVING *⅔ cup: 327 cal., 15g fat (6g sat. fat), 41mg chol., 317mg sodium, 45g carb. (29g sugars, 2g fiber), 5g pro.*

BUTTERNUT SQUASH WITH WHOLE GRAINS

EAT SMART **SLOW COOKER** 🍲

BUTTERNUT SQUASH WITH WHOLE GRAINS

Fresh ingredients shine in this scrumptious slow-cooked side. This dish is great way to spread some holiday cheer.

—*TASTE OF HOME* TEST KITCHEN

PREP: 15 MIN. • **COOK:** 4 HOURS
MAKES: 12 SERVINGS (¾ CUP EACH)

- 1 **medium butternut squash (about 3 pounds), cut into ½-inch cubes**
- 1 **cup uncooked whole grain brown and red rice blend**
- 1 **medium onion, chopped**
- ½ **cup water**
- 3 **garlic cloves, minced**
- 2 **teaspoons minced fresh thyme or ½ teaspoon dried thyme**
- ½ **teaspoon salt**
- ¼ **teaspoon pepper**
- 1 **can (14½ ounces) vegetable broth**
- 1 **package (6 ounces) fresh baby spinach**

1. In a 4-qt. slow cooker, combine the first eight ingredients. Stir in broth.
2. Cook, covered, on low 4-5 hours or until grains are tender. Stir in spinach before serving.
PER SERVING *¾ cup: 97 cal., 1g fat (trace sat. fat), 0 chol., 252mg sodium, 22g carb. (3g sugars, 4g fiber), 3g pro.* **Diabetic Exchanges:** *1½ starch.*

SLOW COOKER 🍲

WESTERN OMELET CASSEROLE

When I'm hosting a big brunch, I make omelets the easy way. From youngest to oldest, the whole family is on board.

—**KATHLEEN MURPHY** LITTLETON, CO

PREP: 15 MIN. • **COOK:** 6 HOURS + STANDING
MAKES: 8 SERVINGS

- 1 **package (30 ounces) frozen shredded hash brown potatoes, thawed**
- 1 **pound cubed fully cooked ham or 1 pound bulk pork sausage, cooked and drained**
- 1 **medium onion, chopped**
- 1 **medium green pepper, chopped**
- 1½ **cups shredded cheddar cheese**
- 12 **large eggs**
- 1 **cup 2% milk**
- 1 **teaspoon salt**
- 1 **teaspoon pepper**

1. In a greased 5- or 6-qt. slow cooker, layer half of each of the following: potatoes, ham, onion, green pepper and cheese. Repeat layers.
2. Whisk together the remaining ingredients; pour over top. Cook, covered, on low until set, 6-7 hours. Turn off slow cooker. Remove insert; let stand, uncovered, 15-30 minutes before serving.
PER SERVING *1⅓ cups: 363 cal., 17g fat (8g sat. fat), 332mg chol., 1166mg sodium, 24g carb. (4g sugars, 2g fiber), 29g pro.*

CHOCOLATE ESPRESSO LAVA CAKE

SAUSAGE WITH
JALAPENO POTATOES

SEAFOOD CIOPPINO

If you want a great seafood recipe for your slow cooker, look no further than this classic fish stew. Brimming with clams, crab, fish and shrimp, pair it with some bakery bread for an elegant meal.
—**LISA MORIARTY** WILTON, NH

PREP: 20 MIN. • **COOK:** 4½ HOURS
MAKES: 8 SERVINGS (2½ QUARTS)

- 1 can (28 ounces) diced tomatoes, undrained
- 2 medium onions, chopped
- 3 celery ribs, chopped
- 1 bottle (8 ounces) clam juice
- 1 can (6 ounces) tomato paste
- ½ cup white wine or ½ cup vegetable broth
- 5 garlic cloves, minced
- 1 tablespoon red wine vinegar
- 1 tablespoon olive oil
- 1 to 2 teaspoons Italian seasoning
- 1 bay leaf
- ½ teaspoon sugar
- 1 pound haddock fillets, cut into 1-inch pieces
- 1 pound uncooked shrimp (41-50 per pound), peeled and deveined
- 1 can (6 ounces) chopped clams, undrained
- 1 can (6 ounces) lump crabmeat, drained
- 2 tablespoons minced fresh parsley

1. In a 4- or 5-qt. slow cooker, combine the first 12 ingredients. Cook, covered, on low 4-5 hours.
2. Stir in seafood. Cook, covered, 20-30 minutes longer or until fish just begins to flake easily with a fork and shrimp turn pink.
3. Remove bay leaf. Stir in parsley.
PER SERVING *1¼ cups: 205 cal., 3g fat (1g sat. fat), 125mg chol., 483mg sodium, 15g carb. (8g sugars, 3g fiber), 29g pro.* ***Diabetic Exchanges:*** *3 lean meat, 2 vegetable.*

SAUSAGE WITH JALAPENO POTATOES

My husband and his friends loved to make this dish on the grill. I modified it for the slow cooker. This one is for meat and potato lovers everywhere.
—**ROSE SMITH** ROYALTON, IL

PREP: 25 MIN. • **COOK:** 5 HOURS
MAKES: 6 SERVINGS

- 3 pounds potatoes (about 6 medium), peeled and cut into 1-inch cubes
- 3 jalapeno peppers, sliced and seeded
- ¼ cup butter, cubed
- 2 tablespoons water
- 3 garlic cloves, minced
- ¾ teaspoon salt
- ¼ teaspoon pepper
- 2 medium sweet red peppers, halved and cut into 1-inch strips
- 2 medium sweet yellow or orange peppers, halved and cut into 1-inch strips
- 1 large onion, halved and thinly sliced
- 1 teaspoon olive oil
- 5 Italian sausage links (4 ounces each)
  Chopped fresh basil, optional

1. Place the first seven ingredients in a 6-qt. slow cooker; toss to combine. Top with sweet peppers and onion.
2. In a large skillet, heat olive oil over medium-high heat. Brown sausages on all sides; place over vegetables. Cook, covered, on low 5-6 hours or until potatoes are tender.
3. Remove sausages; cut diagonally into 2- to 3-in. pieces. Remove the vegetables with a slotted spoon; serve with sausage. If desired, sprinkle with fresh basil.
NOTE *Wear disposable gloves when cutting hot peppers; the oils can burn skin. Avoid touching your face.*
PER SERVING *518 cal., 29g fat (11g sat. fat), 71mg chol., 948mg sodium, 50g carb. (5g sugars, 7g fiber), 16g pro.*

SLOW-COOKED SENSATIONS

SWEET POTATO LENTIL STEW

I fell in love with the spicy aromas in this slow-cooked lentil stew. Add whatever ingredients you have on hand, like zucchini, spinach, kale and corn.
—**HEATHER GRAY** LITTLE ROCK, AR

PREP: 15 MIN. • **COOK:** 5 HOURS
MAKES: 6 SERVINGS

- 1¼ pounds sweet potatoes (about 2 medium), peeled and cut into 1-inch pieces
- 1½ cups dried lentils, rinsed
- 3 medium carrots, cut into 1-inch pieces
- 1 medium onion, chopped
- 4 garlic cloves, minced
- ½ teaspoon ground cumin
- ¼ teaspoon ground ginger
- ¼ teaspoon cayenne pepper
- 1 carton (32 ounces) vegetable broth
- ¼ cup minced fresh cilantro

In a 3-qt. slow cooker, combine the first nine ingredients. Cook, covered, on low 5-6 hours or until vegetables and lentils are tender. Stir in cilantro.
PER SERVING 1⅓ cups: 290 cal., 1g fat (0 sat. fat), 0 chol., 662mg sodium, 58g carb. (16g sugars, 15g fiber), 15g pro.

SWEET POTATO LENTIL STEW

ROSEMARY BEETS

We're a family of beet eaters. For a simple side dish, I use a slow cooker and let the beets mellow with rosemary and thyme.
—**NANCY HEISHMAN** LAS VEGAS, NV

PREP: 20 MIN. • **COOK:** 6 HOURS
MAKES: 8 SERVINGS

- ⅓ cup honey
- ¼ cup white balsamic vinegar
- 1 tablespoon minced fresh rosemary or 1 teaspoon dried rosemary, crushed
- 2 teaspoons minced fresh thyme or ¾ teaspoon dried thyme
- 1 tablespoon olive oil
- 2 garlic cloves, minced
- ¾ teaspoon salt
- ½ teaspoon Chinese five-spice powder
- ½ teaspoon coarsely ground pepper
- 5 large fresh beets (about 3½ pounds), peeled and trimmed
- 1 medium red onion, chopped
- 1 medium orange, peeled and chopped
- 1 cup crumbled feta cheese

1. In a small bowl, whisk the first nine ingredients until blended. Place beets in a greased 4-qt. slow cooker. Add the onion and orange. Pour honey mixture over top.
2. Cook, covered, on low 6-8 hours or until beets are tender. Remove beets; cut into wedges. Return to the slow cooker. Serve warm or refrigerate and serve cold. Serve with a slotted spoon; sprinkle with cheese.
PER SERVING ¾ cup: 200 cal., 4g fat (2g sat. fat), 8mg chol., 511mg sodium, 37g carb. (31g sugars, 5g fiber), 6g pro. *Diabetic Exchanges: 2 vegetable, 1 starch, 1 fat.*

SPICE-BRAISED POT ROAST

I've been serving this gingery roast for years, and it's a treat every time. It has a lot of ingredients, but all you have to do is toss them in the pot!
—**LOREN MARTIN** BIG CABIN, OK

PREP: 15 MIN. • **COOK:** 7 HOURS
MAKES: 8 SERVINGS

- 1 boneless beef chuck roast (2½ pounds)
- 1 can (14½ ounces) diced tomatoes, undrained
- 1 medium onion, chopped
- ¼ cup white vinegar
- 3 tablespoons tomato puree
- 1 tablespoon poppy seeds
- 1 bay leaf
- 2¼ teaspoons sugar
- 2 teaspoons Dijon mustard
- 2 garlic cloves, minced
- ½ teaspoon salt
- ½ teaspoon ground ginger
- ½ teaspoon dried rosemary, crushed
- ½ teaspoon lemon juice
- ¼ teaspoon ground cumin
- ¼ teaspoon ground turmeric
- ¼ teaspoon crushed red pepper flakes
- ⅛ teaspoon ground cloves
  Hot cooked egg noodles

1. Place roast in a 5-qt. slow cooker. Mix all remaining ingredients except noodles; pour over roast. Cook, covered, on low until meat is tender, 7-9 hours.
2. Discard bay leaf. If desired, skim fat and thicken cooking juices. Serve pot roast with noodles and juices.
PER SERVING *276 cal., 14g fat (5g sat. fat), 92mg chol., 305mg sodium, 7g carb. (4g sugars, 2g fiber), 29g pro.* **Diabetic Exchanges:** *4 lean meat, ½ starch.*

WHITE BEAN CHICKEN CHILI

SLOW COOKER

WHITE BEAN CHICKEN CHILI

My sister shared this chili recipe with me. I usually double it and add an extra can of beans. The jalapeno adds just enough heat.
—**KRISTINE BOWLES** RIO RANCHO, NM

PREP: 25 MIN. • **COOK:** 3 HOURS
MAKES: 6 SERVINGS

- ¾ pound boneless skinless chicken breasts, cut into 1¼-inch pieces
- ¼ teaspoon salt
- ¼ teaspoon pepper
- 2 tablespoons olive oil, divided
- 1 medium onion, chopped
- 1 jalapeno pepper, seeded and chopped
- 4 garlic cloves, minced
- 2 teaspoons dried oregano
- 1 teaspoon ground cumin
- 2 cans (15 ounces each) cannellini beans, rinsed and drained, divided
- 2½ cups chicken broth, divided
- 1½ cups shredded cheddar cheese
  Optional toppings: sliced avocado, quartered cherry tomatoes and chopped cilantro

1. Toss chicken with salt and pepper. In a large skillet, heat 1 tablespoon olive oil over medium-high heat; saute chicken until browned. Transfer to a 3-qt. slow cooker.
2. In same skillet, heat remaining oil over medium heat; saute onion until tender. Add jalapeno, garlic, oregano and cumin; cook and stir 2 minutes. Add to slow cooker.
3. In a bowl, mash 1 cup of the beans; stir in ½ cup broth. Stir bean mixture and the remaining whole beans and broth into chicken mixture.
4. Cook, covered, on low until chicken is tender, 3-3½ hours. Stir before serving. Serve with cheese and, if desired, additional toppings.
CHICKEN CORN CHILI *Add 2 cups thawed frozen corn and ½ teaspoon ground coriander to the slow cooker along with the broth. Proceed as directed.*
FREEZE OPTION *Freeze cooled chili in freezer containers. To use, partially thaw in refrigerator overnight. Heat chili through in a saucepan, stirring occasionally and adding a little broth or water if necessary.*
NOTE *Wear disposable gloves when cutting hot peppers; the oils can burn skin. Avoid touching your face.*
PER SERVING *1 cup: 344 cal., 16g fat (6g sat. fat), 62mg chol., 894mg sodium, 23g carb. (1g sugars, 6g fiber), 25g pro.*

OVERNIGHT CHERRY-ALMOND OATMEAL

If you like breakfast ready when the sun comes up, prep this oatmeal with cherries and almond milk the night before. It's good to go when you are.

—GERALDINE SAUCIER ALBUQUERQUE, NM

PREP: 10 MIN. • **COOK:** 7 HOURS
MAKES: 6 SERVINGS

- 4 **cups vanilla almond milk**
- 1 **cup steel-cut oats**
- 1 **cup dried cherries**
- ⅓ **cup packed brown sugar**
- ½ **teaspoon salt**
- ½ **teaspoon ground cinnamon**
  Additional almond milk, optional

1. In a 3-qt. slow cooker coated with cooking spray, combine all ingredients. Cook, covered, on low until oats are tender, 7-8 hours.

2. Stir before serving. If desired, serve with additional milk.

NOTE *Steel-cut oats are also known as Scotch oats or Irish oatmeal.*

PER SERVING *¾ cup: 276 cal., 4g fat (0 sat. fat), 0 chol., 306mg sodium, 57g carb. (35g sugars, 4g fiber), 5g pro.*

HEALTH TIP *Nutritionally, steel cut oats are about the same as rolled oats, so take your pick. Skip instant oatmeal mixes, which have a lot of added sugar.*

CRANBERRY PORK CHOPS

My husband and two kids always ask for these tender chops. You'll want to pour that sweet and tangy gravy over everything on your plate! We like it with mashed potatoes best.

—ROBIN CZACHOR APPLETON, WI

PREP: 15 MIN. • **COOK:** 4 HOURS
MAKES: 6 SERVINGS

- 1 **can (14 ounces) jellied cranberry sauce**
- ½ **cup cranberry or apple juice**
- ¼ **cup sugar**
- 2 **tablespoons spicy brown mustard**
- 6 **bone-in pork loin chops (8 ounces each)**
- 2 **tablespoons cornstarch**
- ¼ **cup cold water**
- ½ **teaspoon salt**
  Dash pepper

1. Whisk together the first four ingredients. Place pork chops in a 3-qt. slow cooker; top with cranberry mixture. Cook, covered, on low until meat is tender, 4-5 hours.

2. Remove chops; keep warm. Strain cooking juices and transfer to a small saucepan. Mix cornstarch and water until smooth; stir into cooking juices. Bring to a boil; cook and stir until thickened, 1-2 minutes. Stir in salt and pepper. Serve with chops.

PER SERVING *472 cal., 18g fat (7g sat. fat), 111mg chol., 357mg sodium, 38g carb. (27g sugars, 1g fiber), 36g pro.*

SLOW COOKER CHICKEN TACO SALAD

PREP: 10 MIN. • **COOK:** 3 HOURS
MAKES: 6 SERVINGS

- 3 **teaspoons chili powder**
- 1 **teaspoon each ground cumin, seasoned salt and pepper**
- ½ **teaspoon each white pepper, ground chipotle pepper and paprika**
- ¼ **teaspoon dried oregano**
- ¼ **teaspoon crushed red pepper flakes**
- 1½ **pounds boneless skinless chicken breasts**
- 1 **cup chicken broth**
- 9 **cups torn romaine**
  Optional toppings: sliced avocado, shredded cheddar cheese, chopped tomato, sliced green onions and ranch salad dressing

1. Mix seasonings; rub over chicken. Place in a 3-qt. slow cooker. Add broth. Cook, covered, on low 3-4 hours or until chicken is tender (a thermometer inserted in the chicken should read at least 165°).

2. Remove chicken; cool slightly. Shred with two forks. Serve over romaine; top as desired.

HEALTH TIP *Switch to a baby kale salad blend for more fiber, vitamin C, calcium and iron.*

PER SERVING *1¾ cups: 143 cal., 3g fat (1g sat. fat), 63mg chol., 516mg sodium, 4g carb. (1g sugars, 2g fiber), 24g pro.* **Diabetic Exchanges:** *3 lean meat, 1 vegetable.*

"Wonderfully simple and simply delicious! I cut the salt in half and used iodized salt. I've made double recipes twice now to use the chicken for this salad, in tacos, over polenta, tossed with spiralizer zucchini...delish!"

—WINEGIRL1959 TASTEOFHOME.COM

OVERNIGHT CHERRY-ALMOND OATMEAL

We use this chicken across several meals including tacos, sandwiches, omelets and enchiladas. My little guys love helping measure seasonings.
—**KARIE HOUGHTON** LYNNWOOD, WA

SLOW COOKER CHICKEN TACO SALAD

SLOW COOKER
PEACH BBQ RIBS

SLOW COOKER 🍲

SLOW COOKER BACON MAC & CHEESE

I'm all about easy slow cooker meals. Using more cheese than ever, I've developed an addictive spin on this casserole favorite.

—KRISTEN HEIGL STATEN ISLAND, NY

PREP: 20 MIN.
COOK: 3 HOURS + STANDING
MAKES: 18 SERVINGS (½ CUP EACH)

- 2 **large eggs, lightly beaten**
- 4 **cups whole milk**
- 1 **can (12 ounces) evaporated milk**
- ¼ **cup butter, melted**
- 1 **tablespoon all-purpose flour**
- 1 **teaspoon salt**
- 1 **package (16 ounces) small pasta shells**
- 1 **cup shredded provolone cheese**
- 1 **cup shredded Manchego or Monterey Jack cheese**
- 1 **cup shredded white cheddar cheese**
- 8 **bacon strips, cooked and crumbled**

1. In a large bowl, whisk the first six ingredients until blended. Stir in pasta and cheeses; transfer to a 4- or 5-qt. slow cooker.

2. Cook, covered, on low 3-3½ hours or until pasta is tender. Turn off slow cooker; remove insert. Let stand, uncovered, 15 minutes before serving. Top with bacon.

PER SERVING *½ cup: 272 cal., 14g fat (8g sat. fat), 59mg chol., 400mg sodium, 24g carb. (5g sugars, 1g fiber), 13g pro.*

SLOW COOKER BACON MAC & CHEESE

SLOW COOKER 🍲

SLOW COOKER PEACH BBQ RIBS

For eat-the-whole-rack ribs, start with a rub of chili powder, cumin, paprika and cayenne. Then slather on sweet, peachy sauce. Keep the napkins stocked.

—SUE RYON SHOREWOOD, WI

PREP: 10 MIN. ● **COOK:** 5 HOURS
MAKES: 8 SERVINGS (3 CUPS SAUCE)

- 2 **tablespoons chili powder**
- 1 **tablespoon brown sugar**
- 2 **teaspoons ground cumin**
- 2 **teaspoons smoked paprika**
- 2 **teaspoons garlic salt**
- ½ **teaspoon cayenne pepper**
- 4 **pounds pork baby back ribs, cut into serving-size pieces**

SAUCE
- 3 **medium ripe peaches, peeled and chopped**
- 1 **bottle (18 ounces) barbecue sauce**
- ¼ **cup water**
- 1 **jalapeno pepper, thinly sliced**

1. In a small bowl, mix seasonings; rub over meaty side of ribs. Place in a 6-qt. slow cooker. Cook, covered, on low for 5-6 hours or until meat is tender.

2. Before serving, combine the peaches, barbecue sauce and water in a saucepan; bring to a boil. Reduce heat; simmer, covered, 15-20 minutes or until peaches are softened, stirring occasionally. If desired, thin with additional water. Stir in jalapeno. Serve with ribs.

PER SERVING *431 cal., 22g fat (8g sat. fat), 81mg chol., 1048mg sodium, 35g carb. (28g sugars, 3g fiber), 24g pro.*

HEALTH TIP *These taste amazing even without the sauce, which loads on most of the sodium. Skip the sauce and use 1 teaspoon garlic powder for the 2 teaspoons garlic salt in the rub and sodium falls to 150 milligrams.*

GINGERBREAD
PUDDING CAKE

GINGERBREAD PUDDING CAKE

Sweet spices and a half cup of molasses give my dessert a delightful old-fashioned flavor. Make it pretty with a dollop of whipped cream.

—**BARBARA COOK** YUMA, AZ

PREP: 20 MIN.
COOK: 2 HOURS + STANDING
MAKES: 8 SERVINGS

- ½ cup molasses
- 1 cup water
- ¼ cup butter, softened
- ¼ cup sugar
- 1 large egg white
- 1 teaspoon vanilla extract
- 1¼ cups all-purpose flour
- ¾ teaspoon baking soda
- ¼ teaspoon salt
- ½ teaspoon ground cinnamon
- ½ teaspoon ground ginger
- ¼ teaspoon ground allspice
- ⅛ teaspoon ground nutmeg
- ½ cup chopped pecans
- 6 tablespoons brown sugar

- ¾ cup hot water
- ⅔ cup butter, melted
  Sweetened whipped cream, optional

1. Mix molasses and 1 cup water. In a bowl, cream softened butter and sugar until light and fluffy; beat in egg white and vanilla. In another bowl, whisk together flour, baking soda, salt and spices; add to creamed mixture alternately with molasses mixture, beating well after each addition. Fold in pecans.

2. Pour into a greased 3-qt. slow cooker. Sprinkle with brown sugar. Mix hot water and melted butter; pour over batter (do not stir).

3. Cook, covered, on high until a toothpick inserted in center comes out clean, 2-2½ hours. Turn off slow cooker; let stand 15 minutes. If desired, serve with whipped cream.

PER SERVING *431 cal., 26g fat (14g sat. fat), 56mg chol., 377mg sodium, 48g carb. (32g sugars, 1g fiber), 3g pro.*

MOIST & TENDER TURKEY BREAST

The first time I slow-cooked turkey was on vacation. It simmered while we were out, and we came back to a spectacularly juicy bird.

—**HEIDI VAWDREY** RIVERTON, UT

PREP: 10 MIN. • **COOK:** 4 HOURS
MAKES: 12 SERVINGS

- 1 bone-in turkey breast (6 to 7 pounds)
- 4 fresh rosemary sprigs
- 4 garlic cloves, peeled
- ½ cup water
- 1 tablespoon brown sugar
- ½ teaspoon coarsely ground pepper
- ¼ teaspoon salt

Place turkey breast, rosemary, garlic and water in a 6-qt. slow cooker. Mix brown sugar, pepper and salt; sprinkle over turkey. Cook, covered, on low for 4-6 hours or until turkey is tender and a thermometer inserted in turkey reads at least 170°.

PER SERVING *5 ounces cooked turkey: 318 cal., 12g fat (3g sat. fat), 122mg chol., 154mg sodium, 2g carb. (1g sugars, 0 fiber), 47g pro.*

**CHEESY HAM &
CORN CHOWDER**

1 can (6 ounces) tomato paste
1 can (2¼ ounces) sliced ripe olives, drained
⅓ cup coarsely chopped fresh basil

1. Place eggplant in a colander over a plate; sprinkle with 1 tablespoon salt and toss. Let stand 45 minutes. Rinse and drain eggplant well; blot dry with paper towels.
2. Place eggplant and remaining vegetables in a 5- or 6-qt. slow cooker. Add oil, dried basil, garlic, pepper and remaining salt; toss to combine.
3. Cook, covered, on low 5-6 hours or until onions are tender. Stir in tomato paste, olives and fresh basil; heat mixture through.
FREEZE OPTION *Freeze cooled ratatouille in freezer containers. To use, partially thaw in refrigerator overnight. Microwave, covered, on high in a microwave-safe dish until heated through, stirring gently.*
PER SERVING *¾ cup: 102 cal., 5g fat (1g sat. fat), 0mg chol., 380mg sodium, 13g carb. (7g sugars, 4g fiber), 3g pro.* **Diabetic Exchanges:** *2 vegetable, 1 fat.*

SLOW COOKER 🍲
CHEESY HAM &
CORN CHOWDER

When the day calls for a warm bowl of chunky soup, we make a big pot of the goods—potatoes, corn, ham and cheese.
—**ANDREA LAIDLAW** SHADY SIDE, MD

PREP: 25 MIN. • **COOK:** 8½ HOURS
MAKES: 12 SERVINGS (3¾ QUARTS)

1½ pounds potatoes (about 3 medium), peeled and cut into ½-inch cubes
4 cups fresh or frozen corn, thawed (about 20 ounces)
4 cups cubed deli ham
2 small onions, chopped
4 celery ribs, chopped
4 garlic cloves, minced
¼ teaspoon pepper
3 cups chicken broth
2 tablespoons cornstarch
2 cups whole milk
2 cups shredded sharp cheddar cheese
1 cup sour cream
3 tablespoons minced fresh parsley

1. Place the first eight ingredients in a 6-qt. slow cooker. Cook, covered, on low 8-10 hours or until potatoes are tender.
2. In a small bowl, mix cornstarch and milk until smooth; stir into soup. Cook, covered, on high 20-30 minutes or until thickened, stirring occasionally. Stir in cheese, sour cream and parsley until cheese is melted.
PER SERVING *1¼ cups: 291 cal., 14g fat (8g sat. fat), 65mg chol., 974mg sodium, 23g carb. (7g sugars, 2g fiber), 19g pro.*

EAT SMART **FREEZE IT** **SLOW COOKER** 🍲
SLOW-COOKED
RATATOUILLE

I get my son to eat veggies by cooking this classic dish low and slow. It's a perfect way to use abundant summer vegetables and herbs.
—**DIANE GOEDDE** RED LODGE, MT

PREP: 25 MIN. + STANDING
COOK: 5 HOURS
MAKES: 10 SERVINGS

1 medium eggplant, peeled and cut into 1-inch cubes
1 tablespoon plus 1 teaspoon salt, divided
2 medium onions, halved and thinly sliced
4 medium tomatoes, chopped
3 medium zucchini, cut into ¾-inch slices
2 celery ribs, chopped
3 tablespoons olive oil
2 teaspoons dried basil or 2 tablespoons minced fresh basil
4 garlic cloves, minced
½ teaspoon pepper

TOP TIP
EASY CLEANUP
Get a squeaky-clean slow cooker insert in just a few simple steps.

• Let the insert cool before getting it wet.
• Wash with hot, soapy water (or in the dishwasher, if allowed). Avoid abrasive cleansers—they may scratch the surface.
• To remove mineral stains, fill with hot water and 1 cup vinegar. Cover and turn the heat to high for two hours. Empty the cooker and wash as directed above.
• To remove water spots, rub the surface with canola oil. Let stand for two hours, then wash as directed above.

ITALIAN SPAGHETTI SQUASH

Here's the easiest spaghetti squash recipe I know. Fill the squash with whatever sauce ingredients score big at your house.

—**MELISSA BROOKS** SPARTA, WI

PREP: 15 MIN. • **COOK:** 6¼ HOURS
MAKES: 4 SERVINGS

- 1 **medium spaghetti squash (3 pounds)**
- 1 **can (14½ ounces) diced tomatoes, undrained**
- 1 **cup sliced fresh mushrooms**
- ½ **teaspoon salt**
- ½ **teaspoon dried oregano**
- ¼ **teaspoon pepper**
- ¾ **cup shredded part-skim mozzarella cheese**

1. Halve squash lengthwise; discard seeds. Fill with the tomatoes and mushrooms; sprinkle with seasonings. Place in an oval 7-qt. slow cooker, tilting one slightly to fit.
2. Cook, covered, on low until squash is tender, 6-8 hours. Sprinkle with cheese. Cook, covered, on low until cheese is melted, 10-15 minutes. To serve, cut each half into two portions.
PER SERVING *¾ cup: 195 cal., 6g fat (3g sat. fat), 14mg chol., 661mg sodium, 31g carb. (4g sugars, 7g fiber), 9g pro.* **Diabetic Exchanges:** *2 starch, 1 medium-fat meat.*

BARBECUE PORK TACOS WITH APPLE SLAW

We celebrate taco Tuesdays, so I like to keep things interesting by switching up the varieties. These pork tacos are really simple to make.

—**JENN TIDWELL** FAIR OAKS, CA

PREP: 15 MIN. • **COOK:** 2¼ HOURS
MAKES: 8 SERVINGS

- 2 **pork tenderloins (1 pound each)**
- 1 **can (12 ounces) root beer**

SLAW
- 6 **cups shredded red cabbage (about 12 ounces)**
- 2 **medium Granny Smith apples, julienned**
- ⅓ **cup cider vinegar**
- ¼ **cup minced fresh cilantro**
- ¼ **cup lime juice**
- 2 **tablespoons sugar**
- ½ **teaspoon salt**
- ½ **teaspoon pepper**

ASSEMBLY
- 1 **bottle (18 ounces) barbecue sauce**
- 16 **taco shells**

1. Place pork in a 3-qt. slow cooker. Pour root beer over top. Cook, covered, on low 2-2½ hours or just until tender (a thermometer inserted in the pork should read at least 145°).
2. Meanwhile, in a large bowl, toss slaw ingredients. Refrigerate, covered, until serving.
3. Remove tenderloins to a cutting board; let stand, covered, 5 minutes. Discard cooking juices.
4. Coarsely chop pork; return to slow cooker. Stir in barbecue sauce; heat through. Serve in taco shells; top with some of the slaw. Serve remaining slaw on the side.
PER SERVING *2 tacos with 1 cup slaw: 396 cal., 9g fat (2g sat. fat), 64mg chol., 954mg sodium, 53g carb. (31g sugars, 3g fiber), 25g pro.*

BARBECUE PORK TACOS WITH APPLE SLAW

**Jerri Gradert's
Oven-Baked Shrimp & Grits**
PAGE 215

Effortless Entertaining

Here they are: some of our most outstanding, company-ready and deceptively easy dishes gathered into one helpful chapter. For fancy or casual affairs that span the seasons, look to these recipes when you host family and friends.

**Jean Ecos'
Snap Pea Salad**
PAGE 207

**Melinda Strable's
Cranberry-Orange
Vodka Slush** *PAGE 211*

**Kristie Schley's
Figgy Apple Brie Tart**
PAGE 216

FAST FIX ▶

BARBARA'S ITALIAN WEDDING SOUP

In a little Italian restaurant in Santa Cruz, my husband and I first tasted this amazing soup with orzo. I tweaked it at home to make it healthier but kept the warm and comforting flavor.

—**BARBARA SPITZER** LODI, CA

START TO FINISH: 30 MIN.
MAKES: 6 SERVINGS

- 1 package (19½ ounces) Italian turkey sausage links, casings removed
- 2 shallots, finely chopped
- 3 garlic cloves, minced
- 1 carton (32 ounces) reduced-sodium chicken broth
- ¾ cup uncooked whole wheat orzo pasta
- ¼ teaspoon pepper
- 10 cups coarsely chopped escarole or spinach
- ½ cup coarsely chopped fresh Italian parsley

1. In a 6-qt. stockpot, cook sausage, shallots and garlic over medium heat 6-8 minutes or until sausage is no longer pink, breaking up sausage into crumbles. Drain.

2. Add broth to sausage mixture; bring to a boil. Stir in orzo, pepper and escarole; return to a boil. Reduce heat; simmer, uncovered, 10-12 minutes or until orzo is tender. Stir in parsley before serving.

PER SERVING *1 cup: 197 cal., 6g fat (1g sat. fat), 34mg chol., 780mg sodium, 20g carb. (1g sugars, 6g fiber), 16g pro.*

BARBARA'S ITALIAN WEDDING SOUP

WHITE ALE POTATO SALAD

WHITE ALE POTATO SALAD

When you use an ale-based dressing instead of mayo, you can take it outside even in the dog days of summer. If you're not sure what to buy, ask someone in your liquor store's beer section to recommend a good white ale.

—**JENNY MACBETH** PITTSBURGH, PA

PREP: 15 MIN. • **COOK:** 20 MIN + CHILLING
MAKES: 12 SERVINGS (¾ CUP EACH)

- 2 pounds fingerling or small red potatoes, cut into 1-inch pieces

DRESSING
- ½ cup white ale
- 3 tablespoons olive oil
- 2 tablespoons balsamic vinegar
- 2 tablespoons Dijon mustard
- 1 package Italian salad dressing mix

SALAD
- 4 cups fresh arugula (about 2½ ounces) or chopped fresh kale
- 1½ cups grape tomatoes
- 6 green onions, chopped
- 10 bacon strips, cooked and crumbled
- 1 cup crumbled Gorgonzola or feta cheese
- ¼ cup minced fresh chives

1. Place potatoes in a large saucepan; add water to cover. Bring to a boil. Reduce heat; cook, uncovered, for 12-15 minutes or until tender. Drain; transfer to a large bowl.

2. In a small bowl, whisk dressing ingredients until blended. Pour over warm potatoes and toss to coat. Cool slightly. Refrigerate, covered, until cold, about 1 hour.

3. To serve, add arugula, tomatoes, green onions and bacon to potatoes; toss gently to combine. Sprinkle with cheese and chives. Serve immediately.

PER SERVING *¾ cup: 185 cal., 9g fat (3g sat. fat), 15mg chol., 536mg sodium, 19g carb. (4g sugars, 2g fiber), 7g pro.*

ASIAN PULLED PORK
SANDWICHES

ASIAN PULLED PORK SANDWICHES

My pulled pork is a happy flavor mash-up of Vietnamese pho noodle soup and a banh mi sandwich. It's one seriously delicious slow cooker dish.
—**STACIE ANDERSON** VIRGINIA BEACH, VA

PREP: 15 MIN. • **COOK:** 7 HOURS
MAKES: 18 SERVINGS

- ½ cup hoisin sauce
- ¼ cup seasoned rice vinegar
- ¼ cup reduced-sodium soy sauce
- ¼ cup honey
- 2 tablespoons tomato paste
- 1 tablespoon Worcestershire sauce
- 2 garlic cloves, minced
- 4 pounds boneless pork shoulder roast
- 18 French dinner rolls (about 1¾ ounces each), split and warmed
  Optional toppings: shredded cabbage, julienned carrot, sliced jalapeno pepper, fresh cilantro or basil and Sriracha Asian hot chili sauce

1. In a small bowl, whisk the first seven ingredients until blended. Place roast in a 4- or 5-qt. slow cooker. Pour sauce mixture over top. Cook, covered, on low for 7-9 hours or until the pork is tender.

2. Remove roast; cool slightly. Skim fat from cooking juices. Coarsely shred pork with two forks. Return pork to slow cooker; heat through. Using tongs, serve pork on rolls, adding toppings as desired.

FREEZE OPTION *Freeze the cooled meat mixture in freezer containers. To use, partially thaw in refrigerator overnight. Heat through in a saucepan, stirring occasionally and adding a little broth or water if necessary. Serve as directed.*

PER SERVING *1 sandwich (calculated without optional toppings): 350 cal., 12g fat (4g sat. fat), 60mg chol., 703mg sodium, 35g carb. (8g sugars, 1g fiber), 23g pro.*

SNAP PEA SALAD

When snap peas are in season, we can't resist making this crunchy salad. I usually serve it cold, but it's also good warm, with the peas straight from the pot.
—**JEAN ECOS** HARTLAND, WI

START TO FINISH: 20 MIN.
MAKES: 12 SERVINGS (¾ CUP EACH)

- ¼ cup white wine vinegar
- ¼ cup Dijon mustard
- 2 tablespoons minced fresh parsley
- 2 tablespoons olive oil
- 2 tablespoons honey
- 1 tablespoon lemon juice
- 1 teaspoon salt
- ½ teaspoon pepper
- 3 pounds fresh sugar snap peas
  Grated lemon peel, optional

1. For vinaigrette, in a small bowl, whisk the first eight ingredients until blended. In a 6-qt. stockpot, bring 16 cups water to a boil. Add snap peas; cook, uncovered, 2-3 minutes or just until peas turn bright green. Remove peas and immediately drop into ice water. Drain and pat dry; place in a large bowl.

2. Drizzle with vinaigrette and toss to coat. Serve immediately or refrigerate, covered, up to 4 hours before serving. If desired, sprinkle with lemon peel.

PER SERVING *¾ cup: 84 cal., 3g fat (trace sat. fat), 0 chol., 322mg sodium, 12g carb. (7g sugars, 3g fiber), 4g pro.* ***Diabetic Exchanges:** 1 vegetable, ½ starch, ½ fat.*

HEALTH TIP *Sugar snap peas are a source of lutein and zeaxanthin, two carotenoids that can reduce the risk of chronic eye diseases.*

REUBEN WAFFLE
POTATO APPETIZERS

SKILLET SEA SCALLOPS

Foods as good as scallops don't need much prep or lots of additional ingredients. Some bread crumbs, garlic and lemon do the trick just beautifully.
—**MARGARET LOWENBERG** KINGMAN, AZ

START TO FINISH: 25 MIN.
MAKES: 4 SERVINGS

- ½ cup dry bread crumbs
- ½ teaspoon salt
- 1 pound sea scallops
- 2 tablespoons butter
- 1 tablespoon olive oil
- ¼ cup white wine or reduced-sodium chicken broth
- 2 tablespoons lemon juice
- 1 garlic clove, minced
- 1 teaspoon minced fresh parsley

1. In a shallow bowl, toss the bread crumbs with the salt. Dip scallops in crumb mixture to coat both sides, patting to help coating adhere.
2. In a large skillet, heat butter and oil over medium-high heat. Add scallops; cook 1½-2 minutes on each side or until firm and opaque. Remove from pan; keep warm.
3. Add wine, lemon juice and garlic to same pan; bring to a boil. Stir in the parsley. Drizzle over scallops; serve immediately.
PER SERVING *249 cal., 11g fat (4g sat. fat), 52mg chol., 618mg sodium, 14g carb. (1g sugars, 1g fiber), 21g pro.* **Diabetic Exchanges:** *3 lean meat, 2 fat, 1 starch.*

REUBEN WAFFLE
POTATO APPETIZERS

I love Reubens, so I turned the classic sandwich into a fun appetizer with corned beef and sauerkraut on waffle fries.
—**GLORIA BRADLEY** NAPERVILLE, IL

PREP: 30 MIN. • **BAKE:** 10 MIN./BATCH
MAKES: ABOUT 4 DOZEN

- 1 package (22 ounces) frozen waffle-cut fries
- 4 ounces cream cheese, softened
- 2 cups shredded fontina cheese, divided
- ⅓ cup Thousand Island salad dressing
- 3 tablespoons chopped sweet onion
- 1½ teaspoons prepared horseradish
- 12 ounces sliced deli corned beef, coarsely chopped
- 1 cup sauerkraut, rinsed, well drained and chopped
- 2 tablespoons minced fresh chives

1. Prepare waffle fries according to package directions for baking. Meanwhile, in a small bowl, beat cream cheese, 1 cup fontina cheese, salad dressing, onion and horseradish until blended.
2. Remove fries from oven; reduce oven setting to 400°. Top each waffle fry with about ¼ ounce corned beef and 1 teaspoon each cream cheese mixture, sauerkraut and fontina cheese. Bake 8-10 minutes or until cheese is melted. Sprinkle with chives.
PER SERVING *1 appetizer: 62 cal., 4g fat (2g sat. fat), 12mg chol., 168mg sodium, 4g carb. (0 sugars, 0 fiber), 3g pro.*

SKILLET SEA SCALLOPS

WHOLE GRAIN CHOW MEIN

WHOLE GRAIN CHOW MEIN

My kids are picky eaters, but a little sweet hoisin works wonders. They love this dish, and I love the goodness of whole grains.

—KELLY SHIPPEY ORANGE, CA

START TO FINISH: 30 MIN.
MAKES: 6 SERVINGS

- 6 **ounces uncooked whole wheat spaghetti**
- 2 **tablespoons canola oil**
- 2 **cups small fresh broccoli florets**
- 2 **bunches baby bok choy, trimmed and cut into 1-inch pieces (about 2 cups)**
- ¾ **cup fresh baby carrots, halved diagonally**
- ½ **cup reduced-sodium chicken broth, divided**
- 3 **tablespoons reduced-sodium soy sauce, divided**
- ¼ **teaspoon pepper**
- 4 **green onions, diagonally sliced**
- 2 **tablespoons hoisin sauce**
- 12 **ounces refrigerated fully cooked teriyaki and pineapple chicken meatballs or frozen fully cooked turkey meatballs, thawed**
- 1 **cup bean sprouts**
- **Additional sliced green onions**

1. Cook spaghetti according to package directions; drain.
2. In a large nonstick skillet, heat oil over medium-high heat. Add the broccoli, bok choy and carrots; stir-fry 4 minutes. Stir in ¼ cup broth, 1 tablespoon soy sauce and pepper; reduce heat to medium. Cook, covered, 3-5 minutes or until vegetables are crisp-tender. Stir in green onions; remove from pan.
3. In same skillet, mix hoisin sauce and the remaining broth and soy sauce; add meatballs. Cook, covered, over medium-low heat for 4-5 minutes or until mixture is heated through, stirring occasionally.
4. Add bean sprouts, spaghetti and broccoli mixture; heat through, tossing to combine. Top with additional green onions.
PER SERVING 1⅓ *cups: 304 cal., 14g fat (3g sat. fat), 54mg chol., 759mg sodium, 31g carb. (4g sugars, 5g fiber), 18g pro.*

SAVORY RUBBED ROAST CHICKEN

A blend of paprika, onion powder, garlic and cayenne go on the skin and inside the cavity to create a delicious, slightly spicy roast chicken.

—MARGARET COLE IMPERIAL, MO

PREP: 20 MIN.
BAKE: 2 HOURS + STANDING
MAKES: 12 SERVINGS

- 2 **teaspoons paprika**
- 1 **teaspoon salt**
- 1 **teaspoon onion powder**
- 1 **teaspoon white pepper**
- 1 **teaspoon cayenne pepper**
- 1 **teaspoon dried thyme**
- ¾ **teaspoon garlic powder**
- ½ **teaspoon pepper**
- 1 **roasting chicken (6 to 7 pounds)**
- 1 **large onion, cut into wedges**

1. Preheat oven to 350°. In a small bowl, mix the first eight ingredients.
2. Pat chicken dry and place on a rack in a roasting pan, breast side up. Rub seasoning mixture over the outside and inside of chicken. Place onion inside cavity. Tuck wings under chicken; tie drumsticks together.
3. Roast 2-2½ hours or until a thermometer inserted in thickest part of thigh reads 170°-175°. (Cover with foil if chicken browns too quickly.) Remove from oven; tent with foil. Let stand 15 minutes before carving.
PER SERVING 4 *ounces cooked chicken: 272 cal., 16g fat (4g sat. fat), 90mg chol., 284mg sodium, 2g carb. (1g sugars, 1g fiber), 29g pro.*

TOP TIP

WHITE PEPPER

White pepper comes from fully ripened peppercorns that have had their skins removed. It has a milder flavor than black pepper and is helpful in dishes like mashed potatoes where you might not want black flecks to show. You can substitute black pepper (perhaps using a bit less than called for).

Smart Tarts

Two dozen pucker-up desserts. Zero stress. Reader Sarah Gilbert from Beaverton, Oregon, calls on simple ingredients to craft these bright little bites in a flash.

LEMON CHEESECAKE TARTS

HOW-TO

MAKE THESE SWEET, EASY TARTS

1. **ROLL & CUT** On a work surface, unroll refrigerated pie pastry sheets. Cut 24 circles with a floured 3-in. round cutter, rerolling the scraps as you go.

2. **PRESS & BAKE** Press circles into muffin cups, smoothing edges. Poke generously with a fork. Bake at 450° for 5-7 minutes, then cool completely on wire racks.

3. **FOLD & FILL** Beat together cream cheese and vanilla; add ¼ cup lemon curd. Gradually fold in whipped topping. Spoon into the tart shells.

4. **DOLLOP & DUST** Top each filled tart with a dab of lemon curd and a few blueberries. Chill until serving. Dust the tarts with confectioners' sugar if you like.

LEMON CHEESECAKE TARTS

To make these cute tarts even quicker, add the filling to store-bought phyllo tart shells.
— **SARAH GILBERT** BEAVERTON, OR

PREP: 30 MIN. • **BAKE:** 10 MIN. + COOLING
MAKES: 2 DOZEN

- 1 **package (14.1 ounces) refrigerated pie pastry**

FILLING
- 1 **package (8 ounces) cream cheese, softened**
- 1 **teaspoon vanilla extract**
- 1 **jar (10 ounces) lemon curd, divided**
- 1 **container (8 ounces) frozen whipped topping, thawed**
- 1 **cup fresh blueberries Confectioners' sugar, optional**

PER SERVING *1 tart: 166 cal., 9g fat (5g sat. fat), 22mg chol., 95mg sodium, 18g carb. (10g sugars, 0 fiber), 1g pro.*

BUTTERY RADISH BAGUETTE

GARLIC BREAD MINI MUFFINS

These little garlic bread bites are a terrific addition to any buffet spread. We make sure to serve them warm.

—KATHY YAROSH APOPKA, FL

PREP: 25 MIN. • **BAKE:** 20 MIN.
MAKES: 2 DOZEN

- 6 ounces cream cheese, softened
- 1 teaspoon garlic powder
- 1 teaspoon onion powder
- ¾ cup shredded Colby-Monterey Jack cheese
- ¾ cup shredded Italian cheese blend
- 1 tube (11 ounces) refrigerated breadsticks
- 1 large egg, lightly beaten
- ½ cup shredded Parmesan cheese

1. Preheat oven to 375°. In a small bowl, beat cream cheese, garlic powder and onion powder until blended. In another bowl, toss Colby-Monterey Jack cheese with Italian cheese blend.
2. On a lightly floured surface, unroll breadstick dough; press perforations together to seal. Roll dough into a 12x8-in. rectangle; cut the dough lengthwise in half.
3. Spread each 12x4-in. rectangle with half of the cream cheese mixture to within ¼ in. of edges. Sprinkle each with half of the combined cheeses; roll up jelly-roll style, starting with a long side. Pinch seam to seal. Cut rolls into 1-in. slices.
4. Place beaten egg and Parmesan cheese in separate shallow bowls. Dip a cut side of each slice in egg, then in Parmesan cheese; place in greased mini-muffin cups, cheese side up.
5. Bake 17-20 minutes or until golden brown. Serve warm.
PER SERVING *1 appetizer: 94 cal., 5g fat (3g sat. fat), 22mg chol., 197mg sodium, 7g carb. (1g sugars, 0 fiber), 4g pro.*

---

(5) INGREDIENTS FAST FIX

BUTTERY RADISH BAGUETTE

My dad and brother are crazy for radishes, and this peppery baguette appetizer is a big-time favorite. Add a sprinkle of fresh dill or parsley on top.

—**KATHY HEWITT** CRANSTON, RI

START TO FINISH: 15 MIN.
MAKES: ABOUT 1½ DOZEN

- 1 sourdough or French bread baguette (about 10 ounces), cut diagonally into ¾-inch slices
- 6 tablespoons unsalted butter, softened
- 2¼ cups thinly sliced radishes (about 18 medium)
  Sea salt
  Snipped fresh dill, optional

Spread baguette slices with butter. Top with radishes; sprinkle lightly with salt and, if desired, top with dill.
PER SERVING *1 appetizer (calculated without sea salt): 76 cal., 4g fat (2g sat. fat), 10mg chol., 107mg sodium, 9g carb. (1g sugars, 0 fiber), 1g pro.*

CRANBERRY-ORANGE VODKA SLUSH

Years ago, my mother made a rosy and refreshing party drink I've never forgotten. The sparkle comes from fruit juices, vodka and lemon-lime soda.

—**MELINDA STRABLE** ANKENY, IA

PREP: 15 MIN. + FREEZING
MAKES: 24 SERVINGS

- 9 cups water
- 2 cups sugar
- 1 can (12 ounces) frozen orange juice concentrate, partially thawed
- 1 can (12 ounces) frozen cranberry juice concentrate, partially thawed
- ¾ cup thawed frozen lemonade concentrate
- 2 cups vodka
- 8 cups lemon-lime soda, chilled

1. In a 5-qt. bowl, mix water and sugar until sugar is dissolved. Stir in juice concentrates and vodka until blended. Transfer to freezer containers; freeze overnight.
2. To serve, place ⅔ cup slush in each glass. Stir in ⅓ cup soda.
PER SERVING *1 cup: 210 cal., 0 fat (0 sat. fat), 0 chol., 10mg sodium, 43g carb. (39g sugars, 0 fiber), 0 pro.*

FAST FIX

SHRIMP WITH COCONUT RICE

Cooking rice with coconut milk makes an incredibly tasty, fragrant dish. I love how this quick-to-make dinner is special enough for company.
—**CHARLA ARNOLD** NORTH BRANCH, MI

START TO FINISH: 30 MIN.
MAKES: 4 SERVINGS

- 1 **can (13.66 ounces) coconut milk**
- 1 **cup uncooked long grain rice**
- 3 **tablespoons butter, divided**
- 1 **garlic clove, minced**
- ½ **teaspoon salt, divided**
- 1 **pound uncooked shrimp (31-40 per pound), peeled and deveined**
- ⅛ **teaspoon pepper**
- 3 **green onions, chopped**
   Lime wedges

1. Place coconut milk in a 2-cup measure; add enough water to measure 2 cups. In a 2-qt. microwave-safe baking dish, combine the rice, 1 tablespoon butter, garlic, ¼ teaspoon salt and the coconut milk mixture. Microwave, uncovered, on high until liquid is absorbed and rice is tender, 20-25 minutes.
2. Meanwhile, in a large skillet, heat remaining butter over medium-high heat; saute shrimp until pink, 5-7 minutes. Stir in pepper and the remaining salt.
3. Stir green onions into rice. Serve with shrimp and lime wedges.
NOTE *This recipe was tested in an 1,100-watt microwave.*
PER SERVING *1 cup shrimp mixture with ½ cup rice: 516 cal., 26g fat (21g sat. fat), 161mg chol., 527mg sodium, 44g carb. (2g sugars, 1g fiber), 24g pro.*

SHRIMP WITH COCONUT RICE

PULLED PORK NACHOS

FREEZE IT **SLOW COOKER**

PULLED PORK NACHOS

While home from college, my daughter made these tempting pork nachos—her first recipe ever. My son and I couldn't get enough of them.
—**CAROL KURPJUWEIT** HUMANSVILLE, MO

PREP: 30 MIN. ● **COOK:** 8 HOURS
MAKES: 16 SERVINGS

- 1 **teaspoon garlic powder**
- 1 **teaspoon mesquite seasoning**
- ¼ **teaspoon pepper**
- ⅛ **teaspoon celery salt**
- 3 **pounds boneless pork shoulder butt roast**
- 1 **medium green pepper, chopped**
- 1 **medium sweet red pepper, chopped**
- 1 **medium onion, chopped**
- 1 **can (16 ounces) baked beans**
- 1 **cup barbecue sauce**
- 1 **cup shredded cheddar cheese**
   Corn or tortilla chips
   Optional toppings: chopped tomatoes, shredded lettuce and chopped green onions

1. In a small bowl, mix seasoning ingredients. Place roast in a 5- or 6-qt. slow cooker; rub with seasonings. Add peppers and onion. Cook, covered, on low 8-10 hours.
2. Remove roast; cool slightly. Strain cooking juices, reserving vegetables and ½ cup juices; discard remaining juices. Skim fat from reserved juices. Shred pork with two forks.
3. Return pork, reserved juices and vegetables to slow cooker. Stir in beans, barbecue sauce and cheese; heat through. Serve over chips and top as desired.
FREEZE OPTION *Freeze cooled pork mixture in freezer containers. To use, partially thaw in the refrigerator overnight. Heat through in a saucepan, stirring occasionally and adding a little broth or water if necessary.*
PER SERVING *½ cup pork mixture (calculated without chips and toppings): 233 cal., 11g fat (5g sat. fat), 60mg chol., 416mg sodium, 14g carb. (6g sugars, 2g fiber), 18g pro.*

JALAPENO POPPER POCKET

For a fresh take on fried jalapeno poppers, we stuff chicken, cheese and jalapenos inside puff pastry and bake.

—**SALLY SIBTHORPE** SHELBY TOWNSHIP, MI

PREP: 15 MIN. • **BAKE:** 20 MIN. + STANDING
MAKES: 12 SERVINGS

- 2 **cups chopped rotisserie chicken (about 10 ounces)**
- 1 **carton (8 ounces) spreadable chive and onion cream cheese**
- 1 **cup shredded pepper jack or Monterey Jack cheese**
- 1 **can (4 ounces) diced jalapeno peppers**
- 1 **sheet frozen puff pastry, thawed**
- 1 **large egg, lightly beaten**

1. Preheat oven to 425°. In a bowl, mix chicken, cream cheese, pepper jack cheese and peppers.
2. On a lightly floured surface, unfold puff pastry; roll into a 13-in. square. Place on a parchment paper-lined baking sheet. Spread one half with chicken mixture to within ½ in. of edges. Fold remaining half over the filling; press edges with a fork to seal.
3. Brush lightly with beaten egg. Cut slits in pastry. Bake 20-25 minutes or until golden brown. Let stand for 10 minutes before cutting.
PER SERVING *1 piece: 237 cal., 15g fat (6g sat. fat), 58mg chol., 252mg sodium, 13g carb. (1g sugars, 2g fiber), 12g pro.*

EAT SMART SLOW COOKER

SPICED HOT APPLE CIDER

During cool-weather season, my husband and I like to take this soul-warming cider outside by the fire pit. It tastes as delicious as it smells.

—**LISA BYNUM** BRANDON, MS

PREP: 10 MIN. • **COOK:** 2 HOURS
MAKES: 10 SERVINGS (¾ CUP EACH)

- 2 **cinnamon sticks (3 inches)**
- 1 **piece fresh gingerroot (about 1 inch), thinly sliced**
- 1 **teaspoon whole allspice**
- 1 **teaspoon whole cloves**
- ½ **teaspoon cardamom pods, crushed**
- 2 **quarts apple cider or juice Rum, optional**

1. Place first five ingredients on a double thickness of cheesecloth. Gather corners of cloth to enclose spice mixture; tie securely with string.
2. Place cider and spice bag in a 3-qt. slow cooker. Cook, covered, to allow flavors to blend, 2-3 hours. Discard spice bag. If desired, stir in rum.
PER SERVING *¾ cup (calculated without rum): 96 cal., 0 fat (0 sat. fat), 0 chol., 20mg sodium, 24g carb. (21g sugars, 0 fiber), 0 pro.*

EAT SMART FAST FIX

PORTOBELLO POLENTA STACKS

My friends and I have recently started growing portobello mushrooms from kits we found at a farmers market. We love to try out new recipes like this one with our harvest.

—**BREANNE HEATH** CHICAGO, IL

START TO FINISH: 30 MIN.
MAKES: 4 SERVINGS

- 1 **tablespoon olive oil**
- 3 **garlic cloves, minced**
- 2 **tablespoons balsamic vinegar**
- 4 **large portobello mushrooms (about 5 inches), stems removed**
- ¼ **teaspoon salt**
- ¼ **teaspoon pepper**
- 1 **tube (18 ounces) polenta, cut into 12 slices**
- 1 **large tomato, cut crosswise into four slices**
- ½ **cup grated Parmesan cheese**
- 2 **tablespoons minced fresh basil**

1. Preheat oven to 400°. In a small saucepan, heat oil over medium heat. Add garlic; cook and stir 1-2 minutes or until tender (do not allow to brown). Stir in vinegar; remove from heat.
2. Place mushrooms, stem sides up, in a 13x9-in. baking dish. Brush with vinegar mixture; sprinkle with salt and pepper. Layer the mushrooms with polenta and tomato; sprinkle with Parmesan cheese.
3. Bake, uncovered, 20-25 minutes or until mushrooms are tender. Sprinkle with basil.
PER SERVING *219 cal., 6g fat (2g sat. fat), 9mg chol., 764mg sodium, 32g carb. (7g sugars, 3g fiber), 7g pro.* **Diabetic Exchanges:** *1½ starch, 1 lean meat, 1 vegetable, 1 fat.*

JALAPENO POPPER POCKET

GARLIC BREAD
PASTA TORTE

GARLIC BREAD PASTA TORTE

My kids love to stuff spiral pasta inside bread for a clever dinner torte. We save the bread crusts to make garlicky croutons for a salad.
—**MELISSA PELKEY HASS** WALESKA, GA

PREP: 40 MIN. • **BAKE:** 25 MIN.
MAKES: 12 SERVINGS

- 1 package (16 ounces) spiral pasta
- 1 package (19½ ounces) Italian turkey sausage links, casings removed
- 8 ounces sliced fresh mushrooms
- 1 medium green pepper, chopped
- 1 medium onion, chopped
- 1 jar (24 ounces) marinara sauce
- 1 tablespoon minced fresh basil or 1 teaspoon dried basil
- 3 teaspoons Italian seasoning
- 2½ cups shredded part-skim mozzarella cheese, divided
- 6 tablespoons butter, cubed
- 6 garlic cloves, minced
- 20 slices white bread, crusts removed
   Additional marinara sauce, warmed, optional

1. Preheat oven to 400°. In a 6-qt. stockpot, cook pasta according to package directions for al dente; drain and return to pot.
2. In a large skillet, cook sausage, mushrooms, green pepper and onion over medium-high heat 7-9 minutes or until the sausage is no longer pink, breaking up sausage into crumbles; drain. Stir in sauce, basil and Italian seasoning. Add to pasta; stir in 2 cups mozzarella cheese.
3. In a microwave, melt butter; stir in garlic. Lightly brush one side of bread with garlic butter. Line bottom and sides of a greased 10-in. springform pan with bread slices, trimming to fit and facing buttered sides against pan. Fill with pasta mixture; press firmly to pack down. Sprinkle with remaining of cheese.
4. Bake, uncovered, 25-30 minutes or until golden brown and cheese is melted. Loosen sides from pan with a knife; remove rim. If desired, serve with additional marinara sauce.
PER SERVING *1 slice (calculated without additional marinara sauce): 409 cal., 16g fat (7g sat. fat), 49mg chol., 752mg sodium, 48g carb. (7g sugars, 3g fiber), 19g pro.*

FRUITED PUNCH

I've made this citrusy drink for years, and it's the best party punch I've found. So good, pretty much everyone who comes over has the recipe now, too.
—**MARLENE MEIMANN** QUEENSBURY, NY

PREP: 20 MIN. + CHILLING
MAKES: 24 SERVINGS (¾ CUP EACH)

- 1½ cups sugar
- 1½ cups water
- 1 bottle (2 liters) ginger ale, chilled
- 3 cups strong brewed tea, chilled
- 3 cups cold orange juice
- 3 cups cold unsweetened pineapple juice
- ½ cup lemon juice
- 3 cups thinly sliced fresh strawberries or frozen unsweetened sliced strawberries

1. For sugar syrup, combine sugar and water in a small saucepan; bring to a boil over medium heat. Reduce heat; simmer, uncovered, 3-4 minutes or until the sugar is dissolved, stirring occasionally. Cool syrup completely. Transfer to a covered container; refrigerate until cold, about 1 hour.
2. To serve, combine ginger ale, tea, fruit juices and sugar syrup in a punch bowl. Or, divide ingredients between two pitchers and stir to combine. Serve with strawberries.
PER SERVING *¾ cup: 107 cal., trace fat (trace sat. fat), 0 chol., 7mg sodium, 27g carb. (25g sugars, trace fiber), trace pro.*

FRUITED PUNCH

CRANBERRY HOT WINGS

OVEN-BAKED SHRIMP & GRITS

On chilly days, I doctor up grits and top them with shrimp for a comfy meal. If you're not a seafood lover, use chicken, ham or both.

—JERRI GRADERT LINCOLN, NE

PREP: 20 MIN. • **BAKE:** 45 MIN.
MAKES: 6 SERVINGS

- 1 **carton (32 ounces) chicken broth**
- 1 **cup quick-cooking grits**
- 1 **can (10 ounces) diced tomatoes and green chilies, drained**
- 1 **cup shredded Monterey Jack cheese**
- 1 **cup shredded cheddar cheese, divided**
  Freshly ground pepper
- 2 **tablespoons butter**
- 1 **medium green pepper, chopped**
- 1 **medium onion, chopped**
- 1 **pound uncooked shrimp (31-40 per pound), peeled and deveined**
- 2 **garlic cloves, minced**

1. Preheat oven to 350°. In a 13x9-in. or 2½-qt. baking dish, combine broth and grits. Bake, uncovered, until liquid is absorbed and the grits are tender, 30-35 minutes.

2. Stir in tomatoes, Monterey Jack cheese and ½ cup cheddar cheese. Bake, uncovered, until heated through, about 10 minutes. Sprinkle with pepper and remaining cheese; let stand 5 minutes.

3. In a large skillet, heat butter over medium-high heat; saute green pepper and onion until tender, 6-8 minutes. Add shrimp and garlic; cook and stir until shrimp turn pink, 2-3 minutes. Spoon over grits.

PER SERVING *1⅔ cups: 360 cal., 18g fat (10g sat. fat), 141mg chol., 1199mg sodium, 26g carb. (2g sugars, 2g fiber), 25g pro.*

HEALTH TIP *A simple switch to reduced-sodium broth will save almost 300 milligrams of sodium.*

SLOW COOKER 🍲
CRANBERRY HOT WINGS

Cranberry wings remind me of all the wonderful celebrations and parties we've had through the years. My daughter's friends can't get enough of them.

—NOREEN MCCORMICK CROMWELL, CT

PREP: 45 MIN. • **COOK:** 3 HOURS
MAKES: 24 SERVINGS

- 1 **can (14 ounces) jellied cranberry sauce**
- ½ **cup orange juice**
- ¼ **cup hot pepper sauce**
- 2 **tablespoons soy sauce**
- 2 **tablespoons honey**
- 1 **tablespoon packed brown sugar**
- 1 **tablespoon Dijon mustard**
- 2 **teaspoons garlic powder**
- 1 **teaspoon dried minced onion**
- 1 **garlic clove, minced**
- 5 **pounds chicken wings (about 24 wings)**
- 1 **teaspoon salt**
- 4 **teaspoons cornstarch**
- 2 **tablespoons cold water**

1. In a small bowl, whisk the first ten ingredients until blended. For chicken, use a sharp knife to cut through two wing joints; discard wing tips. Place wings in a 6-qt. slow cooker; sprinkle with salt. Pour cranberry mixture over top. Cook, covered, on low 3-4 hours or until chicken is tender.

2. Remove wings to a 15x10x1-in. baking pan; arrange in a single layer. Preheat broiler.

3. Transfer cooking juices to a large skillet; skim fat. Bring juices to a boil; cook 15-20 minutes or until mixture is reduced by half, stirring occasionally. In a small bowl, mix cornstarch and water until smooth; stir into juices. Return to a boil, stirring constantly; cook and stir 1-2 minutes or until thickened.

4. Meanwhile, broil wings 3-4 in. from heat for 2-3 minutes or until lightly browned. Brush with some of the glaze; serve with remaining glaze.

PER SERVING *2 pieces with about 1 tablespoon glaze: 142 cal., 7g fat (2g sat. fat), 30mg chol., 244mg sodium, 10g carb. (7g sugars, 0 fiber), 10g pro.*

FIGGY APPLE BRIE TART

Our holiday gatherings often included baked Brie. I transformed it into a dessert that's savory and sweet. It still makes a wonderful appetizer, too.

—KRISTIE SCHLEY SEVERNA PARK, MD

PREP: 25 MIN. • **BAKE:** 15 MIN.
MAKES: 8 SERVINGS

- 3 **tablespoons butter, softened**
- ¾ **cup sugar**
- 2 **large apples**
- 1 **cup dried figs, halved**
- ½ **pound Brie cheese, rind removed, sliced**
- 1 **sheet refrigerated pie pastry**

1. Preheat oven to 425°. Spread butter over bottom of a 10-in. ovenproof skillet; sprinkle evenly with sugar.
2. Peel, quarter and core apples; arrange in a circular pattern over sugar, rounded side down. Place figs around apples. Place skillet over medium heat; cook 10-12 minutes or until sugar is caramelized and apples have softened slightly. Remove from heat; top with cheese.
3. Unroll pastry sheet; place over apples, tucking under edges. Place skillet in oven on an upper rack; bake 15-18 minutes or until crust is golden brown. Cool in pan for 5 minutes. Carefully invert onto a serving plate; serve warm.
PER SERVING *1 piece: 394 cal., 19g fat (11g sat. fat), 45mg chol., 315mg sodium, 50g carb. (33g sugars, 2g fiber), 8g pro.*

FIGGY APPLE BRIE TART

SPAGHETTI SUPPER

FREEZE IT

SPAGHETTI SUPPER

It was such a joy to come home and find my mom making spaghetti and meatballs for dinner. This recipe has always been dear to my heart.

—DEBBIE HEGGIE LARAMIE, WY

PREP: 30 MIN. • **COOK:** 1¾ HOURS
MAKES: 10 SERVINGS

- 2 **cans (28 ounces each) diced tomatoes, undrained**
- 2 **teaspoons sugar**
- 2 **teaspoons dried basil**
- 2 **garlic cloves, minced**
- 1 **teaspoon salt**
- ½ **teaspoon pepper**

MEATBALLS
- 3 **cups soft bread crumbs**
- ½ **cup water**
- 2 **large eggs, lightly beaten**
- ½ **cup grated Parmesan cheese**
- 2 **tablespoons minced fresh parsley**
- 1 **garlic clove, minced**
- 1 **teaspoon salt**
- ¼ **teaspoon pepper**
- 1 **pound ground beef**
- 1 **pound ground pork**
  Hot cooked spaghetti

1. In a 6-qt. stockpot, combine the first six ingredients; bring to a boil.

Reduce heat; simmer, covered, for 1½ hours, stirring occasionally.
2. For meatballs, preheat oven to 400°. In a large bowl, combine bread crumbs and water; let stand 5 minutes. Stir in eggs, cheese, parsley, garlic, salt and pepper. Add beef and pork; mix lightly but thoroughly. Shape into 1-in. balls.
3. Place meatballs on a greased rack in a 15x10x1-in. baking pan. Bake 15-20 minutes or until cooked through. Add meatballs to sauce, stirring gently to combine. Serve with spaghetti.
FREEZE OPTION *Freeze cooled meatball mixture in freezer containers. To use, partially thaw in refrigerator overnight. Heat through in a covered saucepan, stirring gently and adding a little water if necessary.*
NOTE *To make soft bread crumbs, tear bread into pieces and place in a food processor or blender. Cover and pulse until crumbs form. One slice of bread yields ½-¾ cup crumbs.*
PER SERVING *1 cup (calculated without spaghetti): 254 cal., 13g fat (5g sat. fat), 98mg chol., 798mg sodium, 12g carb. (4g sugars, 2g fiber), 21g pro.*

CHICKEN CORDON BLEU BAKE

A friend gave me this awesome hot dish recipe. I freeze several pans to share with neighbors in need or for days when I'm scrambling at mealtime.
—**REA NEWELL** DECATUR, IL

PREP: 20 MIN. • **BAKE:** 40 MIN.
MAKES: 2 CASSEROLES (6 SERVINGS EACH)

- **2** packages (6 ounces each) reduced-sodium stuffing mix
- **1** can (10¾ ounces) condensed cream of chicken soup, undiluted
- **1** cup 2% milk
- **8** cups cubed cooked chicken
- **½** teaspoon pepper
- **¾** pound sliced deli ham, cut into 1-inch strips
- **1** cup shredded Swiss cheese
- **3** cups shredded cheddar cheese

1. Preheat oven to 350°. Prepare stuffing mixes according to package directions. Meanwhile, whisk together soup and milk.

2. Toss chicken with pepper; divide between two greased 13x9-in. baking dishes. Layer with ham, Swiss cheese, 1 cup cheddar cheese, soup mixture and stuffing. Sprinkle with remaining cheddar cheese.

3. Bake, covered, for 30 minutes. Uncover; bake until cheese is melted, 10-15 minutes.

FREEZE OPTION *Cover and freeze unbaked casseroles. To use, partially thaw in refrigerator overnight. Remove from refrigerator 30 minutes before baking. Preheat oven to 350°. Bake, covered, until heated through and a thermometer inserted in center reads 165°, about 45 minutes. Uncover; bake until cheese is melted, 10-15 minutes.*

PER SERVING *1 cup: 555 cal., 29g fat (15g sat. fat), 158mg chol., 1055mg sodium, 26g carb. (5g sugars, 1g fiber), 46g pro.*

STRAWBERRY-BASIL REFRESHER

Strawberries and basil are everywhere in the early summer, so get them together for a cooler that's pure sunshine. Garnish with basil leaves and sip it in the shade.
—**CAROLYN TURNER** RENO, NV

START TO FINISH: 10 MIN.
MAKES: 12 SERVINGS

- **⅔** cup lemon juice
- **½** cup sugar
- **1** cup sliced fresh strawberries Ice cubes
- **1** to 2 tablespoons chopped fresh basil
- **1** bottle (1 liter) club soda, chilled

1. Place the lemon juice, sugar, strawberries and 1 cup ice cubes in a blender; cover and process until blended. Add basil; pulse 1 or 2 times to combine.

2. Divide strawberry mixture among 12 cocktail glasses. Fill with ice; top with club soda.

PER SERVING *40 cal., 0 fat (0 sat. fat), 0 chol., 18mg sodium, 10g carb. (9g sugars, 0 fiber), 0 pro.* **Diabetic Exchanges:** *½ starch.*

TOP TIP

LEMON JUICE

Go for freshly squeezed lemon juice when preparing this summery sipper. Bottled lemon juice, which is from concentrate, won't provide the same bright, fresh flavor. Buy four lemons to get the job done.

CHICKEN CORDON BLEU BAKE

**Diane Bramlett's
Easy Scalloped Potatoes**
PAGE 234

Holiday and Seasonal Pleasers

Special celebrations are for making memories, and the simple menus here will help you maximize the time spent with family and friends. These wow-worthy dishes are easy to prepare. For Easter, Fourth of July, game day, Thanksgiving and Christmas, we've got you covered.

BJ Larsen's Barbecue Sliders
PAGE 228

Katie Stanczak's Garden Cucumber Salad
PAGE 224

Karole Friemann's Citrus Avocado Spinach Salad *PAGE 239*

Easter, Made Easy

Here's a gorgeous Easter spread that's simpler than ever. Readers share their fresh-picked, easy takes on all the standards, from ham with pineapple to asparagus dishes, coconut cake and deviled eggs. Think springtime, streamlined.

ASPARAGUS PASTRY PUFFS

DEVILED EGG SPREAD

FAST FIX

DEVILED EGG SPREAD

I tasted this egg salad at a luncheon and had to have it. I like to punch it up with pickled banana peppers. It's a hit with my kids and my mother.
—**LISA EASLEY** LONGVIEW, TX

START TO FINISH: 20 MIN.
MAKES: 16 SERVINGS (¼ CUP EACH)

- 10 **hard-cooked large eggs**
- 1 **cup Miracle Whip**
- 1 **cup finely shredded cheddar cheese**
- ½ **pound bacon strips, cooked and crumbled**
- ¼ **cup finely chopped pickled banana peppers**
- 2 **teaspoons juice from pickled banana peppers**
- ¼ **teaspoon salt**
- ¼ **teaspoon pepper**
  Ritz crackers and assorted fresh vegetables

1. Place eggs in a large bowl; mash with a fork. Stir in Miracle Whip, cheese, bacon, banana peppers, juice from peppers, salt and pepper.
2. Refrigerate until serving. Serve with crackers and vegetables.
PER SERVING ¼ cup (calculated without crackers and vegetables): 149 cal., 12g fat (4g sat. fat), 134mg chol., 383mg sodium, 3g carb. (2g sugars, 0 fiber), 7g pro.

ASPARAGUS PASTRY PUFFS

When the first asparagus of the season appears, we serve it rolled inside puff pastry with a yummy cheese filling. Our guests always compliment these fresh, lovely treats.
—**CINDY JAMIESON** TONAWANDA, NY

PREP: 30 MIN. • **BAKE:** 25 MIN.
MAKES: 16 SERVINGS

- 1 **pound fresh asparagus, trimmed**
- 4 **ounces cream cheese, softened**
- ¼ **cup grated Parmesan cheese**
- 1 **tablespoon stone-ground mustard**
- 2 **teaspoons lemon juice**
- ¼ **teaspoon salt**
- ¼ **teaspoon pepper**
- 1 **package (17.3 ounces) frozen puff pastry, thawed**
- 1 **large egg**
- 2 **tablespoons water**

1. Preheat oven to 400°. In a large skillet, bring 1½ in. of water to a boil. Add asparagus; cook, uncovered, for 1-3 minutes or until crisp-tender. Remove asparagus and immediately drop into ice water. Drain and pat dry.
2. In a small bowl, mix cream cheese, Parmesan cheese, mustard, lemon juice, salt and pepper until blended. Unfold puff pastry sheets; cut each sheet in half to make a total of four rectangles. Spread each rectangle with a fourth of the cream cheese mixture to within ¼ in. of edges. Arrange asparagus over top, allowing tips to show at each end; roll up jelly-roll style. Using a serrated knife, cut each roll crosswise into four sections.
3. Place on a parchment paper-lined baking sheet, seam side down. In a small bowl, whisk egg with water until blended; brush lightly over tops.
4. Bake 25-30 minutes or until golden brown. Remove from pan to a wire rack; serve warm.
PER SERVING 188 cal., 11g fat (4g sat. fat), 21mg chol., 211mg sodium, 18g carb. (1g sugars, 3g fiber), 4g pro.

STRAWBERRY PASTA SALAD

HAM & PINEAPPLE KABOBS

For a twist on the usual holiday fare, my family turns ham and pineapple into juicy kabobs. The marinade gets its unique zip from hoisin, teriyaki and soy sauces.

—**CHANDRA LANE-SIROIS** KANSAS CITY, MO

PREP: 30 MIN. + MARINATING
BAKE: 15 MIN.
MAKES: 12 SERVINGS

- ¼ **cup hoisin sauce**
- ¼ **cup unsweetened pineapple juice**
- ¼ **cup teriyaki sauce**
- 1 **tablespoon honey**
- 1½ **teaspoons rice vinegar**
- 1½ **teaspoons reduced-sodium soy sauce**

KABOBS

- 2 **pounds fully cooked boneless ham, cut into 1-inch pieces**
- 1 **large fresh pineapple, peeled, cored and cut into 1-in. cubes (about 4 cups)**

1. In a large resealable plastic bag, combine the first six ingredients. Add the ham; seal bag and turn to coat. Refrigerate overnight.
2. Preheat oven to 350°. Drain ham, reserving marinade. For glaze, pour marinade into a small saucepan; bring to a boil. Reduce the heat and simmer, uncovered, 5-7 minutes or until slightly thickened, stirring occasionally. Remove from heat.
3. Meanwhile, on 12 metal or soaked wooden skewers, alternately thread ham and pineapple; place in a foil-lined 15x10x1-in. baking pan. Brush with glaze. Bake, uncovered, 15-20 minutes or until lightly browned.
PER SERVING *1 kabob equals 144 cal., 3g fat (1g sat. fat), 39mg chol., 1109mg sodium, 15g carb., 1g fiber, 15g pro.*

EAT SMART

STRAWBERRY PASTA SALAD

Bow tie pasta with fresh strawberries makes a delicious, refreshing salad, especially with a little chopped mint. I multiply it for brunches, potlucks and even tailgate parties.

—**BARBARA LENTO** HOUSTON, PA

PREP: 20 MIN. ● **COOK:** 15 MIN.
MAKES: 12 SERVINGS (⅔ CUP EACH)

- ½ **pound uncooked mini farfalle or other bow tie pasta**
- ½ **cup (4 ounces) lemon yogurt**
- ¼ **cup canola oil**
- 2 **tablespoons lemon juice**
- ½ **teaspoon sea salt**
- ⅛ **teaspoon cayenne pepper**
- 1 **green onion, thinly sliced**
- 2 **tablespoons crystallized ginger, finely chopped**
- 1 **tablespoon pickled jalapeno slices, finely chopped**
- 1 **pound fresh strawberries, quartered**
- ¼ **cup slivered almonds, toasted**
  Toasted flaked coconut and small fresh mint leaves, optional

1. Cook pasta according to package directions. Drain; rinse with cold water and drain well.
2. In a large bowl, whisk yogurt, oil, lemon juice, salt and cayenne until blended; stir in green onion, ginger and pickled jalapeno. Add pasta and toss to coat.
3. Refrigerate, covered, until serving. Stir in strawberries and sprinkle with almonds just before serving. If desired, sprinkle with coconut and mint.
NOTE *To toast nuts and coconut, bake in separate shallow pans in a 350° oven for 5-10 minutes or until golden brown, stirring occasionally.*
PER SERVING ⅔ *cup (calculated without coconut): 153 cal., 6g fat (1g sat. fat), 1mg chol., 96mg sodium, 21g carb. (5g sugars, 2g fiber), 4g pro.*
Diabetic Exchanges: 1 starch, 1 fat, ½ fruit.

EASY PEASY SLAW

CUMIN-ROASTED CARROTS

PER SERVING *86 cal., 4g fat (3g sat. fat), 0 chol., 277mg sodium, 13g carb. (5g sugars, 4g fiber), 1g pro.* **Diabetic Exchanges:** *1 vegetable, 1 fat.*
HEALTH TIP *The fat in coconut oil includes medium-chain triglycerides, but their health benefits are still unproven. It will give these carrots a subtle coconut flavor, but it probably won't help you shed pounds.*

EAT SMART | (5) INGREDIENTS | FAST FIX ▶

EASY PEASY SLAW

I get tons of compliments when I bring out this slaw brightened up with peas, peanuts and poppy seed dressing. It's fresh and colorful with a satisfying crunch.
—**SUE ORT** DES MOINES, IA

START TO FINISH: 5 MIN.
MAKES: 12 SERVINGS (⅔ CUP EACH)

- 4 **cups frozen peas (about 16 ounces), thawed**
- 1 **package (14 ounces) coleslaw mix**
- 4 **green onions, chopped**
- 1 **cup poppy seed salad dressing**
- 1 **cup sweet and crunchy peanuts or honey-roasted peanuts**

Place peas, coleslaw mix and green onions in a large bowl. Pour dressing over salad and toss to coat. Stir in peanuts just before serving.
PER SERVING *⅔ cup: 202 cal., 12g fat (2g sat. fat), 7mg chol., 178mg sodium, 20g carb. (14g sugars, 4g fiber), 4g pro.* **Diabetic Exchanges:** *2 fat, 1 starch, 1 vegetable.*

TOP TIP

CUT GREEN ONIONS WITH SCISSORS

When a recipe calls for green onions, I find it easier and faster to cut them with kitchen scissors than with a knife. If the recipe calls for quite a few, grab a bunch at one time and snip away. You'll be done before you know it, and there's no need to wash a cutting board.

—**LOUISE B.** COLUMBIA, SC

EAT SMART | (5) INGREDIENTS

CUMIN-ROASTED CARROTS

Carrots make a super side—big on flavor and a breeze to cook. Plus, I can actually get my husband to eat these fragrant, deeply spiced veggies.
—**TAYLOR KISER** BRANDON, FL

PREP: 20 MIN. • **COOK:** 35 MIN.
MAKES: 12 SERVINGS

- 2 **tablespoons coriander seeds**
- 2 **tablespoons cumin seeds**
- 3 **pounds carrots, cut into 4x½-inch sticks**
- 3 **tablespoons coconut oil or butter, melted**
- 8 **garlic cloves, minced**
- 1 **teaspoon salt**
- ½ **teaspoon pepper**
  Minced fresh cilantro, optional

1. Preheat oven to 400°. In a dry small skillet, toast coriander and cumin seeds over medium heat for 45-60 seconds or until aromatic, stirring frequently. Cool slightly. Grind in a spice grinder, or with a mortar and pestle, until finely crushed.
2. Place carrots in a large bowl. Add melted coconut oil, garlic, salt, pepper and ground spices; toss to coat. Divide the carrots between two 15x10x1-in. baking pans coated with cooking spray, spreading evenly.
3. Roast 35-40 minutes or until crisp-tender and lightly browned, stirring and rotating pans halfway. If desired, sprinkle with cilantro before serving.
NOTE *Two tablespoons each ground coriander and ground cumin may be substituted for whole spices. Before using, toast ground spices in a dry skillet until aromatic, stirring frequently.*

COCONUT CAKE WITH WHITE CHOCOLATE FROSTING

COCONUT CAKE WITH WHITE CHOCOLATE FROSTING

My husband adores coconut, but cake? Not so much. When I take this beauty to family potlucks, though, even he takes a slice.
—**SHARON REHM** NEW BLAINE, AR

PREP: 40 MIN. • **BAKE:** 25 MIN. + COOLING
MAKES: 16 SERVINGS

- 1 **package white cake mix (regular size)**
- 1¼ **cups coconut milk (about 10 ounces)**
- 3 **large eggs**
- ⅓ **cup butter, melted**

FROSTING

- 1 **cup butter, cubed**
- 12 **ounces white baking chocolate, chopped**
- ½ **cup coconut milk (about 4 ounces)**
- 2½ **cups confectioners' sugar, sifted**
- 1 **to 2 cups unsweetened coconut flakes**

1. Preheat oven to 350°. Line bottoms of two greased 8-in. round baking pans with parchment paper; grease paper.
2. In a large bowl, combine cake mix, coconut milk, eggs and melted butter; beat on low speed 30 seconds. Beat on medium speed 1½ minutes. Transfer to prepared pans. Bake and cool as package directs.
3. For frosting, in a small saucepan, combine the butter, white chocolate and coconut milk; heat and stir over medium heat until blended. Remove from the heat; gradually stir in the confectioners' sugar until smooth.

4. Transfer mixture to a bowl. Place bowl in an ice-water bath. Using a hand mixer, beat frosting on high speed 6-8 minutes or until spreadable. Spread between layers and over top and sides of cake. Cover with coconut.
NOTE *Look for unsweetened coconut in the baking or health food section.*
HEALTH TIP *To save nearly 10 grams of fat and 150 calories, cut the frosting in half and spread it between the cake layers and over the top—but not the sides—for an elegant look.*
PER SERVING *1 slice: 517 cal., 33g fat (23g sat. fat), 76mg chol., 338mg sodium, 55g carb. (43g sugars, 1g fiber), 5g pro.*

Fabulous Fourth of July

From saucy barbecue chicken and sizzling burgers to garden-fresh salads and classic icebox sweets, this menu's got your summer picnic needs covered. Spread out the checkered tablecloths and make your own fireworks!

WATERMELON SALAD WITH FETA

FAST FIX

WATERMELON SALAD WITH FETA

Our family celebrates the Fourth of July with a watermelon salad that resembles the flag. Here's an all-American centerpiece that's truly red, white and blue.

—**JAN WHITWORTH** ROEBUCK, SC

START TO FINISH: 25 MIN.
MAKES: 12 SERVINGS (¾ CUP EACH)

- ¼ cup red wine vinegar
- 1 tablespoon Dijon mustard
- 1 tablespoon grated lemon peel
- 1 teaspoon sugar
- ¼ teaspoon salt
- ¼ teaspoon pepper
- ⅓ cup olive oil
- ¼ cup finely chopped red onion

SALAD

- 6 cups fresh arugula (about 5 ounces)
- 1½ cups fresh blueberries
- 5 cups cubed seedless watermelon
- 1 package (8 ounces) feta cheese, cut into ½-in. cubes

1. For vinaigrette, in a small bowl, whisk the first six ingredients; gradually whisk in oil until blended. Stir in onion.

2. In a large bowl, lightly toss arugula with ¼ cup vinaigrette. Arrange the salad evenly in a large rectangular serving dish.

3. For stars, place blueberries over arugula at the top left corner. For stripes, arrange watermelon and cheese in alternating rows. Drizzle with remaining vinaigrette. Serve immediately.

PER SERVING ¾ cup salad: 140 cal., 10g fat (4g sat. fat), 17mg chol., 256mg sodium, 10g carb. (7g sugars, 1g fiber), 4g pro.

EAT SMART

GARDEN CUCUMBER SALAD

If you like cucumber salad like I do, this one's a cool pick. It's a mix of fresh veggies, feta cheese and Greek seasoning, and it's so refreshing when the sun's beating down.

—**KATIE STANCZAK** HOOVER, AL

PREP: 10 MIN. + CHILLING
MAKES: 12 SERVINGS (¾ CUP EACH)

- 4 medium cucumbers, cut into ½-inch pieces (about 7 cups)
- 2 medium sweet red peppers, chopped
- 1 cup cherry tomatoes, halved
- 1 cup crumbled feta cheese
- ½ cup finely chopped red onion
- ½ cup olive oil
- ¼ cup lemon juice
- 1 tablespoon Greek seasoning
- ½ teaspoon salt

Place all ingredients in a large bowl; toss gently to combine. Refrigerate, covered, at least 30 minutes before serving.

PER SERVING ¾ cup: 125 cal., 11g fat (2g sat. fat), 5mg chol., 431mg sodium, 5g carb. (3g sugars, 2g fiber), 3g pro. **Diabetic Exchanges:** 2 fat, 1 vegetable.

SAUCY BARBECUE
DRUMSTICKS

MARYLAND CORN POPS

Fresh-picked sweet corn is a big thing in Maryland. Here's my homespun version of Mexican street corn that also includes local Bay flavors.

—KRISTIE SCHLEY SEVERNA PARK, MD

PREP: 25 MIN. • **GRILL:** 10 MIN.
MAKES: 2 DOZEN

- 8 medium ears sweet corn, husks removed
- 2 tablespoons canola oil
- 1½ cups mayonnaise
- 1½ teaspoons garlic powder
- ¼ teaspoon freshly ground pepper
- 24 corncob holders
- 2 cups crumbled feta cheese
- 2 tablespoons seafood seasoning
- ¼ cup minced fresh cilantro
  Lime wedges, optional

1. Brush all sides of corn with oil. Grill, covered, over medium heat 10-12 minutes or until tender and lightly browned, turning occasionally. Remove from grill; cool slightly.
2. Meanwhile, in a small bowl, mix mayonnaise, garlic powder and pepper. Cut each ear of corn into thirds. Insert one corncob holder into each piece. Spread corn with the mayonnaise mixture; sprinkle with feta cheese, seafood seasoning and minced cilantro. If desired, serve with lime wedges.

PER SERVING *1 corn pop: 164 cal., 14g fat (3g sat. fat), 10mg chol., 336mg sodium, 7g carb. (2g sugars, 1g fiber), 3g pro.*

MARYLAND
CORN POPS

SAUCY BARBECUE DRUMSTICKS

After searching for an out-of-this-world bottled barbecue sauce, I threw in the towel and stirred up my own with ketchup, honey, brown mustard—the works.

—KATHLEEN CRIDDLE LAKE WORTH, FL

PREP: 25 MIN. • **GRILL:** 15 MIN.
MAKES: 8 SERVINGS (2 CUPS SAUCE)

- 2 cups ketchup
- ⅔ cup honey
- ⅓ cup packed brown sugar
- 2 tablespoons finely chopped sweet onion
- 2 tablespoons spicy brown mustard
- 4 garlic cloves, minced
- 1 tablespoon Worcestershire sauce
- 1 tablespoon cider vinegar
- 16 chicken drumsticks

1. In a large saucepan, mix the first eight ingredients; bring to a boil. Reduce heat; simmer, uncovered, 15-20 minutes to allow flavors to blend, stirring occasionally. Reserve 2 cups sauce for serving.
2. On a greased grill rack, grill the chicken, covered, over medium heat 15-20 minutes or until a thermometer reads 170°-175°, turning occasionally and brushing generously with the remaining sauce during the final 5 minutes. Serve with reserved sauce.

PER SERVING *2 drumsticks with ¼ cup sauce: 422 cal., 12g fat (3g sat. fat), 95mg chol., 909mg sodium, 49g carb. (48g sugars, 0 fiber), 29g pro.*

EAT SMART

SUMMERTIME TOMATO SALAD

Here is the best of summer in a cool, refreshing salad. Cherry tomatoes make it pretty and colorful, and the blueberries and hint of mint offer a sweet surprise.
—**THOMAS FAGLON** SOMERSET, NJ

PREP: 15 MIN. ● **COOK:** 10 MIN. + CHILLING
MAKES: 12 SERVINGS

- 4 medium ears sweet corn, husks removed
- 2 pounds cherry tomatoes (about 6 cups), halved
- 1 small yellow summer squash, halved lengthwise and sliced
- 1 cup fresh blueberries
- 1 small red onion, halved and thinly sliced
- ¼ cup olive oil
- 2 tablespoons lemon juice
- 1 tablespoon minced fresh mint
- ½ teaspoon salt
- ½ teaspoon freshly ground pepper

1. In a 6-qt. stockpot, bring 8 cups water to a boil. Add corn; cook, uncovered, 2-4 minutes or until crisp-tender. Remove corn and immediately drop into ice water to cool; drain well.

2. Cut corn from cobs and place in a bowl. Add remaining ingredients; toss to combine. Refrigerate, covered, until cold, about 30 minutes.

PER SERVING ¾ cup: 95 cal., 5g fat (1g sat. fat), 0 chol., 108mg sodium, 12g carb. (6g sugars, 2g fiber), 2g pro. **Diabetic Exchanges:** 1 vegetable, 1 fat, ½ starch.

SUMMERTIME TOMATO SALAD

STAR-SPANGLED LEMON ICEBOX PIE

STAR-SPANGLED LEMON ICEBOX PIE

With a little chill time, my no-bake lemon pie turns into a potluck superstar. My kids like to arrange the berries in a star pattern.
—**LAUREN KATZ** ASHBURN, VA

PREP: 35 MIN. + CHILLING
MAKES: 8 SERVINGS

- 15 pecan shortbread cookies (about 8 ounces)
- 1 tablespoon sugar
- 3 tablespoons butter, melted

FILLING

- 8 ounces cream cheese, softened
- ½ cup mascarpone cheese
- 1 tablespoon grated lemon peel
- ½ cup lemon juice
- 1 can (14 ounces) sweetened condensed milk
- 1 cup sliced fresh strawberries
- 1 cup fresh blueberries

1. Preheat oven to 350°. Place cookies and sugar in a food processor; process until cookies are ground. Add melted butter; pulse just until combined. Press mixture onto bottom and up sides of an ungreased 9-in. pie plate. Bake 15-20 minutes or until crust is lightly browned. Cool completely on a wire rack.

2. In a large bowl, beat cream cheese, mascarpone cheese, lemon peel and lemon juice until smooth; gradually beat in milk.

3. Spread into prepared cookie crust. Refrigerate, covered, at least 4 hours or until filling is set. Top with berries before serving.

PER SERVING 1 piece: 591 cal., 41g fat (20g sat. fat), 104mg chol., 310mg sodium, 52g carb. (38g sugars, 1g fiber), 10g pro.

BURGERS WITH SPICY DILL SALSA

When I make burgers or hot dogs for boating or barbecues, I do a topping that tastes like relish meets salsa. Pile it on any grillable you like.

—VALONDA SEWARD COARSEGOLD, CA

PREP: 20 MIN. • **GRILL:** 10 MIN./BATCH
MAKES: 12 SERVINGS (3 CUPS SALSA)

- 1 jar (10 ounces) dill pickle relish
- 3 plum tomatoes, seeded and finely chopped
- 1 small white onion, finely chopped
- ½ cup finely chopped red onion
- ½ cup minced fresh cilantro
- 1 tablespoon olive oil
- 1 to 2 serrano peppers, seeded and chopped

BURGERS

- 3 pounds ground beef
- 2 teaspoons salt
- 1 teaspoon pepper
- 12 hamburger buns, split

1. For salsa, in a bowl, mix the first seven ingredients. In another bowl, combine beef, salt and pepper; mix lightly but thoroughly. Shape into twelve ½-in.-thick patties.

2. In two batches, grill the burgers, covered, over medium heat or broil 4 in. from heat 4-5 minutes on each side or until a thermometer reads 160°. Serve with salsa.

NOTE *Wear disposable gloves when cutting hot peppers; the oils can burn skin. Avoid touching your face.*

PER SERVING *1 burger with ¼ cup salsa: 371 cal., 16g fat (6g sat. fat), 70mg chol., 926mg sodium, 31g carb. (4g sugars, 2g fiber), 25g pro.*

JEN'S BAKED BEANS

FREEZE IT

JEN'S BAKED BEANS

My daughters wanted baked beans, so I gave homemade ones a shot. With mustard, molasses and a dash of heat, I made them absolutely delicious.

—JENNIFER HEASLEY YORK, PA

PREP: 20 MIN. • **BAKE:** 50 MIN.
MAKES: 8 SERVINGS

- 6 bacon strips, chopped
- 4 cans (15½ ounces each) great northern beans, rinsed and drained
- 1⅓ cups ketchup
- ⅔ cup packed brown sugar
- ⅓ cup molasses
- 3 tablespoons yellow mustard
- 2½ teaspoons garlic powder
- 1½ teaspoons hot pepper sauce
- ¼ teaspoon crushed red pepper flakes

1. Preheat the oven to 325°. In an ovenproof Dutch oven, cook and stir bacon over medium heat until crisp. Remove with a slotted spoon; drain on paper towels. Discard drippings.

2. Return bacon to pan. Stir in the remaining ingredients; bring to a boil. Place in oven; bake, covered, 50-60 minutes to allow flavors to blend.

FREEZE OPTION *Freeze cooled baked beans in freezer containers. To use, partially thaw in refrigerator overnight. Heat through in a saucepan, stirring occasionally and adding a little broth or water if necessary.*

PER SERVING *¾ cup: 362 cal., 3g fat (1g sat. fat), 6mg chol., 1000mg sodium, 71g carb. (39g sugars, 11g fiber), 13g pro.*

BURGERS WITH SPICY DILL SALSA

Friday Night Bites

Whip up some game-day greats and you're in for a win any day of the week. Pack these delicious five-ingredient snacks and watch the crowd go wild.

BACON CHEDDAR JALAPENOS

BARBECUE SLIDERS

NOTE *Wear disposable gloves when cutting hot peppers; the oils can burn skin. Avoid touching your face.*
PER SERVING *1 appetizer: 56 cal., 4g fat (2g sat. fat), 13mg chol., 116mg sodium, 1g carb. (1g sugars, 0 fiber), 3g pro.*

FREEZE IT ⑤ INGREDIENTS
BARBECUE SLIDERS

When company dropped in by surprise, all I had was sausage and ground beef defrosted. We combined the two for juicy burgers on the grill.
—**BJ LARSEN** ERIE, CO

START TO FINISH: 25 MIN.
MAKES: 8 SERVINGS

- 1 **pound ground beef**
- 1 **pound bulk pork sausage**
- 1 **cup barbecue sauce, divided**
- 16 **Hawaiian sweet rolls, split**
  Optional toppings: lettuce leaves, sliced plum tomatoes and red onion

1. In a large bowl, mix beef and sausage lightly but thoroughly. Shape into sixteen ½-in.-thick patties.
2. Grill patties, covered, over medium heat or broil 4-5 in. from heat for 3-4 minutes on each side or until a thermometer reads 160°; brush with ¼ cup sauce during the last 2 minutes of cooking. Serve on Hawaiian sweet rolls with remaining barbecue sauce; top as desired.
FREEZE OPTION *Place patties on a plastic wrap-lined baking sheet; wrap and freeze until firm. Remove from pan and transfer to a large resealable plastic bag; return to freezer. To use, grill frozen patties as directed, increasing time as necessary.*
HEALTH TIP *Make these with 90 percent lean ground beef and turkey breakfast sausage, and you'll save nearly 100 calories per serving and more than half the fat.*
PER SERVING *2 sliders: 499 cal., 24g fat (9g sat. fat), 96mg chol., 885mg sodium, 47g carb. (23g sugars, 2g fiber), 24g pro.*

⑤ INGREDIENTS
BACON CHEDDAR JALAPENOS

Take these cheesy, fiery appetizers straight to the grill so you can add a touch of smoke. We pass them with bowls of guacamole and sour cream.
—**WAYNE BARNES** MONTGOMERY, AL

PREP: 20 MIN. • **GRILL:** 10 MIN.
MAKES: 2 DOZEN

- 1 **cup shredded cheddar cheese**
- 3 **ounces cream cheese, softened**
- 24 **jalapeno peppers (3 inches)**
- 12 **bacon strips, halved**
  Guacamole and sour cream, optional

1. In a small bowl, mix cheddar and cream cheese. Cut and discard tops from jalapenos; remove seeds. Fill each with 2 teaspoons cheese mixture. Wrap each with a bacon piece; secure with a toothpick.
2. Grill, covered, over medium heat 8-10 minutes or until bacon is crisp, turning frequently. If desired, serve with guacamole and sour cream.

PARTY PRETZELS

PARTY PRETZELS

Turn pretzels into instant party food with a quick trip to the spice drawer. Use pretzel sticks or minis to whip up an awesome (and healthier) alternative to typical snack mixes.

—CARRIE SHAUB MOUNT JOY, PA

START TO FINISH: 25 MIN.
MAKES: 12 CUPS

- 1 **package (16 ounces) fat-free miniature pretzels**
- ¼ **cup canola oil**
- 3 **teaspoons garlic powder**
- 1 **teaspoon dill weed**
- ½ **teaspoon lemon-pepper seasoning**

1. Preheat oven to 350°. Place pretzels in a 15x10x1-in. baking pan. In a small bowl, mix oil and seasonings; drizzle over pretzels and toss to coat.

2. Bake, uncovered, 12 minutes, stirring twice. Cool on a wire rack. Store in an airtight container.

PER SERVING ½ *cup: 89 cal., 2g fat (trace sat. fat), 0 chol., 290mg sodium, 16g carb. (1g sugars, 1g fiber), 2g pro. Diabetic Exchanges: 1 starch, ½ fat.*

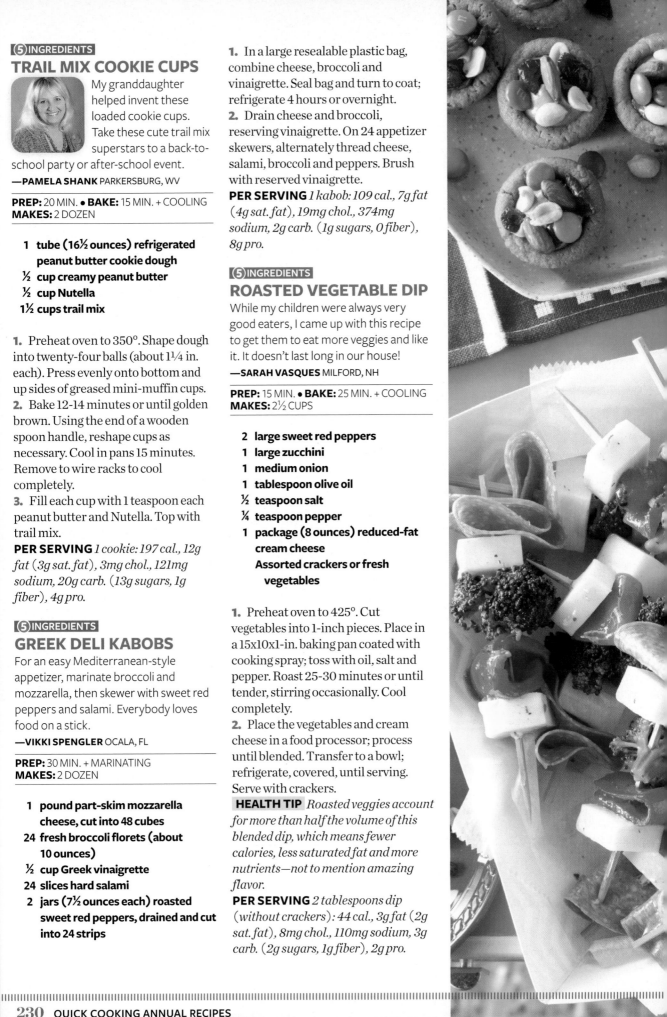

(5) INGREDIENTS
TRAIL MIX COOKIE CUPS

My granddaughter helped invent these loaded cookie cups. Take these cute trail mix superstars to a back-to-school party or after-school event.

—PAMELA SHANK PARKERSBURG, WV

PREP: 20 MIN. • **BAKE:** 15 MIN. + COOLING
MAKES: 2 DOZEN

- 1 tube (16½ ounces) refrigerated peanut butter cookie dough
- ½ cup creamy peanut butter
- ½ cup Nutella
- 1½ cups trail mix

1. Preheat oven to 350°. Shape dough into twenty-four balls (about 1¼ in. each). Press evenly onto bottom and up sides of greased mini-muffin cups.

2. Bake 12-14 minutes or until golden brown. Using the end of a wooden spoon handle, reshape cups as necessary. Cool in pans 15 minutes. Remove to wire racks to cool completely.

3. Fill each cup with 1 teaspoon each peanut butter and Nutella. Top with trail mix.

PER SERVING *1 cookie: 197 cal., 12g fat (3g sat. fat), 3mg chol., 121mg sodium, 20g carb. (13g sugars, 1g fiber), 4g pro.*

(5) INGREDIENTS
GREEK DELI KABOBS

For an easy Mediterranean-style appetizer, marinate broccoli and mozzarella, then skewer with sweet red peppers and salami. Everybody loves food on a stick.

—VIKKI SPENGLER OCALA, FL

PREP: 30 MIN. + MARINATING
MAKES: 2 DOZEN

- 1 pound part-skim mozzarella cheese, cut into 48 cubes
- 24 fresh broccoli florets (about 10 ounces)
- ½ cup Greek vinaigrette
- 24 slices hard salami
- 2 jars (7½ ounces each) roasted sweet red peppers, drained and cut into 24 strips

1. In a large resealable plastic bag, combine cheese, broccoli and vinaigrette. Seal bag and turn to coat; refrigerate 4 hours or overnight.

2. Drain cheese and broccoli, reserving vinaigrette. On 24 appetizer skewers, alternately thread cheese, salami, broccoli and peppers. Brush with reserved vinaigrette.

PER SERVING *1 kabob: 109 cal., 7g fat (4g sat. fat), 19mg chol., 374mg sodium, 2g carb. (1g sugars, 0 fiber), 8g pro.*

(5) INGREDIENTS
ROASTED VEGETABLE DIP

While my children were always very good eaters, I came up with this recipe to get them to eat more veggies and like it. It doesn't last long in our house!

—SARAH VASQUES MILFORD, NH

PREP: 15 MIN. • **BAKE:** 25 MIN. + COOLING
MAKES: 2½ CUPS

- 2 large sweet red peppers
- 1 large zucchini
- 1 medium onion
- 1 tablespoon olive oil
- ½ teaspoon salt
- ¼ teaspoon pepper
- 1 package (8 ounces) reduced-fat cream cheese
  Assorted crackers or fresh vegetables

1. Preheat oven to 425°. Cut vegetables into 1-inch pieces. Place in a 15x10x1-in. baking pan coated with cooking spray; toss with oil, salt and pepper. Roast 25-30 minutes or until tender, stirring occasionally. Cool completely.

2. Place the vegetables and cream cheese in a food processor; process until blended. Transfer to a bowl; refrigerate, covered, until serving. Serve with crackers.

HEALTH TIP *Roasted veggies account for more than half the volume of this blended dip, which means fewer calories, less saturated fat and more nutrients—not to mention amazing flavor.*

PER SERVING *2 tablespoons dip (without crackers): 44 cal., 3g fat (2g sat. fat), 8mg chol., 110mg sodium, 3g carb. (2g sugars, 1g fiber), 2g pro.*

TRAIL MIX
COOKIE CUPS

GREEK DELI KABOBS

ROASTED VEGETABLE DIP

Thanksgiving: Best Meal of the Year

Pucker up for fresh cranberries, savor slow-cooked turkey breast and nail that homemade mac and cheese. The most anticipated meal of the year just got even better.

CRANBERRY FRUIT RELISH

CRANBERRY FRUIT RELISH

My sweet-tart relish is a lifesaver during potluck season. It's terrific on its own, with poultry and as an appetizer: Pour it over a block of cream cheese to spread on crackers.
—**HENRYETTA LEWIS** SANTA FE, NM

PREP: 10 MIN. + CHILLING
MAKES: ABOUT 4 CUPS

- 3½ cups fresh or frozen cranberries
- 1 medium navel orange, peeled and sectioned
- 1 medium apple, cored and cut into wedges
- 1½ cups sugar
- 1 can (8 ounces) crushed pineapple, drained
- ¾ teaspoon ground ginger
- ½ teaspoon ground nutmeg

Pulse cranberries, orange and apple in a blender or food processor until chopped. Remove to a bowl; stir in remaining ingredients. Refrigerate, covered, at least 2 hours.
PER SERVING *¼ cup: 101 cal., 0 fat (0 sat. fat), 0 chol., 1mg sodium, 26g carb. (24g sugars, 2g fiber), 0 pro.*

SLOW-ROASTED ROOT VEGETABLES

When she was a little girl growing up in Italy, my aunt Virginia learned to make a dish called Noodles and Nuts. I tried the topping on carrots and parsnips instead of noodles and haven't looked back.
—**TERRI COLLINS** PITTSBURGH, PA

PREP: 15 MIN. ● **COOK:** 5 HOURS
MAKES: 12 SERVINGS

- 2 pounds fresh baby carrots
- 1 medium onion, halved and thinly sliced
- ¼ cup butter, cubed
- 3 garlic cloves, minced
- ¾ teaspoon salt
- ¼ teaspoon pepper
- 1½ pounds medium parsnips
- 2 tablespoons seasoned bread crumbs
- ¾ cup chopped walnuts, toasted
- 3 tablespoons grated Romano cheese, optional

1. In a 5-qt. slow cooker, combine first six ingredients. Cut parsnips crosswise into 2-in. pieces. Cut thinner pieces in half; cut thicker pieces into quarters. Stir into carrot mixture.
2. Cook, covered, on low until tender, 5-6 hours. To serve, stir in bread crumbs; sprinkle with walnuts and, if desired, cheese.
NOTE *To toast nuts, bake in a shallow pan in a 350° oven for 5-10 minutes or cook in a skillet over low heat until lightly browned, stirring occasionally.*
PER SERVING *⅔ cup: 158 cal., 9g fat (3g sat. fat), 10mg chol., 263mg sodium, 19g carb. (7g sugars, 4g fiber), 3g pro. **Diabetic Exchanges:** 2 fat, 1 starch.*

SLOW-ROASTED ROOT VEGETABLES

TANGY BACON
GREEN BEANS

SPICED BUTTERNUT
SQUASH SOUP

FREEZE OPTION *Freeze cooled soup in freezer containers. To use, partially thaw in refrigerator overnight. Heat through in a saucepan, stirring occasionally and adding a little broth or water if necessary.*
PER SERVING *1 cup: 131 cal., 2g fat (1g sat. fat), 3mg chol., 521mg sodium, 28g carb. (9g sugars, 7g fiber), 4g pro.* **Diabetic Exchanges:** *2 starch, ½ fat.*

FAST FIX ▸
TANGY BACON GREEN BEANS

My grandmother's Pennsylvania Dutch-style recipe turns plain old green beans into a tangy cross between three-bean and German potato salad.
—**SHARON TIPTON** CASSELBERRY, FL

START TO FINISH: 30 MIN.
MAKES: 12 SERVINGS

- 2 pounds frozen whole green beans
- 12 bacon strips, chopped
- 2 medium onions, halved and sliced
- 2 tablespoons cornstarch
- 1¼ cups water
- ¼ cup packed brown sugar
- ¼ cup cider vinegar
- 1½ teaspoons salt
- 1 teaspoon ground mustard

1. Cook beans according to package directions. Meanwhile, in a 6-qt. stockpot, cook bacon over medium heat until crisp, stirring occasionally. With a slotted spoon, remove bacon to paper towels; reserve drippings.
2. In same pan, saute onions in drippings over medium heat until tender and lightly browned, 7-9 minutes. In a bowl, whisk remaining ingredients until smooth; add to pan. Bring to a boil; cook and stir until thickened, 1-2 minutes.
3. Drain beans and add to warm dressing; toss and heat through. Top with bacon.
PER SERVING *173 cal., 11g fat (4g sat. fat), 18mg chol., 483mg sodium, 13g carb. (7g sugars, 2g fiber), 5g pro.*
HEALTH TIP *Not only can using frozen veggies save prep time, they're just as healthy as fresh—sometimes even more nutritious—because they're picked at the peak of ripeness.*

EAT SMART FREEZE IT
SPICED BUTTERNUT SQUASH SOUP

I like to simmer up this recipe year-round, but it's best in the fall and winter months when butternut squash is in season. I love the soup because it's hearty and satisfying, healthy, easy to make, and the leftovers reheat well.
—**JULIE HESSION** LAS VEGAS, NV

PREP: 50 MIN. ● **COOK:** 25 MIN.
MAKES: 12 SERVINGS (3 QUARTS)

- 2 medium butternut squash (about 3 pounds each)
- 1 tablespoon butter
- 1 tablespoon olive oil
- 2 large onions, sliced
- 2 tablespoons brown sugar
- 1 tablespoon minced fresh gingerroot
- 2 garlic cloves, minced
- 2 cinnamon sticks (3 inches)
- 1¼ teaspoons salt
- 3 cans (14½ ounces each) reduced-sodium chicken broth
- 1¾ cups water
   Minced fresh parsley

1. Halve the squash; discard seeds. Place squash in a 15x10x1-in. pan coated with cooking spray, cut side down. Bake at 400° until tender, 40-50 minutes. Cool slightly; scoop out pulp.
2. In a 6-qt. stockpot, heat butter and oil over medium heat; saute onions until tender, about 5 minutes. Add brown sugar, ginger, garlic and cinnamon sticks; cook and stir for 2 minutes. Stir in salt, squash, broth and water; bring to a boil. Reduce the heat; simmer, covered, 10 minutes.
3. Discard cinnamon. Puree soup using an immersion blender. Or, cool slightly and puree soup in batches in a blender; return to pan. If desired, thin with additional water or broth; heat through. Serve with parsley.

EASY SCALLOPED POTATOES

We all loved my mom's super-rich scalloped potatoes. I tweaked her recipe to keep all the flavor but cut the fat. The cheese blend is the clincher. It's all about experimenting.

—**DIANE BRAMLETT** STOCKTON, CA

PREP: 30 MIN. ● **BAKE:** 20 MIN.
MAKES: 12 SERVINGS (½ CUP EACH)

- 3 pounds Yukon Gold potatoes (about 11 medium), peeled and thinly sliced
- ¼ cup water
- ¼ cup butter, cubed
- 1 large sweet onion, chopped
- 4 garlic cloves, chopped
- ¼ cup all-purpose flour
- 1 teaspoon salt
- 1 teaspoon pepper
- ⅛ teaspoon cayenne pepper
- 2 cups chicken broth
- ⅓ cup half-and-half cream
- 1 cup shredded Gruyere or Swiss cheese
- 1 cup shredded Monterey Jack or cheddar cheese
  Minced fresh chives, optional

1. Preheat oven to 400°. Place potatoes and water in a large microwave-safe bowl; microwave, covered, on high until almost tender, 12-14 minutes.

2. In a 6-qt. stockpot, heat butter over medium-high heat; saute onion and garlic until tender, 5-7 minutes. Stir in flour and seasonings until blended; gradually stir in broth and cream. Bring to a boil, stirring occasionally; cook and stir until slightly thickened, 2-3 minutes. Stir in cheeses until melted.

3. Drain potatoes; add to sauce, stirring gently. Transfer to a greased 13x9-in. baking dish. Bake, uncovered, until lightly browned, about 20 minutes. If desired, sprinkle with minced chives.

NOTE *This recipe was tested in an 1,100-watt microwave.*

PER SERVING *½ cup: 245 cal., 11g fat (7g sat. fat), 33mg chol., 526mg sodium, 29g carb. (4g sugars, 2g fiber), 8g pro.*

SLOW COOKER TURKEY BREAST WITH GRAVY

EAT SMART **SLOW COOKER**

SLOW COOKER TURKEY BREAST WITH GRAVY

This quick-prep recipe lets you feast on turkey at any time of year. We save the rich broth for gravy, noodles and soup-making.

—**JOYCE HOUGH** ANNAPOLIS, MD

PREP: 25 MIN.
COOK: 5 HOURS + STANDING
MAKES: 12 SERVINGS

- 2 teaspoons dried parsley flakes
- 1 teaspoon salt
- 1 teaspoon poultry seasoning
- ½ teaspoon paprika
- ½ teaspoon pepper
- 2 medium onions, chopped
- 3 medium carrots, cut into ½-inch slices
- 3 celery ribs, coarsely chopped
- 1 bone-in turkey breast (6 to 7 pounds), skin removed
- ¼ cup all-purpose flour
- ½ cup water

1. Mix first five ingredients in a small bowl. Place vegetables in a 6- or 7-qt. slow cooker; top with turkey. Rub turkey with seasoning mixture.

2. Cook, covered, on low until a thermometer inserted in turkey reads at least 170°, 5-6 hours Remove from slow cooker; let stand, covered, for 15 minutes before slicing.

3. Meanwhile, strain cooking juices into a small saucepan. Mix flour and water until smooth; stir into cooking juices. Bring to a boil; cook and stir until thickened, 1-2 minutes. Serve with turkey.

PER SERVING *6 ounces cooked turkey with 3 tablespoons gravy: 200 cal., 1g fat (0 sat. fat), 117mg chol., 270mg sodium, 2g carb. (0 sugars, 0 fiber), 43g pro. **Diabetic Exchanges:** 6 lean meat.*

BRUSSELS SPROUTS WITH GARLIC & GOAT CHEESE

I wanted to up my veggie game, so I smothered Brussels sprouts with olive oil, garlic and goat cheese. It's really a side dish, but I love to eat a big portion for lunch!

—**BRENDA WILLIAMS** SANTA MARIA, CA

START TO FINISH: 30 MIN.
MAKES: 16 SERVINGS (⅔ CUP EACH)

- 3 pounds Brussels sprouts, trimmed and halved
- ¼ cup olive oil
- 8 garlic cloves, minced
- 1 teaspoon salt
- ½ teaspoon pepper
- 1 package (5.3 ounces) fresh goat cheese, crumbled

Preheat oven to 425°. Toss first five ingredients; spread in a greased 15x10x1-in. pan. Roast until tender, 20-25 minutes, stirring occasionally. Transfer to a bowl; toss with cheese.

PER SERVING *⅔ cup: 81 cal., 5g fat (1g sat. fat), 6mg chol., 205mg sodium, 8g carb. (2g sugars, 3g fiber), 4g pro. **Diabetic Exchanges:** 1 vegetable, 1 fat.*

HEALTH TIP *Brussels sprouts are loaded with fat-soluble vitamin K. It's important to serve with a little fat to help absorb the nutrients—so thank you, goat cheese and olive oil!*

MARINATED MUSHROOMS & ARTICHOKES

I marinate mushrooms and artichokes in fresh tarragon and thyme, and they turn out tart, tangy and irresistible.

—**MARCIA DOYLE** POMPANO, FL

PREP: 15 MIN. + MARINATING
MAKES: 16 SERVINGS (½ CUP EACH)

- 2 pounds medium fresh mushrooms, halved
- 2 cans (14 ounces each) water-packed quartered artichoke hearts, drained
- 1½ cups water
- 1 cup cider vinegar
- ½ cup olive oil
- 1 bay leaf
- 1½ teaspoons salt
- 1½ teaspoons minced fresh tarragon or ½ teaspoon dried tarragon
- 1½ teaspoons minced fresh thyme or ½ teaspoon dried thyme
- 1 garlic clove, minced
- ½ teaspoon pepper
- 1 tablespoon minced fresh parsley
  Additional parsley

In a nonreactive bowl, combine the first twelve ingredients. Refrigerate, covered, to allow flavors to blend, 3-4 hours. Serve with additional parsley.

PER SERVING *½ cup: 43 cal., 1g fat (trace sat. fat), 0 chol., 162mg sodium, 5g carb. (trace sugars, trace fiber), 3g pro. **Diabetic Exchanges:** 1 vegetable.*

BRUSSELS SPROUTS WITH GARLIC & GOAT CHEESE

MARINATED MUSHROOMS & ARTICHOKES

PREPARE MUSHROOMS

To clean mushrooms, gently remove dirt by rubbing with a mushroom brush or a damp paper towel. Do not peel mushrooms. Trim stems. Mushrooms can be eaten raw, marinated, sauteed, stir-fried, baked, broiled or grilled.

POMEGRANATE
PERSIMMON SALAD

POTLUCK MACARONI
AND CHEESE

POMEGRANATE PERSIMMON SALAD

I bring sunshine to the table with a bright salad of persimmons and pomegranate seeds dressed with a puckery vinaigrette.

—LINDA TAMBUNAN DUBLIN, CA

START TO FINISH: 15 MIN
MAKES: 12 SERVINGS

- ½ cup olive oil
- ½ cup maple syrup
- ¼ cup rice vinegar
- 2 tablespoons Dijon mustard
- ¼ teaspoon salt
- ¼ teaspoon pepper

SALAD

- 3 ripe Fuyu persimmons or 3 plums, sliced
- 2 packages (10 ounces each) baby kale salad blend
- 1 cup pomegranate seeds

1. Place first six ingredients in a jar with a lid; shake well. Refrigerate.
2. To serve, shake vinaigrette and toss ½ cup with persimmons. Toss remaining vinaigrette with salad blend. Top with persimmons and pomegranate seeds.

PER SERVING *1½ cups: 175 cal., 9g fat (2g sat. fat), 0 chol., 220mg sodium, 23g carb. (17g sugars, 3g fiber), 2g pro.* **Diabetic Exchanges:** *2 vegetable, 2 fat, ½ starch, ½ fruit.*

PREP POMEGRANATE

1. Cut off crown. Score fruit into quarters, taking care not to cut into the red juice sacs (arils).
2. Soak sections in water for 5 minutes. Gently break them open and separate arils. Discard skin and white membrane. Drain the water, reserving the arils. Dry on paper towels.

POTLUCK MACARONI AND CHEESE

For my all-star mac, I use a bunch of different cheeses to get an ultra creamy sauce. People know me for this recipe!

—JENNIFER BABCOCK CHICOPEE, MA

PREP: 25 MIN. • **COOK:** 2 HOURS
MAKES: 16 SERVINGS (¾ CUP EACH)

- 3 cups uncooked elbow macaroni
- 1 package (16 ounces) process cheese (Velveeta), cubed
- 2 cups shredded Mexican cheese blend
- 2 cups shredded white cheddar cheese
- 1¾ cups whole milk
- 1 can (12 ounces) evaporated milk
- ¾ cup butter, melted
- 3 large eggs, lightly beaten

1. Cook the macaroni according to package directions for al dente; drain. Transfer to a greased 5-qt. slow cooker. Stir in remaining ingredients.
2. Cook, covered, on low until a thermometer reads at least 160°, 2-2½ hours, stirring once.

PER SERVING *¾ cup: 388 cal., 28g fat (17g sat. fat), 122mg chol., 652mg sodium, 16g carb. (6g sugars, 0 fiber), 17g pro.*

TOMATO-BASIL PULL-APART ROLLS

My nephew helped me create these soft and colorful rolls. He named them wheelies because the spiral shapes remind him of his toy trucks.

—DIANNA WARA WASHINGTON, IL

PREP: 30 MIN. + RISING • **BAKE:** 20 MIN.
MAKES: 1 DOZEN

- 1 package (¼ ounce) active dry yeast
- 2 tablespoons sugar
- ¾ cup warm whole milk (110° to 115°)
- 1 large egg
- ¼ cup tomato paste
- 3 tablespoons olive oil
- 1 teaspoon salt
- 2¾ to 3¼ cups bread flour

TOMATO-BASIL PULL-APART ROLLS

FILLING

- 1 cup shredded Italian cheese blend
- 2 teaspoons dried basil
- ½ teaspoon garlic powder

1. Dissolve yeast and sugar in warm milk. In a large bowl, beat egg, tomato paste, oil, salt, yeast mixture and 1 cup flour on medium speed until smooth. Stir in enough remaining flour to form a soft dough (dough will be sticky).
2. Turn dough onto a floured surface; knead until smooth and elastic, about 6-8 minutes. Place in a greased bowl, turning to grease the top. Cover with plastic wrap; let rise in a warm place until doubled, about 45 minutes.
3. In a bowl, toss filling ingredients. Punch down dough; turn onto a lightly floured surface. Roll into a 16x12-in. rectangle. Sprinkle with filling to within ½ in. of edges. Roll up jelly-roll style, starting with a long side; pinch seam to seal. Cut into 12 slices.
4. Place, cut side down, in a parchment paper-lined 10-in. cast-iron skillet. Cover with a kitchen towel; let rise in a warm place until almost doubled, about 45 minutes. Preheat oven to 350°.
5. Bake until golden brown, 20-25 minutes. Remove rolls to a wire rack.

FREEZE OPTION *Securely wrap cooled rolls in foil; place in a resealable plastic freezer bag. To use, partially thaw overnight in refrigerator. Reheat rolls, wrapped in foil, in a 300° oven until warm, about 25 minutes.*

PER SERVING *1 roll: 204 cal., 7g fat (2g sat. fat), 24mg chol., 284mg sodium, 27g carb. (3g sugars, 1g fiber), 7g pro.*

Christmas: The Short List

Roast beef, sweet potatoes, green bean casserole, buttery biscuits, pistachio cake...what could be better than a holiday spread filled with the flavors of Christmas? How about one where every dish is prepped with just a handful of ingredients? Yes, please.

SALT-ENCRUSTED RIB ROAST

ZESTY GARLIC GREEN BEANS

If you've got side-dish duty, change up the usual green bean casserole. These better-for-you beans travel well, too.
—**CHRISTINE BERGMAN** SUWANEE, GA

START TO FINISH: 25 MIN.
MAKES: 10 SERVINGS

- 2 tablespoons oil from oil-packed sun-dried tomatoes
- 1 cup sliced sweet onion
- ½ cup oil-packed sun-dried tomatoes, chopped
- 3 garlic cloves, minced
- 1½ teaspoons lemon-pepper seasoning
- 2 packages (16 ounces each) frozen french-style green beans

1. In a Dutch oven, heat oil over medium heat. Add onion; cook and stir 3-4 minutes or until tender. Add tomatoes, garlic and lemon pepper; cook and stir 2 minutes longer.
2. Stir in frozen green beans; cook, covered 7-9 minutes or until heated through, stirring occasionally. Uncover; cook 2-3 minutes longer or until liquid is almost evaporated.
PER SERVING *⅔ cup: 76 cal., 3g fat (trace sat. fat), 0 chol., 85mg sodium, 9g carb. (3g sugars, 3g fiber), 2g pro.* **Diabetic Exchanges:** *1 vegetable, 1 fat.*

⑤ INGREDIENTS
SALT-ENCRUSTED RIB ROAST

A rib roast is a big part of our holiday dinner traditions. We love the yellow mustard, but you can use your favorite— Dijon and others are fair game.
—**REBECCA WIRTZBERGER** YUMA, AZ

PREP: 15 MIN.
BAKE: 2½ HOURS + STANDING
MAKES: 10 SERVINGS

- 1 bone-in beef rib roast (about 6 pounds)
- ½ cup yellow mustard
- 3 cups kosher salt (about 1½ pounds)
- ½ cup water

1. Preheat oven to 450°. Place rib roast in a roasting pan, fat side up; spread all sides with mustard. In a bowl, mix salt and water to make a dry paste (mixture should be just moist enough to pack); press onto top and sides of roast.
2. Roast 15 minutes. Reduce oven setting to 325°. Roast 2¼-2¾ hours longer or until a thermometer inserted in beef reaches 135° for medium-rare; 150° for medium. (Temperature of roast will continue to rise about 10° upon standing.) Let stand 20 minutes before serving.
3. Remove and discard salt crust. Carve roast into slices.
PER SERVING *5 ounces cooked beef: 320 cal., 18g fat (7g sat. fat), 0 chol., 997mg sodium, 1g carb. (0 sugars, 0 fiber), 37g pro.*

ZESTY GARLIC GREEN BEANS

APPLESAUCE SWEET
POTATOES

(5)INGREDIENTS

CITRUS AVOCADO SPINACH SALAD

Tossing together this salad with creamy avocado and tangy citrus is so simple, and it practically makes a meal in and of itself.

—**KAROLE FRIEMANN** KIMBERLING CITY, MO

PREP: 15 MIN.
MAKES: 8 SERVINGS

- 8 **cups fresh baby spinach (about 6 ounces)**
- 3 **cups refrigerated citrus salad, drained**
- 2 **medium ripe avocados, peeled and sliced**
- 1 **cup crumbled blue cheese**
  Sliced almonds, toasted, optional
  Salad dressing of your choice

Divide spinach among eight plates; top with citrus salad and avocados. Sprinkle with cheese and, if desired, almonds; drizzle with dressing. Serve immediately.

NOTE *This recipe was tested with Del Monte SunFresh Citrus Salad. To toast nuts, bake in a shallow pan in a 350° oven for 5-10 minutes or cook in a skillet over low heat until lightly browned, stirring occasionally.*

PER SERVING *(calculated without almonds and dressing): 168 cal., 10g fat (4g sat. fat), 13mg chol., 231mg sodium, 16g carb. (10g sugars, 3g fiber), 5g pro.*

(5)INGREDIENTS SLOW COOKER

APPLESAUCE SWEET POTATOES

During the holidays, using a slow cooker not only frees up oven space, it saves time, too. Sweet potatoes are a must on our family menu, and this no-fuss version will have everyone thinking you spent hours in the kitchen.

—**PAMELA ALLEN** MARYSVILLE, OH

PREP: 15 MIN. • **COOK:** 4 HOURS
MAKES: 8 SERVINGS

- 3 **pounds sweet potatoes (about 5 medium), peeled and sliced**
- 1½ **cups unsweetened applesauce**
- ⅔ **cup packed brown sugar**
- 3 **tablespoons butter, melted**
- 1 **teaspoon ground cinnamon**
- ½ **cup glazed pecans, chopped, optional**

1. Place the sweet potatoes in a 4-qt. slow cooker. In a small bowl, mix the applesauce, brown sugar, melted butter and cinnamon; pour over potatoes.

2. Cook, covered, on low 4-5 hours or until potatoes are tender. If desired, sprinkle with pecans before serving. Serve with a slotted spoon.

PER SERVING ¾ *cup (calculated without pecans): 303 cal., 5g fat (3g sat. fat), 11mg chol., 57mg sodium, 65g carb. (39g sugars, 6g fiber), 3g pro.*

CHEESE TREES

Mini cheese wedges become a festive forest with pops of sweet pepper, dill sprigs and pretzel sticks. Deck your crackers!

ONION & GARLIC BISCUITS

Bake a dozen of these oniony, herby biscuits for a little something new in the holiday bread basket. They're delicious with a bowl of chili, soup or stew, too.

—L. DOROW FAIRMONT, MN

START TO FINISH: 20 MIN.
MAKES: 1 DOZEN

- 1 tablespoon canola oil
- 1 medium onion, finely chopped
- 2 garlic cloves, minced
- 2 cups biscuit/baking mix
- ½ teaspoon dried thyme
- ⅔ cup 2% milk

1. Preheat oven to 450°. In a skillet, heat oil over medium heat. Add onion; cook and stir 3-4 minutes or until tender. Stir in garlic; cook 1 minute longer. Cool completely.

2. In a large bowl, combine baking mix, thyme and onion mixture; make a well in center. Pour milk into well; stir just until moistened. Drop dough by rounded tablespoonfuls 2 in. apart onto a greased baking sheet.

3. Bake 8-10 minutes or until golden brown. Serve warm.

PER SERVING *1 biscuit: 101 cal., 4g fat (2g sat. fat), 4mg chol., 262mg sodium, 15g carb. (2g sugars, 1g fiber), 2g pro.*

PESTO RICE-STUFFED
CHICKEN

ONION & GARLIC
BISCUITS

PESTO RICE-STUFFED CHICKEN

Juicy stuffed chicken is light, fresh and feels special. The quick prep makes it a good fit for any schedule. Substitute shredded cheese for the pesto if you like.

—RACHEL DION PORT CHARLOTTE, FL

PREP: 20 MIN. ● **BAKE:** 20 MIN.
MAKES: 8 SERVINGS

- ¾ cup uncooked instant rice
- ½ cup chopped seeded tomato
- ¼ cup prepared pesto
- ⅛ teaspoon salt
- 8 boneless skinless chicken breast halves (6 ounces each)
- 2 tablespoons canola oil, divided

1. Preheat oven to 375°. Cook rice according to package directions.

2. In a small bowl, combine tomato, pesto, salt and rice. Cut a pocket horizontally in the thickest part of each chicken breast. Fill each with 3 tablespoons rice mixture; secure with toothpicks.

3. In a large skillet, heat 1 tablespoon oil over medium-high heat. In batches, brown chicken breasts on each side, adding additional oil as needed. Transfer to a greased 15x10x1-in. baking pan.

4. Bake 18-22 minutes or until chicken is no longer pink. Discard toothpicks before serving.

PER SERVING *1 stuffed chicken breast half: 278 cal., 10g fat (2g sat. fat), 94mg chol., 210mg sodium, 9g carb. (1g sugars, 0 fiber), 35g pro.* **Diabetic Exchanges:** *5 lean meat, 1 fat, ½ starch.*

EASY PISTACHIO
BUNDT CAKE

PECAN
ROLL-UPS

PECAN ROLL-UPS

This simple recipe is so tasty, it's sure to become a holiday favorite with your family. The pecans tucked inside make the cookies so rich and special.

—**LEE ROBERTS** RACINE, WI

PREP: 45 MIN. + CHILLING
BAKE: 15 MIN./BATCH + COOLING
MAKES: 8 DOZEN

- 1 cup butter, softened
- 1 package (8 ounces) cream cheese, softened
- ¼ teaspoon salt
- 2 cups all-purpose flour
- 1¼ cups confectioners' sugar, divided
- 96 pecan halves (about 2 cups)

1. In a large bowl, beat the butter, cream cheese and salt until smooth. Gradually beat in flour. Divide dough in half; shape each into a disk. Wrap in plastic; refrigerate 2 hours or until firm enough to roll.

2. Preheat oven to 350°. Dust a work surface with about 2 tablespoons of confectioners' sugar. Roll one portion of dough into an 18x8-in. rectangle; cut dough crosswise into six 3-in.-wide sections. Cut each section crosswise into eight 1-in.-wide strips. Roll each strip around a pecan half; place 1 in. apart on ungreased baking sheets. Repeat with remaining dough and pecans, dusting work surface with an additional 2 tablespoons of confectioners' sugar.

3. Bake for 12-15 minutes or until bottoms are lightly browned. Remove to wire racks to cool completely.

4. Place the remaining confectioners' sugar in a shallow bowl. Roll cookies in sugar, coating well.

FREEZE OPTION *Bake and roll cookies in confectioners' sugar as directed. Freeze in freezer containers, separating layers with waxed paper, up to 3 months. Thaw before serving; dust with additional confectioners' sugar.*

PER SERVING *1 cookie: 51 cal., 4g fat (2g sat. fat), 8mg chol., 30mg sodium, 4g carb. (2g sugars, trace fiber), 1g pro.*

EASY PISTACHIO BUNDT CAKE

Cake and pudding mixes make this cake easy, and a Bundt pan gets it holiday party-ready. Go for the pistachios on top—the extra crunch is worth it.

—**DINA CROWELL** FREDERICKSBURG, VA

PREP: 15 MIN. ● **BAKE:** 35 MIN. + COOLING
MAKES: 12 SERVINGS

- 1 package yellow cake mix (regular size)
- 1 package (3.4 ounces) instant pistachio pudding mix
- 4 large eggs
- 1½ cups water
- ¼ cup canola oil
- ½ teaspoon almond extract
  Confectioners' sugar
  Finely chopped pistachios, optional

1. Preheat oven to 350°. Grease and flour a 10-in. fluted tube pan.

2. In a large bowl, combine the first six ingredients; beat on low speed for 30 seconds. Beat on medium 2 minutes. Transfer to prepared pan. Bake 35-40 minutes or until a toothpick inserted in center comes out clean. Cool in pan 10 minutes before removing to a wire rack to cool completely.

3. Dust with confectioners' sugar. If desired, sprinkle with pistachios.

NOTE *To remove cakes easily, use solid shortening to grease plain and fluted tube pans.*

PER SERVING *1 slice (calculated without pistachios): 266 cal., 10g fat (2g sat. fat), 62mg chol., 416mg sodium, 41g carb. (24g sugars, 0 fiber), 4g pro.*

**Cindy Reams'
Lemon Meringue Floats**
PAGE 251

Delectable Desserts

Rich cheesecakes, dazzling pies, homey fruit crisps and cookie-jar favorites...you'll find all of these and more in this irresistible chapter. Which tasty indulgence will you whip up first?

**Raymonde Bourgeois'
Coconut-Pineapple
Rhubarb Bars** PAGE 246

**Nancy Bruce's
Ice Cream Snowballs with
Raspberry Sauce** PAGE 252

**Suzanne Banfield's
Lemon Ginger Icebox
Cake** PAGE 253

HOT CHOCOLATE PUMPKIN CAKE

Hot chocolate is my go-to winter indulgence. I like to serve it with this moist pumpkin cake dusted with cocoa for an added chocolate boost.

—**COLLEEN DELAWDER** HERNDON, VA

PREP: 20 MIN. • **BAKE:** 55 MIN. + COOLING
MAKES: 16 SERVINGS

- 1 can (15 ounces) pumpkin
- 2 cups sugar
- 3 large eggs
- ½ cup packed brown sugar
- ½ cup butter, melted
- ½ cup canola oil
- 1 tablespoon vanilla extract
- 3 cups all-purpose flour
- 2 teaspoons baking soda
- 2 teaspoons ground cinnamon
- ¼ teaspoon ground nutmeg
- ¼ teaspoon ground chipotle pepper
- ½ teaspoon salt
- 1 package (12 ounces) miniature semisweet chocolate chips
  Baking cocoa or confectioners' sugar, optional

1. Preheat oven to 350°. Generously grease and flour a 10-in. fluted tube pan.
2. Beat first seven ingredients until well blended. In a separate bowl, whisk together flour, baking soda, spices and salt; gradually beat into pumpkin mixture. Stir in chocolate chips.
3. Add to prepared pan. Bake until a toothpick inserted in center comes out clean, 55-65 minutes. Cool in pan for 30 minutes before removing to a wire rack; cool completely. If desired, dust with cocoa.

NOTE *To remove cakes easily, use solid shortening to grease plain and fluted tube pans.*

PER SERVING *1 slice: 450 cal., 20g fat (8g sat. fat), 50mg chol., 298mg sodium, 66g carb. (45g sugars, 3g fiber), 5g pro.*

BERRY & GANACHE CHEESECAKE BARS

BERRY & GANACHE CHEESECAKE BARS

I use fresh raspberries with chocolate ganache to make cheesecake bars that dare you to walk away.

—**CARMELL CHILDS** FERRON, UT

PREP: 35 MIN. • **BAKE:** 25 MIN. + CHILLING
MAKES: 2 DOZEN

- 1½ cups graham cracker crumbs
- ¼ cup finely chopped pecans
- ¼ teaspoon salt
- ¼ cup butter, melted

CHEESECAKE LAYER
- 2 packages (8 ounces each) cream cheese, softened
- ½ cup sugar
- ½ teaspoon vanilla extract
- 2 large eggs, lightly beaten

TOPPING
- 1½ cups (9 ounces) semisweet chocolate chips
- 1 cup heavy whipping cream
- 2 tablespoons balsamic vinegar
- 1 tablespoon light corn syrup
- 1½ cups fresh raspberries or blueberries

1. Preheat oven to 350°. In a bowl, mix cracker crumbs, pecans and salt; stir in melted butter. Press onto bottom of a greased 13x9-in. baking pan. Bake for 8-10 minutes or until lightly browned. Cool on a wire rack.
2. In a large bowl, beat cream cheese and sugar until smooth. Beat in vanilla. Add eggs; beat on low speed just until blended. Spread over crust. Bake for 15-20 minutes or until center is almost set. Cool 1 hour on a wire rack.
3. Place chocolate chips in a small bowl. In a saucepan, bring cream just to a boil. Pour over chocolate; let stand for 5 minutes. Stir with a whisk until smooth. Stir in vinegar and corn syrup; cool slightly, stirring occasionally. Pour over cheesecake layer; let stand 5 minutes. Top with berries.
4. Refrigerate for at least 3 hours, covering when completely cooled. Cut into bars.

PER SERVING *1 bar: 233 cal., 17g fat (9g sat. fat), 55mg chol., 149mg sodium, 19g carb. (14g sugars, 1g fiber), 3g pro.*

APPLE CRUMBLE PIE

The crumb topping is irresistible, which may explain why this pie always disappears fast in our house. Or maybe it's the chunky apple filling. Either way, this dessert is a family tradition.

—VERA BROUWER MAURICE, IA

PREP: 25 MIN. ● **BAKE:** 50 MIN.
MAKES: 10 SERVINGS

**Pastry for single-crust pie
    (9 inches)**
TOPPING
½ cup sugar
½ cup all-purpose flour
½ cup cold butter, cubed
FILLING
½ cup sugar
2 tablespoons all-purpose flour
1 teaspoon ground cinnamon
½ teaspoon ground nutmeg
5 cups chopped peeled tart apples
    (about 5 medium)

1. Preheat oven to 400°. On a lightly floured surface, roll pastry dough to a ⅛-in.-thick circle; transfer to a 9-in. pie plate. Trim pastry to ½ in. beyond rim of plate; flute edge. Refrigerate while preparing topping and filling.

2. For topping, in a small bowl, mix sugar and flour; cut in butter until crumbly. For filling, in a large bowl, mix sugar, flour, cinnamon and nutmeg. Add apples and toss to coat. Transfer to pastry-lined pie plate. Sprinkle with topping.

3. Bake 10 minutes. Reduce oven setting to 375°. Bake 40-45 minutes or until topping is browned and apples are tender. Cover edge loosely with foil during the last 15 minutes if needed to prevent overbrowning. Cool on a wire rack.

NOTE *Pastry for single-crust pie (9 inches): Combine 1¼ cups all-purpose flour and ¼ tsp. salt; cut in ½ cup cold butter until crumbly. Gradually add 3-5 Tbsp. ice water, tossing with a fork until dough holds together when pressed. Wrap in plastic wrap and refrigerate 1 hour.*

PER SERVING *1 slice: 353 cal., 19g fat (12g sat. fat), 49mg chol., 197mg sodium, 45g carb. (26g sugars, 2g fiber), 3g pro.*

APPLE CRUMBLE PIE

LEMON POUND CAKE LOAVES

Next time you're spending the weekend at a friend's, take along these luscious lemon loaves. You can enjoy them for breakfast in the morning!

—LOLA BAXTER WINNEBAGO, MN

PREP: 20 MIN. ● **BAKE:** 35 MIN. + COOLING
MAKES: 2 MINI LOAVES (6 SLICES EACH)

½ cup butter, softened
1 cup sugar
2 large eggs
1 teaspoon grated lemon peel
1 teaspoon vanilla extract
½ teaspoon lemon extract
1¾ cups all-purpose flour
½ teaspoon salt
¼ teaspoon baking soda
½ cup sour cream
ICING
¾ cup confectioners' sugar
½ teaspoon grated lemon peel
1 tablespoon lemon juice

1. Preheat oven to 350°. Grease and flour two 5¾x3x2-in. loaf pans.

2. In a large bowl, cream butter and sugar until light and fluffy. Add eggs, one at a time, beating well after each addition. Beat in the lemon peel and extracts. In another bowl, whisk flour, salt and baking soda; add to creamed mixture alternately with sour cream, beating well after each addition.

3. Transfer to prepared pans. Bake 35-40 minutes or until a toothpick inserted in center comes out clean. Cool in pans 10 minutes before removing to wire racks to cool completely.

4. In a small bowl, mix the icing ingredients. Spoon over loaves.

FREEZE OPTION *Do not make icing. Securely wrap cooled loaves in plastic wrap and foil, then freeze. To use, thaw at room temperature. Prepare icing as directed.*

PER SERVING *1 slice: 262 cal., 10g fat (6g sat. fat), 58mg chol., 201mg sodium, 39g carb. (25g sugars, 1g fiber), 3g pro.*

CHOCOLATE-COVERED
CHERRY DELIGHTS

COCONUT-PINEAPPLE RHUBARB BARS

I make this crunchy, buttery dessert bar with homegrown rhubarb. For an added attraction, serve it warm with frozen yogurt or ice cream.

—RAYMONDE BOURGEOIS SWASTIKA, ON

PREP: 25 MIN. ● **BAKE:** 40 MIN. + COOLING
MAKES: 2 DOZEN

- **3 cups chopped fresh or frozen rhubarb (about ¾ pound)**
- **1 cup coarsely chopped fresh pineapple**
- **½ cup packed brown sugar**
- **4 tablespoons water, divided**
- **1 teaspoon lemon juice**
- **2 tablespoons cornstarch**
- **½ teaspoon coconut extract, optional**

CRUST AND TOPPING

- **2 cups old-fashioned oats**
- **1½ cups all-purpose flour**
- **1 cup flaked coconut**
- **½ cup packed brown sugar**
- **½ teaspoon salt**
- **1 cup butter, melted**

1. Preheat oven to 350°. In a large saucepan, combine the rhubarb, pineapple, brown sugar, 1 tablespoon water and lemon juice; bring to a boil. Reduce heat; simmer, uncovered, for 4-5 minutes or until rhubarb is tender.
2. In a small bowl, mix cornstarch and remaining water until smooth; stir into rhubarb mixture. Return to a boil; cook and stir for 1-2 minutes or until thickened. Remove from heat; if desired, stir in extract.
3. In a large bowl, mix oats, flour, coconut, brown sugar and salt; stir in melted butter until crumbly. Press 3 cups crumb mixture onto bottom of a greased 13x9-in. baking dish. Spread with rhubarb mixture. Sprinkle with remaining crumb mixture.
4. Bake 40-45 minutes or until golden brown. Cool in pan on a wire rack. Cut into bars.
PER SERVING *1 bar: 185 cal., 10g fat (6g sat. fat), 20mg chol., 124mg sodium, 24g carb. (12g sugars, 1g fiber), 2g pro.*

CHOCOLATE-COVERED CHERRY DELIGHTS

Chocolate-covered cherries were my dad's favorite candy, so I designed these cookies for him. They've got a fudgy sauce and a coconut surprise inside.

—DARLENE BRENDEN SALEM, OR

PREP: 35 MIN.
BAKE: 10 MIN./BATCH + COOLING
MAKES: 4 DOZEN

- **1 cup butter, softened**
- **1½ cups sugar**
- **⅓ cup maraschino cherry juice**
- **1 teaspoon vanilla extract**
- **3 cups all-purpose flour**
- **½ cup baking cocoa**
- **1 cup flaked coconut**
- **¾ cup chopped maraschino cherries, drained and patted dry**
- **½ cup miniature semisweet chocolate chips**

TOPPING

- **¾ cup vanilla frosting**
- **48 maraschino cherries with stems, drained and patted dry**
- **1 cup miniature semisweet chocolate chips**
- **1 teaspoon shortening**

1. Preheat oven to 375°. In a large bowl, beat butter and sugar until blended. Gradually beat in cherry juice and vanilla. In another bowl, whisk flour and cocoa; gradually beat into creamed mixture. Stir in coconut, cherries and chocolate chips.
2. Shape dough into 48 balls (about 1¼ in. each); place 2 in. apart on ungreased baking sheets. Press a deep indentation in center of each with the end of a wooden spoon handle. Bake 9-11 minutes or until set and bottoms are lightly browned. Remove from pans to wire racks to cool completely.
3. Fill each cookie with ¾ teaspoon frosting. Top with cherries. In a microwave, melt chocolate chips and shortening; stir until smooth. Spoon over cherries. Let stand until set.
PER SERVING *1 cookie: 160 cal., 7g fat (4g sat. fat), 10mg chol., 47mg sodium, 25g carb. (17g sugars, 1g fiber), 1g pro.*

DOUBLE-LAYER
PUMPKIN CHEESECAKE

FREEZE IT

HONEY-LIME ALMOND COOKIES

Decades ago, my grandmother passed this recipe for buttery lime cookies to me. Through years of baking, our cookie memories keep the family connected although we're miles apart.
—**PAULA MARCHESI** LENHARTSVILLE, PA

PREP: 25 MIN. + CHILLING
BAKE: 10 MIN./BATCH + COOLING
MAKES: ABOUT 3 DOZEN

- 1 cup butter, softened
- ½ cup sugar
- 3 tablespoons honey
- 1 large egg yolk
- 1 tablespoon grated lime peel
- 1 teaspoon lime juice
- 2 cups all-purpose flour
- 1 cup slivered almonds, finely chopped
  Confectioners' sugar, optional

1. In a large bowl, cream butter and sugar until light and fluffy. Beat in honey, egg yolk, lime peel and lime juice. Gradually beat in flour. Stir in almonds.

2. Divide dough in half; shape each into a 5-in.-long roll. Wrap in plastic; refrigerate 1 hour or until firm.

3. Preheat oven to 350°. Unwrap and cut dough crosswise into ¼-in. slices. Place 1 in. apart on ungreased baking sheets. Bake 10-12 minutes or until edges are light brown.

4. Cool on pans 2 minutes. Remove to wire racks to cool completely. If desired, dust with confectioners' sugar.

FREEZE OPTION *Freeze cookies in freezer containers. To use, thaw before serving. If desired, dust with additional confectioners' sugar.*

PER SERVING *1 cookie: 106 cal., 7g fat (3g sat. fat), 19mg chol., 41mg sodium, 10g carb. (4g sugars, 1g fiber), 1g pro.*

DOUBLE-LAYER PUMPKIN CHEESECAKE

I thought that cheesecake and pumpkin pie would be amazing together. This creamy combo won a prize in our local pie contest, so I guess the judges agreed!
—**NOEL FERRY** PERKASIE, PA

PREP: 25 MIN. ● **BAKE:** 55 MIN. + COOLING
MAKES: 10 SERVINGS

- 1½ cups crushed gingersnap cookies (about 30 cookies)
- ¾ cup chopped pecans, toasted
- 1 tablespoon sugar
- ⅛ teaspoon salt
- ¼ cup butter, melted
  CHEESECAKE LAYER
- 1 package (8 ounces) cream cheese, softened
- ⅓ cup sugar
- 1 large egg, lightly beaten
- 1 teaspoon vanilla extract
  PUMPKIN LAYER
- 2 large eggs, lightly beaten
- 1⅓ cups canned pumpkin
- ½ cup sugar
- 1 teaspoon pumpkin pie spice
- ⅛ teaspoon salt
- ⅔ cup heavy whipping cream
  Sweetened whipped cream, optional
  Toasted chopped pecans, optional

1. Preheat oven to 325°. Pulse first four ingredients in a food processor until ground. Add butter; pulse to blend. Press mixture onto bottom and up sides of an ungreased 9-in. deep-dish pie plate. Refrigerate while preparing filling.

2. For cheesecake layer, beat all ingredients until smooth. For the pumpkin layer, whisk together eggs, pumpkin, sugar, pie spice and salt; gradually whisk in cream. Spread cheesecake mixture onto crust; cover with pumpkin mixture.

3. Bake on a lower oven rack until filling is set, 55-65 minutes. Cool at least 1 hour on a wire rack; serve or refrigerate within 2 hours. If desired, top with whipped cream and pecans.

NOTE *To toast nuts, bake in a shallow pan in a 350° oven for 5-10 minutes or cook in a skillet over low heat until lightly browned, stirring occasionally.*

PER SERVING *1 piece: 422 cal., 28g fat (13g sat. fat), 115mg chol., 313mg sodium, 40g carb. (25g sugars, 2g fiber), 6g pro.*

Picture-Perfect Pavlova

Minnesota reader Norma Stevenson shares secrets for her light-as-air meringue shell topped with berries and whipped cream. Anna Pavlova, the famed Russian ballerina, is the namesake of this classic, lovely, better-for-you dessert.

TWO-BERRY PAVLOVA

TWO-BERRY PAVLOVA

Here is a light and airy dessert that I first tried in Ireland. When I got home, I made it for my kids, who loved building their own with their favorite fruits.

—**NORMA STEVENSON** EAGAN, MN

PREP: 20 MIN. + STANDING
BAKE: 45 MIN. + COOLING
MAKES: 12 SERVINGS

- 4 **large egg whites**
- ½ **teaspoon cream of tartar**
- 1 **cup sugar**
- 1 **tablespoon cornstarch**
- 1 **teaspoon lemon juice**

TOPPINGS
- 2 **cups fresh blackberries**
- 2 **cups sliced fresh strawberries**
- ¼ **cup plus 3 tablespoons sugar, divided**
- 1¼ **cups heavy whipping cream**

1. Place egg whites in a large bowl; let stand at room temperature for 30 minutes. Meanwhile, line a baking sheet with parchment paper; draw a 10-in. circle on the paper. Invert paper.

2. Preheat oven to 300°. Add cream of tartar to egg whites; beat on medium speed until soft peaks form. Gradually add sugar, 1 tablespoon at a time, beating on high after each addition until sugar is dissolved. Continue beating until stiff glossy peaks form. Fold in cornstarch and lemon juice.

3. Spoon meringue onto prepared pan; with the back of a spoon, shape into a 10-in. circle, forming a shallow well in the center. Bake 45-55 minutes or until meringue is set and dry. Turn off oven (do not open oven door); leave meringue in oven 1 hour. Remove from oven; cool completely on baking sheet.

4. To serve, toss berries with ¼ cup sugar in a small bowl; let stand for 10 minutes. Meanwhile, in a large bowl, beat cream until it begins to thicken. Add remaining sugar; beat until soft peaks form.

5. Remove meringue from parchment paper; place on a serving plate. Spoon whipped cream over top, forming a slight well in the center. Top with berries.

PER SERVING *1 piece: 208 cal., 9g fat (6g sat. fat), 34mg chol., 29mg sodium, 30g carb. (27g sugars, 2g fiber), 2g pro. **Diabetic Exchanges:** 2 starch, 2 fat.*

HOW-TO

BE A MERINGUE MAVEN

1. Beat egg whites, cream of tartar and sugar until stiff, glossy peaks form. To make sure the sugar has dissolved, rub some meringue between your fingers—it should feel silky smooth. If not, keep whipping.

2. After folding in cornstarch and lemon juice, grab the parchment-covered baking sheet you've prepared with the circle template. Plop the meringue in the center of the circle and spread it outward to create a well, then pop it in the oven.

COCONUT
MACAROON PIE

STRAWBERRY CHEESECAKE ICE CREAM

When I first got my ice cream maker, a friend shared this dreamy recipe.

—**JOAN HALLFORD** NORTH RICHLAND HILLS, TX

PREP: 15 MIN.
PROCESS: 25 MIN. + FREEZING
MAKES: 1½ QUARTS

- 1 **cup half-and-half cream**
- 1 **tablespoon vanilla extract**
- 2 **teaspoons grated lemon peel**
- 2 **teaspoons lemon juice**
- 1 **cup sugar**
- 1 **package (8 ounces) cream cheese, cubed and softened**
- 1 **cup heavy whipping cream**
- 1½ **cups fresh strawberries**
  Sliced fresh strawberries or crushed graham crackers, optional

1. Place the first six ingredients in a blender; cover and process until smooth. Add whipping cream; cover and process until blended. Remove to a large bowl.

2. Add 1½ cups strawberries to blender; cover and process until pureed. Stir into cream mixture.

3. Fill cylinder of ice cream maker no more than two-thirds full; freeze according to manufacturer's directions. (Refrigerate any remaining mixture until ready to freeze.)

4. Transfer ice cream to freezer containers, allowing headspace for expansion. Freeze 4-6 hours or until firm. If desired, serve with sliced strawberries and graham crackers.

PER SERVING ½ *cup: 234 cal., 16g fat (10g sat. fat), 58mg chol., 87mg sodium, 20g carb. (20g sugars, 0 fiber), 2g pro.*

HEALTH TIP *For a lighter way to enjoy this must-have treat, fill a dish with sliced fresh peaches or berries and top them with just a small dollop of ice cream.*

COCONUT MACAROON PIE

Macaroons are divine, but they can be a little messy to make. I turned the batter into a pie filling, and the luscious results speak for themselves.

—**BECKY MOLLENKAMP** ST. LOUIS, MO

PREP: 15 MIN. • **BAKE:** 35 MIN.
MAKES: 10 SERVINGS

- 1 **sheet refrigerated pie pastry**
- 2 **large eggs**
- 1 **can (14 ounces) sweetened condensed milk**
- ¼ **cup butter, melted**
- 1 **teaspoon almond extract**
- ¼ **teaspoon salt**
- ¼ **cup all-purpose flour**
- 1 **package (14 ounces) flaked coconut**

1. Preheat oven to 350°. Unroll pastry sheet into a 9-in. pie plate; flute edge. Refrigerate while preparing filling.

2. In a large bowl, beat eggs, milk, melted butter, extract and salt until blended. Stir in flour. Reserve ½ cup coconut; stir remaining coconut into egg mixture. Transfer to pastry-lined pie plate. Sprinkle with reserved coconut.

3. Bake on a lower oven rack 35-45 minutes or until golden brown and filling is set. Cool on a wire rack.

PER SERVING *1 piece: 490 cal., 29g fat (20g sat. fat), 67mg chol., 344mg sodium, 53g carb. (40g sugars, 2g fiber), 7g pro.*

⑤ INGREDIENTS

EASY ELEPHANT EARS

The cinnamon sugar in these crispy treats is a classic. Plus, the recipe calls for only three ingredients and are so simple to assemble.

—**BOB ROSE** WAUKESHA, WI

PREP: 20 MIN. + FREEZING
BAKE: 15 MIN./BATCH
MAKES: ABOUT 2½ DOZEN

- ½ **cup sugar**
- 2 **teaspoons ground cinnamon**
- 1 **package (17.3 ounces) frozen puff pastry, thawed**

1. Preheat oven to 375°. Mix together sugar and cinnamon.

2. On a lightly floured surface, roll one sheet of pastry into an 11x8-in. rectangle. Sprinkle with ¼ cup cinnamon sugar. Working from short sides, roll up jelly-roll style toward the center. Wrap in plastic; freeze for 10 minutes. Repeat.

3. Unwrap and cut dough into ½-in. slices; place on parchment paper-lined baking sheets. Bake 12-15 minutes or until crisp and golden brown. Remove to wire racks to cool.

PER SERVING *1 elephant ear: 87 cal., 4g fat (1g sat. fat), 0 chol., 51mg sodium, 12g carb. (3g sugars, 1g fiber), 1g pro.*

FAST FIX

BROWNIE AFFOGATO SUNDAE

We can't resist brownie sundaes. I combined an affogato (coffee-based beverage) idea with a brownie to get this decadent sundae that mixes it all in there: warm, cold, sweet and salty.
—**JULIE MERRIMAN** SEATTLE, WA

START TO FINISH: 20 MIN.
MAKES: 6 SERVINGS

- ½ cup heavy whipping cream
- ¼ cup marshmallow creme
- 6 prepared brownies
- 6 tablespoons fudge ice cream topping
- 2 cups coffee ice cream
- ¾ cup hot brewed espresso
- 6 tablespoons Kahlua (coffee liqueur), optional
  Chocolate-covered coffee beans
  Sea salt or smoked salt

1. In a small bowl, beat whipping cream and the marshmallow creme until soft peaks form. Refrigerate until serving.
2. To serve, place each brownie in a dessert dish; top with fudge topping and ice cream. Pour espresso and, if desired, Kahlua over ice cream. Top with cream mixture and coffee beans; sprinkle with salt. Serve immediately.
PER SERVING (*calculated without Kahlua, coffee beans and salt*): 350 cal., 21g fat (10g sat. fat), 62mg chol., 146mg sodium, 38g carb. (23g sugars, 1g fiber), 4g pro.

BROWNIE AFFOGATO SUNDAE

PECAN BUTTER TARTS

PECAN BUTTER TARTS

I searched for the perfect butter tart for ages. After many attempts, I discovered this favorite that begs for a little scoop of ice cream on top.
—**SUSAN KIEBOAM** STREETSBORO, OH

PREP: 30 MIN. • **BAKE:** 10 MIN. + COOLING
MAKES: 1 DOZEN

- 1 package (14.1 ounces) refrigerated pie pastry
  FILLING
- ½ cup raisins
- 1 cup water
- 1 large egg, lightly beaten
- ½ cup packed dark brown sugar
- ½ cup packed light brown sugar
- ⅓ cup butter, melted
- 1½ teaspoons vanilla extract
- ¼ teaspoon salt
- ⅓ cup coarsely chopped pecans
  Vanilla ice cream, optional

1. Preheat oven to 425°. Line 12 muffin cups with foil liners. (Do not use paper-lined foil liners.)
2. On a work surface, unroll pastry sheets. Cut 12 circles with a floured 4-in. round cookie cutter (save the remaining pastry for another use). Gently press pastry circles onto bottom and up sides of foil liners. Refrigerate while preparing filling.
3. In a microwave-safe bowl, combine raisins and water; microwave on high 2 minutes. Drain; cool slightly.
4. In a small bowl, mix egg, brown sugars, melted butter, vanilla and salt until blended; stir in pecans and raisins. Spoon into pastry cups, dividing evenly.
5. Bake on a lower oven rack 7-9 minutes or until filling just begins to bubble up and crusts are light golden brown (do not overbake). Cool completely in pan on a wire rack. If desired, serve with ice cream.
PER SERVING 1 tart: 252 cal., 13g fat (6g sat. fat), 33mg chol., 177mg sodium, 33g carb. (22g sugars, 1g fiber), 2g pro.

CRANBERRY WHITE CHOCOLATE CHUNK CHEESECAKE

My New York-style cheesecake has tart cranberries, white chocolate chunks and a smidge of yuletide red. It's an impressive addition to any holiday dessert table.

—**ANGELA SPENGLER** TAMPA, FL

PREP: 30 MIN. ● **BAKE:** 1 HOUR + CHILLING
MAKES: 16 SERVINGS

- **15** Oreo cookies, finely crushed (about 1½ cups)
- **⅓** cup butter, melted

CHEESECAKE

- **5** packages (8 ounces each) cream cheese, softened
- **1½** cups sugar
- **1** tablespoon cranberry juice or 2% milk
- **1** tablespoon vanilla extract
- **3** large eggs, lightly beaten
- **12** ounces white baking chocolate, cut into ½-in. pieces
- **1** cup dried cranberries

1. Preheat oven to 325°. Place a greased 10-in. springform pan on a double thickness of heavy-duty foil (about 18 in. square). Wrap foil securely around pan.
2. In a small bowl, mix the crushed cookies and melted butter. Press onto bottom of prepared pan.
3. In a large bowl, beat cream cheese and sugar until smooth. Beat in cranberry juice and vanilla. Add eggs; beat on low speed just until blended. Fold in white chocolate and cranberries. Pour over crust. Place springform pan in a larger baking pan; add 1 in. of hot water to larger pan.
4. Bake 60-70 minutes or until center is just set and top appears dull. Remove springform pan from water bath. Cool cheesecake on a wire rack 10 minutes. Loosen sides from pan with a knife; remove foil. Cool 1 hour longer. Refrigerate overnight, covering when completely cooled. Remove rim from pan before serving.
PER SERVING *1 slice: 545 cal., 37g fat (22g sat. fat), 123mg chol., 362mg sodium, 50g carb. (44g sugars, 1g fiber), 7g pro.*

---

⑤INGREDIENTS FAST FIX

LEMON MERINGUE FLOATS

I actually dreamed of this float idea one night, and woke up knowing I needed to make it. Thank you, Mr. Sandman!

—**CINDY REAMS** PHILIPSBURG, PA

START TO FINISH: 5 MIN.
MAKES: 6 SERVINGS

- **3** cups vanilla ice cream, softened if necessary
- **18** miniature meringue cookies
- **6** cups cold pink lemonade

Place ½ cup ice cream and three cookies in each of six tall glasses. Top with lemonade. Serve immediately.
NOTE *Make your floats with frozen yogurt for a slimmed-down treat.*
PER SERVING *1½ cups with 3 cookies: 282 cal., 7g fat (4g sat. fat), 29mg chol., 77mg sodium, 51g carb. (48g sugars, 0 fiber), 3g pro.*

MAPLE-ORANGE PEAR CRISP

In fall, my family loves to kick back after dinner and dig into big bowls of this spiced crisp. It isn't too sweet, but it still satisfies a sweet tooth.

—**NOREEN MCCORMICK** CROMWELL, CT

PREP: 15 MIN. ● **BAKE:** 30 MIN.
MAKES: 8 SERVINGS

- **½** cup chopped pecans
- **¼** cup butter, cubed
- **3** tablespoons brown sugar
- **3** tablespoons all-purpose flour
- **1** teaspoon grated orange peel
- **½** teaspoon ground cinnamon
- **¼** teaspoon salt
- **¼** teaspoon ground ginger
- **⅛** teaspoon ground cloves
- **1** teaspoon butter, softened

FILLING

- **6** medium ripe Bosc pears
- **2** tablespoons lemon juice
- **⅓** cup maple syrup
- **1** tablespoon butter
- **2** teaspoons grated orange peel
- **1** teaspoon ground cinnamon
  Ice cream or whipped cream

1. Preheat oven to 375°. For topping, place first nine ingredients in a food processor; pulse until crumbly. Grease an 8-in. square baking dish with 1 teaspoon of butter.
2. Peel, core and cut each pear lengthwise into eight wedges; toss with lemon juice. Place in prepared baking dish.
3. In a small pan, bring syrup, butter, orange peel and cinnamon to a boil, stirring constantly. Pour over pears. Sprinkle with topping. Bake until golden brown and pears are tender, 30-40 minutes. Serve with ice cream.
PER SERVING *254 cal., 12g fat (5g sat. fat), 19mg chol., 135mg sodium, 38g carb. (26g sugars, 5g fiber), 2g pro.*

CRANBERRY WHITE CHOCOLATE CHUNK CHEESECAKE

PUMPKIN PIE CUPCAKES
WITH WHIPPED CREAM

ICE CREAM SNOWBALLS WITH RASPBERRY SAUCE

I needed a dessert for a church group at Christmas, and snowballs came to mind. For added flavor, toast the coconut before making these frozen treats.

—NANCY BRUCE BIG TIMBER, MT

PREP: 30 MIN. + FREEZING
COOK: 10 MIN. + CHILLING
MAKES: 10 SERVINGS

- 1 cup sugar
- 2 tablespoons cornstarch
- ¼ teaspoon salt
- ⅔ cup orange juice
- ½ cup white grape juice
- 1 package (10 ounces) frozen sweetened raspberries, thawed

SNOWBALLS
- 4 cups flaked coconut
- 5 cups vanilla ice cream

1. In a small saucepan, mix the sugar, cornstarch and salt; stir in juices until smooth. Add raspberries; bring to a boil, stirring constantly. Cook and stir for 1-2 minutes or until thickened. Transfer to a small bowl and cool slightly. Refrigerate, covered, 2 hours or until cold.

2. For snowballs, place coconut in a shallow bowl. Using a ½-cup scoop, drop a scoop of ice cream in coconut; roll in coconut to coat and shape into a ball. Transfer to a wax paper-lined baking pan; place in freezer. Repeat to make a total of 10 snowballs; freeze 1 hour or until firm.

3. To serve, spoon the raspberry sauce into dessert dishes and top with snowballs.

PER SERVING *1 snowball with ¼ cup sauce: 405 cal., 17g fat (13g sat. fat), 29mg chol., 188mg sodium, 62g carb. (55g sugars, 3g fiber), 3g pro.*

PUMPKIN PIE CUPCAKES WITH WHIPPED CREAM

I combined my two loves, cupcakes and pie, into one amazing treat. These pumpkin cupcakes have a pie crust bottom and a snow-white topping.

—JULIE HERRERA-LEMLER ROCHESTER, MN

PREP: 45 MIN. ● **BAKE:** 20 MIN. + COOLING
MAKES: 2 DOZEN

- 1 sheet refrigerated pie pastry
- 1 can (15 ounces) solid-pack pumpkin
- 4 large eggs
- ½ cup canola oil
- ½ cup water
- 2 teaspoons vanilla extract
- 3 cups all-purpose flour
- 2 cups sugar
- 1 tablespoon cornstarch
- 2 teaspoons baking powder
- 1 teaspoon baking soda
- 1 teaspoon pumpkin pie spice
- ½ teaspoon salt

WHIPPED CREAM
- 2 cups heavy whipping cream
- ½ cup confectioners' sugar
  Ground cinnamon

1. Preheat oven to 350°. Line 24 muffin cups with foil liners.

2. On a work surface, unroll pastry sheet. Cut 24 circles with a floured 2¼-in. round cookie cutter, rerolling scraps as necessary. Press one pastry circle into each liner. Bake for 10-12 minutes or until lightly browned. Cool on wire racks.

3. In a large bowl, beat the pumpkin, eggs, oil, water and vanilla until well blended. In another bowl, whisk the flour, sugar, cornstarch, baking powder, baking soda, pie spice and salt; gradually beat into pumpkin mixture. Pour ¼ cup batter into each prepared cup.

4. Bake 20-25 minutes or until a toothpick inserted in center comes out clean, rotating pans halfway through baking. Cool in pans for 10 minutes before removing to wire racks to cool completely.

5. For whipped cream, in a large bowl, beat cream until it begins to thicken. Add confectioners' sugar; beat until soft peaks form. To serve, dollop over cupcakes; sprinkle with cinnamon.

PER SERVING *1 cupcake: 297 cal., 15g fat (6g sat. fat), 60mg chol., 185mg sodium, 37g carb. (21g sugars, 1g fiber), 4g pro.*

ICE CREAM SNOWBALLS
WITH RASPBERRY SAUCE

EASY GRASSHOPPER PIE

NUTTY BUTTER MUNCHIES

My sweet tooth flared up, so I had to get baking. Peanuts and pecans are extremely popular in Louisiana, so I worked them into my buttery drop cookies.

—**ZENOLA FRAZIER** TALLULAH, LA

PREP: 25 MIN. ● **BAKE:** 10 MIN./BATCH
MAKES: ABOUT 8 DOZEN

- 1 cup butter, softened
- ½ cup chunky peanut butter
- 1 cup sugar
- 1 cup packed brown sugar
- 3 large eggs
- 1 teaspoon vanilla extract
- ½ teaspoon almond extract
- 3 cups all-purpose flour
- ½ teaspoon baking soda
- ½ teaspoon salt
- 1½ cups chopped pecans
- ½ cup salted peanuts

1. Preheat oven to 350°. In a large bowl, cream butter, peanut butter and sugars until light and fluffy. Beat in eggs, one at a time, and extracts. In another bowl, whisk flour, baking soda and salt; gradually beat into creamed mixture. Stir in nuts.

2. Drop by tablespoonfuls 2 in. apart onto greased baking sheets. Flatten slightly with bottom of a glass dipped in sugar. Bake 10-12 minutes or until edges are light brown. Remove from pans to wire racks to cool.

PER SERVING *1 cookie: 75 cal., 4g fat (2g sat. fat), 11mg chol., 46mg sodium, 8g carb. (5g sugars, 0 fiber), 1g pro.*

EASY GRASSHOPPER PIE

This pie with chocolate mint candies is a Yuletide classic in our family. It's so tempting, we don't wait until Christmas anymore. I make it throughout the year.

—**MELISSA SOKASITS** WARRENVILLE, IL

PREP: 15 MIN. + CHILLING
MAKES: 8 SERVINGS

- 1½ cups cold 2% milk
- 1 package (3.9 ounces) instant chocolate pudding mix
- 2¾ cups whipped topping, divided
- 1 package (4.67 ounces) Andes mint candies, chopped, divided
- 1 chocolate crumb crust (9 inches)
- ¼ teaspoon mint extract
- 2 drops green food coloring, optional

1. In a small bowl, whisk milk and pudding mix 2 minutes. Stir in ¾ cup whipped topping. Fold in ¾ cup of the mint candies. Spoon into crust.

2. Place remaining whipped topping in another bowl. Fold in extract and, if desired, food coloring. Spread over pudding mixture; top with remaining candies. Refrigerate, covered, 4 hours or until set.

PER SERVING *1 piece: 332 cal., 16g fat (11g sat. fat), 4mg chol., 196mg sodium, 44g carb. (26g sugars, 1g fiber), 4g pro.*

LEMON GINGER ICEBOX CAKE

Everyone searches for grand desserts that have easy ingredients and minimal effort. My lemony ginger icebox cake is the answer. It's a holiday lifesaver.

—**SUZANNE BANFIELD** BASKING RIDGE, NJ

PREP: 20 MIN. + CHILLING
MAKES: 12 SERVINGS

- 1 package (8 ounces) cream cheese, softened
- 2 teaspoons grated lemon peel
- 1 jar (10 ounces) lemon curd
- 2 cups heavy whipping cream
- 2 packages (5¼ ounces each) thin ginger cookies
- 2 tablespoons chopped crystallized ginger

1. In a large bowl, beat cream cheese and lemon peel until creamy. Beat in lemon curd until smooth. Gradually add cream, beating on medium-high speed until soft peaks form.

2. Line bottom of an 8-in. square dish with nine cookies; spread with about ⅔ cup cream cheese mixture. Repeat layers six times. Sprinkle with the crystallized ginger. Refrigerate, covered, 2 hours or overnight.

PER SERVING *1 square: 521 cal., 31g fat (19g sat. fat), 93mg chol., 340mg sodium, 54g carb. (34g sugars, 0 fiber), 4g pro.*

NUTTY BUTTER MUNCHIES

CRANBERRY PECAN OATMEAL COOKIES

I needed a new holiday cookie, so I tweaked an old 4-H recipe. This updated oatmeal cookie with cranberries and nuts is my family's all-time favorite.

—**TAMMY HOGGATT** OMAHA, NE

PREP: 25 MIN. • **BAKE:** 15 MIN./BATCH
MAKES: ABOUT 5 DOZEN

- ½ cup butter, softened
- ½ cup sugar
- ½ cup packed brown sugar
- 1 large egg
- ½ teaspoon vanilla extract
- 1 cup all-purpose flour
- ¾ teaspoon ground cinnamon
- ½ teaspoon salt
- ½ teaspoon baking powder
- ½ teaspoon baking soda
- 1½ cups old-fashioned or quick-cooking oats
- 1 cup dried cranberries, coarsely chopped
- 1 cup chopped pecans

1. Preheat oven to 350°. Cream butter and sugars until light and fluffy; beat in egg and vanilla. In another bowl, whisk together flour, cinnamon, salt, baking powder and baking soda; gradually beat into creamed mixture. Stir in remaining ingredients.

2. Drop by tablespoonfuls 1 in. apart onto ungreased baking sheets. Bake until light golden brown, 12-15 minutes. Cool on pans 2 minutes. Remove to wire racks to cool.

PER SERVING *1 cookie: 62 cal., 3g fat (1g sat. fat), 7mg chol., 47mg sodium, 8g carb. (5g sugars, 1g fiber), 1g pro.*

CRANBERRY PECAN OATMEAL COOKIES

GRANDMA DAVIDSON'S BAKED APPLE PUDDING

GRANDMA DAVIDSON'S BAKED APPLE PUDDING

My savvy grandmother whipped up recipes in the Depression years that many of us still use today, like this homey cinnamon-scented apple pudding.

—**HOLLY SHARP** WARREN, ON

PREP: 15 MIN. • **BAKE:** 40 MIN. + STANDING
MAKES: 6 SERVINGS

- 1 cup packed brown sugar
- 1 cup all-purpose flour
- 2 teaspoons baking powder
- ½ teaspoon salt
- ½ teaspoon ground cinnamon
- ½ cup 2% milk
- 3 medium tart apples, peeled and chopped
- 2 tablespoons butter, cubed
- 2 cups boiling water
  Vanilla ice cream, optional

1. Preheat oven to 400°. In a large bowl, mix the first five ingredients. Add milk; stir just until blended. Fold in apples. Transfer to a greased 2½-qt. deep baking dish. Dot with butter.

2. Pour boiling water over top. Bake, uncovered, 40-45 minutes or until golden brown. Let stand 15 minutes before serving. If desired, serve with ice cream.

PER SERVING *1 cup: 291 cal., 5g fat (3g sat. fat), 12mg chol., 381mg sodium, 61g carb. (43g sugars, 2g fiber), 3g pro.*

EAT SMART **⑤ INGREDIENTS**

APRICOT FRUIT POPS

You may think serving ice pops at a formal dinner party is all wrong, but my guests think these freezer treats loaded with lemon and mint are way cool.

—**AYSHA SCHURMAN** AMMON, ID

PREP: 15 MIN. + FREEZING
MAKES: 6 SERVINGS

- ¼ cup orange juice
- 1 teaspoon grated lemon peel
- ¼ cup lemon juice
- 4 teaspoons sugar
- 1 cup sliced fresh apricots (4-5 medium)
- ½ cup ice cubes
- 1 teaspoon minced fresh mint, optional
- 6 freezer pop molds or 6 paper cups (3 ounces each) and wooden pop sticks

1. Place the first six ingredients in a blender; cover and process until blended. If desired, stir in mint.

2. Pour into molds or paper cups. Top molds with holders. If using cups, top with foil and insert sticks through foil. Freeze until firm.

PER SERVING *1 pop: 31 cal., trace fat (trace sat. fat), 0 chol., trace sodium, 8g carb. (6g sugars, 1g fiber), trace pro.* **Diabetic Exchanges:** *½ fruit.*
  HEALTH TIP *There are only 11 little calories from added sugar in these refreshing fruit pops!*

SHORTCUT TRES LECHES CAKE

My mom's favorite cake is tres leches, a butter cake soaked with three kinds of milk. I developed this no-fuss version that's rich and tender.
—**MARINA CASTLE KELLEY**
CANYON COUNTRY, CA

PREP: 20 MIN. + CHILLING
BAKE: 30 MIN. + COOLING
MAKES: 20 SERVINGS

- 1 **package butter recipe golden cake or yellow cake mix (regular size)**
- 3 **large eggs**
- ⅔ **cup 2% milk**
- ½ **cup butter, softened**
- 1 **teaspoon vanilla extract**

TOPPING
- 1 **can (14 ounces) sweetened condensed milk**
- 1 **can (12 ounces) evaporated milk**
- 1 **cup heavy whipping cream**

WHIPPED CREAM
- 1 **cup heavy whipping cream**
- 3 **tablespoons confectioners' sugar**
- 1 **teaspoon vanilla extract**

1. Preheat oven to 350°. Grease a 13x9-in. baking pan.
2. In a large bowl, combine cake mix, eggs, milk, softened butter and vanilla; beat on low speed 30 seconds. Beat on medium 2 minutes. Transfer to the prepared pan. Bake 30-35 minutes or until a toothpick inserted in center comes out clean.
3. Cool in pan on a wire rack for 20 minutes. In a 4-cup measuring cup, whisk topping ingredients until blended. Using a skewer, generously poke holes in top of warm cake. Pour the milk mixture slowly over the cake, filling holes. Cool 30 minutes longer. Refrigerate, covered, at least 4 hours or overnight.
4. In a bowl, beat cream until it begins to thicken. Add confectioners' sugar and vanilla; beat until soft peaks form. Spread over cake.

PER SERVING *1 piece: 343 cal., 20g fat (12g sat. fat), 89mg chol., 257mg sodium, 36g carb. (28g sugars, 0 fiber), 6g pro.*

SHORTCUT TRES
LECHES CAKE

LEMON-LIME MOUSSE

This citrusy mousse is incredibly refreshing after a home-cooked meal. Use all lime or all lemon if you like.
—**KATHY ANDERSON** WALLKILL, NY

PREP: 20 MIN. • **COOK:** 10 MIN. + CHILLING
MAKES: 6 SERVINGS

- ½ **cup sugar**
- 2 **tablespoons cornstarch**
  Pinch salt
- 3 **large egg yolks**
- ⅔ **cup 2% milk**
- ¼ **cup lemon juice**
- 1 **tablespoon lime juice**
- 1½ **teaspoons grated lemon peel**
- ½ **teaspoon grated lime peel**
- 1 **cup heavy whipping cream**
  Lime slices, optional

1. In a small saucepan, mix sugar, cornstarch and salt; whisk in egg yolks and milk until smooth. Whisk in citrus juices until blended; bring to a boil over medium heat, stirring constantly. Cook and stir 2 minutes longer. Stir in citrus peels.
2. Transfer to a bowl. Cover surface with plastic wrap; chill.
3. To serve, in a small bowl, beat cream until soft peaks form. Fold into citrus mixture. Spoon into serving dishes. If desired, top with lime slices.

PER SERVING *½ cup: 257 cal., 18g fat (10g sat. fat), 149mg chol., 57mg sodium, 23g carb. (20g sugars, 0 fiber), 3g pro.*

HEALTH TIP *Save nearly 40 calories and 5 grams saturated fat per serving with an easy swap: Stir 1 cup fat-free lemon Greek yogurt into the lemon mixture first, then fold in ½ cup heavy cream that's been beaten to soft peaks.*

TOP TIP

CITRUS SUBS

It is often possible to use lemon and lime juice and peel interchangeably in recipes to achieve a different flavor. To substitute orange, though, you'll need to keep a little lemon or lime to brighten the flavor.

CHOCOLATE CAKE WITH
CHOCOLATE FROSTING

EASY LEMON PIE

I've had this one-bowl lemon pie for years. It's my twist on chocolate French silk pie, and it's easy to do with refrigerated pastry.

—**GLENNA TOOMAN** BOISE, ID

PREP: 15 MIN. ● **BAKE:** 40 MIN. + CHILLING
MAKES: 8 SERVINGS

- 1 **sheet refrigerated pie pastry**
- ½ **cup sugar**
- 2 **tablespoons all-purpose flour**
- 4 **large eggs**
- 1 **cup light corn syrup**
- 1 **teaspoon grated lemon peel**
- ⅓ **cup lemon juice**
- 2 **tablespoons butter, melted**

WHIPPED CREAM
- 1 **cup heavy whipping cream**
- 2 **tablespoons confectioners' sugar**

1. Preheat oven to 350°. Unroll pastry sheet into a 9-in. pie plate; flute edge. Refrigerate while preparing filling.
2. In a bowl, mix sugar and flour until blended. Whisk in eggs, corn syrup, lemon peel, lemon juice and melted butter until blended. Pour into pastry-lined pie plate.
3. Bake on a lower oven rack 40-45 minutes or until filling is golden brown and thickened; cover edge loosely with foil during the last 15 minutes if needed to prevent overbrowning. Remove foil; cool 1 hour on a wire rack. Refrigerate, covered, for 2 hours or until cold.
4. For whipped cream, in a bowl, beat cream until it begins to thicken. Add confectioners' sugar; beat until soft peaks form. Serve with pie.
PER SERVING *1 piece: 475 cal., 23g fat (13g sat. fat), 147mg chol., 197mg sodium, 65g carb. (50g sugars, 0 fiber), 5g pro.*

CHOCOLATE CAKE WITH CHOCOLATE FROSTING

I once sent this rich chocolate cake to my kids' teachers, and it vanished, so I had to make another one. (Who swipes a whole cake, anyway?)

—**MEGAN MOELBERT** SPRINGVILLE, NY

PREP: 40 MIN. ● **BAKE:** 30 MIN. + COOLING
MAKES: 16 SERVINGS

- 2 **cups sugar**
- 2 **cups water**
- ⅔ **cup canola oil**
- 2 **tablespoons white vinegar**
- 2 **teaspoons vanilla extract**
- 3 **cups all-purpose flour**
- ⅓ **cup plus 1 tablespoon baking cocoa, sifted**
- 2 **teaspoons baking soda**
- 1 **teaspoon salt**

FROSTING
- 3¾ **cups confectioners' sugar**
- ⅓ **cup baking cocoa**
- 1 **cup butter, softened**
- 1 **teaspoon vanilla extract**
- 3 **to 5 tablespoons 2% milk**

1. Preheat oven to 350°. Line bottoms of two greased 9-in. round baking pans with parchment paper; grease paper.

2. In a large bowl, beat sugar, water, oil, vinegar and vanilla until well blended. In a large bowl, whisk flour, sifted cocoa, baking soda and salt; gradually add to sugar mixture, beating until smooth.
3. Transfer batter to prepared pans. Bake for 30-35 minutes or until a toothpick inserted in center comes out clean. Cool in pans 10 minutes before removing to wire racks; remove paper. Cool completely.
4. For frosting, sift confectioners' sugar and cocoa together. In a large bowl, beat butter and vanilla until blended. Beat in confectioners' sugar mixture alternately with enough milk to reach desired consistency. Spread frosting between layers and over top and sides of cake.

FOR CHOCOLATE SHEET CAKE
Make batter as directed and transfer to a greased 13x9-in. baking pan. Bake in a preheated 350° oven 30-35 minutes or until a toothpick inserted in center comes out clean. Frosting recipe may be halved.
PER SERVING *1 slice: 491 cal., 22g fat (8g sat. fat), 31mg chol., 399mg sodium, 74g carb. (53g sugars, 1g fiber), 3g pro.*

EASY LEMON PIE

KEY LIME CUPCAKES

SACHER TORTE SQUARES

Sacher torte is a classic Viennese cake that requires several steps. My recipe gives you an easy way out that still features the classic apricot and chocolate flavors.

—**ARLENE ERLBACH** MORTON GROVE, IL

PREP: 30 MIN. • **BAKE:** 30 MIN. + CHILLING
MAKES: 20 SERVINGS

- 1 **package devil's food cake mix (regular size)**
- 2 **cans (12 ounces each) apricot cake and pastry filling**
- 3 **large eggs**
- 2 **teaspoons vanilla extract**
- 1 **cup (6 ounces) dark chocolate chips**

TOPPINGS

- ½ **cup apricot preserves**
- 2 **teaspoons vanilla extract**
- ⅓ **cup butter, cubed**
- 1 **cup sugar**
- 1 **cup heavy whipping cream**
- 1 **cup (6 ounces) dark chocolate chips**
- ¼ **cup sliced almonds**

1. Preheat oven to 350°. Grease a 13x9-in. baking pan.
2. In a large bowl, combine cake mix, apricot filling, eggs and vanilla; beat on low speed 30 seconds. Beat on medium 2 minutes. Fold in chocolate chips. Transfer to prepared pan. Bake 30-35 minutes or until a toothpick inserted in center comes out clean.
3. Remove pan from oven and place on a wire rack. In a small bowl, mix preserves and vanilla; spread over warm cake.
4. In a small saucepan, combine butter, sugar and cream; bring to a boil, stirring to dissolve sugar. Remove from heat; stir in chocolate chips until melted. Spread over cake; sprinkle with almonds. Refrigerate until set, about 1 hour.
PER SERVING *1 piece: 410 cal., 17g fat (10g sat. fat), 52mg chol., 275mg sodium, 64g carb. (45g sugars, 3g fiber), 4g pro.*

KEY LIME CUPCAKES

I made these light, tangy cupcakes on a chilly day to remind me of our vacation in southern Florida, where Key lime pies are star attractions.

—**JENNIFER GILBERT** BRIGHTON, MI

PREP: 30 MIN. • **BAKE:** 15 MIN. + COOLING
MAKES: 16 CUPCAKES

- ½ **cup butter, softened**
- ¾ **cup sugar**
- ¼ **cup packed brown sugar**
- 2 **large eggs**
- ½ **teaspoon vanilla extract**
- 2 **cups graham cracker crumbs**
- ¾ **cup all-purpose flour**
- 3 **teaspoons baking powder**
- 1 **teaspoon ground cinnamon**
- ¼ **teaspoon ground nutmeg**
- 1 **cup 2% milk**

FROSTING

- 1 **package (8 ounces) cream cheese, softened**
- ¼ **cup butter, softened**
- 2 **teaspoons grated Key lime peel**
- 2 **teaspoons Key lime juice**
- 1 **teaspoon vanilla extract**
- 3¾ **cups confectioners' sugar**

1. Preheat oven to 350°. Line 16 muffin cups with paper or foil liners.
2. In a large bowl, cream butter and sugars until light and fluffy. Add eggs, one at a time, beating well after each addition. Beat in vanilla. In another bowl, whisk cracker crumbs, flour, baking powder, cinnamon and nutmeg; add to creamed mixture alternately with milk, beating well after each addition.
3. Fill prepared cups two-thirds full. Bake for 15-20 minutes or until a toothpick inserted in center comes out clean. Cool in pans 10 minutes before removing to wire racks to cool completely.
4. For frosting, in a large bowl, beat cream cheese, butter and lime peel until blended. Beat in lime juice and vanilla. Gradually beat in confectioners' sugar until smooth. Pipe or spread onto cupcakes. Refrigerate until serving.
PER SERVING *1 cupcake: 378 cal., 16g fat (9g sat. fat), 63mg chol., 270mg sodium, 57g carb. (45g sugars, 1g fiber), 4g pro.*

**Betty Ann Morgan's
Potato Clam Chowder**
PAGE 265

Lightened-Up Classics

If you're looking to eat healthier by cutting fat, sugar or salt from your diet, these dishes are for you. Discover good-for-you takes on 30+ heartwarming classics, such as chimichangas, clam chowder, pizza and even peach cobbler.

**Kristin Michalenko's
One-Pot Meaty Spaghetti**
PAGE 262

**Marquisha Turner's
Southwest Chicken Dinner**
PAGE 270

**Kimberly Hammond's
No-Fry Black Bean
Chimichangas** *PAGE 264*

SPANISH RICE WITH CHICKEN & PEAS

My mom made this juicy chicken and rice for us every Wednesday. I still make it for my hubby. It reminds me of family dinners growing up.

—**JOSEE LANZI** NEW PORT RICHEY, FL

PREP: 15 MIN. ● **COOK:** 30 MIN.
MAKES: 6 SERVINGS

- 1 **pound boneless skinless chicken breasts, cut into 1½-inch pieces**
- 1 **tablespoon all-purpose flour**
- ½ **teaspoon pepper**
- ½ **teaspoon salt, divided**
- 4 **teaspoons plus 1 tablespoon olive oil, divided**
- 1 **small sweet red pepper, chopped**
- 1 **small onion, chopped**
- 1 **celery rib, chopped**
- 1½ **cups uncooked long grain rice**
- 1 **teaspoon ground cumin**
- 1 **teaspoon chili powder**
- 2¼ **cups chicken broth**
- 1 **can (14½ ounces) diced tomatoes, undrained**
- 1 **cup frozen peas, thawed**

1. In a small bowl, toss chicken with the flour, pepper and ¼ teaspoon salt. In a Dutch oven, heat 4 teaspoons oil over medium-high heat. Brown the chicken, stirring occasionally; remove from pan.

2. In same pan, heat remaining oil over medium heat. Add pepper, onion and celery; cook and stir 2-4 minutes or until onion is tender. Add rice, cumin, chili powder and remaining salt; stir to coat rice. Stir in remaining ingredients; bring to a boil. Reduce heat; simmer, covered, 10 minutes.

3. Place browned chicken over rice (do not stir in). Cook, covered, for 5 minutes longer or until rice is tender and chicken is cooked through.

PER SERVING *1½ cups: 367 cal., 8g fat (1g sat. fat), 44mg chol., 755mg sodium, 50g carb. (5g sugars, 4g fiber), 22g pro.* **Diabetic Exchanges:** *3 starch, 2 lean meat, 1 vegetable, 1 fat.*

WINTERTIME BRAISED BEEF STEW

WINTERTIME BRAISED BEEF STEW

This wonderful beef stew makes an easy Sunday meal. It's even better a day or two later, so we make a double batch to be sure we have leftovers.

—**MICHAELA ROSENTHAL**

WOODLAND HILLS, CA

PREP: 40 MIN. ● **BAKE:** 2 HOURS
MAKES: 8 SERVINGS (2 QUARTS)

- 2 **pounds boneless beef sirloin steak or chuck roast, cut into 1-inch pieces**
- 2 **tablespoons all-purpose flour**
- 2 **teaspoons Montreal steak seasoning**
- 2 **tablespoons olive oil, divided**
- 1 **large onion, chopped**
- 2 **celery ribs, chopped**
- 2 **medium parsnips, peeled and cut into 1½-inch pieces**
- 2 **medium carrots, peeled and cut into 1½-inch pieces**
- 2 **garlic cloves, minced**
- 1 **can (14½ ounces) diced tomatoes, undrained**
- 1 **cup dry red wine or reduced-sodium beef broth**
- 2 **tablespoons red currant jelly**
- 2 **bay leaves**
- 2 **fresh oregano sprigs**
- 1 **can (15 ounces) white kidney or cannellini beans, rinsed and drained**
- **Minced fresh parsley, optional**

1. Preheat oven to 350°. Toss beef with flour and steak seasoning.

2. In an ovenproof Dutch oven, heat 1 tablespoon oil over medium heat. Brown beef in batches; remove with a slotted spoon.

3. In same pan, heat remaining oil over medium heat. Add onion, celery, parsnips and carrots; cook and stir until onion is tender. Add garlic; cook 1 minute longer. Stir in tomatoes, wine, jelly, bay leaves, oregano and beef; bring to a boil.

4. Bake, covered, 1½ hours. Stir in beans; bake, covered, 30-40 minutes longer or until beef is tender. Remove the bay leaves and oregano sprigs. If desired, sprinkle with parsley.

FREEZE OPTION *Freeze cooled stew in freezer containers. To use, partially thaw in refrigerator overnight. Heat through in a saucepan, stirring occasionally and adding a little broth or water if necessary.*

PER SERVING *1 cup: 310 cal., 9g fat (3g sat. fat), 64mg chol., 373mg sodium, 26g carb. (8g sugars, 5g fiber), 25g pro.* **Diabetic Exchanges:** *3 lean meat, 1 starch, 1 vegetable, 1 fat.*

BARLEY BEEF BURGERS

I stirred cooked barley and barbecue sauce into hamburger patties to make them moist and flavorful. It's an ingenious way to work grains into a meal.

—**ROSELLA PETERS** GULL LAKE, SK

START TO FINISH: 30 MIN.
MAKES: 2 SERVINGS

- ½ cup water
- ¼ cup quick-cooking barley
- ½ small onion, halved
- 1 tablespoon barbecue sauce
- 1½ teaspoons all-purpose flour
- ¼ teaspoon salt
- ⅛ teaspoon pepper
- ½ pound lean ground beef
- 2 hamburger buns, split
  Optional toppings: lettuce leaves, tomato slices and onion slices

1. In a small saucepan, bring water to a boil. Stir in the barley. Reduce heat; simmer, covered, 8-10 minutes or until barley is tender. Remove from heat; let stand 5 minutes. Cool slightly.

2. Place onion and barley in a food processor; process until finely chopped. Remove to a bowl; stir in barbecue sauce, flour, salt and pepper. Add beef; mix lightly but thoroughly. Shape into two ½-in. thick patties.

3. Grill, covered, over medium heat 4-5 minutes on each side or until a thermometer reads 160°. Serve on buns with toppings as desired.

PER SERVING *1 burger (calculated without toppings): 395 cal., 12g fat (4g sat. fat), 69mg chol., 625mg sodium, 42g carb. (5g sugars, 5g fiber), 29g pro.* **Diabetic Exchanges:** *3 lean meat, 2 starch, 2 fat.*

PROVOLONE ZITI BAKE

Instead of waiting for water to boil, I threw the makings for ziti in the oven. After a long day, I'm more than happy to make the oven do the work.

—**VICKY PALMER** ALBUQUERQUE, NM

PREP: 20 MIN. • **BAKE:** 65 MIN.
MAKES: 8 SERVINGS

- 1 tablespoon olive oil
- 1 medium onion, chopped
- 3 garlic cloves, minced
- 2 cans (28 ounces each) Italian crushed tomatoes
- 1½ cups water
- ½ cup dry red wine or reduced-sodium chicken broth
- 1 tablespoon sugar
- 1 teaspoon dried basil
- 1 package (16 ounces) ziti or small tube pasta
- 8 slices provolone cheese

1. Preheat oven to 350°. In a 6-qt. stockpot, heat oil over medium-high heat. Add onion; cook and stir for 2-3 minutes or until tender. Add garlic; cook 1 minute longer. Stir in tomatoes, water, wine, sugar and basil. Bring to a boil; remove from the heat. Stir in the uncooked ziti.

2. Transfer to a 13x9-in. baking dish coated with cooking spray. Bake, covered, 1 hour. Top with cheese. Bake, uncovered, for 5-10 minutes longer or until the ziti is tender and the cheese is melted.

PER SERVING *1½ cups: 381 cal., 8g fat (4g sat. fat), 15mg chol., 763mg sodium, 60g carb. (13g sugars, 4g fiber), 16g pro.*

CURRY SHRIMP

I created this Indian-style shrimp when we were entertaining some friends, one of our favorite things to do.

—**SHANA CONRADT** GREENVILLE, WI

START TO FINISH: 15 MIN.
MAKES: 4 SERVINGS

- 1 tablespoon olive oil
- ¼ cup finely chopped onion
- 1 pound uncooked shrimp (31-40 per pound), peeled and deveined
- 1 garlic clove, minced
- 1 teaspoon curry powder
- ⅓ cup fat-free plain Greek yogurt
- 2 tablespoons chopped fresh cilantro
- 1 tablespoon water
- ¼ teaspoon salt
- ¼ teaspoon pepper
  Hot cooked rice, optional

1. In a large skillet, heat the oil over medium-high heat. Add onion; cook and stir 1-2 minutes or until tender. Add shrimp; cook and stir 2 minutes. Add garlic and curry powder; cook and stir for 30-60 seconds longer or until shrimp turn pink.

2. Remove from heat. Stir in the remaining ingredients. If desired, serve with rice.

PER SERVING *½ cup: 147 cal., 5g fat (1g sat. fat), 138mg chol., 293mg sodium, 3g carb. (1g sugars, 1g fiber), 21g pro.* **Diabetic Exchanges:** *3 lean meat, ½ fat.*

BARLEY BEEF BURGERS

SPINACH-FETA CHICKEN PENNE

EAT SMART **FAST FIX**

SPINACH-FETA CHICKEN PENNE

I wanted a light sauce for pasta, so I cooked tomatoes with garlic, wine and olive oil. It's a blockbuster combo for seafood, too.

—**GERALYN SIPOS** BLANDON, PA

START TO FINISH: 30 MIN.
MAKES: 6 SERVINGS

- 1   package (12 ounces) whole wheat penne pasta
- 1½ pounds boneless skinless chicken breasts, cut into ¼-in.-thick strips
- 3   tablespoons olive oil, divided
- ¾   teaspoon salt, divided
- ¼   teaspoon pepper
- 3   garlic cloves, minced
- ½   cup reduced-sodium chicken broth
- ½   cup dry white wine or additional broth
- 6   plum tomatoes, chopped
- 2   cups fresh baby spinach
- ¾   cup crumbled feta cheese

1. In a 6-qt. stockpot, cook pasta according to the package directions. Drain; return to pot.
2. Meanwhile, toss chicken with 2 tablespoons oil, ½ teaspoon salt and pepper. In a large skillet, cook and stir chicken, half at a time, over medium-high heat for 3-5 minutes or until no longer pink; remove from pan.
3. In same skillet, heat remaining oil over medium heat. Add garlic; cook and stir 1-2 minutes or until tender. Add broth and wine. Bring to a boil, stirring to loosen browned bits from

pan; cook 2 minutes. Stir in tomatoes and the remaining salt; cook until tomatoes are softened. Stir in spinach until wilted.
4. Add chicken and tomato mixture to the pasta; heat through, tossing to combine. Serve with cheese.
PER SERVING *1½ cups: 455 cal., 13g fat (3g sat. fat), 70mg chol., 552mg sodium, 46g carb. (3g sugars, 8g fiber), 36g pro. Diabetic Exchanges: 3 lean meat, 2½ starch, 2 fat, 1 vegetable.*

EAT SMART

SUNDAY BRUNCH CASSEROLE

My favorite brunch dish got a makeover with egg substitute and lower-fat cheese. The lightened-up version still tastes delicious, but it won't weigh you down!

—**ALICE HOFMANN** SUSSEX, WI

PREP: 20 MIN. • **BAKE:** 30 MIN.
MAKES: 8 SERVINGS

- 6   bacon strips, chopped
- 1   teaspoon canola oil
- 1   small green pepper, chopped
- 1   small onion, chopped
- 4   large eggs
- 2   cartons (8 ounces each) egg substitute
- 1   cup fat-free milk
- ¾   teaspoon salt
- ½   teaspoon pepper
- ¼   teaspoon dill weed
- 4   cups frozen shredded hash brown potatoes, thawed
- 1   cup shredded reduced-fat cheddar cheese

1. Preheat oven to 350°. In a large skillet, cook bacon over medium heat until crisp, stirring occasionally. Remove with a slotted spoon; drain on paper towels. Discard drippings.
2. In the same skillet, heat oil over medium-high heat. Add pepper and onion; cook and stir until tender. Remove from heat.
3. In a large bowl, whisk eggs, egg substitute, milk and seasonings until blended. Stir in potatoes, cheese, bacon and pepper mixture.
4. Transfer to a 13x9-in. baking dish coated with cooking spray. Bake for 30-35 minutes or until a knife inserted

in the center comes out clean.
PER SERVING *1 piece: 181 cal., 8g fat (3g sat. fat), 122mg chol., 591mg sodium, 11g carb. (4g sugars, 1g fiber), 16g pro. Diabetic Exchanges: 2 lean meat, 1 starch.*

EAT SMART **FAST FIX**

ONE-POT MEATY SPAGHETTI

I used to help my mom make this when I was growing up, and the recipe stuck. It was a beloved comfort food at college, and now the same dish is a weeknight staple for my fiance and me.

—**KRISTIN MICHALENKO** SEATTLE, WA

START TO FINISH: 30 MIN.
MAKES: 6 SERVINGS

- 1   pound extra-lean ground beef (95% lean)
- 2   garlic cloves, minced
- 1   teaspoon sugar
- 1   teaspoon dried basil
- ½   teaspoon dried oregano
- ¼   teaspoon salt
- ¼   teaspoon paprika
- ¼   teaspoon pepper
- 1   can (28 ounces) diced tomatoes, undrained
- 1   can (15 ounces) tomato sauce
- 2   cups water
- ¼   cup chopped fresh parsley
- 8   ounces uncooked whole wheat spaghetti, broken in half
- ¼   cup grated Parmesan cheese
      Additional chopped parsley

1. In a 6-qt. stockpot, cook and crumble beef with garlic over medium heat until no longer pink, 5-7 minutes; drain. Stir in sugar and seasonings. Add tomatoes, tomato sauce, water and ¼ cup parsley; bring to a boil. Reduce the heat; simmer, covered, 5 minutes.
2. Stir in spaghetti, a little at a time; return to a boil. Reduce the heat to medium-low; cook, uncovered, until spaghetti is al dente, 8-10 minutes, stirring occasionally. Stir in cheese. Sprinkle with additional parsley.
PER SERVING *1⅓ cups: 292 cal., 6g fat (2g sat. fat), 46mg chol., 737mg sodium, 40g carb. (6g sugars, 8g fiber), 24g pro. Diabetic Exchanges: 3 starch, 2 lean meat.*

FLOURLESS DARK
CHOCOLATE CAKE

ROASTED CHICKEN
WITH POTATO WEDGES

I grow herbs and dry them for use all
year. Knowing that the rosemary and
thyme are from our garden makes this
cozy roast chicken dinner even better.
—**TANYA BORKHOLDER** MILFORD, IN

PREP: 10 MIN. • **BAKE:** 30 MIN.
MAKES: 4 SERVINGS

- 2 **large potatoes (about 1½ pounds)**
- 2 **teaspoons olive oil**
- 2 **teaspoons Montreal steak**
  seasoning

CHICKEN
- 4 **bone-in chicken thighs**
- 4 **chicken drumsticks**
- 1 **tablespoon hot water**
- 2 **teaspoons butter**
- 1 **teaspoon dried rosemary, crushed**
- 1 **teaspoon dried thyme**
- ¼ **teaspoon kosher salt**
- ¼ **teaspoon pepper**

1. Preheat the oven to 450°. Cut each
potato lengthwise into 12 wedges; toss
with oil and steak seasoning. Arrange
in a single layer in a greased 15x10x1-
in. baking pan. Roast on a lower oven
rack 30-35 minutes or until tender and
lightly browned, turning occasionally.
2. Place chicken in a large bowl. In
a small bowl, mix the remaining
ingredients; add to chicken and toss to
coat. Transfer to a rack in a broiler pan,
skin side up. Place on an oven rack
above potatoes; roast 30-35 minutes
or until a thermometer inserted in
chicken reads 170°-175°. Serve with
potato wedges.
PER SERVING *1 thigh and 1 drumstick
(skin removed) with 6 potato wedges:
447 cal., 17g fat (5g sat. fat), 133mg
chol., 596mg sodium, 33g carb. (1g
sugars, 4g fiber), 41g pro.* **Diabetic
Exchanges:** *5 lean meat, 2 starch,
2 fat.*

FLOURLESS DARK
CHOCOLATE CAKE

Here's a simple cake to
make that's rich, elegant
and over-the-top
chocolaty. For finishing
touches, add powdered
sugar, cocoa or flavored whipped cream.
—**MARIE PARKER** MILWAUKEE, WI

PREP: 25 MIN. • **BAKE:** 30 MIN. + COOLING
MAKES: 12 SERVINGS

- 4 **large eggs, separated**
- 3 **tablespoons butter**
- 8 **ounces dark baking chocolate,**
  chopped
- ⅓ **cup plus ¼ cup sugar, divided**
- 1 **container (2½ ounces) prune baby**
  food
- 1½ **teaspoons vanilla extract**
  Confectioners' sugar

1. Place the egg whites in a small bowl;
let stand at room temperature for
30 minutes. Preheat the oven to 350°.
Coat a 9-in. springform pan with
cooking spray; place on a baking sheet.
2. In a small saucepan, melt butter
and chocolate over low heat, stirring
constantly. Remove from heat; cool
slightly. In a large bowl, beat egg yolks
on high speed 3 minutes or until
slightly thickened. Gradually add
⅓ cup sugar, beating until thick and
lemon-colored. Beat in baby food,
vanilla and chocolate mixture.
3. With clean beaters, beat egg whites
on medium until soft peaks form.
Gradually add the remaining sugar,
1 tablespoon at a time, beating on high
after each addition until the sugar is
dissolved. Continue beating until stiff
glossy peaks form. Fold a fourth of the
whites into chocolate mixture, then
fold in remaining whites.
4. Pour into prepared pan. Bake for
30-35 minutes or until a toothpick
inserted in center comes out with
moist crumbs. Cool on a wire rack for
20 minutes. Loosen sides from pan
with a knife; remove rim from pan.
Cool cake completely. Dust with
confectioners' sugar before serving.
PER SERVING *1 slice: 188 cal., 11g
fat (6g sat. fat), 78mg chol., 50mg
sodium, 22g carb. (18g sugars, 2g
fiber), 4g pro.*

NO-FRY BLACK BEAN CHIMICHANGAS

Chimichangas are typically deep-fried burritos. My version gets lovin' from the oven, so they're healthier. Black beans and corn make it a hearty meatless meal. If you have 2 cups of leftover rice, here's a great way to use it.

—KIMBERLY HAMMOND KINGWOOD, TX

START TO FINISH: 25 MIN.
MAKES: 6 SERVINGS

- 2 **cans (15 ounces each) black beans, rinsed and drained**
- 1 **package (8.8 ounces) ready-to-serve brown rice**
- ⅔ **cup frozen corn**
- ⅔ **cup minced fresh cilantro**
- ⅔ **cup chopped green onions**
- ½ **teaspoon salt**
- 6 **whole wheat tortillas (8 inches), warmed if necessary**
- 4 **teaspoons olive oil, divided Guacamole and salsa, optional**

1. Preheat the broiler. In a large microwave-safe bowl, mix beans, rice and corn; microwave, covered, for 4-5 minutes or until heated through, stirring halfway. Stir in cilantro, green onions and salt.
2. To assemble, spoon ¾ cup bean mixture across the center of each tortilla. Fold bottom and sides of tortilla over the filling and roll up. Place on a greased baking sheet, seam side down.
3. Brush tops with 2 teaspoons oil. Broil 3-4 inches from heat for 45-60 seconds or until golden brown. Turn over; brush tops with remaining oil. Broil 45-60 seconds longer or until golden brown. If desired, serve with guacamole and salsa.
PER SERVING *1 chimichanga (calculated without guacamole and salsa): 337 cal., 5g fat (0 sat. fat), 0 chol., 602mg sodium, 58g carb. (2g sugars, 10g fiber), 13g pro.*

LIGHT HAM TETRAZZINI

LIGHT HAM TETRAZZINI

Creamy pasta is an easy way to serve a hungry crowd. If you're bringing this tetrazzini to a potluck, cook and add the spaghetti to the slow cooker just before heading to the gathering.

—SUSAN BLAIR STERLING, MI

PREP: 15 MIN. • **COOK:** 4 HOURS
MAKES: 10 SERVINGS

- 2 **cans (10¾ ounces each) reduced-fat reduced-sodium condensed cream of mushroom soup, undiluted**
- 2 **cups cubed fully cooked ham**
- 2 **cups sliced fresh mushrooms**
- 1 **cup fat-free evaporated milk**
- ¼ **cup white wine or water**
- 2 **teaspoons prepared horseradish**
- 1 **package (14½ ounces) multigrain spaghetti**
- 1 **cup shredded Parmesan cheese**

1. In a 5-qt. slow cooker, mix the first six ingredients. Cook, covered, on low 4-5 hours or until heated through.
2. To serve, cook spaghetti according to package directions; drain. Add spaghetti and cheese to slow cooker; toss to combine.
PER SERVING *1 cup: 279 cal., 5g fat (2g sat. fat), 26mg chol., 734mg sodium, 37g carb. (5g sugars, 4g fiber), 20g pro.* **Diabetic Exchanges:** *2½ starch, 1 lean meat, ½ fat.*

GARLIC MASHED CAULIFLOWER

I ordered cauliflower mash every time we were at our favorite restaurant. One night, I figured out how to make it at home and couldn't believe how easy it was. Lucky us!

—JEAN KEISER WEST CHESTER, PA

START TO FINISH: 25 MIN.
MAKES: 4 SERVINGS

- 5 **cups fresh cauliflowerets**
- 1 **garlic clove, thinly sliced**
- 3 **tablespoons fat-free milk**
- 3 **tablespoons reduced-fat mayonnaise**
- ½ **teaspoon salt**
- ⅛ **teaspoon white pepper Cracked black pepper and minced fresh chives, optional**

1. Place 1 in. of water in a large saucepan; add cauliflower and garlic. Bring to a boil. Reduce heat; simmer, covered, until tender, 10-15 minutes, stirring occasionally. Drain cauliflower and garlic; return to pan.
2. Mash the cauliflower mixture to desired consistency. Stir in the milk, mayonnaise, salt and white pepper. If desired, sprinkle with cracked pepper and chives.
PER SERVING *½ cup: 74 cal., 4g fat (1g sat. fat), 4mg chol., 428mg sodium, 8g carb. (4g sugars, 3g fiber), 3g pro.* **Diabetic Exchanges:** *1 vegetable, 1 fat.*

CHICKEN WITH MUSHROOM SAUCE

This saucy chicken looks impressive, but it comes together in no time. I think its flavor rivals that of many full-fat entrees found in fancy restaurants.

—JENNIFER PEMBERTON MUNCIE, IN

START TO FINISH: 25 MIN.
MAKES: 4 SERVINGS

- 2 teaspoons cornstarch
- ½ cup fat-free milk
- 4 boneless skinless chicken breast halves (4 ounces each)
- 1 tablespoon olive oil
- 1 tablespoon butter
- ½ pound sliced fresh mushrooms
- ½ medium onion, thinly sliced
- ¼ cup sherry or chicken broth
- ½ teaspoon salt
- ⅛ teaspoon pepper

1. Mix cornstarch and milk until smooth. Pound chicken with a meat mallet to ¼-in. thickness.
2. In a large nonstick skillet, heat oil over medium heat; cook chicken until no longer pink, 5-6 minutes per side. Remove from pan.
3. In the same pan, heat butter over medium-high heat; saute mushrooms and onion until tender. Stir in the sherry, salt and pepper; bring to a boil. Stir the cornstarch mixture and add to the pan. Return mixture to a boil; cook and stir until thickened, for about 1-2 minutes. Return chicken to pan and heat through.
PER SERVING *225 cal., 9g fat (3g sat. fat), 71mg chol., 541mg sodium, 8g carb. (4g sugars, 1g fiber), 26g pro.* **Diabetic Exchanges:** *3 lean meat, 1½ fat, 1 vegetable.*

POTATO CLAM CHOWDER

I ran across this recipe in one of my antique cookbooks. It's a timeless classic I like to prepare for friends and family throughout the year, especially during the holidays.

—BETTY ANN MORGAN UPPER MARLBORO, MD

PREP: 10 MIN. • **COOK:** 35 MIN.
MAKES: 6 SERVINGS

- 2 cans (6½ ounces each) minced clams
- 2 bacon strips, chopped
- 1 medium onion, chopped
- 2 tablespoons all-purpose flour
- 1 cup water
- 1¾ pounds potatoes (about 4 medium), peeled and cut into ¾-in. cubes
- ½ teaspoon salt
- ¼ to ½ teaspoon dried thyme
- ¼ teaspoon dried savory
- ⅛ teaspoon pepper
- 2 cups 2% milk
- 2 tablespoons minced fresh parsley

1. Drain clams, reserving clam juice. In a large saucepan, cook bacon over medium heat until crisp, stirring occasionally. Remove bacon with a slotted spoon; drain on paper towels.
2. Add onion to drippings; cook and stir 4-6 minutes or until tender. Stir in flour until blended. Gradually stir in water and reserved clam juice; cook and stir until bubbly.
3. Add the potatoes and seasonings; bring to a boil, stirring frequently. Reduce the heat; simmer, covered, for 20-25 minutes or until potatoes are tender, stirring occasionally.
4. Stir in the milk, parsley and clams; heat through. Top with bacon.
PER SERVING *1 cup: 201 cal., 6g fat (2g sat. fat), 34mg chol., 615mg sodium, 27g carb. (6g sugars, 2g fiber), 11g pro.* **Diabetic Exchanges:** *2 starch, 2 lean meat.*

CHICKEN WITH
MUSHROOM SAUCE

SPICED PEACH
COBBLER

SPICED PEACH COBBLER

Because this warm cobbler with cinnamon and cardamom is a slimmed-down dessert, flirt with the possibility of ice cream on top.

—MARY RELYEA CANASTOTA, NY

PREP: 20 MIN. • **BAKE:** 30 MIN.
MAKES: 8 SERVINGS

- ½ cup sugar
- 3 tablespoons cornstarch
- ½ teaspoon ground cinnamon
- ¼ teaspoon ground cardamom
- 12 medium peaches, peeled and sliced (about 8 cups)
- 1 tablespoon lemon juice

TOPPING

- 1 cup all-purpose flour
- ¼ cup sugar
- 2 teaspoons grated orange peel
- ¾ teaspoon baking powder
- ¼ teaspoon salt
- ¼ teaspoon baking soda
- 3 tablespoons cold butter
- ¾ cup buttermilk

1. Preheat oven to 375°. In a large bowl, mix sugar, cornstarch, cinnamon and cardamom. Add the peaches and lemon juice; toss to combine. Transfer to an 11x7-in. baking dish coated with cooking spray.
2. In a small bowl, whisk the first six topping ingredients; cut in butter until the mixture resembles coarse crumbs. Add the buttermilk; stir just until mixture is moistened. Drop the batter by tablespoonfuls over peach mixture.
3. Bake, uncovered, 30-35 minutes or until topping is golden brown. Serve cobbler warm.

PER SERVING *246 cal., 5g fat (3g sat. fat), 12mg chol., 206mg sodium, 49g carb. (32g sugars, 3g fiber), 4g pro.*

HEALTH TIP *To dollop or not to dollop? Calories per ¼ cup: whipped topping, 50; light ice cream, 50; ice cream, 70; sweetened whipped cream, 114.*

SKILLET BEEF & POTATOES

Sirloin strips with red potatoes and fresh rosemary are seriously amazing and ready in a flash. The key is precooking potatoes in the microwave to speed up the process.

—TASTE OF HOME TEST KITCHEN

START TO FINISH: 25 MIN.
MAKES: 4 SERVINGS

- 1½ pounds red potatoes (about 5 medium), halved and cut into ¼-in. slices
- ⅓ cup water
- ½ teaspoon salt
- 1 pound beef top sirloin steak, cut into thin strips
- ½ cup chopped onion
- 3 tablespoons olive oil, divided
- 2 teaspoons garlic pepper blend
- 1½ teaspoons minced fresh rosemary

1. Place potatoes, water and salt in a microwave-safe dish; microwave, covered, on high for 7-9 minutes or until potatoes are tender. Drain.
2. Meanwhile, toss beef with onion, 2 tablespoons oil and pepper blend. Place a large skillet over medium-high heat. Add half of the beef mixture; cook and stir 2-3 minutes or until no longer pink. Remove from pan; repeat with remaining beef mixture.
3. In a clean skillet, heat remaining oil over medium-high heat. Add potatoes; cook for 4-5 minutes or until lightly browned, turning occasionally. Stir in beef mixture and rosemary.

PER SERVING *1½ cups: 320 cal., 16g fat (4g sat. fat), 63mg chol., 487mg sodium, 20g carb. (2g sugars, 2g fiber), 23g pro.* **Diabetic Exchanges:** *3 lean meat, 2 fat, 1 starch.*

BLACK BEAN TURKEY CHILI

This busy-day chili is packed with flavor. We make it ahead and freeze some to eat later.

—MARISELA SEGOVIA MIAMI, FL

START TO FINISH: 30 MIN.
MAKES: 6 SERVINGS

- 1 pound lean ground turkey
- 1 large green pepper, chopped
- 1 medium onion, chopped
- 2 tablespoons chili powder
- ½ teaspoon salt
- ¼ teaspoon pepper
- ⅛ to ¼ teaspoon cayenne pepper
- 1 can (15 ounces) no-salt-added tomato sauce
- 1 can (15 ounces) black beans, rinsed and drained
- 1½ cups frozen corn (about 8 ounces), thawed
- 1 large tomato, chopped
- ½ cup water
  Shredded cheddar cheese, optional

1. In a 6-qt stockpot, cook turkey with green pepper and onion over medium-high heat until no longer pink, stirring and breaking the meat into crumbles, about 5-7 minutes. Stir in seasonings; cook 1 minute.
2. Stir in tomato sauce, beans, corn, tomato and water; bring to a boil. Reduce heat; simmer, uncovered, to allow flavors to blend, about 10 minutes, stirring occasionally. If desired, serve with cheese.

FREEZE OPTION *Freeze cooled chili in freezer containers. To use, partially thaw in refrigerator overnight. Heat chili through in a saucepan, stirring occasionally and adding a little water if necessary.*

PER SERVING *1 cup: 247 cal., 7g fat (2g sat. fat), 52mg chol., 468mg sodium, 27g carb. (7g sugars, 7g fiber), 21g pro.* **Diabetic Exchanges:** *3 lean meat, 1½ starch, 1 vegetable.*

FRUIT & ALMOND BITES

EASY WHITE CHICKEN CHILI

Chili is one of our favorite cold-weather strategies. We use chicken and white beans for a twist on the regular bowl of red. It's soothing comfort food.

—**RACHEL LEWIS** DANVILLE, VA

START TO FINISH: 30 MIN.
MAKES: 6 SERVINGS

- 1 pound lean ground chicken
- 1 medium onion, chopped
- 2 cans (15 ounces each) cannellini beans, rinsed and drained
- 1 can (4 ounces) chopped green chilies
- 1 teaspoon ground cumin
- ½ teaspoon dried oregano
- ¼ teaspoon pepper
- 1 can (14½ ounces) reduced-sodium chicken broth
  Optional toppings: reduced-fat sour cream, shredded cheddar cheese and chopped fresh cilantro

1. In a large saucepan, cook chicken and onion over medium-high heat for 6-8 minutes or until chicken is no longer pink, breaking up the chicken into crumbles.
2. Place one can of beans in a small bowl; mash slightly. Stir mashed beans, remaining can of beans, chilies, seasonings and broth into chicken mixture; bring to a boil. Reduce heat; simmer, covered, 12-15 minutes or until flavors are blended. Serve with toppings as desired.

FREEZE OPTION *Freeze cooled chili in freezer containers. To use, partially thaw in refrigerator overnight. Heat through in a saucepan, stirring occasionally and adding a little broth if necessary.*

PER SERVING *1 cup: 228 cal., 5g fat (1g sat. fat), 54mg chol., 504mg sodium, 23g carb. (1g sugars, 6g fiber), 22g pro. Diabetic Exchanges: 3 lean meat, 1½ starch.*

EAT SMART

FRUIT & ALMOND BITES

With big handfuls of dried apricots, cherries, almonds and pistachios, these are some seriously tasty and satisfying no-bake treats. You can take them anywhere.

—**DONNA POCHODAY-STELMACH**
MORRISTOWN, NJ

PREP: 30 MIN. + CHILLING
MAKES: ABOUT 4 DOZEN

- 3¾ cups sliced almonds, divided
- ¼ teaspoon almond extract
- ¼ cup honey
- 2 cups finely chopped dried apricots
- 1 cup finely chopped dried cherries or cranberries
- 1 cup finely chopped pistachios, toasted

1. Place 1¼ cups almonds in a food processor; pulse until finely chopped. Remove almonds to a shallow bowl; reserve for coating.
2. Add remaining 2½ cups almonds to food processor; pulse until finely chopped. While processing, gradually add extract and honey. Remove to a large bowl; stir in the apricots and cherries. Divide mixture into six portions; shape each portion into a ½-in.-thick roll. Wrap in plastic wrap; refrigerate 1 hour or until firm.
3. Unwrap and cut rolls into 1½-in. pieces. Roll half of the pieces in reserved almonds, pressing gently to help nuts adhere. Roll remaining half in the pistachios. Store bites between waxed paper in airtight containers.
NOTE *To toast nuts, bake in a shallow pan in a 350° oven for 5-10 minutes or cook in a skillet over low heat until lightly browned, stirring occasionally.*
PER SERVING *1 piece: 86 cal., 5g fat (0 sat. fat), 0 chol., 15mg sodium, 10g carb. (7g sugars, 2g fiber), 2g pro. Diabetic Exchanges: 1 fat, ½ starch.*
HEALTH TIP *Per ounce, almonds contain more fiber and protein than any other tree nut.*

BOW TIES WITH
SAUSAGE & ASPARAGUS

BOW TIES WITH SAUSAGE & ASPARAGUS

We love asparagus, so I am always looking for ways to go green. This veggie pasta comes together fast on hectic nights and makes wonderful leftovers.
—CAROL A. SUTO LIVERPOOL, NY

START TO FINISH: 30 MIN.
MAKES: 6 SERVINGS

- 3 **cups uncooked whole wheat bow tie pasta (about 8 ounces)**
- 1 **pound fresh asparagus, trimmed and cut into 1½-inch pieces**
- 1 **package (19½ ounces) Italian turkey sausage links, casings removed**
- 1 **medium onion, chopped**
- 3 **garlic cloves, minced**
- ¼ **cup shredded Parmesan cheese**
  Additional shredded Parmesan cheese, optional

1. In a large saucepan, cook pasta according to the package directions, adding asparagus during the last 2-3 minutes of cooking. Drain pasta, reserving ½ cup pasta water. Return pasta to pan.
2. Meanwhile, in a large skillet, cook sausage, onion and garlic over medium heat 6-8 minutes or until sausage is no longer pink, breaking up sausage into crumbles. Using a slotted spoon, add sausage mixture to pasta.
3. Stir in ¼ cup cheese and enough reserved pasta water to moisten. If desired, serve with additional cheese.
PER SERVING 1⅓ cups (*calculated without additional cheese*): 247 cal., 7g fat (2g sat. fat), 36mg chol., 441mg sodium, 28g carb. (2g sugars, 4g fiber), 17g pro. **Diabetic Exchanges:** 2 lean meat, 1½ starch, 1 vegetable.

SAUCY PORK CHOP SKILLET

Skillet pork chops make easy comfort food. We have them with a salad and fruit. If you've got fresh green beans or steamed broccoli, go for it.
—DONNA ROBERTS MANHATTAN, KS

START TO FINISH: 30 MIN.
MAKES: 6 SERVINGS

- 3 **cups uncooked instant brown rice**
- 2 **teaspoons canola oil**
- 6 **boneless pork loin chops (6 ounces each)**
- 1 **small onion, sliced**
- 1 **cup canned diced tomatoes**
- 1 **cup reduced-sodium beef broth**
- 1 **tablespoon dried parsley flakes**
- ½ **teaspoon salt**
- ¼ **teaspoon pepper**
- ⅛ **teaspoon dried basil**
- ⅛ **teaspoon dried oregano**
- 2 **tablespoons all-purpose flour**
- ½ **cup water**

1. Cook rice according to package directions. Meanwhile, in a large nonstick skillet coated with cooking spray, heat oil over medium-high heat. Brown the pork chops on both sides; remove from pan.
2. Add onion to drippings; cook and stir until tender. Stir in tomatoes, broth, parsley and seasonings; bring to a boil. Return pork to pan. Reduce heat; simmer, covered, 6-8 minutes or until a thermometer inserted in pork reads 145°.
3. Remove pork to a serving plate; keep warm. In a small bowl, mix flour and water until smooth; stir into sauce. Bring to a boil, stirring constantly; cook and stir for 2 minutes or until thickened. Spoon over pork chops; serve with rice.
PER SERVING 1 pork chop with ⅔ cup cooked rice and ⅓ cup sauce: 436 cal., 13g fat (4g sat. fat), 83mg chol., 382mg sodium, 39g carb. (2g sugars, 3g fiber), 38g pro. **Diabetic Exchanges:** 5 lean meat, 2½ starch.

EGG ROLL NOODLE BOWL

We love Asian egg rolls, but they can be challenging to make. Simplify everything with this deconstructed version made on the stovetop.
—COURTNEY STULTZ WEIR, KS

START TO FINISH: 30 MIN.
MAKES: 4 SERVINGS

- 1 **tablespoon sesame oil**
- ½ **pound ground pork**
- 1 **tablespoon soy sauce**
- 1 **garlic clove, minced**
- 1 **teaspoon ground ginger**
- ½ **teaspoon salt**
- ¼ **teaspoon ground turmeric**
- ¼ **teaspoon pepper**
- 6 **cups shredded cabbage (about 1 small head)**
- 2 **large carrots, shredded (about 2 cups)**
- 4 **ounces rice noodles**
- 3 **green onions, thinly sliced**
  Additional soy sauce, optional

1. In a large skillet, heat the oil over medium-high heat; cook and crumble pork until browned, 4-6 minutes. Stir in the soy sauce, garlic and seasonings. Add cabbage and carrots; cook for 4-6 minutes longer or until vegetables are tender, stirring occasionally.
2. Cook rice noodles according to the package directions; drain and immediately add to pork mixture, tossing to combine. Sprinkle with green onions. If desired, serve with additional soy sauce.
PER SERVING 1½ cups: 302 cal., 12g fat (4g sat. fat), 38mg chol., 652mg sodium, 33g carb. (2g sugars, 4g fiber), 14g pro. **Diabetic Exchanges:** 2 medium-fat meat, 2 vegetable, 1½ starch, ½ fat.

TOP TIP

TURMERIC

This spice contributes a bright yellow color and slightly bitter, pungent taste. It's the main ingredient in yellow curry powder, which you can substitute for turmeric if you like.

SOUTHWEST CHICKEN DINNER

My family loves to order gigantic takeout Tex-Mex burritos, but they can be expensive, and we always have leftovers. I created a lighter, no-guilt alternative that skips the tortilla but still has all the flavors they love.

—**MARQUISHA TURNER** AURORA, CO

START TO FINISH: 30 MIN.
MAKES: 4 SERVINGS

- 2 cups water
- 2 tablespoons olive oil, divided
- ½ teaspoon salt
- ¼ teaspoon pepper
- 1 cup uncooked long grain rice
- 1 tablespoon taco seasoning
- 4 boneless skinless chicken breast halves (4 ounces each)
- 1 cup canned black beans or pinto beans, rinsed and drained
- ¼ cup chopped fresh cilantro
- 1 teaspoon grated lime peel
- 2 tablespoons lime juice
  Optional toppings: pico de gallo, shredded Mexican cheese blend and sour cream

1. In a large saucepan, combine water, 1 tablespoon oil, salt and pepper; bring to a boil. Stir in rice. Reduce the heat; simmer, covered, 15-17 minutes or until liquid is absorbed and the rice is tender.

2. Meanwhile, sprinkle taco seasoning over both sides of chicken. In a large skillet, heat the remaining oil over medium heat. Add chicken; cook for 4-5 minutes on each side or until a thermometer reads 165°.

3. In a microwave, heat beans until warmed. To serve, gently stir cilantro, lime peel and lime juice into rice; divide among four bowls. Cut chicken into slices. Place chicken and beans over rice; top as desired.

PER SERVING (*calculated without optional toppings*): *398 cal., 7g fat (1g sat. fat), 63mg chol., 678mg sodium, 52g carb. (1g sugars, 3g fiber), 30g pro.*

SPINACH-BASIL LASAGNA

SPINACH-BASIL LASAGNA

In the kitchen, my husband and I like to use classic ingredients in new ways. I came up with this lasagna one day and haven't made another type since. We both love it!

—**CHARLOTTE GEHLE** BROWNSTOWN, MI

PREP: 20 MIN. ● **BAKE:** 45 MIN.
MAKES: 9 SERVINGS

- 1 large egg, lightly beaten
- 2 cups reduced-fat ricotta cheese
- 4 ounces crumbled feta cheese
- ¼ cup grated Parmesan cheese
- ¼ cup chopped fresh basil
- 2 garlic cloves, minced
- ¼ teaspoon pepper
- 1 jar (24 ounces) pasta sauce
- 9 no-cook lasagna noodles
- 3 cups fresh baby spinach
- 2 cups (8 ounces) shredded part-skim mozzarella cheese

1. Preheat oven to 350°. In a small bowl, mix the first seven ingredients.

2. Spread ½ cup pasta sauce into a greased 13x9-in. baking dish. Layer with three lasagna noodles, ¾ cup ricotta mixture, 1 cup spinach, ½ cup mozzarella cheese and ⅔ cup sauce. Repeat layers twice. Sprinkle with the remaining mozzarella cheese.

3. Bake, covered, for 35 minutes. Uncover; bake 10-15 minutes longer or until cheese is melted. Let stand for 5 minutes before serving.

FREEZE OPTION *Cover and freeze unbaked lasagna. To use, partially thaw in refrigerator overnight. Remove from refrigerator 30 minutes before baking. Preheat oven to 350°. Bake lasagna as directed, increasing time as necessary to heat through and for a thermometer in center to read 165°.*

PER SERVING *1 piece: 292 cal., 12g fat (6g sat. fat), 59mg chol., 677mg sodium, 27g carb. (10g sugars, 3g fiber), 18g pro.* **Diabetic Exchanges:** *2 starch, 2 medium-fat meat.*

BLACKENED PORK CAESAR SALAD

When I cook, my goal is to have enough leftovers for lunch the next day. This Caesar with pork has fantastic flavor even when the meat is chilled.

—PENNY HEDGES DEWDNEY, BC

START TO FINISH: 30 MIN.
MAKES: 2 SERVINGS

- 2 tablespoons mayonnaise
- 1 tablespoon olive oil
- 1 tablespoon lemon juice
- 1 garlic clove, minced
- ⅛ teaspoon seasoned salt
- ⅛ teaspoon pepper

SALAD
- ¾ pound pork tenderloin, cut into 1-inch cubes
- 1 tablespoon blackened seasoning
- 1 tablespoon canola oil
- 6 cups torn romaine
  Salad croutons and shredded Parmesan cheese, optional

1. For dressing, in a small bowl, mix the first six ingredients until blended.
2. Toss pork with the blackened seasoning. In a large skillet, heat oil over medium-high heat. Add the pork; cook and stir 5-7 minutes or until tender.

3. Place romaine in bowl; add dressing and toss to coat. Top with pork, and, if desired, croutons and cheese.
PER SERVING *2½ cups (calculated without croutons and cheese): 458 cal., 31g fat (5g sat. fat), 100mg chol., 464mg sodium, 8g carb. (2g sugars, 3g fiber), 36g pro.*

ZUCCHINI CRUST PIZZA

My mother-in-law shared the recipe for this unique pizza with me. Its nutritious zucchini crust makes it just right for brunch, lunch or a light supper.

—RUTH DENOMME ENGLEHART, ON

PREP: 15 MIN. • **BAKE:** 25 MIN.
MAKES: 6 SLICES

- 3 cups shredded zucchini
- ¾ cup egg substitute
- ⅓ cup all-purpose flour
- ½ teaspoon salt
- 2 cups (8 ounces) shredded part-skim mozzarella cheese
- 2 small tomatoes, halved and thinly sliced
- ½ cup chopped onion
- ½ cup julienned green pepper
- 1 teaspoon dried oregano
- ½ teaspoon dried basil
- 3 tablespoons shredded Parmesan cheese

1. In a large bowl, combine zucchini and egg substitute. Stir in flour and salt. Spread onto a 12-in. pizza pan coated with cooking spray.
2. Bake at 450° for 8 minutes. Reduce the heat to 350°. Sprinkle with the mozzarella, tomatoes, onion, green pepper, oregano, basil and Parmesan cheese. Bake 15-20 minutes or until onion is tender and cheese is melted.
PER SERVING *1 slice: 185 cal., 9g fat (5g sat. fat), 26mg chol., 555mg sodium, 13g carb. (4g sugars, 2g fiber), 15g pro. Diabetic Exchanges: 2 lean meat, 2 vegetable, ½ fat.*

DIJON-HONEY PORK CHOPS

Lemon-pepper is our seasoning of choice for these chops. With the flavorful orange and Dijon-honey sauce, there's no need to pass the salt.

—SHIRLEY GOEHRING LODI, CA

START TO FINISH: 20 MIN.
MAKES: 4 SERVINGS

- 4 boneless pork loin chops (5 ounces each)
- 1 teaspoon salt-free lemon-pepper seasoning
- 2 teaspoons canola oil
- ½ cup orange juice
- 1 tablespoon Dijon mustard
- 1 tablespoon honey

1. Sprinkle pork chops with lemon pepper. In a large nonstick skillet coated with cooking spray, heat oil over medium heat. Brown chops on both sides.
2. In a small bowl, whisk orange juice, mustard and honey until blended; pour over the chops. Bring to a boil. Reduce the heat; simmer, covered, for 5-8 minutes or until a thermometer inserted in pork reads 145°.
3. Remove chops from the pan; keep warm. Bring sauce to a boil; cook until mixture is reduced to ¼ cup, stirring occasionally. Serve with chops.
PER SERVING *1 pork chop with 1 tablespoon sauce: 244 cal., 11g fat (3g sat. fat), 68mg chol., 134mg sodium, 9g carb. (7g sugars, trace fiber), 28g pro. Diabetic Exchanges: 4 lean meat, ½ starch.*

BLACKENED PORK CAESAR SALAD

SLOW-COOKED PORK ROAST DINNER

EAT SMART SLOW COOKER

SLOW-COOKED PORK ROAST DINNER

This recipe will give you the most tender pork you have ever tasted! You can cut it with a fork, and it's just as moist and tender the next day...if there are any leftovers.

—JANE MONTGOMERY PIQUA, OH

PREP: 25 MIN. • **COOK:** 6 HOURS
MAKES: 8 SERVINGS

- 1 cup hot water
- ¼ cup sugar
- 3 tablespoons cider vinegar
- 2 tablespoons reduced-sodium soy sauce
- 1 tablespoon ketchup
- ½ teaspoon salt
- ½ teaspoon pepper
- ¼ teaspoon garlic powder
- ¼ teaspoon chili powder
- 1 large onion, halved and sliced
- 1 boneless pork loin roast (2½ pounds), halved
- 4 medium potatoes (about 1¾ pounds), peeled and cut into 1-inch pieces
- 1 package (16 ounces) frozen sliced carrots, thawed
- 2 tablespoons cornstarch
- 2 tablespoons cold water

1. In a small bowl, whisk the first nine ingredients until blended. Place onion in a 5-qt. slow cooker. Place the roast, potatoes and carrots over onion. Pour sauce mixture over top. Cook, covered, on low for 6-8 hours or until pork and potatoes are tender.
2. Remove roast and vegetables from slow cooker; keep warm. Transfer cooking juices to a small saucepan; skim fat. Bring juices to a boil. In a small bowl, mix cornstarch and water until smooth; stir into cooking juices. Bring to a boil; cook and stir for 1-2 minutes or until thickened. Serve with roast and vegetables.

PER SERVING *4 ounces cooked pork with ⅔ cup vegetables and ⅓ cup sauce: 304 cal., 7g fat (2g sat. fat), 70mg chol., 401mg sodium, 30g carb. (11g sugars, 3g fiber), 29g pro.*
***Diabetic Exchanges:** 4 lean meat, 1½ starch, 1 vegetable.*

EAT SMART FAST FIX

GREEK SAUSAGE PITAS

I nicknamed my sandwich "Thor's Pita" because it's robust and lightning-quick. The ingredient amounts don't really matter. Use more or less depending on what you have.

—TERESA ALEKSANDROV YPSILANTI, MI

START TO FINISH: 20 MIN.
MAKES: 4 SERVINGS

- 4 whole wheat pita breads (6 inches)
- 1 cup plain yogurt
- 2 green onions, chopped
- 2 tablespoons minced fresh parsley
- 1 teaspoon lemon juice
- 1 garlic clove, minced
- ¾ pound Italian turkey sausage links or other sausage links of your choice, casings removed
- 1 medium cucumber, seeded and chopped
- 1 medium tomato, chopped
  Additional minced fresh parsley

1. Preheat oven to 325°. Wrap pita breads in foil; warm in oven while preparing toppings.
2. In a small bowl, mix yogurt, green onions, parsley, lemon juice and garlic. In a large skillet, cook sausage over medium heat 4-6 minutes or until no longer pink, breaking into crumbles.
3. To assemble, spoon sausage over pitas. Top with cucumber, tomato and yogurt mixture; sprinkle with additional parsley.

PER SERVING *1 open-faced sandwich: 309 cal., 9g fat (3g sat. fat), 39mg chol., 667mg sodium, 42g carb. (5g sugars, 6g fiber), 19g pro.* ***Diabetic Exchanges:** 3 starch, 2 lean meat.*

EAT SMART FAST FIX

JAMAICAN CHICKEN WITH COUSCOUS

Fantabulous is a word I reserve for fantastic dishes like this jerk-seasoned chicken. Fresh pineapple and cilantro are delicious, delightful counterpoints to the warm spices.

—JONI HILTON ROCKLIN, CA

START TO FINISH: 30 MIN.
MAKES: 6 SERVINGS

- 1 can (20 ounces) unsweetened pineapple tidbits, undrained
- 1 teaspoon salt, divided
- 1 cup uncooked whole wheat couscous
- ⅓ cup all-purpose flour
- 2 tablespoons minced fresh cilantro
- 1½ pounds boneless skinless chicken breasts, cut into ½-inch-thick strips
- 2 teaspoons Caribbean jerk seasoning
- 3 tablespoons olive oil, divided
  Additional minced fresh cilantro, optional

1. In a large saucepan, combine pineapple and ½ teaspoon salt; bring to a boil. Stir in couscous. Remove from heat; let stand, covered, for 5 minutes or until liquid is absorbed. Fluff with a fork.
2. Meanwhile, in a shallow bowl, mix flour and 2 tablespoons cilantro. Toss chicken with the jerk seasoning and remaining salt. Add to flour mixture, a few pieces at a time, and toss to coat lightly; shake off any excess.
3. In a large skillet, heat 1 tablespoon oil. Add a third of the chicken; cook for 1-2 minutes on each side or until no longer pink. Repeat twice with the remaining oil and chicken. Serve with couscous. If desired, sprinkle with additional cilantro.

PER SERVING *3 oz. chicken with ⅔ cup couscous: 374 cal., 10g fat (2g sat. fat), 63mg chol., 542mg sodium, 42g carb. (12g sugars, 5g fiber), 29g pro.*
***Diabetic Exchanges:**
3 starch, 3 lean meat, 1 fat.*

SHRIMP PANZANELLA SALAD

WEEKNIGHT BEEF SKILLET

This mild but hearty family fare is chock-full of veggies and good nutrition. It just might become one of your family's favorites!

—CLARA COULSON MINNEY
WASHINGTON COURT HOUSE, OH

START TO FINISH: 25 MIN.
MAKES: 4 SERVINGS

- 3 cups uncooked yolk-free whole wheat noodles
- 1 pound lean ground beef (90% lean)
- 1 medium green pepper, finely chopped
- 1 can (15 ounces) tomato sauce
- 1 tablespoon Worcestershire sauce
- 1½ teaspoons Italian seasoning
- 1 teaspoon sugar, optional
- 1 package (16 ounces) frozen mixed vegetables, thawed and drained
- ¼ cup minced fresh parsley

1. Cook noodles according to package directions; drain. Meanwhile, in a large nonstick skillet, cook beef and pepper over medium heat 5-7 minutes or until beef is no longer pink, breaking up beef into crumbles; drain.
2. Add tomato sauce, Worcestershire sauce, Italian seasoning and, if desired, sugar to beef mixture; bring to a boil. Stir in vegetables; heat through. Serve with noodles; sprinkle with parsley.
   FREEZE OPTION *Do not cook the noodles. Freeze cooled meat mixture in a freezer container. To use, partially thaw in refrigerator overnight. Cook noodles according to the package directions. Place meat mixture in a large saucepan; heat through, stirring occasionally and adding a little broth or water if necessary. Serve as directed.*
PER SERVING *1¼ cups beef mixture with ¾ cup noodles : 400 cal., 11g fat (4g sat. fat), 71mg chol., 638mg sodium, 48g carb. (8g sugars, 11g fiber), 31g pro.* **Diabetic Exchanges:** *3 starch, 3 lean meat, 1 vegetable.*

SHRIMP PANZANELLA SALAD

These days I'm cooking for two. After working in the garden, I can dash indoors and have this shrimp and bread salad on the table pronto.

—KALLEE KRONG-MCCREERY ESCONDIDO, CA

START TO FINISH: 20 MIN.
MAKES: 2 SERVINGS

- 1 cup cubed French bread (¾ inch)
- 1 teaspoon olive oil
- ⅛ teaspoon garlic salt
- 1 teaspoon butter
- ½ pound uncooked shrimp (31-40 per pound), peeled and deveined
- 1 garlic clove, minced
- 3 cups fresh baby spinach
- ½ medium ripe avocado, peeled and cubed
- 1 medium tomato, chopped
- 2 tablespoons Italian salad dressing
- 1 tablespoon grated Parmesan cheese

1. In a large nonstick skillet, toss bread cubes with oil and garlic salt. Cook over medium heat 3-4 minutes or until the bread is toasted, stirring frequently. Remove from pan.
2. In same skillet, heat butter over medium heat. Add shrimp and garlic; cook and stir 2-3 minutes or until shrimp turn pink. Remove from heat.
3. In a large bowl, combine spinach, avocado, tomato, toasted bread and shrimp; drizzle with dressing and toss gently to coat. Sprinkle with cheese; serve immediately.
PER SERVING *306 cal., 16g fat (3g sat. fat), 145mg chol., 567mg sodium, 19g carb. (4g sugars, 5g fiber), 23g pro.* **Diabetic Exchanges:** *3 lean meat, 2 vegetable, 1 fat, ½ starch.*

HEALTH TIP *Whole wheat French bread is becoming more popular, but can still be hard to find. Substitute cubed bread from a crusty whole wheat dinner roll to increase fiber in this salad.*

**Connie Craig's
No-Bake Cereal Cookie Bars**
PAGE 277

Cooking for Kids

Whether you're feeding your children or grandchildren or planning a family-friendly party, turn here to be inspired by fun twists on hot dogs, s'mores indoors, healthy fruit pops, and homemade fish sticks and chicken nuggets no kid can resist.

**Virginia Krites'
Slow Cooker Pizza
Casserole** PAGE 292

**Danielle Green's
S'mores Nachos**
PAGE 279

**Scott Woodward's
Makeover Tater-Topped
Casserole** PAGE 291

BLUEBERRY CREAM POPS

Blueberries and cream are such a fun after-school snack. Make it in the morning so the pops are ready to go when the kids come in the door.

—**CINDY REAMS** PHILIPSBURG, PA

PREP: 15 MIN. + FREEZING
MAKES: 8 POPS

- ⅔ **cup sugar**
- ⅔ **cup water**
- 2 **cups fresh or frozen blueberries, thawed**
- ¼ **cup heavy whipping cream**
- 8 **freezer pop molds or 8 paper cups (3 ounces each) and wooden pop sticks**

1. For sugar syrup, in a small saucepan, combine sugar and water; bring to a boil, stirring to dissolve sugar. Cool completely.
2. Meanwhile, in a bowl, coarsely mash blueberries; stir in cream and sugar syrup. Spoon into molds or paper cups. Top molds with holders. If using cups, top with foil and insert sticks through foil. Freeze until firm. To serve, let pops stand at room temperature 10 minutes before unmolding.

PER SERVING *1 pop: 112 cal., 3g fat (2g sat. fat), 10mg chol., 3mg sodium, 22g carb. (21g sugars, 1g fiber), 0 pro.*

BLUEBERRY CREAM POPS

BEEFY CHILI DOGS

BEEFY CHILI DOGS

For years, I've made the best hot dog chili out there. It's timeless, it's family friendly, and I carry the recipe with me because people always request it.

—**VICKI BOYD** MECHANICSVILLE, VA

START TO FINISH: 30 MIN.
MAKES: 8 SERVINGS (2 CUPS CHILI)

- 1 **pound ground beef**
- 1 **teaspoon chili powder**
- ½ **teaspoon garlic powder**
- ½ **teaspoon paprika**
- ¼ **teaspoon cayenne pepper**
- 1 **cup ketchup**
- 8 **hot dogs**
- 8 **hot dog buns, split**
  Shredded cheddar cheese and chopped onion, optional

1. For chili, in a large skillet, cook beef over medium heat 5-7 minutes or until no longer pink, breaking into crumbles; drain. Transfer beef to a food processor; pulse until finely chopped.
2. Return beef to skillet; stir in seasonings and ketchup. Bring to a boil. Reduce heat; simmer, covered, 15-20 minutes to allow flavors to blend, stirring occasionally.
3. Meanwhile, cook hot dogs according to package directions. Serve in buns with chili. If desired, top with cheese and onion.

FREEZE OPTION *Freeze cooled chili in a freezer container. To use, partially thaw in refrigerator overnight. Heat through in a saucepan, stirring occasionally and adding a little water if necessary.*

PER SERVING *1 hot dog with ¼ cup chili: 400 cal., 22g fat (9g sat. fat), 60mg chol., 1092mg sodium, 31g carb. (11g sugars, 1g fiber), 19g pro.*

PIZZA PANCAKES

Anything goes in these pancakes for pizza lovers. We add pepperoni and mozzarella to the batter, but garlic, onions and mushrooms are crazy good, too.

—**MAXINE SMITH** OWANKA, SD

START TO FINISH: 30 MIN.
MAKES: 14 PANCAKES

- 2 **cups biscuit/baking mix**
- 2 **teaspoons Italian seasoning**
- 2 **large eggs**
- 1 **cup 2% milk**
- ½ **cup shredded part-skim mozzarella cheese**
- ½ **cup chopped pepperoni**
- 1 **plum tomato, chopped and seeded**
- ¼ **cup chopped green pepper**
- 1 **can (8 ounces) pizza sauce, warmed**

1. In a bowl, combine biscuit mix and Italian seasoning. In another bowl, whisk eggs and milk until blended. Add to dry ingredients, stirring just until moistened. Stir in cheese, pepperoni, tomato and pepper.

2. Preheat griddle over medium heat; grease lightly. Pour batter by ¼ cupfuls onto griddle; cook until bubbles on top begin to pop and bottoms are golden brown. Turn; cook until second side is golden brown. Serve with pizza sauce.

PER SERVING *2 pancakes with about 2 tablespoons pizza sauce: 272 cal., 13g fat (5g sat. fat), 70mg chol., 827mg sodium, 28g carb. (4g sugars, 2g fiber), 10g pro.*

NO-BAKE CEREAL COOKIE BARS

We pull out goodies like raisins and coconut for these chewy bars. For additional color, sprinkle the M&M's on after the bars are in the pan, then press them in.

—**CONNIE CRAIG** LAKEWOOD, WA

PREP: 10 MIN. ● **COOK:** 15 MIN. + COOLING
MAKES: 3 DOZEN

- 4½ **cups Rice Krispies**
- 3¼ **cups quick-cooking oats**
- ½ **cup cornflakes**
- ½ **cup flaked coconut**
- ½ **cup butter, cubed**
- 1 **package (16 ounces) miniature marshmallows**
- ¼ **cup honey**
- ½ **cup M&M's minis**
- ¼ **cup raisins**

1. Grease a 15x10x1-in. pan. Place Rice Krispies, oats, cornflakes and coconut in a large bowl; toss to combine.

2. In a large saucepan, melt butter over low heat. Add marshmallows; stir until completely melted. Stir in honey until blended. Pour over cereal mixture; stir until evenly coated. Cool 5 minutes.

3. Stir in M&M's and raisins. Using a greased spatula, press evenly into prepared pan. Let stand 30 minutes before cutting. Store between layers of waxed paper in an airtight container.

PER SERVING *1 bar: 137 cal., 4g fat (3g sat. fat), 8mg chol., 58mg sodium, 24g carb. (13g sugars, 1g fiber), 2g pro. Diabetic Exchanges: 1½ starch, ½ fat.*

HEALTH TIP *The M&M's only add 15 calories, so go ahead and add them.*

DAD'S FAVORITE
BARBECUE MEAT LOAVES

FROZEN HOT CHOCOLATE

⑤ INGREDIENTS

Chocolate lovers will swoon over this icy treat. Freeze for a full 8 hours for a stiffer consistency. Serve in frosted glasses and top with whipped cream and chocolate syrup for a pretty touch.

—LILY JULOW LAWRENCEVILLE, GA

PREP: 15 MIN. + FREEZING
MAKES: 4 SERVINGS

- ¾ **cup sugar**
- ½ **cup baking cocoa**
- 2¾ **cups 2% milk, divided**
- ¼ **cup reduced-fat whipped topping**
- 4 **teaspoons chocolate syrup**

1. In a large saucepan, combine the sugar and cocoa. Gradually add milk, reserving 2 tablespoons for blending; cook and stir until heated through and sugar is dissolved. Remove from the heat and let cool.

2. Transfer to an 8-in. square dish. Freeze 2 hours or until edges begin to firm. Stir and return to freezer. Freeze 4 hours longer or until firm.

3. Just before serving, transfer to a food processor; cover and process with remaining milk until smooth. Garnish with whipped topping and chocolate syrup.

PER SERVING *1 cup: 285 cal., 5g fat (3g sat. fat), 13mg chol., 88mg sodium, 57g carb. (49g sugars, 2g fiber), 8g pro.*

FREEZE IT | FAST FIX

DAD'S FAVORITE BARBECUE MEAT LOAVES

It may sound old-fashioned, but it warms my heart to serve dishes that make my family and friends happy. This recipe does just that, and then some.

—LETA WINTERS JOHNSON CITY, TN

START TO FINISH: 30 MIN.
MAKES: 4 SERVINGS

- 1 **large egg, lightly beaten**
- ½ **cup stuffing mix, crushed**
- 3 **tablespoons 2% milk**
- 2 **tablespoons grated Parmesan cheese**
- 1 **tablespoon plus ¼ cup barbecue sauce, divided**
- 1 **pound ground beef**

1. Preheat oven to 425°. In a large bowl, combine the egg, stuffing mix, milk, Parmesan and 1 tablespoon barbecue sauce. Add beef; mix lightly but thoroughly. Shape mixture into four 4x2-in. loaves in a foil-lined 15x10x1-in. baking pan.

2. Bake for 15-20 minutes or until a thermometer reads 160°. Spread meat loaves with remaining barbecue sauce before serving.

FREEZE OPTION *Individually wrap cooled meat loaves in plastic and foil, then freeze. To use, partially thaw meat loaves in the refrigerator overnight. Unwrap loaves; reheat in a greased 15x10x1-in. baking pan in a preheated 350° oven until heated through and a thermometer inserted in center reads 165°. Top each with 1 tablespoon barbecue sauce before serving.*

PER SERVING *1 mini meat loaf: 305 cal., 16g fat (6g sat. fat), 120mg chol., 449mg sodium, 15g carb. (8g sugars, 1g fiber), 24g pro.*

BAKED BANANA BOATS

Cut 4 medium unpeeled bananas lengthwise ½ in. deep, leaving ½ in. uncut at ends. Place each banana on a 12-in. square of foil; crimp foil around bananas so they sit flat. Pull banana peels open, forming a pocket. Fill each with 2 tablespoons unsweetened crushed pineapple, 1 tablespoon each granola and chopped pecans, and 1 teaspoon mini chocolate chips. Place on a baking sheet. Bake at 350° 10-12 minutes or until chips are softened.

—REBEKAH VIERS TAYLORS, SC

GHOST CUPCAKE CONES

1. Preheat oven to 350°. Pour ¼ cup buttermilk into a shallow bowl; add chicken. Turn to coat. Place flour in a resealable plastic bag. In another shallow bowl, whisk eggs and remaining buttermilk. In a third bowl, combine cornflakes, onion powder, garlic salt, salt, oregano and pepper.
2. Add chicken to flour and shake to coat. Dip floured chicken into egg mixture, then into cornflake mixture, turning to coat. Arrange chicken in a greased 15x10x1-in. baking pan.
3. Bake until juices run clear, 15-18 minutes. In a small bowl, combine the apricot preserves and mustard. Serve with chicken.

PER SERVING *1 piece with 2 teaspoons sauce: 102 cal., 1g fat (0 sat. fat), 26mg chol., 163mg sodium, 18g carb. (7g sugars, 0 fiber), 6g pro.* **Diabetic Exchanges:** *1 starch, 1 lean meat.*

EAT SMART (5)INGREDIENTS

GHOST CUPCAKE CONES

Scare up a good treat using prepared cake mix, ice cream cones and whipped topping. These ghosts are as easy as child's play.
—**TASTE OF HOME** **TEST KITCHEN**

PREP: 25 MIN. • **BAKE:** 20 MIN. + COOLING
MAKES: 2½ DOZEN

- 1 **package yellow cake mix (regular size)**
- 30 **ice cream cake cones (about 3 inches tall)**
- 1 **carton (12 ounces) frozen whipped topping, thawed Black decorating icing**

1. Preheat oven to 350°. Tightly cover two 13x9-in. pans with foil, securing edges around pan. For each pan, cut fifteen small holes in foil, about 2½ in. apart. Carefully stand an ice cream cone in each hole.
2. Prepare cake mix according to package directions. Fill the cones to within ½ in. of tops (scant 3 tablespoons); do not overfill. Bake until a toothpick inserted in center comes out clean, 17-20 minutes. Cool completely on wire racks.
3. To serve, pipe or dollop whipped topping over tops for ghosts; decorate with black icing. Refrigerate leftovers.

PER SERVING *1 cupcake cone: 139 cal., 6g fat (3g sat. fat), 19mg chol., 119mg sodium, 18g carb. (8g sugars, trace fiber), 2g pro.* **Diabetic Exchanges:** *1 starch, 1 fat.*

EAT SMART

CHICKEN NUGGETS WITH APRICOT SAUCE

Satisfying a hungry crowd is easy with these oven-baked morsels. The crispy bite-size chicken pieces are served with an incredibly easy sauce made of apricot preserves and mustard.
—**MICHELLE KRZMARCZICK**
REDONDO BEACH, CA

PREP: 25 MIN. • **BAKE:** 15 MIN.
MAKES: 2 DOZEN (1 CUP SAUCE)

- ½ **cup buttermilk, divided**
- 1 **pound boneless skinless chicken breasts, cut into 1-inch cubes**
- ¾ **cup all-purpose flour**
- 2 **large eggs**
- 2 **cups crushed cornflakes**
- ½ **teaspoon onion powder**
- ½ **teaspoon garlic salt**
- ¼ **teaspoon salt**
- ¼ **teaspoon dried oregano**
- ⅛ **teaspoon pepper**
- 1 **cup apricot preserves**
- 2 **tablespoons prepared mustard**

(5)INGREDIENTS FAST FIX ▶

S'MORES NACHOS

In my nacho-style version of s'mores, I use pita chips instead of graham crackers and bake up the nachos in a skillet with plenty of sweet toppings.
—**DANIELLE GREEN** GRACEVILLE, MN

START TO FINISH: 15 MIN.
MAKES: 8 SERVINGS

- 1 **package (8 ounces) cinnamon sugar pita chips**
- 1¼ **cups milk chocolate chips, divided**
- 3 **cups miniature marshmallows**
- 1 **teaspoon canola oil**

1. Preheat oven to 350°. In a large ovenproof skillet, arrange half of the pita chips in an even layer. Sprinkle with ½ cup chocolate chips and 1½ cups marshmallows. Repeat layers. Bake 8-10 minutes or until the marshmallows are lightly toasted.
2. Meanwhile, in a microwave, melt remaining chocolate chips with oil; stir until smooth. Drizzle over top.

PER SERVING *345 cal., 13g fat (5g sat. fat), 6mg chol., 152mg sodium, 51g carb., 3g fiber, 5g pro.*

CHEWY HONEY
GRANOLA BARS

EAT SMART

CHEWY HONEY GRANOLA BARS

 Sweet honey, chewy raisins, crunchy nuts and a hint of chocolate and cinnamon are sure to please. To save a few for later, wrap individual bars in plastic and place in a resealable freezer bag. When you want a satisfying treat on short notice, just grab one and let it thaw for a few minutes.
—**TASHA LEHMAN** WILLISTON, VT

PREP: 10 MIN. • **BAKE:** 15 MIN. + COOLING
MAKES: 20 SERVINGS

- 3 **cups old-fashioned oats**
- 2 **cups unsweetened puffed wheat cereal**
- 1 **cup all-purpose flour**
- ⅓ **cup chopped walnuts**
- ⅓ **cup raisins**
- ⅓ **cup miniature semisweet chocolate chips**
- 1 **teaspoon baking soda**
- 1 **teaspoon ground cinnamon**
- 1 **cup honey**
- ¼ **cup butter, melted**
- 1 **teaspoon vanilla extract**

1. Preheat oven to 350°. In a large bowl, combine the first eight ingredients. In a small bowl, combine honey, butter and vanilla; pour over oat mixture and mix well. (Batter will be sticky.)
2. Press into a 13x9-in. baking pan coated with cooking spray. Bake for 14-18 minutes or until set and edges are lightly browned. Cool on a wire rack. Cut into bars.

PER SERVING *1 bar: 178 cal., 5g fat (2g sat. fat), 6mg chol., 81mg sodium, 32g carb. (17g sugars, 2g fiber), 3g pro. Diabetic Exchanges: 2 starch, ½ fat.*

ICE CREAM WAFFLEWICHES

With chewy waffles, smooth ice cream, gooey caramel syrup and crunchy pecans, a wafflewich is a masterpiece of textures. This is cold-storage comfort food.
—*TASTE OF HOME* TEST KITCHEN

PREP: 20 MIN. + COOLING
COOK: 5 MIN. + COOLING
MAKES: 1 DOZEN

- 24 **frozen mini waffles, unseparated**
- 2 **tablespoons butter**
- 1½ **cups chopped pecans**
- 2 **tablespoons brown sugar**
- ½ **teaspoon chili powder**
- ½ **teaspoon vanilla extract**
- ¼ **cup caramel sundae syrup**
- 1½ **cups dulce de leche or vanilla ice cream**

1. Toast waffles according to package directions; separate into mini waffles and cool completely.
2. In a large skillet, melt butter over low heat; stir in pecans, brown sugar, chili powder and vanilla. Cook and stir for 4-6 minutes or until the nuts are toasted. Transfer to a shallow bowl; cool completely.
3. To assemble, spread 1 teaspoon caramel syrup over a mini waffle; top with 2 tablespoons ice cream. Top with a second waffle, pressing to spread ice cream to edges. Roll sides into spiced pecans; place on a plate. Freeze, covered, until firm.
PER SERVING *1 wafflewich: 213 cal., 15g fat (4g sat. fat), 17mg chol., 151mg sodium, 19g carb. (10g sugars, 2g fiber), 3g pro.*

GRILLED BANANA BROWNIE SUNDAES

My niece Amanda Jean and I have a lot of fun in the kitchen creating different dishes. One of us will start with a recipe idea and it just grows from there—as does the mess. We always have a blast. That's exactly what happened with these sundaes.
—**CAROL FARNSWORTH** GREENWOOD, IN

PREP: 10 MIN. • **GRILL:** 5 MIN. + COOLING
MAKES: 8 SERVINGS

- 2 **medium bananas, unpeeled**
- 4 **ounces cream cheese, softened**
- ¼ **cup packed brown sugar**
- 3 **tablespoons creamy peanut butter**
- 8 **prepared brownies (2-in. squares)**
- 4 **cups vanilla ice cream**
- ½ **cup hot fudge ice cream topping, warmed**
- ½ **cup chopped salted peanuts**

1. Cut unpeeled bananas crosswise in half, then lengthwise in half. Place quartered bananas on an oiled grill rack, cut side down. Grill, covered, over medium-high heat 2-3 minutes on each side or until lightly browned. Cool slightly.
2. In a small bowl, beat cream cheese, brown sugar and peanut butter until mixture is smooth.
3. To serve, remove bananas from peel; place over brownies. Top with cream cheese mixture, ice cream, fudge topping and peanuts.
PER SERVING *505 cal., 28g fat (11g sat. fat), 62mg chol., 277mg sodium, 57g carb. (33g sugars, 3g fiber), 10g pro.*

TOP TIP

EASY-PEASY GRILLED DESSERTS

For a three-ingredient dessert, grill sliced pound cake and serve with whipped cream and your favorite berry sauce, pie filling or fruit curd. Or, sandwich mini marshmallows and chocolate chips between frozen waffles; wrap in foil and grill.

ICE CREAM
WAFFLEWICHES

GRILLED BANANA
BROWNIE SUNDAES

MUFFIN TIN LASAGNAS

PARMESAN FISH STICKS

I wanted a healthier approach to fish sticks so I developed this baked tilapia with a slightly peppery bite. My husband and sons love the crispy coating.

—**CANDY SUMMERHILL** ALEXANDER, AR

START TO FINISH: 25 MIN.
MAKES: 4 SERVINGS

⅓ **cup all-purpose flour**
½ **teaspoon salt**
⅛ **to ¼ teaspoon pepper**
2 **large eggs**
1 **cup panko (Japanese) bread crumbs**
⅓ **cup grated Parmesan cheese**
2 **tablespoons garlic-herb seasoning blend**
1 **pound tilapia fillets**
 Cooking spray

1. Preheat oven to 450°. In a shallow bowl, mix flour, salt and pepper. In another bowl, whisk eggs. In a third bowl, toss bread crumbs with cheese and seasoning blend.
2. Cut fillets into 1-in.-wide strips. Dip fish in flour mixture to coat both sides; shake off excess. Dip in eggs, then in crumb mixture, patting to help coating adhere.
3. Place on a foil-lined baking sheet coated with cooking spray. Spritz tops with cooking spray until crumbs appear moistened. Bake 10-12 minutes or until golden brown and fish just begins to flake easily with a fork.
PER SERVING *281 cal., 11g fat (3g sat. fat), 154mg chol., 641mg sodium, 16g carb. (1g sugars, 1g fiber), 28g pro.* **Diabetic Exchanges:** *3 lean meat, 1 starch, 1 fat.*

PARMESAN FISH STICKS

MUFFIN TIN LASAGNAS

This is a super fun way to serve lasagna for potlucks or other fun get-togethers. My daughter took some of these to work and by noon was emailing me for the recipe.

—**SALLY KILKENNY** GRANGER, IA

START TO FINISH: 30 MIN.
MAKES: 6 SERVINGS

1 **large egg, lightly beaten**
1 **carton (15 ounces) part-skim ricotta cheese**
2 **cups shredded Italian cheese blend, divided**
1 **tablespoon olive oil**
24 **wonton wrappers**
1 **jar (24 ounces) garden-style pasta sauce**
 Minced fresh parsley, optional

1. Preheat oven to 375°. In a bowl, mix egg, ricotta cheese and 1¼ cups Italian cheese blend.
2. Generously grease 12 muffin cups with oil; line each with a wonton wrapper. Fill each with 1 tablespoon ricotta mixture and 1½ tablespoons pasta sauce. Top each with a second wrapper, rotating corners and pressing down centers. Repeat ricotta and sauce layers. Sprinkle with remaining cheese blend.
3. Bake 20-25 minutes or until cheese is melted. If desired, sprinkle with minced parsley.
PER SERVING *2 mini lasagnas: 431 cal., 20g fat (9g sat. fat), 83mg chol., 979mg sodium, 38g carb. (10g sugars, 2g fiber), 22g pro.*

MINI S'MORES

MINI S'MORES

I created these s'mores at a time when I couldn't afford store-bought gifts. They're awesome for parties and bake sales, and kids love to help make them.
—**STEPHANIE TEWELL** ELIZABETH, IL

PREP: 50 MIN. + STANDING • **COOK:** 5 MIN.
MAKES: ABOUT 4 DOZEN

- 2 **cups milk chocolate chips**
- ½ **cup heavy whipping cream**
- 1 **package (14.4 ounces) graham crackers, quartered**
- 1 **cup marshmallow creme**
- 2 **cartons (7 ounces each) milk chocolate for dipping**
- 4 **ounces white candy coating, melted, optional**

1. Place chocolate chips in a small bowl. In a small saucepan, bring cream just to a boil. Pour over chocolate; stir with a whisk until smooth. Cool to room temperature or until mixture reaches spreading consistency, about 10 minutes.
2. Spread chocolate mixture over half of the graham crackers. Spread marshmallow creme over remaining graham crackers; place over chocolate-covered crackers, pressing to adhere.
3. Melt dipping chocolate according to package directions. Dip each s'more halfway into dipping chocolate; allow excess to drip off. Place on waxed paper-lined baking sheets; let stand until dipping chocolate is set.
4. If desired, drizzle tops with melted white candy coating; let stand until set. Store s'mores in an airtight container in the refrigerator.
PER SERVING *1 piece: 145 cal., 7g fat (4g sat. fat), 5mg chol., 66mg sodium, 19g carb. (13g sugars, 1g fiber), 2g pro.*

POTATO CHIP CRUNCHIES

When my family comes home, I like having treats ready for them. No matter what's on the cookie tray, these are always the first to vanish.
—**DOROTHY BUITER** WORTH, IL

PREP: 15 MIN. • **BAKE:** 15 MIN./BATCH
MAKES: ABOUT 8 DOZEN

- 2 **cups butter, softened**
- 1½ **cups sugar**
- 1 **large egg**
- 1 **teaspoon vanilla extract**
- 4 **cups all-purpose flour**
- 1 **cup chopped pecans**
- 1 **cup coarsely crushed potato chips**
  Additional crushed potato chips, optional

1. Preheat oven to 350°. In a large bowl, cream butter and sugar until light and fluffy. Beat in egg and vanilla. Gradually beat in flour. Stir in pecans and 1 cup potato chips.
2. Drop by tablespoonfuls 1½ in. apart onto ungreased baking sheets. Flatten with a fork. If desired, top cookies with additional chips.
3. Bake 12-14 minutes or until golden brown. Remove from pans to wire racks to cool.
PER SERVING *1 cookie (calculated without optional chips): 77 cal., 5g fat (3g sat. fat), 12mg chol., 35mg sodium, 8g carb. (3g sugars, 0 fiber), 1g pro.*

FREEZE IT

PIZZA-SYLE MANICOTTI

Ham, pepperoni and string cheese make little bundles that are stuffed into manicotti shells. It's a fun recipe that the kids will enjoy helping to prepare.

—JUDY ARMSTRONG PRAIRIEVILLE, LA

PREP: 20 MIN. • **BAKE:** 25 MIN.
MAKES: 4 SERVINGS

- 8 uncooked manicotti shells
- 1 jar (24 ounces) spaghetti sauce
- 8 slices deli ham (about 6 ounces)
- 8 fresh basil leaves
- 8 pieces string cheese
- 24 slices pepperoni
- 1 can (2¼ ounces) sliced ripe olives, drained
- 1 cup shredded Parmesan cheese

1. Cook manicotti according to package directions for al dente; drain. Preheat oven to 350°.

2. Pour 1 cup sauce into an 11x7-in. baking dish. On a short side of each ham slice, layer one basil leaf, one piece string cheese and three slices pepperoni; roll up. Insert in manicotti shells; arrange in a single layer in baking dish.

3. Pour remaining sauce over top. Sprinkle with olives and Parmesan cheese. Bake, uncovered, 25-30 minutes or until heated through.

FREEZE OPTION *Cover unbaked casserole; freeze up to 3 months. Thaw in refrigerator overnight. Remove from refrigerator 30 minutes before baking. Cover and bake at 375° for 25-30 minutes or until pasta is tender. Let stand 10 minutes before serving.*

PER SERVING *2 stuffed manicotti: 618 cal., 32g fat (15g sat. fat), 87mg chol., 2427mg sodium, 43g carb. (13g sugars, 4g fiber), 40g pro.*

READER RAVE

Very flavorful! Will make again. I lightened it with low-fat cheese and turkey pepperoni.

—KATIEBROWNKY TASTEOFHOME.COM

TATER TOT-CHOS

FAST FIX

TATER TOT-CHOS

Playing with food is loads of fun when you have Tater Tots and taco toppings. Let kids build their own for smiles all around.

—ELEANOR MIELKE MITCHELL, SD

START TO FINISH: 30 MIN.
MAKES: 6 SERVINGS

- 4 cups frozen miniature Tater Tots
- 1 pound ground beef
- 1 envelope reduced-sodium taco seasoning
- ⅔ cup water
- ½ cup shredded cheddar cheese
- 2 cups shredded lettuce
- ¼ cup sliced ripe olives, optional
- ¼ cup taco sauce
- ½ cup sour cream

1. Bake Tater Tots according to package directions.

2. Meanwhile, in a large skillet, cook beef over medium heat 6-8 minutes or until no longer pink, breaking into crumbles; drain. Stir in taco seasoning and water. Bring to a boil; cook and stir 2 minutes or until thickened.

3. To serve, top Tater Tots with beef mixture, cheese, lettuce and, if desired, olives. Serve with taco sauce and sour cream.

PER SERVING *375 cal., 23g fat (9g sat. fat), 70mg chol., 828mg sodium, 27g carb. (4g sugars, 2g fiber), 18g pro.*

EAT SMART **⑤INGREDIENTS** **FAST FIX**

TOAD IN THE HOLE

This is one of the first recipes I had my children prepare when they were learning to cook. My little ones are now grown (and have advanced to more difficult recipes), but this continues to be a standby in all our homes.

—RUTH LECHLEITER BRECKENRIDGE, MN

START TO FINISH: 15 MIN.
MAKES: 1 SERVING

- 1 slice of bread
- 1 teaspoon butter
- 1 large egg
  Salt and pepper to taste

1. Cut a 3-in. hole in the middle of the bread and discard. In a small skillet, melt the butter; place the bread in the skillet.

2. Place egg in the hole. Cook for about 2 minutes over medium heat until the bread is lightly browned. Turn and cook the other side until egg yolk is almost set. Season with salt and pepper.

PER SERVING *183 cal., 10g fat (4g sat. fat), 196mg chol., 244mg sodium, 15g carb. (2g sugars, 1g fiber), 9g pro.* **Diabetic Exchanges:** *1 starch, 1 medium-fat meat, 1 fat.*

EASY CONFETTI PIE

Sugar cone crust and a colorful, creamy no-bake confetti filling makes a pie that tastes like birthday cake.

—*TASTE OF HOME* TEST KITCHEN

PREP: 25 MIN. + CHILLING
MAKES: 10 SERVINGS

- 2¾ cups crushed ice cream sugar cones
- 2 tablespoons plus ½ cup sugar, divided
- ½ cup butter, melted
- 1 envelope unflavored gelatin
- ¼ cup cold water
- 2 packages (8 ounces each) cream cheese, softened
- 2 cups heavy whipping cream
- 2 teaspoons butter flavoring
- 1 teaspoon almond extract
- ⅓ cup assorted sprinkles

1. Preheat oven to 350°. Combine crushed sugar cones and 2 tablespoons sugar with melted butter. Using the bottom of a glass, press cone mixture onto bottom and up the sides of a greased 9-in. deep-dish pie plate. Bake until set, 12-15 minutes. Cool crust completely on a wire rack.

2. Meanwhile, sprinkle gelatin over cold water; let stand 5 minutes. Beat cream cheese and remaining sugar until smooth. Slowly beat in cream, butter flavoring and extract. In a microwave, heat gelatin on high until melted, about 10 seconds; beat into the cream cheese mixture. Fold in sprinkles; transfer filling to crust. Refrigerate, covered, until set, about 3 hours.

3. Top with additional sprinkles.

PER SERVING *1 piece: 568 cal., 44g fat (26g sat. fat), 125mg chol., 290mg sodium, 38g carb. (24g sugars, 0 fiber), 7g pro.*

EASY CONFETTI PIE

CRISPY ALMOND TILAPIA

CRISPY ALMOND TILAPIA

Since changing to a healthier style of cooking, I've come up with new coatings for baked fish. I use almonds, panko bread crumbs and a smidge of hot sauce to add crunchy texture with nice heat.

—**AMANDA FLINNER** BEAVER, PA

START TO FINISH: 30 MIN.
MAKES: 4 SERVINGS

- 1 large egg
- ¼ cup Louisiana-style hot sauce
- ¾ cup slivered almonds, chopped and toasted
- ⅓ cup panko (Japanese) bread crumbs
- 1 teaspoon grated lemon peel
- 1 teaspoon seafood seasoning
- ¼ teaspoon garlic powder
- 4 tilapia fillets (4 ounces each)
- ½ teaspoon salt
- ¼ teaspoon pepper

1. Preheat oven to 400°. Whisk egg and hot sauce in a shallow bowl. In a separate shallow bowl, toss almonds, bread crumbs, lemon peel and spices.

2. Halve fillets lengthwise; sprinkle with salt and pepper. Dip in egg mixture, then in almond mixture, patting to adhere; place on a greased or parchment paper-lined baking sheet. Bake until lightly browned and fish just begins to flake easily with a fork, 12-15 minutes.

NOTE *To toast nuts, bake in a shallow pan in a 350° oven for 5-10 minutes or cook in a skillet over low heat until lightly browned, stirring occasionally.*

PER SERVING *2 fillet pieces: 251 cal., 13g fat (2g sat. fat), 102mg chol., 537mg sodium, 9g carb. (1g sugars, 3g fiber), 28g pro.* **Diabetic Exchanges:** *4 lean meat, 2 fat.*

WALKING TACOS

PECAN-CRUSTED CHICKEN NUGGETS

I loved chicken nuggets as a kid. This baked version is healthier than a restaurant's, and it's a great meal for kids.

—HAILI CARROLL VALENCIA, CA

START TO FINISH: 30 MIN.
MAKES: 6 SERVINGS

- 1½ **cups cornflakes**
- 1 **tablespoon dried parsley flakes**
- 1 **teaspoon salt**
- ½ **teaspoon garlic powder**
- ½ **teaspoon pepper**
- ½ **cup panko (Japanese) bread crumbs**
- ½ **cup finely chopped pecans**
- 3 **tablespoons 2% milk**
- 1½ **pounds boneless skinless chicken breasts, cut into 1-inch pieces**
  Cooking spray

1. Preheat oven to 400°. Place the cornflakes, parsley, salt, garlic powder and pepper in a blender; cover and pulse until finely ground. Transfer to a shallow bowl; stir in bread crumbs and pecans. Place milk in another shallow bowl. Dip chicken in milk, then roll in crumb mixture to coat.

2. Place on a greased baking sheet; spritz chicken with cooking spray. Bake 12-16 minutes or until chicken is no longer pink, turning once halfway through cooking.

PER SERVING *3 ounces cooked chicken: 206 cal., 9g fat (1g sat. fat), 63mg chol., 290mg sodium, 6g carb. (1g sugars, 1g fiber), 24g pro.* **Diabetic Exchanges:** *3 lean meat, 1 fat, ½ starch.*

PECAN-CRUSTED CHICKEN NUGGETS

WALKING TACOS

This chili is perfect on game nights. All the ingredients go right into the chips bag so no dishes to wash. While the chili simmers, enjoy a round of Texas Hold'em.

—BEVERLY MATTHEWS PASCO, WA

PREP: 10 MIN. • **COOK:** 30 MIN.
MAKES: 5 SERVINGS

- 1 **pound ground beef**
- 1 **envelope reduced-sodium chili seasoning mix**
- ¼ **teaspoon pepper**
- 1 **can (10 ounces) diced tomatoes and green chilies**
- 1 **can (15 ounces) Ranch Style beans (pinto beans in seasoned tomato sauce)**
- 5 **packages (1 ounce each) corn chips**

Toppings: shredded cheddar cheese, sour cream and sliced green onions

1. In a large skillet, cook beef over medium heat 6-8 minutes or until no longer pink, breaking into crumbles; drain. Stir in chili seasoning mix, pepper, tomatoes and beans; bring to a boil. Reduce heat; simmer, uncovered, 20-25 minutes or until thickened, stirring occasionally.

2. Just before serving, cut open corn chip bags. Add beef mixture and toppings as desired.

PER SERVING (*calculated without toppings*): *530 cal., 28g fat (6g sat. fat), 56mg chol., 1017mg sodium, 44g carb. (5g sugars, 6g fiber), 24g pro.*

PIGS IN A POOL

My kids love sausage and pancakes, but making them for breakfast on a busy weekday was out of the question. My homemade version of pigs in a blanket is a great alternative to the packaged kind, and they freeze like a dream.

—LISA DODD GREENVILLE, SC

PREP: 45 MIN. • **BAKE:** 20 MIN.
MAKES: 4 DOZEN

- 1 pound reduced-fat bulk pork sausage
- 2 cups all-purpose flour
- ¼ cup sugar
- 1 tablespoon baking powder
- 1 teaspoon salt
- ½ teaspoon ground cinnamon
- ¼ teaspoon ground nutmeg
- 1 large egg, lightly beaten
- 2 cups fat-free milk
- 2 tablespoons canola oil
- 2 tablespoons honey
  Maple syrup, optional

1. Preheat oven to 350°. Coat mini-muffin cups with cooking spray.

2. Shape sausage into forty-eight ¾-in. balls. Place meatballs on a rack coated with cooking spray in a shallow baking pan. Bake 15-20 minutes or until cooked through. Drain on paper towels. In a large bowl, whisk flour, sugar, baking powder, salt and spices. In another bowl, whisk egg, milk, oil and honey until blended. Add to flour mixture; stir just until moistened.

3. Place a sausage ball into each mini-muffin cup; cover with batter. Bake 20-25 minutes or until lightly browned. Cool 5 minutes before removing from pans to wire racks. Serve warm with syrup if desired.

FREEZE OPTION *Freeze cooled muffins in resealable plastic freezer bags. To use, microwave each muffin on high for 20-30 seconds or until heated through.*

PER SERVING *4 pieces (calculated without syrup): 234 cal., 10g fat (3g sat. fat), 45mg chol., 560mg sodium, 26g carb. (9g sugars, 1g fiber), 10g pro.* **Diabetic Exchanges:** *1½ starch, 1 medium-fat meat, ½ fat.*

STUFFED PIZZA BURGERS

For years, I used this recipe to make pizza meat loaf, which was absolutely killer. I decided to try it as burgers for a party, and they were a smashing success. Everyone left with the recipe.

—DENNIS BARTER REEDSBURG, WI

PREP: 30 MIN. • **GRILL:** 10 MIN.
MAKES: 8 SERVINGS

- 2 large eggs, lightly beaten
- 1 medium onion, finely chopped
- 1 medium green pepper, finely chopped
- ½ cup crushed cornflakes
- ½ cup chopped fresh mushrooms
- 1 tablespoon minced fresh basil or 1 teaspoon dried basil
- 1 tablespoon minced fresh oregano or 1 teaspoon dried oregano
- 2 garlic cloves, minced
- 2 pounds lean ground turkey
- 1 cup pizza sauce, divided
- ½ cup finely chopped turkey pepperoni
- ½ cup shredded part-skim mozzarella cheese
- 8 hamburger buns, split

1. In a large bowl, combine the first eight ingredients. Crumble turkey over mixture and mix well. Shape into 16 patties. Layer 1 tablespoon pizza sauce, pepperoni and cheese onto the center of each of eight patties. Top with remaining patties and press edges firmly to seal.

2. On a greased grill rack, grill burgers, covered, over medium heat or broil 4 in. from the heat for 4-6 minutes on each side or until a meat thermometer reads 165° and juices run clear. Serve on buns with remaining pizza sauce.

PER SERVING *1 each: 385 cal., 14g fat (4g sat. fat), 155mg chol., 613mg sodium, 32g carb. (6g sugars, 2g fiber), 31g pro.* **Diabetic Exchanges:** *4 lean meat, 2 starch, 1 fat.*

PIGS IN A POOL

BANANA CHOCOLATE
CHIP MUFFINS

1. Preheat the broiler. Arrange marshmallows in a single layer on a greased foil-lined baking sheet. Broil 3-4 in. from heat 15-30 seconds on each side or until golden brown. Cool completely.

2. Place the milk and ice cream in a blender; cover and process just until combined. Add 10 toasted marshmallows; cover and pulse until blended.

3. Divide milk shake among four glasses; top with crushed crackers and remaining toasted marshmallows. Drizzle with chocolate syrup; serve immediately.

PER SERVING *¾ cup (calculated without chocolate syrup) equals 327 cal., 12g fat (7g sat. fat), 46mg chol., 142mg sodium, 50g carb., 1g fiber, 5g pro.*

FREEZE IT

BANANA CHOCOLATE CHIP MUFFINS

These tender banana muffins are a big hit at our house. I use mini muffin tins because they are a better size for children, but you can make them full-size, too. I sprinkle a few mini chips on top before baking because the muffins look prettier that way.

—**MARCIE TREBE** SANTA ROSA, CA

PREP: 25 MIN. • **BAKE:** 20 MIN.
MAKES: 1½ DOZEN

- ½ **cup butter, softened**
- ½ **cup sugar**
- ½ **cup packed brown sugar**
- 2 **large eggs**
- 1¼ **cups mashed ripe bananas (about 3 medium)**
- 1 **teaspoon vanilla extract**
- 1½ **cups white whole wheat flour**
- ½ **cup all-purpose flour**
- 1 **teaspoon baking soda**
- ½ **teaspoon salt**
- ¼ **cup sour cream**
- ½ **cup 2% milk**
- ¾ **cup miniature semisweet chocolate chips, divided**

1. Preheat oven to 350°. In a large bowl, cream butter and sugars until light and fluffy. Add eggs, one at a time, beating well after each addition. Beat in bananas and vanilla.

2. In another bowl, whisk flours, baking soda and salt. Add to creamed mixture, alternating with sour cream and milk; stir just until moistened. Fold in ½ cup chocolate chips.

3. Fill greased or paper-lined muffin cups two-thirds full. Sprinkle with remaining chocolate chips.

4. Bake 18-20 minutes or until a toothpick inserted in center comes out clean. Cool 5 minutes before removing from pans to a wire rack. Serve warm.

FREEZE OPTION *Freeze cooled muffins in resealable plastic freezer bags. To use, thaw muffins at room temperature or, if desired, microwave each muffin on high for 20-30 seconds or until heated through.*

PER SERVING *1 muffin: 210 cal., 9g fat (5g sat. fat), 37mg chol., 191mg sodium, 31g carb. (18g sugars, 2g fiber), 3g pro.*

---

(5) INGREDIENTS FAST FIX

S'MORES MILK SHAKE

When cabin fever hits, we whip up a beverage that tastes like s'mores. Oven-toasted marshmallows and a blender make it happen.

—**SARAH MCKENNA** CENTENNIAL, CO

START TO FINISH: 15 MIN.
MAKES: 4 SERVINGS

- 14 **large marshmallows**
- ½ **cup 2% milk**
- 3 **cups vanilla ice cream**
- ¼ **cup coarsely crushed graham crackers**
  Chocolate syrup

---

(5) INGREDIENTS FAST FIX

S'MORES CRESCENT ROLLS

Here's how to score indoor s'mores fast: Grab crescent dough and Nutella. Invite the kids to help with this rolled-up version of the campfire classic.

—**CATHY TROCHELMAN** BROOKFIELD, WI

START TO FINISH: 25 MIN.
MAKES: 8 SERVINGS

- 1 **tube (8 ounces) refrigerated crescent rolls**
- ¼ **cup Nutella, divided**
- 2 **whole graham crackers, broken up**
- 2 **tablespoons milk chocolate chips**
- ⅔ **cup miniature marshmallows**

1. Preheat oven to 375°. Unroll crescent dough; separate into eight triangles. Place 1 teaspoon Nutella at the wide end of each triangle; sprinkle with graham crackers, chocolate chips and marshmallows. Roll up and place on ungreased baking sheets, point side down; curve to form crescents. Bake 9-11 minutes or until golden brown.

2. In a microwave, warm the remaining Nutella until it achieves a drizzling consistency; spoon over rolls. Serve warm.

PER SERVING *1 roll equals 201 cal., 10g fat (3g sat. fat), 1mg chol., 256mg sodium, 25g carb., 1g fiber, 3g pro.*

S'MORES MILK SHAKE

S'MORES CRESCENT ROLLS

SNICKERDOODLE ICE
CREAM SANDWICH MINIS

FAST FIX ▶

STRAWBERRY CREAM FLOATS

When it starts warming up in Colorado, my kids ask for ice-cold treats. This rosy float is one of our household favorites.

—**CRYSTAL JO BRUNS** ILIFF, CO

START TO FINISH: 25 MIN.
MAKES: 8 SERVINGS

- 1 **cup heavy whipping cream**
- 2 **tablespoons confectioners' sugar**
STRAWBERRY SODA
- 2 **packages (14 ounces each) frozen unsweetened sliced strawberries (about 6 cups), thawed**
- 1 **cup sugar**
- ⅓ **cup lime juice**
- 2 **cups chilled carbonated water**
ASSEMBLY
- 4 **cups vanilla ice cream**
  Sliced fresh strawberries, optional

1. In a small bowl, beat cream until it begins to thicken. Add confectioners' sugar; beat until soft peaks form. Refrigerate until serving.
2. Place strawberries, sugar and lime juice in a blender; cover and process until pureed. Press through a fine-mesh strainer into a pitcher; discard seeds. Stir in carbonated water.
3. Divide ice cream among eight glasses. Pour strawberry soda over ice cream. Top with whipped cream and, if desired, fresh strawberries; serve immediately.
PER SERVING (*calculated without fresh strawberries*): *383 cal., 18g fat (11g sat. fat), 70mg chol., 65mg sodium, 54g carb. (46g sugars, 3g fiber), 3g pro.*

STRAWBERRY
CREAM FLOATS

SNICKERDOODLE ICE CREAM SANDWICH MINIS

My husband absolutely loves ice cream sandwiches and snickerdoodles, so I combined them into one fun treat. Here's how we build this cool dessert.

—**HEATHER PILON** WINSLOW, ME

PREP: 50 MIN. + FREEZING
MAKES: ABOUT 16 SERVINGS

- ½ **cup butter, softened**
- ¾ **cup plus 3 tablespoons sugar, divided**
- 1 **large egg**
- 1½ **cups all-purpose flour**
- 1 **teaspoon cream of tartar**
- ½ **teaspoon baking soda**
- ⅛ **teaspoon salt**
- 1 **tablespoon brown sugar**
- 2 **teaspoons ground cinnamon**
- 2 **cups vanilla ice cream**

1. Preheat oven to 400°. In a bowl, beat butter and ¾ cup sugar until blended. Beat in egg. In another bowl, whisk flour, cream of tartar, baking soda and salt; gradually beat into creamed mixture.
2. In a small bowl, mix brown sugar, cinnamon and remaining sugar until blended. Shape rounded tablespoons of dough into 1-in. balls; roll in brown sugar mixture. Place 2 in. apart on ungreased baking sheets.
3. Bake 7-9 minutes or until set and edges are lightly browned. Remove cookies from pans to wire racks to cool completely.
4. Using a small scoop, place 2 tablespoons ice cream on bottom of a cookie; top with a second cookie, pressing gently to flatten ice cream. Wrap in plastic and freeze. Repeat with remaining ingredients. Freeze sandwiches overnight.
PER SERVING *1 ice cream sandwich: 182 cal., 8g fat (5g sat. fat), 34mg chol., 122mg sodium, 26g carb. (16g sugars, 1g fiber), 2g pro.*

MINI MAC & CHEESE DOGS

I love Tater Tots, and my casserole is a delicious version, but I wanted it to be healthier. The experts at *Taste of Home* slashed the fat in this favorite dish, while keeping all the Tater Tots my family loves!

—SCOTT WOODWARD ELKHORN, WI

PREP: 15 MIN. • **BAKE:** 55 MIN.
MAKES: 8 SERVINGS

- 1 pound lean ground beef (90% lean)
- ½ pound extra-lean ground turkey
- 1 package (16 ounces) frozen mixed vegetables, thawed and drained
- ¾ cup French-fried onions
- 1 can (10¾ ounces) reduced-fat reduced-sodium condensed cream of celery soup, undiluted
- 1 can (10¾ ounces) reduced-fat reduced-sodium condensed cream of chicken soup, undiluted
- ½ cup fat-free milk
- 4 cups frozen Tater Tots, thawed

1. In a large skillet, cook the beef and turkey over medium heat until no longer pink, breaking meat into crumbles. In a 13x9-in. baking dish coated with cooking spray, layer the meat mixture, vegetables and onions.
2. In a small bowl, combine soups and milk; spread over onions. Top with Tater Tots. Bake, uncovered, at 350° 55-60 minutes or until golden brown.
PER SERVING *1 cup: 340 cal., 14g fat (4g sat. fat), 44mg chol., 657mg sodium, 33g carb. (4g sugars, 4g fiber), 22g pro.*

---

⑤INGREDIENTS

MINI MAC & CHEESE DOGS

We wanted to get creative with hot dogs, so we made them mac-and-cheesy. Pile on the extra cheese, relish and even bacon to gussy up these dogs.

—JULIE PETERSON CROFTON, MD

PREP: 25 MIN. + RISING
BAKE: 15 MIN. + COOLING
MAKES: 2 DOZEN

- 1 package (16 ounces) frozen bread dough dinner rolls (12 count), thawed but still cold
- ½ cup panko (Japanese) bread crumbs
- 2 tablespoons chopped onion
- 1 tablespoon canola oil
- ¼ teaspoon salt
- ⅛ teaspoon pepper
- 12 bun-length beef hot dogs
- 1 package (7¼ ounces) macaroni and cheese dinner mix

1. Let the dough stand at room temperature 15-20 minutes or until soft enough to shape. Cut each roll in half; shape each half into a 3-in.-long mini hot dog bun. Place 2 in. apart on greased baking sheets.

2. Cover with greased plastic wrap; let rise in a warm place until almost doubled, about 45 minutes. Preheat oven to 350°.
3. Bake buns 12-15 minutes or until golden brown. Remove from pans to wire racks to cool completely.
4. In a 15x10x1-in. baking pan, toss bread crumbs with onion, oil, salt and pepper. Bake at 350° for 5-7 minutes or until golden brown, stirring once.
5. Cook hot dogs and macaroni and cheese according to their package directions. To serve, cut hot dogs crosswise in half. Split buns; fill with hot dogs and macaroni and cheese. Sprinkle with toasted crumbs.
PER SERVING *1 appetizer: 198 cal., 12g fat (5g sat. fat), 25mg chol., 446mg sodium, 18g carb. (2g sugars, 1g fiber), 6g pro.*

LOVE SQUARED

A sprinkle of strawberries on a cloud of frosting makes your favorite brownies the sweetest valentine of all.

To make happy little hearts, cut a strawberry in half, core with a V-shaped cut, then slice it up.

SLOW COOKER

SLOW COOKER PIZZA CASSEROLE

A comforting casserole with mass appeal is just what you need when cooking for a crowd. For added convenience, it stays warm in a slow cooker.

—VIRGINIA KRITES CRIDERSVILLE, OH

PREP: 20 MIN. • **COOK:** 2 HOURS
MAKES: 12-14 SERVINGS

- 1 package (16 ounces) rigatoni or large tube pasta
- 1½ pounds ground beef
- 1 small onion, chopped
- 4 cups shredded part-skim mozzarella cheese
- 2 cans (15 ounces each) pizza sauce
- 1 can (10¾ ounces) condensed cream of mushroom soup, undiluted
- 1 package (8 ounces) sliced pepperoni

1. Cook pasta according to package directions. Meanwhile, in a skillet, cook beef and onion over medium heat until meat is no longer pink; drain.
2. Drain pasta; place in a 5-qt. slow cooker. Stir in the beef mixture, cheese, pizza sauce, soup and pepperoni. Cover and cook on low for 2-3 hours or until heated through.
PER SERVING *1 cup: 329 cal., 19g fat (8g sat. fat), 57mg chol., 885mg sodium, 16g carb. (5g sugars, 2g fiber), 22g pro.*

SLOW COOKER PIZZA CASSEROLE

CITRUS-HONEY CHICKEN

FAST FIX

CITRUS-HONEY CHICKEN

We raise heirloom-breed chickens, so I'm always looking for chicken recipes. This one with orange and honey is tops at our house.

—BETH NAFZIGER LOWVILLE, NY

START TO FINISH: 30 MIN.
MAKES: 6 SERVINGS

- 1 cup dry bread crumbs
- 1 tablespoon grated orange peel
- 1 teaspoon salt
- ½ teaspoon pepper
- 1½ pounds chicken tenderloins
- ¼ cup orange juice
  Olive oil-flavored cooking spray

SAUCE
- ¼ cup butter, cubed
- ½ cup honey
- 2 tablespoons water
- 1 teaspoon chicken bouillon granules

1. Preheat oven to 425°. In a shallow bowl, mix bread crumbs, orange peel, salt and pepper. In another bowl, toss chicken with orange juice. Dip chicken in crumb mixture, patting to help the coating adhere; place on a greased foil-lined baking sheet.
2. Spritz tops with cooking spray until crumbs appear moistened. Bake for 10-12 minutes or until light golden brown and chicken is no longer pink.
3. Meanwhile, in a small saucepan, combine sauce ingredients. Bring to a boil over medium heat, stirring constantly; cook and stir 1-2 minutes or until blended. Serve with chicken.
PER SERVING *2 chicken tenders with 2 tablespoons sauce: 326 cal., 10g fat (5g sat. fat), 76mg chol., 663mg sodium, 34g carb. (24g sugars, 1g fiber), 29g pro.*

FROZEN BERRY & YOGURT SWIRLS

FROZEN BERRY & YOGURT SWIRLS

These are a great treat to have on a warm summer day! They're a favorite at our summer block party.

—COLLEEN LUDOVICE WAUWATOSA, WI

PREP: 15 MIN. + FREEZING
MAKES: 10 POPS

- 2¾ cups fat-free honey Greek yogurt
- 10 plastic or paper cups (3 ounces each) and wooden pop sticks
- 1 cup mixed fresh berries
- ¼ cup water
- 2 tablespoons sugar

1. Divide yogurt among cups. Place berries, water and sugar in a food processor; pulse until combined. Spoon over yogurt. Using a pop stick, stir mixture to swirl.
2. Top cups with foil and insert sticks through foil. Freeze until firm.
FROZEN CLEMENTINE & YOGURT SWIRLS: *Use 1 cup clementine segments (about 5 medium; seeded if necessary) and ¼ cup orange juice in place of berries, water and sugar; proceed as directed.*
PER SERVING *1 pop: 60 cal., 0 fat (0 sat. fat), 0 chol., 28mg sodium, 9g carb. (8g sugars, 1g fiber), 6g pro.* ***Diabetic Exchanges:*** *1 starch.*

MACARONI SCRAMBLE

This simple dinner made with macaroni, cheese, ground beef and tomato sauce is sure to be a family classic. Serve it with a green salad and crusty French bread, and you'll have a surefire hit.

—PATRICIA KILE ELIZABETHTOWN, PA

START TO FINISH: 25 MIN.
MAKES: 3 SERVINGS

- 1 cup uncooked cellentani (spiral pasta) or elbow macaroni
- ½ pound lean ground beef (90% lean)
- 1 small onion, chopped
- 1 celery rib, chopped
- 1 small green pepper, chopped
- 1 garlic clove, minced
- 1 can (10¾ ounces) reduced-sodium condensed tomato soup, undiluted
- 1 tablespoon minced fresh parsley or 1 teaspoon dried parsley flakes
- 1 teaspoon dried oregano
- ¼ teaspoon salt
- ¼ teaspoon pepper
- ½ cup shredded reduced-fat cheddar cheese

1. Cook pasta according to package directions. Meanwhile, in a large skillet, cook the beef, onion, celery and green pepper over medium heat until meat is no longer pink. Add garlic; cook 1 minute longer. Drain.
2. Drain pasta; add to beef mixture. Stir in the soup, parsley, oregano, salt and pepper. Bring to a boil. Reduce the heat; simmer, uncovered, for 4-5 minutes or until heated through. Sprinkle with cheese.
PER SERVING *1⅓ cup: 351 cal., 11g fat (5g sat. fat), 50mg chol., 758mg sodium, 38g carb. (13g sugars, 3g fiber), 24g pro.* ***Diabetic Exchanges:*** *3 medium-fat meat, 2 starch, 1 vegetable.*

**Angela Leinenbach's
Herbed Grilled Corn on the Cob**
PAGE 306

Hot Off the Grill

When the days are long and the kitchen's hot, take a fresh approach to dinner by cooking it outdoors. From fiery kabobs and lip-smacking ribs to the best marinades, sides and more, these are dishes to cheer for.

Helen Vail's Spinach Steak Pinwheels *PAGE 299*

Christine Hadden's Grilled Chicken Chopped Salad *PAGE 304*

Leah Lenz's Lime-Rosemary Shrimp Skewers *PAGE 300*

FAST FIX ▸

GRILLED ORANGE CHICKEN THIGHS

This orangey chicken was the first meal I served my future husband. I chose it because it's easy, but he thought it was amazing and gobbled it up. We were married three months later, so I guess it worked.

—**LEAH HARVATH** HEBER CITY, UT

START TO FINISH: 30 MIN.
MAKES: 6 SERVINGS

- 1 **cup orange juice**
- ⅓ **cup sugar**
- ⅓ **cup packed light brown sugar**
- ¼ **teaspoon salt**
- 1 **tablespoon Dijon mustard**
- 2 **teaspoons grated orange peel**

CHICKEN

- 6 **boneless skinless chicken thighs (about 1½ pounds)**
- ½ **teaspoon lemon-pepper seasoning**

1. In a small saucepan, combine juice, sugars and salt; bring to a boil, stirring to dissolve sugar. Cook, uncovered, 10-15 minutes or until mixture reaches a glaze consistency. Remove from heat; stir in mustard and orange peel.

2. Moisten a paper towel with cooking oil; using long-handled tongs, rub on grill rack to coat lightly. Sprinkle the chicken with lemon pepper. Grill chicken, covered, over medium heat 6-8 minutes on each side or until a thermometer reads 170°, brushing occasionally with some of the sauce during the last 5 minutes. Serve with remaining sauce.

PER SERVING *1 chicken thigh with about 1 tablespoon sauce: 277 cal., 8g fat (2g sat. fat), 76mg chol., 256mg sodium, 29g carb. (27g sugars, 0 fiber), 21g pro.*

GRILLED ORANGE CHICKEN THIGHS

GRILLED GARDEN PIZZA

FAST FIX ▸

GRILLED GARDEN PIZZA

Dazzle your family and friends with pizzas fresh off the grill. We top them with Asiago, Parmesan, veggies and fresh basil. Pile on the toppings you love.

—**TERI RASEY** CADILLAC, MI

START TO FINISH: 30 MIN.
MAKES: 6 SERVINGS

- 2 **plum tomatoes, thinly sliced**
- ½ **teaspoon sea salt or kosher salt**
- 1 **loaf (1 pound) frozen pizza dough, thawed**
- 2 **tablespoons olive oil, divided**
- ½ **cup shredded Parmesan or Asiago cheese**
- ½ **cup fresh or frozen corn, thawed**
- ¼ **cup thinly sliced red onion**
- 8 **ounces fresh mozzarella cheese, sliced**
- ½ **cup thinly sliced fresh spinach**
- 3 **tablespoons chopped fresh basil**

1. Sprinkle tomatoes with salt; set aside. On a lightly floured surface, divide dough in half. Roll or press each to ¼-in. thickness; place each on a greased sheet of foil (about 10 in. square). Brush tops with 1 tablespoon of oil.

2. Carefully invert crusts onto grill rack, removing foil. Brush tops with remaining oil. Grill, covered, over medium heat 2-3 minutes or until bottom is golden brown. Remove from grill; reduce grill temperature to low.

3. Top grilled sides of crusts with Parmesan cheese, tomatoes, corn, onion and mozzarella cheese. Grill, covered, on low heat 4-6 minutes or until cheese is melted. Sprinkle with spinach and basil.

PER SERVING *1 piece: 375 cal., 16g fat (7g sat. fat), 35mg chol., 680mg sodium, 40g carb. (4g sugars, 1g fiber), 15g pro.*

HEALTH TIP *Fresh mozzarella has about the same calories and fat as part-skim; both kinds of mozzarella are lighter than cheeses like cheddar, Muenster and provolone.*

PLUM-GLAZED PORK KABOBS

START TO FINISH: 30 MIN.
MAKES: 6 SERVINGS

- ⅓ cup plum jam
- 2 tablespoons reduced-sodium soy sauce
- 1 garlic clove, minced
- ½ teaspoon ground ginger
- 1 medium sweet red pepper
- 1 medium green pepper
- 1 small red onion
- 1½ pounds pork tenderloins

1. For glaze, in a small bowl, mix jam, soy sauce, garlic and ginger. Cut the vegetables and pork into 1-in. pieces. On six metal or soaked wooden skewers, alternately thread pork and vegetables.

2. Moisten a paper towel with cooking oil; using long-handled tongs, rub on grill rack to coat lightly. Grill kabobs, covered, over medium heat for 12-15 minutes or until the pork is tender, turning occasionally and brushing with ¼ cup glaze during the last 5 minutes. Brush with remaining glaze before serving.

PER SERVING *1 kabob: 196 cal., 4g fat (1g sat. fat), 64mg chol., 239mg sodium, 15g carb. (12g sugars, 1g fiber), 24g pro.* **Diabetic Exchanges:** *3 lean meat, 1 starch.*

MANGO & GRILLED CHICKEN SALAD

We live in the hot South, and this fruity chicken salad is a weeknight standout. I buy salad greens and add veggies for color and crunch.
—**SHERRY LITTLE** SHERWOOD, AR

START TO FINISH: 25 MIN.
MAKES: 4 SERVINGS

- 1 pound chicken tenderloins
- ½ teaspoon salt
- ¼ teaspoon pepper

SALAD

- 6 cups torn mixed salad greens
- ¼ cup raspberry or balsamic vinaigrette
- 1 medium mango, peeled and cubed
- 1 cup fresh sugar snap peas, halved lengthwise

1. Toss chicken with salt and pepper. Moisten a paper towel with cooking oil; using long-handled tongs, rub on grill rack to coat lightly. Grill chicken, covered, over medium heat or broil 4 in. from heat 3-4 minutes on each side or until no longer pink. Cut the chicken into 1-in. pieces.

2. Divide salad greens among four plates; drizzle with vinaigrette. Top with the chicken, mango and peas; serve immediately.

PER SERVING *210 cal., 2g fat (trace sat. fat), 56mg chol., 447mg sodium, 22g carb. (16g sugars, 4g fiber), 30g pro.* **Diabetic Exchanges:** *3 lean meat, 2 vegetable, ½ starch, ½ fat.*
HEALTH TIP *Keep a cold at bay (or at least shorten its duration) with vitamin C-rich mango.*

Get out there and fire up the grill for pork kabobs, a tasty alternative to chicken and beef. These sweet and gingery beauties make dinnertime great.
—**TONYA BURKHARD** PALM COAST, FL

PLUM-GLAZED PORK KABOBS

ZESTY GRILLED CHOPS

TOP TIP

FIVE-STAR MARINADES

1. CAJUN SEAFOOD

Mix ¾ cup canola oil, 1 finely chopped medium onion, 2 tablespoons Cajun seasoning, 6 minced garlic cloves, 2 teaspoons ground cumin and 1 teaspoon each minced fresh rosemary and thyme. Makes about 1 cup, enough for 4 pounds seafood.

—**DWAYNE VERETTO** ROSWELL, NM

2. SWEET MUSTARD FOR PORK

Whisk ½ cup mayonnaise, ½ cup red wine vinegar, ¼ cup each packed brown sugar and prepared mustard, and 2 teaspoons seasoned salt. Makes about 1 cup, enough for 4 pounds pork.

—**DEANN ALLEVA** COLUMBUS, OH

3. BARBECUED CHICKEN

Mix 1 chopped large onion, ⅔ cup melted butter, ⅓ cup cider vinegar, 4 teaspoons sugar, 1 tablespoon chili powder, 2 teaspoons each salt and Worcestershire sauce, 1½ teaspoons each ground mustard and pepper, 2 minced garlic cloves and ½ teaspoon hot sauce. Makes about 1⅓ cups, enough for 5 pounds chicken.

—**BARBARA BLICKENS DERFER** EDGEWATER, FL

4. TERIYAKI BEEF

Mix ½ cup reduced-sodium soy sauce, ¼ cup cider vinegar, 2 tablespoons each brown sugar and finely chopped onion, 1 tablespoon canola oil, 1 minced garlic clove, ½ teaspoon ground ginger and ⅛ teaspoon pepper. Makes about ¾ cup, enough for 3 pounds beef.

—**JERI DOBROWSKI** BEACH, ND

EAT SMART

ZESTY GRILLED CHOPS

These pork chops make a quick company dish. Our family enjoys them on the grill, as the summer weather in our part of the country is hot and muggy. In the wintertime, they're just as wonderful prepared under the broiler.

—**BLANCHE BABINSKI** MINTO, ND

PREP: 10 MIN. + MARINATING
GRILL: 10 MIN.
MAKES: 6 SERVINGS

- ¾ cup soy sauce
- ¼ cup lemon juice
- 1 tablespoon chili sauce
- 1 tablespoon brown sugar
- 1 garlic clove, minced
- 6 bone-in pork loin or rib chops (about 1½ inches thick)

1. In a large resealable plastic bag, combine first five ingredients; reserve ⅓ cup mixture for brushing over pork chops. Add chops to bag; seal bag and turn to coat. Refrigerate overnight.

2. Drain pork, discarding marinade. Grill chops, covered, over medium heat or broil 4 in. from heat until a thermometer reads 145°, 6-8 minutes per side. Brush occasionally with reserved soy mixture during the last 5 minutes. Let stand for 5 minutes before serving.

PER SERVING *1 pork chop: 214 cal., 8g fat (3g sat. fat), 86mg chol., 614mg sodium, 1g carb. (1g sugars, trace fiber), 31g pro.* **Diabetic Exchanges:** *5 lean meat.*

SWEET GINGER RIBS

SPINACH STEAK PINWHEELS

Bacon and spinach bring plenty of flavor to these sirloin steak spirals. It's an easy dish to make and great to grill at a backyard cookout. I get lots of compliments on it, no matter how many times I serve it.

—HELEN VAIL GLENSIDE, PA

START TO FINISH: 25 MIN.
MAKES: 6 SERVINGS

- 1½ **pounds beef top sirloin steak**
- 8 **bacon strips, cooked**
- 1 **package (10 ounces) frozen chopped spinach, thawed and squeezed dry**
- ¼ **cup grated Parmesan cheese**
- ½ **teaspoon salt**
- ⅛ **teaspoon cayenne pepper**

1. Lightly score steak by making shallow diagonal cuts at 1-in. intervals into top of steak; repeat cuts in the opposite direction. Cover steak with plastic wrap; pound with a meat mallet to ½-in. thickness. Remove plastic.

2. Place bacon widthwise at center of steak. In a bowl, mix the remaining ingredients; spoon over bacon. Starting at a short side, roll up steak jelly-roll style; secure with toothpicks. Cut into six slices.

3. Moisten a paper towel with cooking oil; using long-handled tongs, rub on grill rack to coat lightly. Grill the pinwheels, covered, over medium heat for 5-6 minutes on each side or until beef reaches desired doneness (for medium-rare, a thermometer should read 145°; medium, 160°). Discard toothpicks before serving.

PER SERVING *1 pinwheel: 227 cal., 10g fat (4g sat. fat), 60mg chol., 536mg sodium, 3g carb. (0 sugars, 1g fiber), 31g pro. Diabetic Exchanges: 4 lean meat, 1 fat.*

HEALTH TIP *Spinach is loaded with vitamin K, which plays an important role in bone health.*

SWEET GINGER RIBS

People ask what's in the marinade of my glazed ribs with ginger, garlic and peach preserves. Now you know! Psst: It works on steaks and chicken, too.

—GRACE MCKEONE SCHENECTADY, NY

PREP: 15 MIN. + MARINATING
GRILL: 1½ HOURS • **MAKES:** 8 SERVINGS

- ½ **cup soy sauce**
- ½ **cup red wine vinegar**
- ½ **cup ketchup**
- ½ **cup peach preserves**
- ⅓ **cup minced fresh gingerroot**
- 2 **tablespoons stone-ground mustard**
- 2 **tablespoons brown sugar**
- 6 **garlic cloves, minced**
- ½ **teaspoon crushed red pepper flakes**
- ½ **teaspoon coarsely ground pepper**
- 4 **pounds pork baby back ribs**

1. In a small bowl, whisk the first 10 ingredients until blended. Reserve 1 cup marinade for basting. Divide ribs and remaining marinade between two large resealable plastic bags; seal bags and turn to coat. Refrigerate the ribs and the reserved marinade, covered, overnight.

2. Remove ribs, discarding remaining marinade in bags. Grill ribs, covered, over indirect medium heat for 1½ to 2 hours or until tender, basting occasionally with reserved marinade during the last half hour.

PER SERVING *338 cal., 21g fat (8g sat. fat), 81mg chol., 721mg sodium, 13g carb. (10g sugars, 0 fiber), 24g pro.*

SIMPLE GRILLED
STEAK FAJITAS

EAT SMART FAST FIX
SIMPLE GRILLED STEAK FAJITAS

After moving to a new state with two toddlers in tow, I came up with these effortless fajitas. They make a great meal on the grill or in a cast-iron skillet.
—SHANNEN MAHONEY ODESSA, MO

START TO FINISH: 30 MIN.
MAKES: 4 SERVINGS

- 1 **beef top sirloin steak (¾ inch thick and 1 pound)**
- 2 **tablespoons fajita seasoning mix**
- 1 **large sweet onion, cut crosswise into ½-inch slices**
- 1 **medium sweet red pepper, halved**
- 1 **medium green pepper, halved**
- 1 **tablespoon olive oil**
- 4 **whole wheat tortillas (8 inches), warmed**
   Optional ingredients: sliced avocado, chopped fresh cilantro and lime wedges

1. Rub steak with seasoning mix. Brush onion and peppers with oil.
2. Grill steak and vegetables, covered, over medium heat 4-6 minutes on each side or until the meat reaches desired doneness (for medium-rare, a thermometer should read 145°; medium, 160°; well-done, 170°) and vegetables are tender. Remove from grill. Let steak stand, covered, for 5 minutes before slicing.
3. Cut vegetables and steak into strips; serve in tortillas. If desired, serve with avocado, cilantro and lime.
PER SERVING *363 cal., 13g fat (4g sat. fat), 54mg chol., 686mg sodium, 34g carb. (6g sugars, 5g fiber), 27g pro.* **Diabetic Exchanges:** *3 lean meat, 2 starch, 1 vegetable, ½ fat.*

EAT SMART
LIME-ROSEMARY SHRIMP SKEWERS

I had a big bunch of rosemary, so I turned the stems into skewers for grilling shrimp. Serve the skewers with rice or couscous and lime wedges.
—LEAH LENZ LOS ANGELES, CA

PREP: 20 MIN. + MARINATING
COOK: 5 MIN.
MAKES: 6 SERVINGS

- 2 **tablespoons minced fresh parsley**
- 2 **tablespoons dry white wine or orange juice**
- 4 **garlic cloves, minced**
- 1 **tablespoon olive oil**
- 1 **teaspoon grated lime peel**
- 1 **tablespoon lime juice**
- ½ **teaspoon salt**
- ½ **teaspoon pepper**
- 12 **fresh rosemary sprigs (4-6 inches)**
- 1½ **pounds uncooked shrimp (26-30 per pound), peeled and deveined**
   Lime wedges, optional

1. In a large bowl, mix the first eight ingredients. For skewers, strip leaves from bottom portion of rosemary sprigs, leaving 1-2 in. of leaves attached at top; reserve 1 tablespoon of the removed leaves. Finely chop reserved leaves; add to parsley mixture. Add shrimp; toss to coat. Refrigerate, covered, 30 minutes.
2. Thread shrimp onto rosemary stems; discard remaining marinade. Grill, covered, 2-3 minutes on each side or until shrimp turn pink. If desired, serve with lime wedges.
NOTE *Six metal or soaked wooden skewers may be substituted for rosemary stems; grill as directed.*
PER SERVING *2 rosemary skewers: 103 cal., 2g fat (0 sat. fat), 138mg chol., 184mg sodium, 1g carb. (0 sugars, 0 fiber), 18g pro.* **Diabetic Exchanges:** *3 lean meat.*
 HEALTH TIP *Shrimp are a lean source of high-quality protein. Three ounces of cooked shrimp have 18 grams protein and just over 80 calories.*

EAT SMART FAST FIX
CHICKEN WITH MANGO-CUCUMBER SALSA

I put this dish together after looking for something quick and easy without too much indoor cooking. My husband likes that it's a little spicy.
—LINDA TRINGALI MONROE TOWNSHIP, NJ

START TO FINISH: 30 MIN.
MAKES: 4 SERVINGS (4 CUPS SALSA)

- 2 **tablespoons lemon juice**
- 1 **tablespoon lime juice**
- 2 **teaspoons minced fresh cilantro or parsley**
- ¼ **teaspoon ground cumin**
- ¼ **teaspoon salt**
- ⅛ **teaspoon pepper**
- 1 **medium cucumber, diced**
- 1 **medium mango, peeled and diced**
- 1 **medium tomato, chopped**
- ¼ **cup finely chopped red onion**

CHICKEN
- 4 **boneless skinless chicken breast halves (6 ounces each)**
- 1 **tablespoon olive oil**
- 1 **teaspoon chili powder**
- ½ **teaspoon salt**
- ¼ **teaspoon pepper**

1. For dressing, in a small bowl, mix the first six ingredients. Place the cucumber, mango, tomato and onion in a large bowl; toss with dressing.
2. Brush chicken with oil; sprinkle with seasonings. Grill chicken, covered, over medium heat or broil 4 in. from heat 4-5 minutes on each side or until a thermometer reads 165°. Serve with salsa.
PER SERVING *1 chicken breast half with 1 cup salsa: 285 cal., 8g fat (2g sat. fat), 94mg chol., 547mg sodium, 18g carb. (14g sugars, 3g fiber), 36g pro.* **Diabetic Exchanges:** *5 lean meat, 1 starch, ½ fat.*
 HEALTH TIP *Stir 3 cups cooked whole wheat couscous into the colorful salsa to make a hearty side dish for the chicken. Per serving, the meal would contain: 413 cal., 8 g fat (2 g sat. fat), 94 mg chol., 547 mg sodium, 45 g carb., 7 g fiber, 42 g pro.*

CHICKEN WITH MANGO-CUCUMBER SALSA

TOMATO-HERB
GRILLED TILAPIA

GRILLED PORK TACOS

My family raves about this moist pork with smoked paprika and pineapple. I dish it up next to brown rice and a salad of avocado and tomatoes.

—E. GELESKY BALA CYNWYD, PA

START TO FINISH: 30 MIN.
MAKES: 4 SERVINGS

- 1 **pound boneless pork ribeye chops, cut into ¾-inch cubes**
- 2 **tablespoons plus 2 teaspoons lime juice, divided**
- 1 **teaspoon smoked or regular paprika**
- ½ **teaspoon salt**
- ¼ **teaspoon pepper**
- ¾ **cup canned black beans, rinsed and drained**
- ½ **cup canned unsweetened pineapple tidbits plus 1 tablespoon reserved juice**
- 2 **tablespoons finely chopped red onion**
- 2 **tablespoons chopped fresh cilantro**
- 4 **flour tortillas (6 to 8 inches), warmed**
  Reduced-fat sour cream or plain yogurt, optional

1. In a large bowl, toss the pork with 2 tablespoons lime juice and the seasonings; let stand 5 minutes. Meanwhile, in a small bowl, mix beans, pineapple with reserved juice, onion, cilantro and remaining lime juice.

2. Thread pork onto four metal or soaked wooden skewers. Moisten a paper towel with cooking oil; using long-handled tongs, rub on grill rack to coat lightly. Grill kabobs, covered, over medium heat 6-8 minutes or until tender, turning occasionally.

3. Remove pork from skewers; serve in tortillas. Top with bean mixture and, if desired, sour cream.

PER SERVING *1 taco with ¼ cup salsa: 383 cal., 16g fat (6g sat. fat), 66mg chol., 636mg sodium, 31g carb. (6g sugars, 4g fiber), 27g pro.*
Diabetic Exchanges: 3 starch, 3 medium-fat meat.

TOMATO-HERB GRILLED TILAPIA

Trust me: This super tilapia with ginger and lemon takes dinner over the top with minimal prep. Grilling the fish in foil is about as easy as it gets.

—TRISHA KRUSE EAGLE, ID

START TO FINISH: 30 MIN.
MAKES: 4 SERVINGS

- 1 **cup fresh cilantro leaves**
- 1 **cup fresh parsley leaves**
- 2 **tablespoons olive oil**
- 2 **teaspoons grated lemon peel**
- 2 **tablespoons lemon juice**
- 1 **tablespoon coarsely chopped fresh gingerroot**
- ¾ **teaspoon sea salt or kosher salt, divided**
- 2 **cups grape tomatoes, halved lengthwise**
- 1½ **cups fresh or frozen corn (about 8 ounces), thawed**
- 4 **tilapia fillets (6 ounces each)**

1. Place the first six ingredients in a food processor; add ½ teaspoon salt. Pulse until mixture is finely chopped.

2. In a bowl, combine tomatoes and corn; stir in 1 tablespoon herb mixture and remaining salt.

3. Place each fillet on a piece of heavy-duty foil (about 12-in. square). Top with herb mixture; spoon tomato mixture alongside fish. Fold foil around fish and vegetables, sealing tightly.

4. Grill, covered, over medium-high heat 6-8 minutes or until fish just begins to flake easily with a fork. Open foil carefully to allow steam to escape.

PER SERVING *270 cal., 9g fat (2g sat. fat), 83mg chol., 443mg sodium, 15g carb. (6g sugars, 3g fiber), 35g pro.*
Diabetic Exchanges: 5 lean meat, 1½ fat, 1 vegetable, ½ starch.

SPICY SHRIMP &
WATERMELON KABOBS

EAT SMART **FAST FIX**

SESAME BEEF SKEWERS

A bottle of sesame-ginger dressing makes this amazing dish doable on any weeknight. My pine-appley salad easily caps off dinner. You can broil the beef, too, but we live in the South where people grill pretty much all year long.
—**JANICE ELDER** CHARLOTTE, NC

START TO FINISH: 30 MIN.
MAKES: 4 SERVINGS

- 1 **pound beef top sirloin steak, cut into 1-inch cubes**
- 6 **tablespoons sesame ginger salad dressing, divided**
- 1 **tablespoon reduced-sodium soy sauce**

SALAD
- 1 **tablespoon sweet chili sauce**
- 1 **tablespoon lime juice**
- ¼ **teaspoon pepper**
- 2 **medium apples, chopped**
- 2 **cups chopped fresh pineapple**
- 1 **tablespoon sesame seeds, toasted**

1. In a bowl, toss the beef with 3 tablespoons dressing and soy sauce; let stand 10 minutes. Meanwhile, in a large bowl, mix chili sauce, lime juice and pepper; gently stir in the apples and pineapple.
2. Thread beef on four metal or soaked wooden skewers; discard remaining marinade. Grill kabobs, covered, over medium heat or broil 4 in. from heat 7-9 minutes or until desired doneness, turning kabobs occasionally; brush generously with remaining dressing during the last 3 minutes. Sprinkle with sesame seeds. Serve with salad.
PER SERVING *1 kabob with 1 cup salad: 311 cal., 11g fat (3g sat. fat), 46mg chol., 357mg sodium, 28g carb. (21g sugars, 3g fiber), 25g pro.*
Diabetic Exchanges: 3 lean meat, 1 starch, 1 fruit, ½ fat.

EAT SMART **FAST FIX**

SPICY SHRIMP &
WATERMELON KABOBS

My three sons can polish off a whole watermelon in one sitting. Before they dig in, I grab a few slices to make these zesty shrimp kabobs.
—**JENNIFER FISHER** AUSTIN, TX

START TO FINISH: 30 MIN.
MAKES: 4 SERVINGS

- 1 **tablespoon reduced-sodium soy sauce**
- 1 **tablespoon Sriracha Asian hot chili sauce**
- 1 **tablespoon honey**
- 1 **garlic clove, minced**
- 4 **cups cubed seedless watermelon (1 inch), divided**
- 1 **pound uncooked shrimp (16-20 per pound), peeled and deveined**
- 1 **medium red onion, cut into 1-inch pieces**
- ½ **teaspoon sea salt**
- ¼ **teaspoon coarsely ground pepper**
  Minced fresh cilantro, optional

1. For glaze, place soy sauce, chili sauce, honey, garlic and 2 cups of watermelon in a blender; cover and process until pureed. Transfer to a small saucepan; bring to a boil. Cook, uncovered, over medium-high heat until mixture is reduced by half, about 10 minutes. Reserve ¼ cup glaze for serving.
2. On four metal or soaked wooden skewers, alternately thread shrimp, onion and remaining watermelon. Sprinkle with salt and pepper.
3. Place kabobs on an oiled grill rack over medium heat. Grill, covered, 3-4 minutes on each side or until shrimp turns pink, brushing with remaining glaze during the last 2 minutes. If desired, sprinkle with cilantro. Serve with reserved glaze.
A serving of fruit with dinner? Check... along with 20 percent of the daily value for vitamin C.
PER SERVING *1 shrimp kabob with 1 tablespoon glaze: 172 cal., 2g fat (0 sat. fat), 138mg chol., 644mg sodium, 23g carb. (19g sugars, 2g fiber), 20g pro. Diabetic Exchanges: 3 lean meat, 1 fruit, ½ starch.*

FAJITA IN A BOWL

FAST FIX

FAJITA IN A BOWL

Pull out the skewers and take a stab at grilling peppers, onions and corn for an awesome steak salad that's pure summer.
—**PEGGY WOODWARD** SHULLSBURG, WI

START TO FINISH: 30 MIN.
MAKES: 4 SERVINGS

- 1 **tablespoon brown sugar**
- 1 **tablespoon chili powder**
- ½ **teaspoon salt**
- 1 **beef flank steak (1 pound)**
- 12 **miniature sweet peppers, halved and seeded**
- 1 **medium red onion, cut into thin wedges**
- 2 **cups cherry tomatoes**
- 2 **medium ears sweet corn, husks removed**

SALAD

- 12 **cups torn mixed salad greens**
- 1 **cup fresh cilantro leaves**
- ½ **cup reduced-fat lime vinaigrette Optional ingredients: cotija cheese, lime wedges and tortillas**

1. In a small bowl, combine the brown sugar, chili powder and salt. Rub onto both sides of steak.

2. Place peppers and onion on a grilling grid; place on grill rack over medium heat. Grill, covered, 9-11 minutes or until crisp-tender, stirring occasionally; add tomatoes during the last 2 minutes. Remove from grill.

3. Place steak and corn directly on grill rack; close lid. Grill the steak for 8-10 minutes on each side or until a thermometer reads 145° for medium rare; grill corn 10-12 minutes or until lightly charred, turning occasionally.

4. Divide greens and cilantro among four bowls. Cut corn from cobs and thinly slice steak across the grain; place in bowls. Top with vegetables and steak; drizzle with vinaigrette. If desired, serve with cheese, lime and tortillas.

NOTE *If you do not have a grilling grid, use a disposable foil pan with holes poked into the bottom with a meat fork.*
PER SERVING (*calculated without optional ingredients*): *351 cal., 14g fat (5g sat. fat), 54mg chol., 862mg sodium, 33g carb. (16g sugars, 7g fiber), 28g pro.*

GRILLED CHICKEN CHOPPED SALAD

Layered desserts always grab my family's attention, but salads? Not so much. I wondered, if I presented a healthy salad in an eye-catching way, could I get everyone on board? I'm happy to report that I did!
—**CHRISTINE HADDEN** WHITMAN, MA

START TO FINISH: 30 MIN.
MAKES: 4 SERVINGS

- 1 **pound chicken tenderloins**
- 6 **tablespoons zesty Italian salad dressing, divided**
- 2 **medium zucchini, quartered lengthwise**
- 1 **medium red onion, quartered**
- 2 **medium ears sweet corn, husks removed**
- 1 **bunch romaine, chopped**
- 1 **medium cucumber, chopped Additional salad dressing, optional**

1. Toss chicken with 4 tablespoons dressing. Brush zucchini and onion with 2 tablespoons dressing.
2. Place corn, zucchini and onion on a grill rack over medium heat; close lid. Grill corn 10-12 minutes or until tender, turning occasionally. Grill zucchini and onion 2-3 minutes on each side or until tender.
3. Drain the chicken, discarding the marinade. Grill chicken, covered, over medium heat 3-4 minutes on each side or until no longer pink.
4. Cut corn from cobs; cut zucchini, onion and chicken into bite-size pieces. In a 3-qt. trifle bowl or other glass bowl, layer romaine, cucumber, grilled veggies and chicken. If desired, serve with additional dressing.
PER SERVING *3 cups: 239 cal., 5g fat (0 sat. fat), 56mg chol., 276mg sodium, 21g carb. (9g sugars, 5g fiber), 32g pro.* **Diabetic Exchanges:** *3 lean meat, 2 vegetable, ½ starch, ½ fat.*

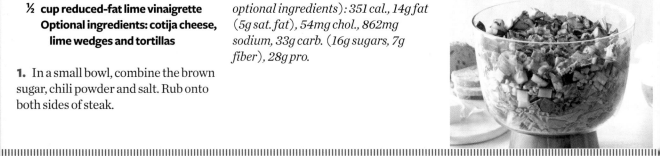

GRILLED CHICKEN CHOPPED SALAD

STRAWBERRY MINT CHICKEN

STEAK WITH CHIPOTLE-LIME CHIMICHURRI

Chimichurri is a parsley-based sauce that complements most any grilled meat, poultry or fish. When I serve it with steak, I add chipotle for a little firepower.

—LAUREEN PITTMAN RIVERSIDE, CA

START TO FINISH: 30 MIN.
MAKES: 8 SERVINGS

- 2 **cups fresh parsley leaves**
- 1½ **cups fresh cilantro leaves**
- ½ **medium red onion, coarsely chopped**
- 1 **to 2 chipotle peppers in adobo sauce**
- 5 **garlic cloves, sliced**
- ½ **cup olive oil**
- ¼ **cup white wine vinegar**
- 1 **teaspoon grated lime peel**
- ¼ **cup lime juice**
- 3 **teaspoons dried oregano**
- 1¼ **teaspoons salt, divided**
- ¾ **teaspoon pepper, divided**
- 2 **pounds beef flat iron steaks or 2 beef top sirloin steaks (1 pound each)**

1. For chimichurri, place the first five ingredients in a food processor; pulse until finely chopped. Add oil, vinegar, lime peel, lime juice, oregano, ½ teaspoon salt and ¼ teaspoon pepper; process until blended. Transfer to a bowl; refrigerate chimichurri, covered, until serving.

2. Sprinkle steaks with the remaining salt and pepper. Grill, covered, over medium heat 5-8 minutes on each side or until meat reaches desired doneness (for medium-rare, a thermometer should read 145°; medium, 160°; well-done, 170°). Let stand 5 minutes before slicing. Serve with chimichurri.

PER SERVING *3 ounces cooked steak with 3 tablespoons sauce: 336 cal., 26g fat (7g sat. fat), 73mg chol., 462mg sodium, 4g carb. (1g sugars, 1g fiber), 22g pro.*

STRAWBERRY MINT CHICKEN

I hand-picked wild strawberries for this saucy chicken dish. We love it with fresh spring greens and a sweet white wine. What a perfect spring meal.

—ALICIA DUERST MENOMONIE, WI

START TO FINISH: 30 MIN.
MAKES: 4 SERVINGS

- 1 **tablespoon cornstarch**
- 1 **tablespoon sugar**
- ⅛ **teaspoon ground nutmeg**
- ⅛ **teaspoon pepper**
- ½ **cup water**
- 1 **cup fresh strawberries, coarsely chopped**
- ½ **cup white wine or white grape juice**
- 2 **teaspoons minced fresh mint**

CHICKEN

- 4 **boneless skinless chicken breast halves (6 ounces each)**
- ½ **teaspoon salt**
- ¼ **teaspoon pepper**
- **Sliced green onion**

1. In a small saucepan, mix the first five ingredients until smooth; stir in strawberries and wine. Bring to a boil. Reduce heat; simmer, uncovered, for 3-5 minutes or until thickened and strawberries are softened, stirring occasionally. Remove from heat; stir in mint.

2. Moisten a paper towel with cooking oil; using long-handled tongs, rub on grill rack to coat lightly. Sprinkle the chicken with salt and pepper.

3. Grill the chicken, covered, over medium heat 5-7 minutes on each side or until a thermometer reads 165°; brush occasionally with ¼ cup sauce during the last 4 minutes. Serve with the remaining sauce. Sprinkle with green onion.

PER SERVING *1 chicken breast half with ¼ cup sauce: 224 cal., 4g fat (1g sat. fat), 94mg chol., 378mg sodium, 8g carb. (5g sugars, 1g fiber), 35g pro.*
Diabetic Exchanges: *5 lean meat, ½ starch.*

TILAPIA WITH LEMON-BASIL VINAIGRETTE

EAT SMART (5)INGREDIENTS FAST FIX

TILAPIA WITH LEMON-BASIL VINAIGRETTE

We aren't big fish eaters, but a friend made this for us, and we couldn't believe how wonderful it was! Now we eat it regularly. I love cooking it for guests because it's simple, looks lovely and tastes like it came from a restaurant.

—BETH COOPER COLUMBUS, OH

START TO FINISH: 25 MIN.
MAKES: 4 SERVINGS

- ½ teaspoon grated lemon peel
- 3 tablespoons lemon juice
- 2 tablespoons olive oil
- 2 garlic cloves, minced
- 2 teaspoons capers, drained
- 3 tablespoons minced fresh basil, divided
- 4 tilapia fillets (6 ounces each)
- ½ teaspoon salt
- ¼ teaspoon pepper

1. In a small bowl, whisk the lemon peel, lemon juice, oil and garlic until blended; stir in the capers and 2 tablespoons basil. Reserve 2 tablespoons mixture for drizzling cooked fish. Brush the remaining mixture onto both sides of tilapia; sprinkle with salt and pepper.

2. Moisten a paper towel with cooking oil; using long-handled tongs, rub on grill rack to coat lightly. Grill tilapia, covered, over medium heat or broil 4 in. from heat 3-4 minutes on each side or until fish just begins to flakes easily with a fork. Drizzle with the reserved lemon mixture; sprinkle with the remaining basil.

PER SERVING *1 fillet: 206 cal., 8g fat (2g sat. fat), 83mg chol., 398mg sodium, 2g carb. (trace sugars, trace fiber), 32g pro.* **Diabetic Exchanges:** *5 lean meat, 1½ fat.*

HEALTH TIP *Look for Canadian or U.S. tilapia that's been farmed in closed tanks for the least impact on the environment.*

(5)INGREDIENTS

HERBED GRILLED CORN ON THE COB

My sister-in-law cooked grilled corn for us. I'd never served it before, but now it's a must on the summertime menu. We dress it with fresh basil and parsley.

—ANGELA LEINENBACH MECHANICSVLLE, VA

PREP: 20 MIN. + SOAKING • **GRILL:** 25 MIN.
MAKES: 8 SERVINGS

- 8 medium ears sweet corn
- ½ cup butter, softened
- 2 tablespoons minced fresh basil
- 2 tablespoons minced fresh parsley
- ½ teaspoon salt

1. Place corn in a stockpot; cover with cold water. Soak 20 minutes; drain. Carefully peel back corn husks to within 1 in. of bottoms; remove silk.

2. In a small bowl, mix remaining ingredients; spread over the corn. Rewrap corn in husks; secure with kitchen string.

3. Grill corn. covered, over medium heat 25-30 minutes or until tender, turning often. Cut string and peel back husks.

GARLIC-BUTTER PARMESAN CORN *Omit last four ingredients. Soak corn as directed. In a small saucepan, combine ⅓ cup butter, 1 minced garlic clove and ¼ teaspoon salt. Cook and stir over medium heat until butter is melted; set aside 2 tablespoons. Carefully peel back corn husks to within 1 in. of bottoms; remove silk. Brush with remaining butter mixture. Rewrap corn in husks and secure with kitchen string. Grill as directed. After husks are removed, drizzle with the reserved butter mixture and sprinkle with ¼ cup grated Parmesan.*

PER SERVING *1 ear of corn with 1 tablespoon butter mixture: 178 cal., 12g fat (7g sat. fat), 31mg chol., 277mg sodium, 17g carb. (5g sugars, 2g fiber), 3g pro.*

CAN-CAN CHICKEN

CAN-CAN CHICKEN

Once the bird is on the grill, the work's basically done. And cleanup is a cinch—a must for a guy like me.

—**STEVE BATH** LINCOLN, NE

PREP: 30 MIN. + CHILLING
GRILL: 1¼ HOURS + STANDING
MAKES: 6 SERVINGS

- 1 tablespoon kosher salt
- 1 teaspoon sugar
- 1 teaspoon onion powder
- 1 teaspoon garlic powder
- 1 teaspoon cayenne pepper
- 1 teaspoon paprika
- 1 teaspoon ground mustard
- 1 broiler/fryer chicken (3½ to 4 pounds)
- 1 can (12 ounces) beer

1. In a small bowl, mix the first seven ingredients. With fingers, carefully loosen skin from the chicken; rub seasoning mixture under and over skin. Tuck wings under chicken. Refrigerate, covered, 1 hour.
2. Completely cover all sides of an 8- or 9-in. baking pan with foil. Place a beer-can chicken rack securely in pan. Remove half of the beer from can. Using a can opener, make additional large holes in top of can; place can in the rack.

3. Stand chicken vertically on rack; place on grill rack. Grill, covered, over indirect medium heat 1¼ to 1½ hours or until a thermometer inserted in thickest part of thigh reads 170°-175°.
4. Carefully remove pan from grill; tent chicken with foil. Let stand for 15 minutes before carving.
PER SERVING *377 cal., 20g fat (5g sat. fat), 122mg chol., 1067mg sodium, 4g carb. (3g sugars, 0 fiber), 39g pro.*

FAST FIX
MESQUITE SALMON

Smoky mesquite chips oomph up our salmon as it grills. Then we slather on a dill, parsley and lemon sauce that makes dinner nothing short of heavenly.

—**JERI KILPATRICK** HOODSPORT, WA

START TO FINISH: 30 MIN.
MAKES: 4 SERVINGS

- ½ cup mayonnaise
- 2 tablespoons brown sugar
- 2 tablespoons minced fresh parsley
- 1 tablespoon minced fresh dill
- ½ teaspoon grated lemon peel
- 1 tablespoon lemon juice
- ¼ teaspoon salt
- ⅛ teaspoon pepper
- 2 cups soaked mesquite wood chips
- 1 salmon fillet (1½ pounds)

1. In a small bowl, mix the first eight ingredients. Add wood chips to grill according to the manufacturer's directions.
2. Place salmon on oiled grill rack, skin side down. Grill, covered, over medium heat 7 minutes. Spoon mayonnaise mixture over salmon. Grill, covered, 7-10 minutes longer or until fish just begins to flake easily with a fork.
PER SERVING *493 cal., 38g fat (6g sat. fat), 95mg chol., 386mg sodium, 7g carb. (7g sugars, 0 fiber), 29g pro.*

(5) INGREDIENTS FAST FIX
GRILLED EGGPLANT PARMESAN STACKS

We love eggplant Parmesan, but when it's hot outside, the dish feels too heavy. Grilled eggplant slices topped with tomato, mozzarella and Parm satisfy everyone.

—**JOANN PARLIN** LITTLE EGG HARBOR, NJ

START TO FINISH: 25 MIN.
MAKES: 4 SERVINGS

- 1 large eggplant (about 2 pounds)
- ½ teaspoon salt
- 1 tablespoon olive oil
- ½ teaspoon pepper
- 1 log (1 pound) fresh mozzarella cheese, cut into sixteen slices
- 1 large tomato, cut into eight slices
- ½ cup shredded Parmesan cheese
  Chopped fresh basil or parsley

1. Trim ends of eggplant; cut eggplant crosswise into eight slices. Sprinkle with salt; let stand 5 minutes.
2. Blot the eggplant dry with paper towels; brush both sides with oil and sprinkle with pepper. Grill, covered, over medium heat 4-6 minutes on each side or until tender. Remove from grill.
3. Top eggplant with mozzarella cheese, tomato and Parmesan cheese. Grill, covered, 1-2 minutes longer or until the cheese begins to melt. Top with basil.
PER SERVING *2 eggplant stacks: 449 cal., 31g fat (18g sat. fat), 96mg chol., 634mg sodium, 15g carb. (10g sugars, 5g fiber), 26g pro.*

**Julie Merriman's
Bagel with a Veggie Schmear**
PAGE 313

Easy Odds & Ends

Here's a roundup of new favorites to discover this year. Homemade jam and pickles? Check. A fancified brunch spread that elevates store-bought bagels? Check. All this and a Sunday pasta dinner, too!

**Gwen Frankhouser's
Strawberry Peach Jam**
PAGE 310

**Caroline Munoz's
Hearty Veggie Sandwiches**
PAGE 312

**Cynthia Huff's
Chicken Mac & Cheese**
PAGE 315

Refrigerator Jams & Condiments

Savor the season's bounty with quick homemade pickles and jams. Make the most of your haul from the farmers market with easy, gift-worthy recipes featuring berries, peaches, rhubarb and rainbow chard.

STRAWBERRY PEACH JAM

(5)INGREDIENTS
STRAWBERRY PEACH JAM

You'll definitely capture the flavors of summer with this chunky, luscious toast-topper. Best of all, this jam freezes well for up to a year, and it makes a great housewarming or hostess gift.
—**GWEN FRANKHOUSER** EL CAJON, CA

PREP: 25 MIN. + STANDING
MAKES: ABOUT 5 CUPS

- **2 cups sliced fresh strawberries**
- **1¼ cups finely chopped peeled peaches**
- **1 package (1¾ ounces) powdered fruit pectin**
- **5 cups sugar**

1. Rinse five 1-cup freezer-safe containers and lids with boiling water. Dry thoroughly.

2. In a large saucepan, mix the strawberries, peaches and pectin; bring to a full rolling boil over high heat, stirring constantly. Stir in sugar; return to a full rolling boil. Boil and stir 1 minute longer. Remove from heat; skim off any foam.

3. Immediately fill containers to within ½ in. of tops. Wipe off edges of containers; immediately cover with lids. Let stand at room temperature 24 hours.

4. Jam is now ready to use. Refrigerate for up to 3 weeks or freeze for up to 12 months. Thaw frozen jam in the refrigerator before serving.
PER SERVING *2 tablespoons: 102 cal., 0 fat (0 sat. fat), 0 chol., 0 sodium, 26g carb. (26g sugars, 0 fiber), 0 pro.*

(5)INGREDIENTS
FIRE-AND-ICE PICKLES

These sweet and spicy pickles are great on a sandwich or all by themselves as a snack. The recipe is an easy way to dress up store-bought pickles and make them a special treat. I like to wrap a pretty ribbon around the tops of the jars and give them as gifts.
—**MYRA INNES** AUBURN, KS

PREP: 10 MIN. + CHILLING
MAKES: 3 PINTS

- **2 jars (32 ounces each) dill pickle slices or spears**
- **4 cups sugar**
- **1 tablespoon hot pepper sauce**
- **½ teaspoon crushed red pepper flakes**
- **3 garlic cloves, peeled**

Drain and discard juice from pickles. In a large bowl, combine pickles, sugar, pepper sauce and pepper flakes; mix well. Cover and let stand 2 hours, stirring occasionally. Spoon pickle mixture into 3 pint-size jars; add a garlic clove to each. Cover and refrigerate 1 week before serving. Store in the refrigerator up to 1 month.
PER SERVING *¼ cup: 134 cal., 0 fat (0 sat. fat), 0 chol., 362mg sodium, 34g carb. (33g sugars, 0 fiber), 0 pro.*

FIRE-AND-ICE PICKLES

BLUEBERRY-RHUBARB REFRIGERATOR JAM

I think the best recipes come from good friends...and that's where I got this jam recipe. It's a great way to use an abundant supply of rhubarb.

—**ARLOIA LUTZ** SEBEWAING, MI

PREP: 10 MIN. ● **COOK:** 20 MIN. + CHILLING
MAKES: 4½ PINTS

- 5 **cups chopped fresh or frozen rhubarb, thawed**
- ½ **cup water**
- 5 **cups sugar**
- 1 **can (21 ounces) blueberry pie filling**
- 2 **cups fresh or frozen blueberries**
- 3 **tablespoons lemon juice**
- 2 **packages (3 ounces each) raspberry gelatin**

In a large kettle, cook rhubarb and water over medium-high heat for 3-5 minutes or until rhubarb is tender. Add sugar. Bring to a boil; boil for 2 minutes. Stir in pie filling, blueberries and lemon juice. Return to a boil. Reduce heat; cook and stir for 10 minutes. Remove from heat; stir in gelatin until dissolved. Cool slightly. Pour into refrigerator containers. Cool to room temperature. Cover and refrigerate.

PER SERVING *2 tablespoon: 142 cal., 0 fat (0 sat. fat), 0 chol., 11mg sodium, 36g carb. (34g sugars, 1g fiber), 1g pro.*

TOP TIP

FREEZE-AHEAD RHUBARB

"In spring, I clean and chop fresh rhubarb, then place 3-cup portions in freezer bags. In summer, I do the same with strawberries. With the premeasured ingredients, I can make strawberry-rhubarb jam whenever we want it."

—**HARRIET M.** STEWARTVILLE, MN

PICKLED RAINBOW CHARD

PICKLED RAINBOW CHARD

Pickling adds pop to fresh foods, especially Swiss chard stems. In this easy fridge method, sweet meets tart and it all balances out overnight.

—*TASTE OF HOME* TEST KITCHEN

PREP: 10 MIN. ● **COOK:** 5 MIN. + CHILLING
MAKES: 8 SERVINGS

- 2 **bunches rainbow Swiss chard**
- 1 **small onion, halved and sliced**
- 2 **teaspoons mixed pickling spices**
- ½ **teaspoon celery seed**
- ½ **teaspoon mustard seed**
- 1 **cup sugar**
- 1 **cup cider vinegar**
- ⅓ **cup water**

1. Trim leaves from Swiss chard; save for another use. Cut stems into 2-in. pieces; place in a large heatproof nonreactive bowl. Add onion, pickling spices, celery seed and mustard seed.
2. In a small saucepan, combine sugar, vinegar and water; bring to a boil. Cook 1 minute, stirring to dissolve sugar; pour carefully over chard mixture. Cool completely. Refrigerate, covered, overnight, stirring occasionally.

PER SERVING *48 cal., 0 fat (0 sat. fat), 0 chol., 211mg sodium, 11g carb. (8g sugars, 2g fiber), 2g pro.*

Just Add Bagels

Whether you're cooking up a casual lunch for friends, a special brunch for family, or treating co-workers to a morning-time nosh, bakery-fresh bagels make the perfect starter.

HEARTY VEGGIE
SANDWICHES

FAST FIX
HEARTY VEGGIE SANDWICHES

My sister and I created this delicious sandwich one day when we had some everything bagels on hand. I have often served it to friends as a casual lunch. The total lack of fussiness lets me spend quality time with my guess.
—**CAROLINE MUNOZ** AUSTIN, MN

START TO FINISH: 15 MIN.
MAKES: 2 SERVINGS

- 2 tablespoons mayonnaise
- 2 teaspoons Dijon mustard
- 2 bagels, split
- 2 lettuce leaves
- 1 medium ripe avocado, peeled and sliced
- 2 large slices tomato
- 1 slice sweet onion, separated into rings
  Salt and pepper to taste

In a small bowl, combine mayonnaise and mustard; spread over cut sides of bagels. On the bagel bottoms, layer lettuce, avocado, tomato and onion. Sprinkle with salt and pepper. Replace bagel tops.
PER SERVING *1 sandwich: 440 cal., 26g fat (4g sat. fat), 5mg chol., 525mg sodium, 46g carb. (5g sugars, 8g fiber), 9g pro.*

EASY BAGEL DIP

The longer this creamy blend chills, the better it tastes. I usually have to make a double batch when I bring it to family gatherings. It's good not only with bite-size bagel pieces, but also with veggies.
—**MARY MERKWAN** WAGNER, SD

PREP: 15 MIN. + CHILLING
MAKES: 4¼ CUPS

- 2 cups (16 ounces) sour cream
- 1½ cups mayonnaise
- 2 tablespoons dried parsley flakes
- 2 tablespoons minced chives
- 2 teaspoons dill weed
- ¼ teaspoon garlic salt
- 1 medium onion, finely chopped
- 2 packages (2½ ounces each) thinly sliced dried beef, chopped
  Plain bagels, split and cut into bite-size pieces

In a large bowl, combine sour cream and mayonnaise. Add the parsley, chives, dill and garlic salt. Stir in onion and dried beef. Cover and refrigerate overnight. Serve with bagels.
PER SERVING *¼ cup: 215 cal., 20g fat (5g sat. fat), 32mg chol., 376mg sodium, 2g carb. (2g sugars, 0 fiber), 4g pro.*

TOP TIP
CRUNCHY BAGEL CHIPS

"I have a super way to use up bagels. I slice them very thin, place them in a baking pan, spritz with cooking spray and sprinkle with different seasonings. For instance, I use garlic powder or basil on egg or onion bagels, and sugar and cinnamon on raisin bagels. Bake at 350° for 15-20 minutes or until crispy. They're delicious with dips, and they're less expensive than bagel chips from the store."
—**DONNA M.** BUTLER, PA

BAGEL WITH A
VEGGIE SCHMEAR

BAGEL WITH A VEGGIE SCHMEAR

I got this recipe from my favorite bagel shop in New York City. Now I make this every time I'm craving a quick and healthy breakfast. I like to add chopped pitted green olives to the schmear.

—**JULIE MERRIMAN** SEATTLE, WA

START TO FINISH: 20 MIN.
MAKES: 4 SERVINGS

- 4 **ounces fat-free cream cheese**
- 4 **ounces fresh goat cheese**
- ½ **teaspoon grated lime peel**
- 1 **tablespoon lime juice**
- ⅔ **cup finely chopped cucumber**
- ¼ **cup finely chopped celery**
- 3 **tablespoons finely chopped carrot**
- 1 **radish, finely chopped**
- 2 **tablespoons finely chopped red onion**
- 2 **tablespoons thinly sliced fresh basil**
- 4 **whole wheat bagels, split and toasted**
- 8 **slices tomato**
  Coarsely ground pepper, optional

In a bowl, beat cheeses, lime peel and lime juice until blended. Fold in the chopped vegetables and basil. Serve on bagels with tomato slices. If desired, sprinkle with pepper.
PER SERVING *2 open-faced sandwiches: 341 cal., 6g fat (3g sat. fat), 22mg chol., 756mg sodium, 56g carb. (15g sugars, 10g fiber), 20g pro.*

5 HOMEMADE SPREADS IN A HURRY

Whip up a couple of these toppings and pop them in the fridge the day before your brunch party. Then all you have to do is ask someone to pick up bagels on their way. Done and done!

1. BEER CHEESE Combine 1 cup softened cream cheese, ½ cup shredded cheddar cheese, 3 tablespoons beer and ½ envelope ranch dressing mix. Add salt and pepper to taste.

2. PECAN PIE Combine 1 cup softened cream cheese, ½ cup toasted chopped pecans and ¼ cup caramel sauce.

3. INSIDE-OUT "EVERYTHING" Combine 1 cup cream cheese, 1 tablespoon each poppy seeds and sesame seeds, 2 teaspoons each dried minced garlic and dried minced onion and 1 teaspoon Worcestershire sauce. Season with salt and pepper to taste.

4. MEDITERRANEAN GOAT CHEESE Combine 1 cup softened cream cheese, ⅓ cup goat cheese, ¼ cup chopped olives, ¼ cup chopped roasted red peppers and 2 teaspoons grated lemon peel. Season with salt and pepper to taste.

5. ORANGE MARMALADE Combine 1 cup softened cream cheese with ⅓ cup orange marmalade.

Pasta for Company

Nothing says "gather around the table" like a big, hearty platter of steaming pasta. Each of these company-worthy dishes features a homemade sauce, plenty of tender meat, and a larger yield to serve eight or more for dinner.

SHRIMP ALFREDO FETTUCCINE

SHRIMP ALFREDO FETTUCCINE

Fettuccine Alfredo's been around for ages. I give it an update by adding tender shrimp and a pop of lemon.
—**TONYA BURKHARD** DAVIS, IL

PREP: 20 MIN. • **COOK:** 25 MIN.
MAKES: 8 SERVINGS

- 1 **package (16 ounces) fettuccine**
- ½ **cup butter, cubed**
- 3 **medium onions, halved and thinly sliced (about 3 cups)**
- 8 **garlic cloves, minced**
- 4 **teaspoons all-purpose flour**
- 1 **teaspoon salt**
- 1 **teaspoon pepper**
- 1 **cup half-and-half cream**
- 2 **pounds uncooked shrimp (26-30 per pound), peeled and deveined**
- 1 **tablespoon grated lemon peel**
- 2 **tablespoons lemon juice**
- 1 **cup grated Parmesan cheese**
- 2 **tablespoons minced fresh parsley**

1. In a 6-qt. stockpot, cook fettuccine according to package directions. Drain; return to pot.
2. Meanwhile, in a large skillet, heat butter over medium heat. Add onions; cook and stir 8-10 minutes or until tender. Add garlic; cook 1 minute longer. Stir in flour, salt and pepper until blended; gradually stir in cream. Bring to a boil, stirring constantly; cook and stir 2-4 minutes or until thickened.
3. Stir in shrimp, lemon peel and lemon juice; cook 3-4 minutes or until shrimp turn pink. Stir in cheese and parsley. Add to fettuccine and toss to combine.
PER SERVING *1½ cups: 503 cal., 20g fat (11g sat. fat), 192mg chol., 738mg sodium, 49g carb. (5g sugars, 3g fiber), 31g pro.*

BACON BOLOGNESE

Pasta with ground beef was a house staple when I was growing up. I've added bacon, white wine and juicy tomatoes to make it a next-level meal.
—**CARLY TERRELL** GRANBURY, TX

PREP: 15 MIN. • **COOK:** 3¼ HOURS
MAKES: 10 SERVINGS

- ½ **pound ground beef**
- ½ **pound ground pork**
- ½ **teaspoon salt**
- ¼ **teaspoon pepper**
- 2 **medium carrots, chopped**
- 1 **medium onion, chopped**
- 6 **thick-sliced bacon strips, chopped**
- 8 **garlic cloves, minced**
- 1 **cup dry white wine**
- 1 **can (28 ounces) whole tomatoes, crushed slightly**
- 1½ **cups chicken stock or reduced-sodium chicken broth**
- 1 **package (16 ounces) spaghetti**
- 3 **tablespoons butter, cubed**
- 1 **cup grated Parmesan cheese**

1. In a 6-qt. stockpot, cook beef and pork over medium heat 5-7 minutes or until no longer pink, breaking into crumbles. Stir in salt and pepper. Remove from pot with a slotted spoon; pour off drippings.
2. Add carrots, onion and bacon to same pot; cook and stir over medium heat 6-8 minutes or until vegetables are softened. Add garlic; cook 1 minute longer. Return meat to pot; add wine. Bring to a boil, stirring to loosen browned bits from pan; cook until liquid is almost evaporated.
3. Add tomatoes and stock; return to a boil. Reduce heat; simmer, covered, 3-4 hours to allow flavors to blend, stirring occasionally.
4. To serve, cook spaghetti according to package directions for al dente; drain. Stir butter into meat sauce; add spaghetti and toss to combine. Serve with cheese.
PER SERVING *1 cup: 483 cal., 26g fat (11g sat. fat), 61mg chol., 686mg sodium, 41g carb. (4g sugars, 3g fiber), 20g pro.*

CHICKEN MAC & CHEESE

In my family, a stick-to-your-ribs supper includes protein, pasta and a good cheese like cheddar. This loaded mac works like a charm at potlucks.
—**CYNTHIA HUFF** FLORA, IL

PREP: 15 MIN. • **COOK:** 25 MIN.
MAKES: 12 SERVINGS (1 CUP EACH)

- 1 **package (16 ounces) elbow macaroni**
- 2 **cups fresh broccoli florets**
- 1 **tablespoon canola oil**
- 1 **pound boneless skinless chicken breasts, cut into 1-inch pieces**
- 1 **medium onion, chopped**
- ½ **teaspoon salt**
- ¼ **teaspoon pepper**
- 3 **tablespoons butter**
- 3 **tablespoons all-purpose flour**
- 1 **teaspoon paprika**
- ¼ **teaspoon cayenne pepper**
- 3 **cups 2% milk**
- 1 **cup chicken broth**
- 3 **cups shredded cheddar cheese**
- 1 **tablespoon Dijon mustard**

1. Cook macaroni according to package directions, adding the broccoli during the last 5 minutes of cooking. Drain.

2. Meanwhile, in a Dutch oven, heat oil over medium-high heat. Add chicken, onion, salt and pepper; cook and stir 6-8 minutes or until chicken is no longer pink. Remove from pan.

3. In same pan, melt butter. Stir in flour, paprika and cayenne until smooth; gradually whisk in milk and broth. Bring to a boil, stirring constantly; cook and stir 2-3 minutes or until thickened. Stir in cheese and mustard until cheese is melted.

4. Add macaroni mixture and chicken to sauce. Heat through, stirring to combine.

PER SERVING *1 cup: 374 cal., 17g fat (9g sat. fat), 63mg chol., 467mg sodium, 34g carb. (5g sugars, 2g fiber), 22g pro.*

General Recipe Index

This handy index lists every recipe by food category, major ingredient and cooking method, so you can easily locate the recipes that suit your needs.

||||||||||||||||||||||||||||||||||||||||||||||||||||||||||||||||||||||||||||||||||||||||||||||||||

SLOW COOKER PEACH
BBQ RIBS, PAGE 200

APPLESAUCE MINI MUFFINS,
PAGE 159

APPLE-SAGE SAUSAGE
PATTIES, PAGE 178

CHICKEN RANCH
FLATBREADS, PAGE 92

MARYLAND CORN
POPS, PAGE 225

**TWO-BERRY
PAVLOVA, PAGE 248**

BARBARA'S ITALIAN
WEDDING SOUP, PAGE 206

S'MORES CRESCENT
ROLLS, PAGE 288

GENERAL RECIPE INDEX

GREEN SALAD WITH
BERRIES, PAGE 31

SAUSAGE WITH JALAPENO
POTATOES, PAGE 195

GARLIC TILAPIA WITH
SPICY KALE, PAGE 131

BUTTERNUT
SQUASH
WITH WHOLE
GRAINS, PAGE 194

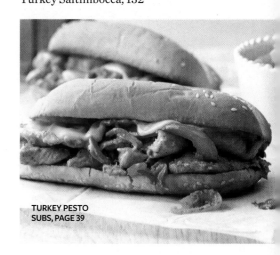

**TURKEY PESTO
SUBS, PAGE 39**

ASPARAGUS & CHEESE FRITTATA, PAGE 187

CRANBERRY WHITE CHOCOLATE CHUNK CHEESECAKE, PAGE 251

Alphabetical Recipe Index

This index lists every recipe in alphabetical order so you can easily find all of your favorites.

||||||||||||||||||||||||||||||||||||||||||||||||||||||||||||||||||||||||||||||||||||||||||

BLACK BEAN & SWEET POTATO
TOSTADAS, PAGE 135

C

CHORIZO & GRITS BREAKFAST BOWLS, PAGE 183

D

JEN'S BAKED BEANS, PAGE 227

LOUISIANA PECAN
BACON BREAD, PAGE 171

ONE-POT SAUCY BEEF
ROTINI, PAGE 63

ALPHABETICAL RECIPE INDEX

SOUTHERN PORK & RICE,
PAGE 121

WALKING TACOS, PAGE 286